MW01074792

Saudi Arabia

Anthony Ham, Martha Brekhus Shams, Andrew Madden

Contents

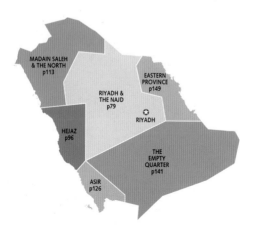

MADAIN SALEH & THE NORTH p113

EASTERN PROVINCE p149

RIYADH & THE NAJD p79

RIYADH

HEJAZ p96

THE EMPTY QUARTER p141

ASIR p126

Destination: Saudi Arabia

Saudi Arabia could be one of *the* great travel destinations of the Middle East.

For 19th century explorers, Arabia was a forbidden kingdom of legend, a land worth visiting because it was so unknown and was furnished with exotic impossibility. Today Saudi Arabia is still difficult to enter, and perhaps not a country you'd normally think of spending your holidays in. But the home of Islam is as diverse as it is surprising – from its traditional Bedouin encampments deep in one of the world's greatest deserts, to its modern cities replete with stunning symbols of the Kingdom's headlong rush into the future.

Madain Saleh, sister-city to Petra in Jordan, is Arabia's greatest treasure – a breathtaking rock-hewn monument to the ingenuity of the ancients. Other wonders abound, from echoes of TE Lawrence ('of Arabia') and the Arab Revolt along the abandoned tracks of the Hejaz Railway, to the mud-brick ruins of Dir'aiyah where Saudi Arabia was born. Jeddah, the gateway to the holy cities of Mecca and Medina where pilgrims have thronged for fourteen centuries, has an enchanting old city made of coral, while the fairy-tale mud towers of Najran belong to an altogether different world of ancient camel caravans laden with frankincense.

Saudi Arabia is also a land of astonishing natural beauty. The spectacular, plunging landscapes of the Asir Mountains around Abha yield to the sculpted sand dunes of the Empty Quarter and the palm trees of the largest oasis in the world at Al-Hofuf, while the waters of the Red Sea offer some of the best diving anywhere on earth.

There are few places left in the world that can be said to represent the last frontier of tourism. Whether you're an expat, here on business or a traveller, Saudi Arabia is one of them.

CHRIS MELLOR

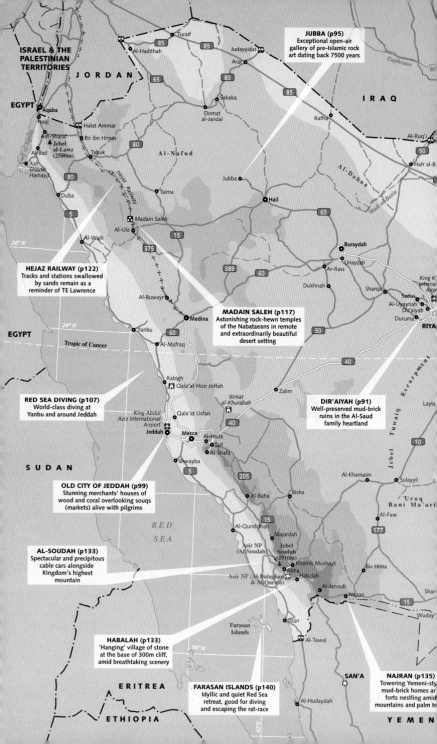

ISRAEL & THE PALESTINIAN TERRITORIES

JORDAN

85 · Turaif

85

Al-Hadithah

Judayyidat

Arar

65

80

Sakaka

Domat al-Jandal

IRAQ

Rafha

EGYPT

Aqaba

Haql

Ash-Sharaf

Halat Ammar

Jebel al-Lawz (2580m)

Bir ibn Himas

Al-Bad

Ash Shaykh Hamayd

Tabuk

Al-Nafud

Al-Ruq'i

50

Hafr al-B

80

JUBBA (p95)
Exceptional open-air gallery of pre-Islamic rock art dating back 7500 years

Duba

Hejaz Railway

Taima

Jubba

Hail

Al-Dahna

Wadi al-Batin

5

Madain Saleh

Al-Ula

65

26° N

Al-Wajh

15

Buraydah

Unayzah

375

HEJAZ RAILWAY (p122)
Tracks and stations swallowed by sands remain as a reminder of TE Lawrence

Ar-Rass

King K interna Airp

389

60

Dukhnah

Sharqa

Sadus

Al-Uyaynah

Dir'aiyah

24° N

Al-Buwayr

Medina

MADAIN SALEH (p117)
Astonishing rock-hewn temples of the Nabataeans in remote and extraordinarily beautiful desert setting

Duruma

RIYA

EGYPT

Yanbu

60

Tropic of Cancer

Al-Mafraq

50

40

Rabigh

Qala'at Hisn Joffah

Zalim

Birkat al-Khurabah

DIR'AIYAH (p91)
Well-preserved mud-brick ruins in the Al-Saud family heartland

Layla

RED SEA DIVING (p107)
World-class diving at Yanbu and around Jeddah

King Abdul Aziz International Airport

Qala'at Usfan

40

10

Jeddah

Mecca

Al-Hada

Taif

Al-Shafa

SUDAN

Shwayba

5

OLD CITY OF JEDDAH (p99)
Stunning merchants' houses of wood and coral overlooking souqs (markets) alive with pilgrims

205

Al-Khamasin

Sulayyil

Bisha

Al-Baha

'Uruq Bani Ma'ar

RED SEA

15

Al-Faw

177

Al-Qundiqhah

Majardah

AL-SOUDAH (p133)
Spectacular and precipitous cable cars alongside Kingdom's highest mountain

Asir NP (Al-Soudah)

Jebel Soudah (2910m)

Khamis Mushayt

Biv Hima

Abha

Habalah

Asir NP (Al-Dalaghan & Al-Qarah)

Al-Janoub

Najran

15

Shar

Wuday'

Farasan Islands

Jizan

16° N

Al-Tawal

HABALAH (p133)
'Hanging' village of stone at the base of 300m cliff, amid breathtaking scenery

ERITREA

SAN'A

NAJRAN (p135)
Towering Yemeni-sty mud-brick homes ar forts nestling amid mountains and palm tr

FARASAN ISLANDS (p140)
Idyllic and quiet Red Sea retreat, good for diving and escaping the rat-race

Al-Hudaydah

ETHIOPIA

YEMEN

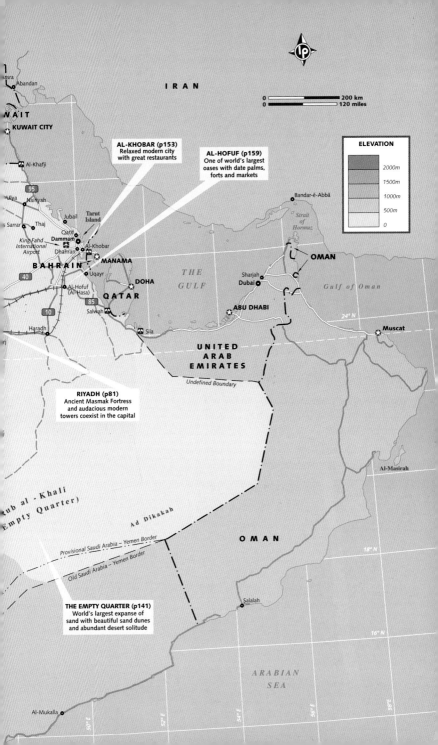

IRAN

0 ————— 200 km
0 ————— 120 miles

ELEVATION

	2000m
	1500m
	1000m
	500m
	0

AL-KHOBAR (p153)
Relaxed modern city
with great restaurants

AL-HOFUF (p159)
One of world's largest
oases with date palms,
forts and markets

KUWAIT CITY

Basra

Abadan

Al-Khafji

95

Ulya

Nairiyah

Bandar-ê-Abbā

Strait
of
Hormuz

s Sarrar

Thaj

Jubail

Tarut
Island

Qatif

Dammam

King Fahd
International
Airport

Dhahran

Al-Khobar

BAHRAIN

40

MANAMA

OMAN

Uqayr

DOHA

THE
GULF

Sharjah

Dubai

Gulf of Oman

Al-Hofuf
(Al-Hasa)

QATAR

85

Salwah

10

Haradh

Sila

ABU DHABI

Muscat

24° N

Harj

UNITED
ARAB
EMIRATES

Undefined Boundary

RIYADH (p81)
Ancient Masmak Fortress
and audacious modern
towers coexist in the capital

Al-Masirah

Rub al - Khali
(Empty Quarter)

Ad Dikakah

OMAN

18° N

Provisional Saudi Arabia – Yemen Border

Old Saudi Arabia – Yemen Border

Salalah

THE EMPTY QUARTER (p141)
World's largest expanse of
sand with beautiful sand dunes
and abundant desert solitude

16° N

ARABIAN
SEA

Al-Mukalla

50° E

52° E

54° E

56° E

58° E

Highlights

Saudi Arabia is a surprising land of contrasts, with jaw-dropping mountain scenery at **Al-Soudah** (p133) and **Habalah** (p133); expanses of sand dunes near **Shararah** (p146); and the idyllic **Farasan Islands** (p140). Arabia's architectural heritage is equally diverse, you'll find pre-Islamic wonders such as **Al-Faw** (p146); mud-brick buildings including **Masmak Fortress** (p86) and the houses of **Najran** (p135); a Portuguese-era fort on **Tarut Island** (p157); and old oasis towns such as **Al-Hofuf** (p159). The **National Museum** (p85) and **Aramco Exhibit** (p156) inform and entertain, while the relatively liberal cities of **Taif** (p107) and **Al-Khobar** (p153) make relaxing destinations.

TONY WHEELER

Be transported to another era among the mud architecture of Dir'aiyah (p91)

Admire the beautiful rock-hewn temples, built by the Nabataeans, in Madain Saleh (p117)

Wander among wood-and-coral houses in old Jeddah (p99)

CHRIS MELLOR

TON

WORLD RELIGIONS PHOTO LIBRARY/ALAMY

Complete your haj (p62), if a Muslim, at Al-Masjid al-Haram in Mecca

Witness the emergence of modern
Arabia at Riyadh's Kingdom Tower (p87)

ANTHONY HAM

ANTHONY HAM

Discover ancient, pre-Islamic
Arabia in the rock art of
Jubba (p95)

ANTHONY HAM

Follow the abandoned tracks and
stations of the Hejaz Railway (p122)

Dive into the blue of the magical Red Sea (p107)

Contemplate the solitude of the world's largest expanse of sand
in the Empty Quarter (p141)

Getting Started

Obtaining a Saudi Arabian visa involves negotiating numerous bureaucratic obstacles (see p172). But, you'll be pleased to know, tracking down good books and websites about the country is a whole lot easier.

For help in planning your itinerary, see p6 and p12.

WHEN TO GO

The ideal time to visit Saudi Arabia is between November and February when the summer heat is over. From mid-April until October you'll swelter under average daily temperatures of more than 40°C, with high humidity in the coastal regions. It's appreciably milder in the Asir Mountains and around Taif year-round, which makes these places popular summer retreats. In the dead of winter (December to January) temperatures in the main cities (except Jeddah) will drop into the teens during the day and even hit zero in some places overnight (particularly in the central deserts). During winter the mountains can also be shrouded in fog.

The Kingdom's Islamic holidays (p37) are another important factor in deciding when to go. Unless you've no choice, Ramadan is to be avoided at all costs: getting a daytime meal can be difficult, opening hours are kept to a minimum and officials can be decidedly (if understandably) surly. During the haj pilgrimage, most forms of transport and some accommodation are busier than normal and prices increase, although usually only in the Hejaz region.

See Climate Charts (p165) for more information.

For a full listing of Islamic holidays in Saudi Arabia, see p168.

COSTS & MONEY

Saudi Arabia isn't a budget destination. Staying in reasonable hotels with satellite TV (singles/doubles from around SR100/150), eating from time to time in an upmarket restaurant (from SR40 per person) and travelling quite often by bus will cost you at least SR200 a day.

It is possible to travel relatively cheaply if you choose to, however. Eating well for SR20 or less per day is never a problem. You can also find a bed for as little as SR10 (youth hostels) or from SR40 (hotels). The

---

DON'T LEAVE HOME WITHOUT...

We assume that you'll remember to bring clothes to keep you warm in winter, so the following list is a somewhat tongue-in-cheek take on what you may need to get through the idiosyncrasies of life in the Kingdom:

- a good book (cinemas are banned, and as for nightclubs, dream on)
- for women, something to throw over your head to ward off the mutawwa (religious police; p174)
- a visa (p173)
- a full stomach if you're arriving on a Ramadan morning (p166)
- a close look at the travel advisory warnings of Western governments (p166)
- your *iqama* (residence permit) if you live in Saudi Arabia; not having it with you at all times will cause untold hassles (p52)
- patience – you'll need it in abundance.

minimum you could get by on is around SR80 per day, although SR125 is more realistic, especially once you factor in travel.

If you plan on staying in top-end hotels, taking tours, travelling around the country by plane or hiring a car, and purchasing the occasional souvenir, you'll need to budget about SR400 per day.

TRAVEL LITERATURE

The Arabian peninsula, the lands of Islam, have held a rare fascination for Western explorers for centuries. This fact is reflected in the rich variety of travel narratives available, many of which are well worth reading before you set out.

Arabian Sands, by Wilfred Thesiger, is one of the finest pieces of travel literature ever written and a classic of desert exploration; Thesiger spent years living and travelling with the Bedouin.

Arabia of the Bedouins, by Marcel Kurpershoek, is a nuanced and fascinating account of a Dutch diplomat's search for the magic of poetry among Bedouin nomads while learning their language. Highly recommended.

Personal Narrative of a Pilgrimage to Al-Madinah and Meccah, by Richard Burton, is a rare (and politically incorrect) Western insight into the holy cities of Mecca and Medina. Another classic.

Hashish (Smuggling Under Sail in the Red Sea), by Henri de Montfried, has everything: Red Sea drug smugglers, fascinating observations about 1920s Arabia, and a lively writing style. It may even be true.

The Adventures of Ibn Battuta: A Muslim Traveller of the 14th Century, by Ross Dunn, brings the 14th century 'Arab Marco Polo' to life, including Ibn Battuta's time in Mecca as a pilgrim.

Crossing Borders: An American Woman in the Middle East, by Judith Caesar, chronicles the author's expat days in Saudi Arabia and handles deftly the complexities faced by women in the region.

At the Drop of a Veil, by Marianne Alireza, is a portrait of Saudi Arabia through the eyes of an American woman who married a Jeddah merchant and lived there in the 1940s and 1950s.

Travelling the Sands: Sagas of Exploration in the Arabian Peninsula, by Andrew Taylor, provides fascinating descriptions of journeys undertaken by haj pilgrims and Western adventurers through the centuries.

Sandstorms: Days and Nights in Arabia, by Peter Theroux, describes the life of the (male) American expat (the author was based in Riyadh); it's a mass-market paperback but contains some interesting observations.

INTERNET RESOURCES

There's not a lot of variety in the information about Saudi Arabia on the web; much of what is there is business-oriented. The following are recommended:

About Saudi Arabia (www.saudia.com) Devoted to news and commerce, with a definite focus on the latter.

BBC News – Middle East (http://news.bbc.co.uk/2/hi/middle_east/default.stm) Impartial news about the Kingdom.

LonelyPlanet.com (www.lonelyplanet.com) Succinct summaries on travel in Saudi Arabia, postcards from other travellers and the Thorn Tree bulletin board.

Saudi Arabian Information Resource (www.saudinf.com) Run by the Ministry of Culture & Information. Contains nearly 2000 pages ranging from history and economics to recommended reading and useful addresses.

The Country & People of Saudi Arabia (www.hejleh.com/countries/saudi.html) Another good site for links (some in Arabic) to all aspects of Saudi Arabia.

HOW MUCH?

Cup of coffee in a Bedouin tent, free

International newspaper SR15-35

Plane fare Riyadh–Jeddah SR280

Bus fare Riyadh–Jeddah SR140

Entry to ancient sites, free; permit required

LONELY PLANET INDEX

One litre of petrol SR0.91

1.5 litres of bottled water SR2-3

Bottle of nonalcoholic beer SR3-4

Bedouin dagger SR100-25,000

Shwarma (beef or chicken in pita bread) SR1-3

TOP TENS

OUR FAVOURITE SOUQS

Saudi Arabia may not fulfil your dreams of exotic Arabian bazaars, but here is a selection of souqs (markets) that retain their traditional character or offer a range of handicrafts worth seeking out:

- Afghan Souq, Jeddah (p105)
- Bedouin Market, Nairiyah (p158)
- Dagger Souq, Najran (p138)
- Gold Souq, Jeddah (p105)
- Old Souq, Jizan (p139)
- Qaisariyah Souq, Al-Hofuf (p161)
- Souq al-Alami, Jeddah (p100)
- Souq al-Harim, Najran (p138)
- Souq al-Thumairi, Riyadh (p89)
- Taif Souq, Taif (p109)

BEST-VALUE HOTELS

Although the international chains in the big cities have all the luxuries you'll need, we think the following places offer the best value in terms of comfort, service and value for money from across the country:

- Abha Palace Hotel, Abha (p131)
- Al-Ahsa Intercontinental, Al-Hofuf (p161)
- Al-Baia Hotel, Jeddah (p103)
- Al-Faisaliah Hotel, Riyadh (p88)
- Al-Nusl Hotel, Sakaka (p123)
- Al-Sharafi Hotel, Nairiyah (p158)
- Farasan Hotel, Farasan Islands (p140)
- Madain Saleh Hotel & Resort, Al-Ula (p117)
- Red Sea Palace Hotel, Jeddah (p103)
- White Palace Hotel, Riyadh (p88)

SAUDI ARABIA FOR KIDS

Saudi Arabia has a wealth of activities which kids (and their parents) will never forget. Our favourites include:

- camel markets, Al-Hofuf (p161) and camel races, Riyadh (p91)
- diving programmes for kids, Red Sea (p107)
- fairy-tale fortresses and houses, Najran (p135)
- hanging village of Habalah (p133)
- Hejaz Railway (p122)
- interactive National Museum, Riyadh (p85)
- Jebel al-Akhdar cable car (p129)
- Kingdom Tower, Riyadh (p87)
- Nabataean rock-hewn tombs of Madain Saleh (p117)
- prehistoric rock art, Jubba (p95)

Itineraries
CLASSIC ROUTES

SAUDI CIRCUIT   One Month

One month in Saudi Arabia will enable you to see the best of the Kingdom.
Allow three days in **Riyadh** (p81) to contrast the super-modern architecture
of the **Al-Faisaliah Tower** and **Kingdom Tower** (p87) with the **Masmak Fortress** (p86)
and nearby **Dir'aiyah** (p91), and to visit the wonderful **National Museum** (p85).
From the capital, head into southern Arabia to **Najran** (p135), with its fairy-
tale houses and forts. North along the mountains takes you to **Abha** (p129),
gateway to the Kingdom's most breathtaking scenery, including Arabia's
highest mountain, **Jebel Soudah** (p133), and the precarious ancient village of
Habalah (p133). Continue north to pleasant **Taif** (p107), also in the mountains.
Jeddah (p98) is Saudi Arabia's most interesting city, with an enchanting **old
town** (p99), pleasant **corniche** (p102) and decidedly cosmopolitan air. From
here, make your way to **Al-Ula** (p161), the evocative base for exploring **Madain
Saleh** (p117), arguably Saudi Arabia's single most impressive site. Backtrack
to Medina airport, then fly to the capital, from where you can explore the
Eastern Province – the culinary delights of **Al-Khobar** (p154), the sentinel-like
Tarut Island (p157), and the oasis charms of **Al-Hofuf** (p153).

This 3000km route
takes you on a tour
of Saudi Arabia's
highlights, from
the contrasts of
old and modern
Riyadh, to the
rock-hewn city of
Madain Saleh.

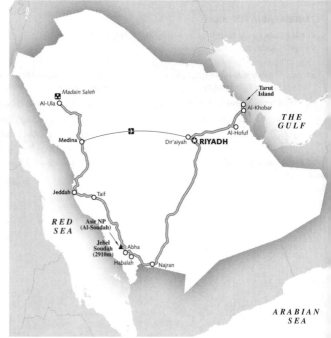

DESERT, SEA & MOUNTAIN   Two Weeks

Flying to **Sharurah** (p146) from Riyadh or Jeddah is like being dropped into an altogether less clamorous world. Getting there by road takes a lot longer but allows you to see the transition from city, to desert fringe to the heart of one of the world's most evocative deserts. If you're coming from Riyadh, don't fail to stop at the isolated but worthwhile pre-Islamic ruins at **Al-Faw** (p146) en route. **Najran** (p135) should be the next stop on your itinerary; spend as long as you can here exploring the distinctive local mud-brick architecture strung out along Wadi Najran, not to mention shopping for silver jewellery and daggers in the souq. **Abha** (p129) is not far to the north and also rewards the time spent exploring the extraordinary mountain panoramas of the **Asir National Park** (p132), most notably around **Habalah** (p133) and **Al-Soudah** (p133) where the cable cars afford the best views. On your way to Jeddah, surround yourself with the greenery of the Shahba and Raghdan Forests around **Al-Baha** (p128), then pause in **Taif** (p107) long enough to enjoy the last of the mild mountain climate before descending to the steaming plains along the Red Sea coastline. The small village of **Al-Hada** (p111) carries traces of ancient Hejaz and has some fine views down off the escarpment. Catching a breeze along the corniche in **Jeddah** (p98) is a great way to beat the summer heat. Even better, organise your diving expedition in the waters of the **Red Sea** (see Red Sea Diving p107), whether it be off the corniche or further afield at **Al-Nakheel** (p106), **Shwayba** (see Red Sea Diving p107), **Rabigh** (see Red Sea Diving p107) or **Yanbu** (p111).

Experience the highs and lows of the Saudi Arabian landscape on this 2100km route (2700km if you drive from Riyadh) that takes you from cool mountain ranges, through steaming plains, to the relief of the Red Sea.

ROADS LESS TRAVELLED

EASTERN & NORTHERN PROVINCES
Two Weeks

Amid the oil fields of the Eastern Province, you'll find hidden vestiges of Arabia's great trading past. Start at **Al-Khobar** (p153) sampling the wonderful food of this most liberal of Saudi cities, stocking up for your journey off-the-beaten-track and arranging the transport for it. The industrial port of **Jubail** (p158) is home to an ancient and little-visited **Nestorian church** (p158). The Bedouin market of **Nairiyah** (p158) is one of the best traditional markets left in Arabia, drawing traders from across the deserts and from neighbouring countries. To the south at **Thaj** (p159), you can track down the once-fabulously wealthy trading city of **Gherra** (p159), one of Arabia's richest archaeological prizes. To reach the north, you could fly to **Sakaka** (p123) from Dammam (via Riyadh) or you could follow the pipelines and drive there via Arar, shadowing the Iraqi border all the way to reach the mysterious **Standing Stones of Rajajil** (p124) and the old mosques and fortresses of **Domat al-Jandal** (p124). **Madain Saleh** (p117) is impossible to bypass with its stone carved monuments due to the ingenuity of the Nabataeans. Continue north to **Tabuk** (p120) with its fort and Hejaz Railway Station before completing a circuit north to **Wadi Hisma** (p122) and then south to more Nabataean ruins at **Al-Bad** (p122), the controversial other Mt Sinai at **Jebel al-Lawz** (p124) and then the pretty Red Sea village of **Duba** (p122).

This 2750km route (less if you fly to Sakaka) takes you off the beaten track to visit some of Saudi Arabia's archaeological gems.

SOUTHERN GATES OF ARABIA   10 Days

If you start your journey in **Najran** (p135), surrounded by mountains and with its architecture strongly reminiscent of Yemen, you shouldn't have too much difficulty imagining the frankincense-laden camel caravans emerging from the highlands of the southern Arabian peninsula. Before heading north, drive between the sand dunes along one of the most evocative desert roads on earth to **Sharurah** (p146), from where you could launch an expedition into the desert's heart (three days is a minimum to get into the best country). If you thought Sharurah was remote, head to **Wuday'ah** (p148), which could just be as close to the end of the earth as you'll ever find yourself. Not far from here was where British explorer Wilfred Thesiger crossed the Empty Quarter from south to north. From Sharurah, drive or fly to **Abha** (p129) and head into the **Al-Soudah region** (p133), descending the cable car to **Rijal Almaa** (p133) where you'll find a wonderful museum, not to mention architecture and local culture unlike anywhere else in the Kingdom. Back up in the mountains, twist along the ridges to **Taif** (p107), a base for visiting the lovely small village of **Al-Shafa** (p111) which has wonderful views and few Western visitors. Unless you have the time to drive, you'll probably have to travel to **Jeddah** (p98) to take a flight south to **Jizan** (p139). From there, make the short crossing to the wonderfully idyllic **Farasan Islands** (p140) where you can go diving (see Red Sea Diving p107) or just enjoy the fact that these rarely visited islands are what the rest of the Red Sea must once have been like.

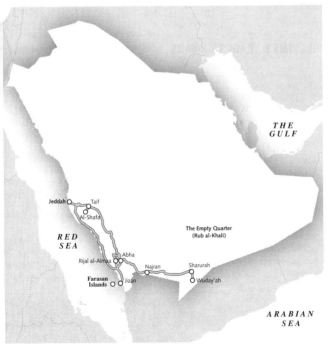

Imagine the camel caravans of by-gone eras as you travel evocative desert roads on this 2700km journey, terminating in the idyllic Farasan Islands.

TAILORED TRIPS

PRE-ISLAMIC ARABIA

10 Days to Two Weeks

This route covers 4000km, exploring the remnants of a rich variety of pre-Islamic ancient civilisations, and requires flying between some towns. The very modern Saudi capital of **Riyadh** (p81) is the best place to start, not least for its transport connections and the opportunity to see the contrast with what lies ahead. Examples of Arabia's finest pre-Islamic **rock art** (see The Rock Art of Arabia p94), some of it dating back to 5500 BC and including stylised and stylish human figures, are to be found at **Jubba** (p95). To get here from Riyadh, drive (704km) or fly to **Hail** (p93) and continue the last

100km by road. From Hail, fly to **Sakaka** (p123) to see the **Standing Stones of Rajajil** (p124), the mysterious 'Stonehenge of Arabia'. Don't miss the astonishing rock-hewn Nabataean city of **Madain Saleh** (p117), nor the Lihyanite, Thamudic inscriptions of **Al-Ula** (p115). **Elephant Rock** (p117), near Al-Ula, has been a cause of wonder since human beings settled the area. Through a mixture of road and air travel (preferably more of the latter), make your way to **Najran** (p135), a base for travelling to some more exceptional rock art at **Bir Hima** (p146). On your way back to Riyadh, stop off at lonely **Al-Faw** (p146), a once flourishing desert city now in ruins and almost 2000 years old.

PILGRIMS & TRADE CARAVANS

Two to Three Weeks

This 2200km route takes you on an adventure to Saudi Arabia's historical sites, from 1000-year-old cisterns to a 20th-century abandoned railway. The ancient trade caravan routes from the south once branched into two at **Najran** (p135). If you follow the northeastern route, you can stop off at the rock art of **Bir Hima** (p146), then at **Al-Faw** (p146), which grew wealthy by supplying the caravans crossing the deserts of the Arabian interior. **Sulayyil** (p144) is on the fringe of the Empty Quarter. As pilgrims crossed Arabia and left behind the **Jebel Tuwaiq Escarpment** (p93), many thirsty desert

miles lay ahead of them on the road to Mecca. The modern traveller can instead enjoy the **Red Sands** (p93), before making a detour to the stone cisterns of **Birkat al-Khurabah** (p111), part of the early Islamic **Darb Zubaydah** (see The Zubaydah Road p111). Circle Mecca (it's as close as you'll get unless you're a Muslim) to **Jeddah** (p98) where the souqs still throng with white-robed pilgrims. The Turkish forts, including **Qala'at Usfan** (p107), of the Hejaz are reminders of when pilgrims travelled by land, while the remnants of the **Hejaz Railway** (see The Hejaz Railway p122) are evocative of TE Lawrence ('of Arabia') and follow the old pilgrimage routes from the north and the trade routes from the south.

The Author

ANTHONY HAM
Coordinating Author

Anthony worked as a refugee lawyer for three years, during which time he represented asylum seekers from across the Middle East and completed a Masters Degree in Middle Eastern politics. After tiring of daily battles with a mean-spirited Australian Government, he set off to write and photograph his way around the world, particularly the Middle East. Saudi Arabia was always the last frontier (he spent four years trying to get a visa) to which Anthony was drawn by a Wilfred Thesiger–inspired love of the Empty Quarter. The longer he waited, the more his fascination grew for Arabia, and its relationship with the rest of the world. Anthony wrote this book apart from the Haj and Health chapters.

My Favourite Trip

There's something about Riyadh (p81) which draws me back. From the ruins of old Dir'aiyah (p91) to the summit of the Kingdom Tower (p87), I'd retrace in microcosm the fast-forward speed of Saudi Arabia's history. From there, I'd head for Najran (p135), that enchanting reminder of Yemen, then pass between the sand dunes to Sharurah (p146), before immersing myself in the solitude of the Empty Quarter (p141). Next stop Abha (p129), and the astonishing landscapes around Habalah (p133), before pressing on to Jeddah, (p98) with its enchanted old city. I couldn't leave the Kingdom without visiting the ghosts of the Hejaz Railway (p122); marvelling at the ingenuity of the ancients at Madain Saleh (p117); and experiencing the other side of desert life at Al-Hofuf oasis (p159).

CONTRIBUTING AUTHORS

Andrew Madden has a Bachelor of Nursing, which was his ticket into Saudi Arabia. He had long been fascinated with the country after travelling through Africa and the Middle East, and reading accounts of Lawrence and Thesiger. After completing two years in the Riyadh Military Hospital, Andrew returned to Australia to study for a degree in Art History and Archaeology. Andrew contributed to the Expats chapter.

Dr Caroline Evans studied medicine at the University of London, and completed General Practice training in Cambridge. She is the medical adviser to Nomad Travel clinic, a private travel health clinic in London, and also a GP specialising in travel medicine. She has been an expedition doctor for Raleigh International and Coral Cay expeditions. Dr Evans wrote the health chapter.

Martha Brekhus Shams has studied Middle Eastern culture for 25 years, including at the University of Maryland and University of Tehran and has lived in Iran for the last 15 years. She has worked with the Iranian Cultural Heritage Organization for 10 years and in the Iranian film industry. As an American with Muslim credentials, she opens the doors to the haj with a Western perspective. Martha wrote the Haj chapter.

Snapshot

Modern Saudi Arabia is a nation at odds with itself and with the outside world, a country with its feet firmly planted in tradition and an eye cast uneasily on the future.

As the Kingdom struggles to strike a balance between its proud Islamic heritage and the demands for reform by a young and restless population, the tensions are evident everywhere. Islamic conservatives and pro-Western moderates take divergent views on many issues – women's rights, for example, are defined in radically different ways by Wahhabi Islam, liberal Saudis and the West. Rapid modernisation in this deeply traditional society poses profound challenges, as Western commercialism increasingly impinges upon traditional Islamic values.

Indeed, the contradictions of modern Saudi Arabia are legion. It's a country with a fiercely Islamic character, but one which is eager to maintain a long-standing friendship with the West; a secretive kingdom which is among the most difficult places in the world to visit, yet welcomes millions of foreign workers and pilgrims; and a place where custodians of the holy cities of Islam depend upon the latest Western technology to ensure their state's continued viability.

These are troubled times for Saudi Arabia's royal family and it's people who have been buffeted by the extraordinary winds of change which have swept across Arabia during the last 70 years. Discoveries of new sources of oil in the Kingdom have largely ceased. At the same time, the population is growing at an extraordinary rate. Oil money no longer guarantees wealth for all and the complicated systems of patronage which once buttressed the power of the Al-Saud dynasty can no longer be sustained. Disillusionment among the young, many of whom are university educated, has reached unprecedented levels. With not enough jobs to go around, there is clamour for change even as people feel themselves pulled in several directions at once. Some have been caught up within a siege mentality, drawn to the ideals of Al-Qaeda, a return to Wahhabi roots and a utopian 18th-century world where Islam reigned supreme and from which foreigners were excluded. Others whisper a desire for democracy, great admiration for the West and anger at those who practise terrorism in the name of Islam (even as they express anger at Western misunderstandings of their country).

And yet Saudi Arabia's future will be defined, in part, by events beyond its control. US disillusion about Saudi Arabian involvement in the September 11 terrorist attacks has prompted a diversification away from the Kingdom's sources of oil and, for the first time in 50 years, Saudi Arabia is in danger of returning to the margins of international power. The sense of helplessness which that will engender, when coupled with the disillusionment of Saudi Arabia's young, may well determine the future of the Kingdom.

With an ailing king, a powerful history and a fascinating, if uncertain future, Saudi Arabia could be the place where many of the great questions of the 21st century are addressed, not least among these will be how to define the complex relationship between Islam and the West.

FAST FACTS

Population: 25 million (over 60% under 15)

Unemployment: 27%

Inflation: 0.8%

GDP per capita: US$7834 (1980s: US$22,000)

Life expectancy: women 70.2; men 66.7

Export income from petroleum products: 90%

External debt: US$23.8 billion (2001)

Literacy: 78% (women 69.5%; men 84.2%)

Health professionals per 100,000: doctors 160; nurses 330

Annual 'tourists' (mostly performing haj or umrah): more than 3.5 million

Share of the world's proven oil reserves: 26%

History

audi Arabia's history has the aroma of frankincense, the stamp of a proud nd nomadic Bedouin heritage and the bountiful legacy of oil wealth. But reater than all of these is Islam – the call to prayer has echoed across the ingdom for fourteen centuries.

For the last 130 years, members of the Al-Saud dynasty have been the overseers of Arabia's unique heritage, trying to balance the demands of modernisation and their custodianship over the land where Islam was orn and to which all Muslims are called. But this has always been the tory of Saudi Arabia's history – the struggle for the legitimacy of its rulers mid the interplay of religion and politics.

PRE-ISLAMIC ARABIA

t's difficult to imagine Arabia without Islam, so dominant is the shadow t casts over modern Saudi Arabia.

One of the earliest mentions of the Arab people came from Sargon II, he King of Assyria from 722 to 705 BC, who wrote that 'the distant Arabs dwelling in the desert…know neither overseers nor officials…all alike are warriors of equal rank…ranging widely with the help of swift horses and slender camels'.

In the millennia before Islam, inhabitants of the central Arabian peninsula consisted of nomadic pastoralists, settled cultivators around the oases, and raders and artisans in small market towns. Here, an early form of Arabic, lingua franca, was spoken. The nomadic groups, effectively tribes, wielded considerable power over sedentary communities. They were well-armed, sufficiently mobile to keep a controlling eye over trade routes and fiercely loyal o each other. They habitually swore allegiance to kinship or family chiefs, exercised their authority from the oases and forged strong links with the traders of the towns. The social structure of the Bedouins – see the Bedu (Bedouin) p148 – has its fledgling roots in the social organisation of these times.

Arabia's remoteness from the great empires of the Mediterranean (the Romans and Greeks) and the northern Middle East (the Assyrians and Babylonians) ensured that the peninsula was left largely to its own devices.

Arabia in antiquity was not solely a chaotic land of tribal wars, territorial disputes and blood feuds. Rather, the peninsula became a place of fabulous wealth, home to the lucrative and legendary trade in frankincense and myrrh (see The Frankincense Trade p135), which lured a Roman legion to march on Arabia in an attempt to wrest control of the trade in 25 BC.

Most trade routes to Egypt, Babylon and Rome took this precious commodity north across the Arabian peninsula. The camel (which had been domesticated in around 1500 BC) enabled trade caravans to reach the Mediterranean from southern Arabia in just over 60 days.

Empires that controlled key staging posts along the way were also enriched. Most notable among these were the Nabataeans (see Who Were The Nabataeans? p123) who controlled trade routes from their splendid rock-hewn cities of Madain Saleh (p117) and Petra (in Jordan) from the 4th century BC until AD 106.

Arabia and the Arabs: From the Bronze Age to the Coming of Islam, by Robert G Hoyland, is one of the few histories of Saudi Arabia to consider in detail the pre-Islamic period, albeit in a rather dry style.

Frankincense and Myrrh: A Study of the Arabian Incense Trade, by Nigel Groom, relates how frankincense and myrrh made Arabia rich, and examines connections with great empires of the time.

Find out everything you needed to know about the history of the Nabataeans and their trading civilisation at http://nabataea.net /who.html.

TIMELINE

6th century BC–AD 106	2nd century AD
Rise and fall of Nabataean empire	Peak of frankincense trade originating in southern Arabia

DID YOU KNOW?

In the 1st century AD, Pliny, the renowned Roman writer and philosopher, wrote that the people of southern Arabia were the richest people on earth.

The decline of the southern Arabian kingdoms of the Sabaeans (see p135) over a number of centuries, and the Roman conquest of the Nabataean cities, ensured ever-diminishing wealth and influence for the tribes of Arabia. The Byzantines and other northern empires began to trade directly with the Indians, bypassing the Arabians in the process. Arabia fell into obscurity.

THE RISE OF ISLAM

With the decline of the caravan trade, increasing difficulties associated with agriculture and the fall of the southern kingdoms, Arabia had come to exist only as a geographical designation, with no overarching sense of identity, political power or spiritual direction.

It was into this atmosphere of political obscurity and multiplicity of faiths that the Prophet Mohammed was born in AD 570. Mohammed's birth would give rise to a new religion, Islam, and transform the destiny of the Arabian Peninsula and beyond. For details, see p33.

DID YOU KNOW?

Contrary to popular belief, Arabs are a Semitic people who share a common ancestry with the Babylonians, Assyrians and Jews.

In the first centuries of Islam, power shifted from Arabia to the Umayyads in Damascus (661–750) and then the Abbasids in Baghdad (749–1258). Although loosely united by Islam and nominally under the suzerainty of distant empires, Arabian tribes who had once gone to war over trade routes now battled one another in an unending quest to be considered the true custodians of Mohammed's legacy (for more on Islamic sects, see p36). As Islamic civilisations elsewhere became the most advanced societies of the day – Damascus, Baghdad, Cairo, Constantinople and Cordoba became tolerant cities of splendour and unprecedented sophistication – Arabia descended into political infighting and was saved from obscurity only by its unparalleled spiritual significance.

With the prize of controlling the holy lands of Islam at stake, and in the absence of cohesive political power in Arabia, Muslim empires from the north and west began to vie with each other for control. The peninsula was invaded by the Seljuk Turks in 1174.

By the early 16th century, Arabia was under the control of the Egyptian Mamluks, but they were quickly swept aside by the forces of the Ottoman Empire. By 1517 the Ottomans, under Salim I, had established their authority over Hejaz (the area around Mecca and Medina). Salim I's position granted guardianship over the Muslim holy lands and the keys to the holy

---

THE YEAR OF THE ELEPHANT

It's not unusual to hear Muslims saying that Mohammed was born in the Year of the Elephant. Far from being some bizarre astrological designation, the name comes from an unusual series of events which took place in the year of the Prophet's birth. By the 6th century AD, the Himyarites (the conquerors of the Sabaeans) controlled much of southwestern Arabia. Their repression of southern Arabia's Christians (see The Trench p139) prompted an Axumite (Ethiopian) invasion. In AD 570, the extraordinary Marib Dam (a 550m-long dam built by the Sabaeans to regulate the waters of the Wadi Sadd) collapsed. Axumite King Abraha and his army marched on Mecca astride elephants – the first (and possibly the last) elephants ever to be seen in Arabia. They failed in their conquering mission and returned to the south, unaware that at the time of their expedition the Prophet who would transform the region and beyond was being born.

AD 570

Birth of Prophet Mohammed

610

Prophet Mohammed receives first revelations from Allah

ities of Mecca and Medina. The idea of the holy cities of Islam being under foreign, albeit Muslim, domination was anathema to many of the inhabitants of Arabia.

Attempts by the Ottoman-appointed sherifs of Mecca to assert their control in the regions of Najd and Hasa met with limited success. Standing once again at the edge of someone else's empire, much of Arabia fell under the effective control of local emirs who controlled the oases.

THE BIRTH OF SAUDI ARABIA

Mohammed ibn Abd al-Wahhab was born into one such oasis, Al-Uyaynah in Najd, in 1703. He belonged to an innocuous family of sedentary oasis dwellers and had nothing in his origins to suggest that he would play a defining role in the future of Arabia.

Al-Wahhab was a man of limited means – three wives and very little money. Driven by poverty and the religious piety of his family, he travelled to Mecca, Medina, Basra and Hasa to try his hand at religious scholarship. Upon his return to Al-Uyaynah, he began to preach a zealous message calling for the purification of Islam (see Wahhabi Islam p34 for more details).

Mohammed ibn Abd al-Wahhab and his reformist zeal were tolerated by the local authorities for a time, until he meted out severe punishments to those who didn't engage in communal prayer. He also led the stoning of a woman accused of adultery.

Al-Wahhab was expelled from the town, whereafter he sought refuge in the settlement of Dir'aiyah (p91), some 40 miles from Al-Uyaynah where he was granted protection by Mohammed ibn al-Saud, the local emir.

Building on the sense of affront, felt throughout the peninsula, that the holy cities of Mecca and Medina were under foreign tutelage, the Saudi-Wahhabi call to religious purity quickly took root and the emirate expanded rapidly. In addition to the spiritual dimension, there is very little doubt that many settlements accepted the new power more through fear of coercion than any sense of devotion. Whatever the motivation, fighters from oases across the Najd launched a jihad (holy war) which appealed to both nomads and city dwellers alike.

Upon his death, Mohammed ibn Saud was succeeded by his son Abdul Aziz, who captured Riyadh (south of Dir'aiyah; see p81) in 1765. The Saudi-Wahhabi emirate made further gains, taking much of Qasim in 1780, and southern Najd 12 years later. In 1792 Mohammed ibn Abd al-Wahhab died, having laid the foundations for the future interdependency of religious and political power in Saudi Arabia.

The slow but inexorable expansion of the Saudi-Wahhabi emirate continued, including a raid into Mesopotamia (Iraq) and the holy Shiite city of Kerbala in 1801. Two years later, the Saudi army marched on the Hejaz and defeated Sherif Hussain of Mecca in a famous victory. The same year, Abdul Aziz was assassinated by a Shiite fanatic in the mosque of Dir'aiyah in revenge for the sacking of the Shiite cities of Iraq. Despite losing their political leader, the Saudi-Wahhabi emirate was recognised by the Mecca authorities as ruler. The First Saudi Empire stretched from Hasa in the east to Hejaz in the west and to Najran in the south.

For the first time in history, the Arabian peninsula was united under a single political and religious authority.

A dry but comprehensive study of Saudi Arabian history up until 1992, drawn from the archives of the US Library of Congress can be found at www.countryreports .org/history/sauhist.htm.

THE SAUDI-WAHHABI PACT

The fact that much of the Arabian peninsula is called Saudi Arabia is due to the ambition, vision and astute political skills of a one-time obscure local ruler – Mohammed ibn al-Saud. Indeed, without him, Saudi Arabia would never have existed.

When the rebellious fugitive Mohammed ibn Abd al-Wahhab arrived in the Al-Saud stronghold of Dir'aiyah, it was a small settlement of less than 100 houses. Its rulers, the Al-Saud family, were a sedentary tribe of landowning merchants who had ruled the town only since 1727. Sufficiently wealthy to maintain large landholdings and finance merchants engaged in long distance trade, the Al-Sauds were able to secure the allegiance of the townspeople. Their rule over the population was also made possible by Mohammed ibn Al-Saud's political mediation skills and ability to defend the town from hostile forces; for this latter role he was paid tribute by the inhabitants. That said, the Al-Saud realm extended little beyond the outskirts of the oasis.

It was apparent to al-Wahhab that, in order to be successful, his reforms required the support of some form of political authority. It was similarly important for Al-Saud ambitions that their cause be distinguished from other minor emirates by some form of doctrinal Islamic legitimacy.

Mohammed ibn al-Saud quickly adopted Wahhabi Islam as the ruling ideology in Dir'aiyah. In 1744, not long after al-Wahhab's arrival, Mohammed ibn Abd al-Wahhab and Mohammed ibn al-Saud pledged an alliance, the overarching aim of which was nothing less than political and religious reform for the entire Arabian peninsula. Under the agreement, founded on the twin pillars of piety and patronage, Al-Saud accepted the role of imam, the leader of the Muslim community to whom zakat (alms or tax) must be paid, while al-Wahhabi was granted leadership in all religious matters and questions of Islamic interpretation. It is an arrangement which largely endures in Saudi Arabia 260 years later.

THE OTTOMAN BACKLASH

The Saudi embassy brushes lightly and uncritically over Saudi history and provides the authorized (ie Saudi government) view of history at www.saudiembassy.net /profile/history/hist _intro.html.

It didn't last long. Understanding all too well the symbolic importance of controlling Mecca and Medina, the Ottoman sultan Mahmoud II ordered his viceroy in Egypt, Mohammed Ali, to retake the Hejaz in the Ottoman sultan's name. In their favour was the fact that many rulers and tribes across Arabia had come to resent the harsh rule of their Saudi-Wahhabi overlords. Regular raids by the Wahhabis served several purposes within the emirate – regenerating the power base, shifting focus from economic difficulties and bolstering the confidence of those already within its realm – but they also alienated ordinary people with the exactions required as evidence of allegiance, and the destruction of the tombs of revered saints.

Consequently, when the Ottomans' largely Egyptian force launched their assault in 1811, many tribal enemies of the Al-Sauds fought alongside the Ottoman army.

With the overwhelming military superiority of an Empire behind them, the Ottoman armies made rapid gains. After taking Mecca and Medina, the Ottomans targeted the Saudi-Wahhabi stronghold of Dir'aiyah which fell on 11 September 1818. Abdullah ibn al-Saud, the contemporary Saudi leader, was carried off to Istanbul, where he was executed. Ottoman sovereignty over the peninsula was re-established.

THE BATTLE WITHIN

With the battle won, the Ottomans focused their attention on protecting pilgrimage routes to the Hejaz and left the areas to the east with only a

632	1517
Death of Prophet Mohammed	Ottoman authority established over the Hejaz (including Mecca and Medina)

nominal military force. In 1824 Turki ibn Abdullah, the son of the executed Abdullah, sought to pick up the pieces of Saudi pre-eminence by retaking Riyadh, all the while avoiding any confrontation which would draw the Ottomans in the Hejaz into an encounter. This second Saudi-Wahhabi emirate made some gains in the eastern region of Hasa, but the tribe soon descended into infighting. In 1834 Turki ibn Abdullah was assassinated by his cousin Mishaari. Turki's son Faisal killed his father's murderer, and claimed the title of emir of Riyadh.

The family squabbles inevitably attracted the attention of the Ottomans who captured the Saudi leader and sent him into exile in Cairo. In Faisal's absence, the Ottomans installed a more compliant member of the Al-Saud family in his place.

Six years later, Faisal escaped from his prison, marched on Riyadh and regained the throne, a position he would hold for another 22 years. When Faisal died, in a rerun of earlier events, the death threw the community into a succession of family squabbles.

Faisal had killed Mishaari with the assistance of the Rashidi emirate which came to prominence in 1836, the power of which rested with nobles of the Shammar tribe based in the northern Najd oasis of Hail (p93). After Faisal died, and after years of al-Rashid expansion throughout Najd and Hasa, the al-Rashidi began to eye Riyadh. In the early 1890s, Riyadh fell to the al-Rashidi. Most of the Al-Saud family sought protection in Kuwait.

FROM WARRING TRIBES TO ISLAMIC STATE

The decisive battle for the future of Arabia came in 1902 when the 21-year-old Abdul Aziz ibn Abdul Rahman ibn al-Saud (Ibn Saud) – the designated head of the family – and a small band of followers stormed Riyadh at night (see The Recapture of Riyadh p85). The religious authorities in Riyadh swore allegiance to the returned family and reinforced Al-Saud legitimacy through a series of religious edicts.

From that moment, Saudi authority over the peninsula became an unstoppable force. The al-Rashids were defeated and Al-Saud armies conquered Qasim and Hasa territories, including many Shiite towns (a fact that would further strain the future relations between the Sunni Wahhabi rulers and Shiite minority). Meanwhile, in 1908, the Ottomans appointed Hussain ibn Ali Sherif as the supreme religious authority in Mecca.

The outbreak of WWI sealed the decline of the ageing and decadent Ottoman Empire. Their Saudi territories proved impossible to defend for any length of time. After the war, Ibn Saud added Hail and Najd to the Al-Saud portfolio of conquered territories and turned his attention to the holy cities and the pilgrimage routes which connected them to the world beyond.

With deft skills of diplomacy and the momentum of successful military campaigns, Ibn Saud called a conference of Islamic clergy. Freed from the patronage of the Ottoman authorities and under immense pressure from Ibn Saud, the conference condemned Sherif Hussain as a foreign puppet. Sherif Hussain responded by proclaiming himself King of the Arabs.

The tide of history was with Ibn Saud. In 1924 Sherif Ali replaced his father Sherif Hussain in Mecca and Taif fell to Ibn Saud. With British support, Ibn Saud took Mecca and Medina in 1925, more than a century

A History of Saudi Arabia, by Madawi al-Rasheed, can get a bit dry but it's comprehensive and, importantly, written by a woman who draws on her own personal experience.

Lord of Arabia, King Saud: An Intimate Study of a King, by Harold Courtenay Armstrong, is a lively history-cum-biography of Ibn Saud; essential for understanding the drive and power of the Al-Sauds in the founding of Saudi Arabia.

1744	1811–1818
Pact between Mohammed Ibn al-Saud and Mohammed ibn Abd al-Wahhab in Dir'aiyah laying foundation for modern Saudi Arabia	Ottoman Egyptian forces capture Hejaz and Saudi emir sent into exile

DID YOU KNOW?

In 1915 the British government (colonial kingmakers in the region) recognised Ibn Saud as the ruler of Najd and Hasa and thereby gave legitimacy to the rule of the Saud's.

after having lost control over those holy cities of Islam. He then quickly mopped up the last vestiges of opposition in Jeddah. The following year Ibn Saud proclaimed himself King of the Hejaz and Sultan of Najd.

Troublesome revolts by the *ikhwan* (tribal orders of Muslim Brothers originally set up by Ibn Saud) were quashed with British help. Such rebellions, and the question of the involvement of foreign armies on Saudi soil gave the Al-Saud's a foretaste of the precarious tightrope they would have to walk as custodians of the holy places of Islam.

But for now, nothing could slow the Saudi ascension. On 22 September 1932, Ibn Saud announced the formation of the Kingdom of Saudi Arabia.

THE POWER OF OIL

DID YOU KNOW?

Saudi Arabia's first revenue from the oil industry in the 1930s was used to build a palace for the Saudi royal family.

The economic viability of the new kingdom was almost instantly secured by a series of fortuitous events. These began when Ibn Saud welcomed underground exploration – some reports claim that he hoped quantities of untapped artesian water would be discovered. Whatever his motivations, in 1933 Saudi Arabia signed its first oil concession and four years later the Standard Oil Company of California (Socal), operating as the Arabian American Oil Company (Aramco), discovered oil in commercial quantities near Riyadh and in the area around Dammam in the east. In 1939 the first oil tanker carrying Saudi oil left Ras Tannura.

The economic importance of Saudi Arabia transformed the desert kingdom from a political backwater to one of the most sought-after allies in the world. After an initial period of neutrality during World War II, Saudi Arabia declared war on Germany. The policy bore fruit in 1943 when President Roosevelt stated grandly that the Kingdom was 'vital for the defence of the USA'. In 1945 Ibn Saud met President Roosevelt and Winston Churchill, both of whom followed up with extravagant gifts and trade concessions.

As financial gains and expectations began to rise in unforeseen quantities, Riyadh's population almost doubled between 1940 and 1950. Even more exponential was the rise in government revenue which stood at US$13.5 million in 1946, rising to US$212 million in 1952.

DID YOU KNOW?

Saudi Arabia has the largest onshore oilfield in the world (al-Ghawar in Eastern Saudi Arabia – 250km long and 35km wide and 70 billion barrels of reserves) and the world's largest offshore field (as-Saffaniyah, near Kuwait).

Fearing a backlash from conservative elements within Saudi society, both Aramco (who was responsible for building much of the Kingdom's oil industry infrastructure) and the royal family ensured that contact between Americans and traditional Saudi communities was almost nonexistent. There was, nonetheless, an underlying resentment among the population that non-Muslims were present in the Kingdom and playing such a significant role in Saudi Arabian life.

For more on Saudi Arabia's oil industry, see The World's Largest Oil Producer p157.

THE MODERNISATION OF THE KINGDOM

Despite simmering discontent among Aramco's Saudi workforce and growing solidarity with Palestinians made homeless by the creation of the state of Israel, the last years of Ibn Saud's rule were ones of relative stability and he is still remembered fondly as a proud Najdi, strong in battle but always close to his subjects.

Upon Ibn Saud's death on 9 November 1953, his extravagant son Saud became king. Whatever his failures of economic management, the

1811–1818	Early 1890s
Ottoman Egyptian forces capture Hejaz and Saudi emir sent into exile	Riyadh falls to rival Rashidi tribe and the Al-Sauds seek protection in Kuwait

unpredictable Saud endeared himself to the 'Arab on the street' when he supported Egypt in the Suez Crisis of 1956 by sending them financial support, thereby tapping into the rising sense of Arab nationalism which was sweeping the region. He also unveiled the first Saudi oil embargo, this time against England and France.

Such grand flourishes could not stave off the creeping anxiety concerning the state of the Kingdom's finances. In 1964 Saud abdicated in favour of his brother Faisal.

Faisal proved adept at providing Saudis with a stake in the economic benefits of the oil industry, using a series of five-year economic plans to introduce a free health service for all Saudis. It was the start of the Saudi welfare state, a shrewd move which broadened support for the Al-Saud dynasty. This was also the dawn of the Saudi building boom which has transformed Saudi Arabia from an impoverished desert kingdom into a nation of modern infrastructure.

Following the debacle for the Palestinians in the 1967 and 1973 wars with Israel, attention shifted again to the nascent sense of Arab nationalism gaining widespread support in the Arab World. Largely secular in its orientation, this ideology was viewed with suspicion, even as a threat by a regime with deep roots in conservative Islamic orthodoxy, although Faisal understood the importance of paying lip service to the cause. In response to America's unflinching support for Israel, Saudi Arabia imposed an oil embargo on the United States in 1974, a move which quadrupled world oil prices, drew support from across the region and reminded the international community of the pivotal role played by Saudi Arabia in a world economy dependent on oil.

It was during Faisal's rule that so many of Saudi Arabia's most divisive issues also came to the fore for the first time: its willingness to use its political and financial weight as a significant regional player; its unwillingness to compromise the monarchical roots of the Al-Saud dynasty; and the tightrope it had to walk between the need for modernisation and the demands of a conservative Islamic constituency. As important as each of these issues were, they paled in comparison with the unease felt over the presence of foreign workers and military personnel in the land of Islam.

SIGNS OF DISSENT

On 25 March 1975 King Faisal was assassinated by a nephew, Prince Faisal ibn Musa'id. Official reports put out by the Saudi authorities claimed that the assassin was suffering from some form of psychological disorder. However, there was much unofficial speculation that the killing was an act of revenge for the death of the prince's brother who had been shot while protesting against the opening of the Kingdom's first television station ten years earlier. Although the throne passed to Faisal's brother Khaled, a man known for his piety, ascetic lifestyle and closeness to his subjects, the real power behind the throne was another of Faisal's brothers, Fahd.

In November 1979, the Great Mosque of Mecca was overrun by 250 fanatical followers of Juhaiman ibn Saif al-Otai, a militant Wahhabi leader, who claimed that the *Mahdi* (messiah) would appear in the mosque on that very day – the first day of the Muslim year 1400. Such a belief in black and white certainties soon descended into the altogether more messy reality

The Remaking of Saudi Arabia: The Struggle Between King Sa'ud and Crown Prince Faysal, 1953–1962, by S Izraeli and Sarah Yizraeli, covers quite well the all important years when oil wealth was growing and the Sauds set about modernising the Kingdom.

A History of the Arab Peoples, by Albert Hourani, is a sweeping and nuanced history of the Arab World and Islam, and is infinitely preferable to books which try to get inside 'the Arab mind'; essential reading.

1902	**1925**
Ibn Saud retakes Riyadh and religious authorities swear allegiance to the Al-Saud family	Ibn Saud recaptures Mecca and Medina and asserts Al-Saud dominion over the Hejaz

---

KING FAHD

Saudi Arabia's king was born in Riyadh in 1921 (some sources say 1923), the son of Ibn Saud. He was the eldest of seven full brothers who were known collectively as the Sudeiri Seven because their mother came from the Sudeiri clan. At the time of Fahd's birth, his father was busy unifying the peninsula under Saudi rule. Reports suggest, however, that the young prince – who was nine years old when the Kingdom of Saudi Arabia came into existence – was close to his legendary father.

Fahd's childhood was one of privilege. He was educated at the 'Princes' School' in Riyadh, a school established by Ibn Saud to provide carefully controlled guidance to the sons of important Saudi notables. From Riyadh, Fahd moved to Mecca where he studied at the Religious Knowledge Institute where classes were led by the Kingdom's leading Islamic scholars. For all of that, Fahd as a young man had a reputation for being something of a social playboy and political progressive.

Since then he has risen through the upper echelons of power in Saudi Arabia. From 1953 until 1960 Fahd was Minister for Education, before becoming Interior Minister in 1962, Second Deputy Prime Minister in 1967 and Deputy Prime Minister two years later. In 1975 he became Crown Prince.

For many, King Fahd will be remembered as the man who invited US troops onto Saudi soil to help remove Iraq from Kuwait, although he, perhaps more than any other Saudi king, has been responsible for reasserting the close ties between the monarchy and the Islamic religious institutions.

Despite suffering a stroke in 1995, Fahd has remained king, but has been little more than a figurehead.

Oil, God and Gold: The Story of Aramco and the Saudi Kings, by Anthony Cave Brown, is a slightly sensationalist account of the Saudi oil industry and its Western patrons, and is loaded with conspiracy theories.

of two bloody weeks of fighting, during which 129 people were killed. The conflict was a devastating blow to the credibility of a regime which had prided itself on being the preservers of the Wahhabi heritage (see Wahhabi Islam p34), and the rulers best able to safeguard the holy places.

The following year in December, riots broke out in the towns of the Qatif Oasis, the heartland of the Kingdom's 300,000 Shiites. This was inspired by the revolutionary fervour of their coreligionists in Iran and the exhortations of the Ayatollah Khomeini to export the Shiite revolution. But Saudi Shiites also remembered with anger the Al-Saud raids on the holy Shiite city of Kerbala in the early 19th century. On the Saudi side, fears of Iran's popular revolution sweeping aside the Sunni monarchies of the Gulf pushed the Kingdom into supporting Iraq in its war with Iran. The riots were brutally put down.

In May 1981, in a more considered bid to combat radicalism in the region, Saudi Arabia joined with the United Arab Emirates, Bahrain, Oman, Qatar and Kuwait to form the Gulf Cooperation Council (GCC) with its headquarters in Riyadh.

On 14 June 1982 the figurehead King Khaled died aged 69. Fahd became king, ensuring that the transition was a smooth one in a kingdom facing important challenges.

Backed by the legitimacy of his new title, King Fahd set about reinforcing the twin pillars (and contradictions) of modern Al-Saud rule. He made a priority of strengthening economic and military links with the United States, purchasing sophisticated weaponry and proving himself a moderate and reliable friend of the West, while in 1986 proclaiming himself the 'Custodian of the Two Holy Mosques'.

During the 1987 haj, bloody clashes broke out between Iranian Shiite pilgrims and Saudi security forces, further straining relations between the

1932	1933
Formation of the Kingdom of Saudi Arabia	Saudi Arabia signs its first oil concession

two Islamic powers. Some 400 people were killed and diplomatic relations between the two, which had never been close, soured further. In July 1990 the Saudi conduct of the haj, and hence its custodianship of Mecca and Medina, were again called into question when almost 1500 pilgrims suffocated or were trampled to death during a stampede in a pedestrian tunnel. It was one of numerous such incidents during the 1990s, including in 1996 (346 killed), 1998 (more than 100 killed) and March 2001 (35 killed).

THE GULF WAR

When Iraq invaded Kuwait in August 1990, the threat, both territorial and symbolic, to the Al-Saud dynasty was obvious. Saddam Hussein came to be seen across the Arab World as a strong leader willing to stand up to the West and issue a direct challenge to the inherited wealth and power of the compliant, conservative Gulf monarchies. The invasion also brought to the fore widespread resentment among impoverished Arab communities who had seen few benefits of the region's oil wealth spent so conspicuously by many Gulf Arabs.

Saudi Arabia's response was to open its doors to foreign military forces, especially those of the United States. The US government, for its part, feared that almost half of the known oil reserves in the region would soon be under Iraqi (rather than Saudi-Kuwaiti-US) control. Saudi forces took part in ejecting the Iraqi army from Kuwait, as well as offering critical logistical and financial support. The Saudi economic commitment placed serious strains on the country's foreign reserves and prompted cutbacks in expenditure on public welfare. This cost to the country for supporting the Americans heightened discontent.

During the conflict in early 1991, Iraq fired Scud missiles at Saudi Arabia. Of greater threat to the long-term security of the Kingdom, the decision to allow the large-scale presence of US and other foreign troops brought to the surface long-simmering dissatisfaction that non-Muslims

Saudi Arabia and the Politics of Dissent, by Mamoun Fandy, gives an excellent background on Islamic opposition in the Kingdom, drawing on the sermons, strategies and backgrounds of Saudi Islamic activists.

Saudi-US Relations Information Service maintains a series of articles and links which cover the history of Saudi-US relations over the last eight decades at www.saudi-us-rela tions .org/history/saudi -history.html.

RELATIONSHIP WITH ISRAEL & THE PALESTINIAN TERRITORIES

Although Saudi Arabia has never gone to war with Israel, the Kingdom's financial power, its role as custodian of the holy cities of Mecca and Medina, and its historical friendship with Washington place Saudi Arabia at the centre of the debate. Far from being the obstructionist power that many believe, Saudi Arabia actually has a history of important peace initiatives.

As early as 1981 Crown Prince Fahd put forward a plan demanding that Israel pull out of the West Bank, Gaza Strip and Golan Heights, abandoning all Jewish settlements and land seized since 1967 in the process. In return, Arab governments would have recognised Israel's right to exist within secure borders, leading to an eventual establishment of diplomatic relations. The same year, Fahd's proposal was adopted as policy by the Arab League. In September 1993, Saudi Arabia announced its support for the Israeli-PLO peace accords and proceeded to fund, almost single-handedly, the fragile Palestinian economy. Pro-Palestinian demonstrations in Al-Jouf and Riyadh in October 2000 prompted the Saudis to pledge US$800 million to preserve the Islamic identity of Jerusalem and US$200 million to families who suffered as a result of the *intifada* (Palestinian uprising against Israeli authorities). Most recently, in early 2002, Crown Prince Abdullah announced a peace plan that was almost identical in scope to that offered by Crown Prince Fahd in 1981.

1943	9 November 1953
US President Franklin D Roosevelt declares Saudi Arabia to be 'vital for the defence of the USA'	Death of Ibn Saud

were allowed to operate so openly and aggressively against a Muslim nation from the country of the holy cities of Mecca and Medina.

It was the decision to allow foreign troops to operate from Saudi soil which would propel Osama bin Laden, a Saudi Arabian, and his Al-Qaeda movement onto the world stage.

STRUGGLE FOR THE SOUL OF SAUDI ARABIA

Pressures within the Kingdom were most apparent in 1991 when Saudi women, spurred on by witnessing female American soldiers driving, defied the ban on female drivers. That year a petition calling for reforms and greater openness was sent to King Fahd by liberal intellectuals. It was quickly followed by a contrary petition by conservative Islamic scholars.

In early 1992 a written constitution was announced. On 20 August 1993, after much fanfare, the Majlis ash-Shoura (Consultative Council) was opened on 20 August 1993. Its 60 members (all men appointed by the king) consisted of university teachers, government officials, religious leaders, media figures, former military officers, and businessmen, but, significantly, not one of the more than 3000 princes of the ruling Al-Saud family. In July 1996 the Council was increased to 90 members, including four (instead of the previous one) Shiite members and a number of Sunni opponents of the regime. It was estimated at the time that 81 of the members held doctoral degrees, mostly from US universities.

Critics of the reforms claimed that it amounted to little more than a codification of absolute royal power, cementing the ruling family's control over all aspects of the Kingdom; the Consultative Council possessed no law-making powers. Supporters of the reforms argued that it was the most important initiative since 1932 and as much as the finely balanced forces in the country would realistically allow.

To satisfy Islamic opponents of greater liberalisation, the authorities announced in July 1992 that a new Ministry of Islamic Affairs was to be set up, with full status in the executive Council of Ministers. This was followed in October 1994 with the formation of a new religious council, the Supreme Council of Islamic Affairs. Headed by the Defence Minister, it was a thinly veiled attempt to regain control over the country's religious affairs and to counter the authority of the deeply conservative Council of Senior Ulema.

Such moves notwithstanding, dissent within Saudi Arabia was coming into the open more frequently than ever before. On 14 October 2000, two Saudi security officers hijacked a London-bound Saudia airlines flight and demanded that it be flown to Baghdad. The key demands included nothing less than the abolition of the Saudi monarchy and the removal of US

THE MAJLIS

For centuries in Arabia, the *majlis* was a traditional meeting where oasis emirs and tribal sheikhs held public audiences. These were designed to receive petitions from subjects, mediate disputes, renew allegiances and demonstrate the power of the presiding ruler. When the Majlis ash-Shoura (Consultative Council) was inaugurated in 1993, the name chosen suggested that the Al-Sauds were attempting to mould traditional Bedouin institutions to modern imperatives for Saudi survival in the face of internal tensions.

1982	1990–91
Fahd becomes king after seven years as the power behind the throne	Saudi Arabia welcomes US troops on Saudi soil to expel Iraq from Kuwait

and UK military forces from the Kingdom. The hijackers gave themselves up to the Iraqi authorities and were granted asylum.

In the midst of this unease, effective power was transferred from King Fahd, who had suffered a stroke, to Crown Prince Abdullah on 1 January 1996. The move sparked fresh concerns about Saudi Arabia's direction. The crown prince, a half brother of Fahd and head of the National Guard, was widely seen as more conservative and less pro-Western than King Fahd, although this is disputed in some circles.

Despite intermittent attacks on Western interests, most notably in Riyadh in November 1995 and Al-Khobar in June 1996, tension within Saudi Arabia largely remained an internal matter.

SAUDI ARABIA AND THE WEST

Following the discovery of oil in the Kingdom in the 1930s, Saudi Arabia enjoyed a special relationship with the West. 'September 11' would prove the catalyst for this close relationship coming to an end, but it had already begun to unravel in the 1990s.

In 1994 two Saudi diplomats had caused great embarrassment by seeking asylum in the West and denouncing the Kingdom's record of human rights. At around the same time, the world media and human rights organisations led a chorus of disapproval with accusations of corruption, widespread religious and political persecution, discriminatory treatment of foreign workers and ill-treatment of women. Saudi Arabia's image in the West as a repressive, totalitarian state was further enhanced when figures were published in 1995 suggesting that 148 people, mostly foreigners, had been executed in the first eight months of the year.

The new hesitancy in Saudi-US relations was reflected in the fact that the US-led Operation Desert Fox attacks on Iraq in December 1998 were not launched from the Kingdom, although US bases in Saudi Arabia continued to be used for patrolling the no-fly zones in Iraq. In the meantime, Saudi Arabia quietly bought US$115 million worth of US missiles.

And then the September 11 terrorist attacks happened. Fifteen of the nineteen hijackers were Saudi citizens and Osama bin Laden – the spiritual leader and alleged mastermind of the attacks – is Saudi Arabian by birth. Saudi unwillingness to commit troops to the US-led war on Iraq in 2003 hardly helped their cause. Allegations of collusion and financial support for terrorists by prominent members of the royal family, the perceived failure to act against Al-Qaeda cells supposedly operating in the country, and suggestions of a covert Saudi pact of non-aggression with Al-Qaeda further deepened the crisis.

In May 2003 suicide bombers attacked targets across Riyadh, killing dozens of people just hours before US Secretary of State Colin Powell was due to arrive in the Kingdom. A month earlier, the US government had announced that it would withdraw almost all of its troops from Saudi Arabia and close many of its military bases. A further bombing occurred in November.

Although both the US and Saudi Arabia stress that they remain strong allies, Saudi Arabia continues to experience unprecedented criticism from the Western media and politicians. The response of the Saudi government has been to crack-down hard on militants within the Kingdom and to launch a public relations offensive, spending millions of dollars in advertising and lobbying in an attempt to restore its reputation as a reliable friend of the West. At the same time, Western governments have actively begun to look elsewhere – most notably Africa and the former Soviet states – for an alternative source of oil, leaving many to wonder whether, after more than 60 years, Saudi Arabia's special relationship with the West is over.

1995	11 September 2001
Fahd suffers a stroke, and Crown Prince Abdullah effectively assumes power	Saudi-US relations weaken following World Trade Centre terrorist attacks: 15 of the 19 attackers were Saudi

The Culture

THE NATIONAL PSYCHE

Saudis are fiercely proud of their Islamic heritage, deeply religious, and you'll be hard-pressed to have a conversation which doesn't turn at some point to Islam. Yet they're also drawn to satellite TV and the Internet with all the exposure it brings from a corrupting, secular outside world. Many Saudis speak proudly of their Bedouin desert heritage, but few happily forsake the comforts of city life and a lot even look down their noses at Bedouins as uncouth reminders of an uncivilised past. Saudis are deeply wary of Western encroachment onto Islamic values and lands (Iraq, Saudi Arabia), but they also love American fast-food restaurants and American-made fast cars. Deeply fearful of the social dislocation wrought by declining family values and the consequences of terrorism, the Saudi people equally long for the respect of the outside world and speak as if resistant to change even as they embrace it. You'll also meet many Saudis, particularly among the young, who hold firmly to their conservative Wahhabi Islamic roots even as they express a desire to study in the West. Outsiders are viewed with a very Saudi reserve that can dissolve into the most generous hospitality.

LIFESTYLE

Saudi society is strictly segregated between the public (male) and private (female) domains. Women are allowed in public, but with strong restrictions (see p174). Young Saudis are gently pushing the boundaries of these social norms (see Shebab & Shopping Mall Culture p90), but it's done very discreetly.

Apart from Islam, the family is the bedrock of Saudi society and family members only leave the family home once married. Tribes, once so important in Saudi Arabia, have become a lesser source of loyalty through the judicious cultivation of alliances under the Al-Sauds.

The Saudi educational system has, over the last two generations, been a battleground between conservatives and reformers. Educating women is particularly problematic; the first girls' school was opened in 1956 by the wife of the future King Faisal, but it had to be disguised as an orphanage.

DOS & DON'TS

- Always dress conservatively. Shorts in public are absolutely out of the question. The exceptions to the rule are the private beaches operated by top-end hotels (see p163), compounds where expatriates live, and some hotels and tourist sites (eg Madain Saleh). For advice on the dress code for women, see p174.

- Take things offered to you with the right, not the left, hand and avoid showing the soles of your feet to people.

- When offered coffee or tea in someone's home or at a business meeting, it is considered impolite to refuse.

- Don't attempt to enter a mosque unless you are a Muslim.

- Don't expect your foreign newspaper to include all its pages; censors routinely extract articles about Saudi Arabia and any photos considered vaguely risqué.

- Never make contact with a Saudi woman unless expressly invited to do so and with the full knowledge of her male relatives.

In September 1963 the news that a girls' school was to open in Buraydah sparked riots in the city. From these difficult beginnings has grown a system of free (though strictly segregated) primary and secondary education for all Saudi citizens. At last count, there were around 100,000 students in Saudi Arabia's seven universities; male professors sometimes lecture their female students via video link.

The Saudi curriculum has been widely criticised for its overwhelming focus on Islam (at least one third of all subjects relate to the Quran). Many young Saudis leave school unprepared for jobs and, according to some, susceptible to religious extremism.

Foreign children are not allowed to attend Saudi schools. Most foreign communities in the Kingdom run schools following their own systems; children of Western expatriates usually attend US or British-system international schools.

POPULATION

Discussing the population of Saudi Arabia is hardly an exact science – a comprehensive census has never been held in the Kingdom. Nonetheless, it's believed that more than 75% of Saudi Arabia's population live in urban areas, with one-third of the population living in the urban agglomerations centred on Riyadh, Jeddah and Mecca. Overall population density is around 12 people per sq km, although desert regions have fewer than one person per sq km. Despite the urbanising impact of oil wealth and modernisation, around 1.8 million Saudi Bedouins still claim to live a nomadic lifestyle.

Rapid population growth is one of the Kingdom's most enduring long-term problems. With around 45% of the population under 15 years old and an annual population growth rate of over 3% (which means that the population doubles every twenty years), the Saudi authorities are increasingly confronted with the dilemma of providing for a disaffected, young population with not enough jobs (or money) to go around. According to the World Bank, the average annual income (2001) for Saudis was US$8,460.

SPORT

The most popular sports in Saudi Arabia are the traditional forms of desert entertainment: falconry, horse and camel racing.

Camel races are held every Thursday afternoon (and some Fridays) just outside Riyadh (p91). The most prestigious is the Jenadriyah National Festival (p87), where up to 2000 camels compete over an 18km track.

MULTICULTURALISM

Modern Saudi Arabia is a paradox: one of the most insular societies on earth where nearly one third of the population is not Saudi Arabian, but is expats/foreign workers.

Traditional Arabian society was loosely divided into nomadic desert dwellers (the Bedouin; see The Bedu (Bedouin) p148), traders and sedentary town-dwellers. In this pre-oil world, tribes were the main source of cultural identification and loyalty. Foreigners were seen as infidels and admitted only grudgingly. The people of the Najd (from Riyadh to Sakaka) considered themselves to be the true Arabs with their ancestral roots in Bedouin nobility, while those of the Hejaz were more cosmopolitan as a result of 14 centuries spent receiving Islamic pilgrims, many of whom remained upon completion of the haj. The tribes of the Eastern Province were similarly exposed to cultural differences, while the people of the southwest were culturally part of Yemen.

DID YOU KNOW?

In 1985 40% of Saudi students attending primary and secondary school were female.

Saudi-American Forum offers useful cross-cultural dialogue with articles discussing the Saudi-American relationship and changes taking place within Saudi society at www.saudi-american-forum.org/index.html.

DID YOU KNOW?

The hunting art of falconry has been practised since ancient times in Arabia; it was born out of a need to hunt for food in the desert, and has long since become one of Saudi Arabia's favourite and most prestigious pastimes.

THE ARABIAN HORSE

Decked out fair to men is the love of lusts: women, children, heaped up heaps of gold and silver, horses of mark, cattle, and tillage. That is the enjoyment of the present life.
The Quran, sura 3:14

Few things are held in higher esteem in the Kingdom than the Arabian horse.

The true homeland of the Arabian is the Najd Plateau in central Arabia where the breed was first developed almost 3500 years ago by nomadic tribes. These horses became creatures of prestige, but were also highly adaptable to desert conditions and possessed many of the qualities revered by the Bedouin: beauty, endurance, intelligence, speed, courage in battle and loyalty to its owners.

When Islamic armies spread the new religion across the world, they rode astride Arabian horses, introducing the breed to China and Spain and all places in between; Arabians would go on to be the horse of choice for everyone from Spanish conquistadors and Native Americans to American presidents.

Ironically, such was the popularity of the Arabian horse that demands by breeding programmes across the world caused numbers to dwindle in Saudi Arabia itself, necessitating an urgent export moratorium. The Saudi authorities are now at the forefront of breeding the Arabian horse in the Kingdom, including research and accreditation programmes for pure bloodlines. Saudis are encouraged to participate by lucrative purebred race prize money, particularly for the King's Cup and Crown Prince's Cup at the annual Jenadriyah National Festival.

If you're planning on buying an Arabian horse, remember that at a 1997 auction for 52 pure-breed Arabians, the average price was US$84,000 per horse.

Cities of Salt, by Abdelrahman Munif, is a novel exploring the discovery of oil and subsequent American interest on a small Bedouin community; its setting is fictional although believed by many to be Saudi Arabia (where it is banned).

Since the discovery of oil, many former nomads have flocked to the city and multiculturalism has been forced upon the Saudis, although they have developed their own special arms-length variety whereby foreigners are allowed to enter the Kingdom to enable its wealth to be developed, but any integration (or even interaction beyond that which is necessary) is rigorously discouraged.

Official figures place the number of foreign expatriates living and working in the Kingdom on temporary visas at around six million (for more details on the division within expat circles, see The Great Divide p56). A process of Saudisation is perennially underway, but a comprehensive process of replacing foreign workers with Saudis continually founders on an education system which privileges religious instruction over technical or professional development, and an unwillingness among young Saudis to work for the wages that non-Western expats are willing to work for.

MEDIA

All media outlets are heavily restricted by Saudi government rules and Islamic sensibilities (the Saudi Press Agency is as responsible for controlling information in the public sphere as it is for disseminating it). All media outlets must obtain government approval, as must all editorial appointments.

For media published within Saudi Arabia, the greatest concern is to avoid all criticism of the royal family or religious authorities, as well as promoting support for popular causes in the Arab World. At the same time, the Saudi authorities are very keen to project an image to the outside world of a modern, stable country, ever-vigilant against terrorism. This complicated balancing act also has to accommodate the heralding of the Al-Sauds as the worthy guardians of the holy places of Islam. The end result? Even vaguely controversial news stories of significance are rarely reported.

The Internet is strictly policed, with over 2000 sites blocked at last count. Most of these are pornographic, but they also include sites discussing politics, health, women's rights and education. For a full list of Internet topics prohibited by the Saudi authorities, visit www.al-bab.com /media/docs/saudi.htm.

Most Saudis get around these restrictions by the use of satellite dishes for televisions and even for dial-up Internet connections. That's just as well because the most interesting programmes otherwise are occasional folk music recordings which are infinitely more entertaining (at least for non-Muslims) than mullahs (religious scholars, teachers or leaders) reading aloud from the Quran, or Islamic scholars discussing the intricacies of Quranic interpretation.

The most popular TV station is undoubtedly Al-Jazeera, which legally operates within the Kingdom, but has a tenuous relationship with the Saudi royal family. Crown Prince Abdullah launched an attack on the station at the beginning of 2003 for threatening the stability of the Arab World.

DID YOU KNOW?

Internet sites are prohibited if they portray 'anything damaging to the dignity of heads of states or heads of credited diplomatic missions in the Kingdom, or harms relations with those countries.'

RELIGION

Islam is more than the state religion in Saudi Arabia – it's an all-encompassing way of life. Officially, all Saudis are Muslim. Among the large population of expats living in the Kingdom, many are Hindu or Christian, but the practice of other religions is forbidden in Saudi Arabia.

DID YOU KNOW?

The modern Saudi state refers to the pre-Islamic period as *jahiliyah* or 'the Period of Ignorance'.

Islam
THE BIRTH OF ISLAM

In the 6th century AD, Arabia was a world of disparate nomadic tribes who felt keenly the loss of influence they had once enjoyed through trade (p20). This loss of purpose created a cultural vacuum, and existential and spiritual angst stood at the centre of the Arabian existence.

Abdul Qasim Mohammed ibn Abdullah ibn Abd al-Muttalib ibn Hashim (the Prophet Mohammed) was born in AD 570. Mohammed's family belonged to the Quraysh tribe, a trading family with links to Syria and Yemen. By the time he was six, Mohammed's parents had both died and he came into the care of his grandfather, the custodian of the Kaaba in Mecca. At around 25 years of age, Mohammed married Khadija, a widow and a merchant, and he worked at running her business.

At the age of 40, in 610, Mohammed retreated into the desert and began to receive divine revelations from Allah (God) via the voice of the Archangel Gabriel. Three years later, Mohammed began imparting Allah's message to the Meccans. Mohammed soon gathered a significant following in his

---

PRESS FREEDOM – THE FIRST STEPS

One positive outcome of the widespread access to satellite programmes has been a discernible relaxation in press censorship. Indeed, long-term expats have noted how, in the last ten years, critical articles have begun to appear on just about every topic, with only criticism of the royal family and Islam considered taboo. Articles now appear regularly in the Arabic- and English-language press discussing hitherto off-limits topics, including unemployment, corruption and the extravagance of rich Saudis when abroad. Significant developments came in March 2003, when the press published unprecedented investigations into (and criticisms of) the death of 15 girls in a fire at their school in Mecca. Eyewitness accounts were reproduced stating that religious police forbade the unveiled girls from escaping the burning school. The information and interior ministries soon clamped down on the story, but not before a top religious official was forced to resign and education matters were transferred to the aegis of the education ministry.

campaign against Meccan idolaters and his movement appealed especially to the poorer, disenfranchised sections of society.

Islam provided a simpler alternative to the established faiths which had become complicated by hierarchical orders, sects and complex rituals, offering instead a direct relationship with God based only on the believer's submission to God (Islam means 'submission').

Among Mecca's ruling families, however, there was a dawning recognition of the new faith's potential to sweep aside the old order. By 622, these families had forced Mohammed and his followers to flee north to Medina. There, Mohammed's supporters rapidly grew in number. By 630, Mohammed returned triumphantly to Mecca to seize control of the city and establish it as the spiritual home of Islam. Many of the surrounding tribes quickly swore allegiance to him and the new faith.

When Mohammed died in 632, the Arab tribes spread quickly across the Middle East with missionary zeal, quickly conquering all of what now constitutes Jordan, Syria, Iraq, Lebanon, Israel and the Palestinian territories. Persia and India soon found themselves confronted by the new army of believers and the unrelenting conquest also swept across North Africa. By the end of the 7th century, the Muslims had reached the Atlantic and then marched on Spain in AD 710, an astonishing achievement given the religion's humble desert roots.

THE QURAN

For Muslims, the Quran is the word of Allah (God), directly communicated to the Prophet Mohammed. It comprises 114 suras (chapters) which govern all aspects of a Muslim's life from a Muslim's relationship to Allah to minute details about daily living.

In addition to drawing on moral ideas prevalent in 7th century Arabia, some of the Quran's laws closely resemble those of the other monotheistic faiths, particularly the doctrinal elements of Judaism and the piety of

WAHHABI ISLAM

The prevailing Islamic orthodoxy in Saudi Arabia is Wahhabi Islam, named after Mohammed ibn Abd al-Wahhab who, in the 18th century, preached a 'new' message which was essentially a call to return to the roots and purity of Islam (also known as the Hanbali or literalist school of Islamic interpretation). With its ties to the power of the Al-Sauds (p21), Wahhabi Islam has been unassailable in Arabia ever since.

At the heart of the Wahhabi doctrine lies the denunciation of all forms of mediation between Allah and believers and a puritanical reassertion of *tawhid*, the oneness of God. Under the Wahhabis, only the Quran, the Sunnah (words and deeds of Mohammed) and the Hadith (Mohammed's sayings) are acceptable sources of Islamic orthodoxy. Worship of saints and the reverence towards tombs belonging to holy men (especially by the Sufis) are seen as acts of egregious heresy.

Obligations espoused by al-Wahhab included the requirement to pay zakat, a tax payable to the leader of a Muslim community and calculated according to a person's wealth. Communal prayers were also considered a religious duty, and rulings on personal matters were interpreted according to Sharia'a law which had changed little in the eleven centuries since it was revealed by the Prophet Mohammed. The austere and puritanical message also came with a sharp edge – the obligation of believers to respond with a holy war or jihad against all who didn't heed the Wahhabi call.

One of the central questions in modern Saudi Arabia is the battle over who can be considered the true inheritors of the legacy of Mohammed ibn Abd al-Wahhab. In November 1979, militant Wahhabis took over the Great Mosque in Mecca and demanded reforms (see p25). At its heart, the ongoing fight by Al-Qaeda is also to prove that Al-Qaeda, not the Saudi royal family, are the modern guardians of the austere and fundamentalist Wahhabi vision.

early eastern Christianity. The suras contain many references to the earlier prophets – Adam, Abraham (Ibrahim), Noah, Moses (Moussa) and Jesus are all recognised as prophets in a line that ends definitively with the greatest of them all, the Prophet Mohammed. Muslims traditionally attribute a place of great respect to Christians and Jews as *ahl al-kitab*, the people of the book (sura 2: 100-115). However, Muslims believe that the Quran is the final expression of Allah's will and the ultimate and definitive guide to his intentions for humankind and fanatical Wahhabi orthodoxy is unusually hostile to any deviations (whether they be Shiite or Christian) from Sunni Islam.

It's not known whether the revelations were written down during Mohammed's lifetime. The third caliph (successor of Mohammed), Uthman (644–656), gathered together everything written by the scribes (parchments, stone tablets, the memories of Mohammed's followers) and gave them to a panel of editors under the caliph's aegis. A Quran printed today is identical to that agreed upon by Uthman's compilers fourteen centuries ago.

Another important aspect of the Quran is the language in which it is written. Some Muslims believe that the Quran must be studied in its original classical Arabic form ('an Arabic Quran, wherein there is no crookedness', sura 39:25) and that translations dilute the holiness of its sacred texts. For Muslims, the language of the Quran is known as *sihr halal* (lawful magic). Apart from its religious significance, the Quran – lyrical and poetic – is considered one of the finest literary masterpieces in history.

THE FIVE PILLARS OF ISLAM

In order to live a devout life, Muslims are expected to observe, as a minimum, the Five Pillars of Islam:

shahada This is the profession of faith, Islam's basic tenet: 'There is no god but Allah, and Mohammed is the Prophet of Allah'; this phrase forms an integral part of the call to prayer and is used at all important events in a Muslim's life.

salat (sura 11: 115) This is the obligation of prayer, ideally five times a day.

zakat (sura 107) Giving of alms to the poor, an essential part of the social teaching of Islam.

Sawm (sura 2: 180-185) Ramadan, the ninth month of the Muslim calendar, commemorates the revelation of the Quran to Mohammed. As Muslims' renewal of faith, nothing may pass their lips (food, cigarettes, drinks) and they must refrain from sex from dawn until dusk. For more information see p37 and Ramadan in Saudi Arabia p47).

haj (sura 2: 190-200) The pinnacle of a devout Muslim's life is the pilgrimage by Muslims of able body and sufficient means to the holy sites in and around Mecca. The high point is the visit to the Kaaba, the construction housing the stone of Ibrahim in the centre of the haram (the sacred area). The faithful, dressed only in white robes, circle the Kaaba seven times and kiss the Black Stone. See p62 for a personal exploration of the haj.

THE CALL TO PRAYER

> *Allahu akbar, Allahu akbar*
> *Ashhadu an la Ilah ila Allah*
> *Ashhadu an Mohammed rasul Allah*
> *Haya ala as-salat*
> *Haya ala as-salat*

This haunting invocation will soon become the soundtrack to your visit to Saudi Arabia, a ritual whose essential meaning and power remain largely unchanged in fourteen centuries. Indeed, for the non-Muslim, the sight of hundreds of believers praying in unison can be a profoundly moving experience.

Muhammad: A Biography of the Prophet, by Karen Armstrong, is a sensitive, well-researched and highly readable biography of the Prophet Mohammed set against the backdrop of modern misconceptions and stereotypes about Islam.

A fairly balanced and detailed coverage of the history and central tenets of Wahhabi Islam can be found at http://reference.all refer.com/country-guide -study/saudi-arabia /saudi-arabia40.html.

DID YOU KNOW?

Depending upon your interpretation, the charging of interest is prohibited by the Quran (sura 2: 275-280).

Five times a day, Muslims are called to prayer – if not actually to enter a mosque to pray, then at least to take the time to do so where they are. The midday prayers on Friday, when the imam (religious teacher) of the mosque delivers his *khutba* (weekly sermon), are considered the most important. For Muslims, prayer is less a petition to Allah (in the Christian sense) than a ritual re-affirmation of Allah's power and a reassertion of the brotherhood and equality of all believers.

When the call to prayer is heard in Saudi Arabia, everything stops and all businesses close for the duration (from 25 to 30 minutes; see Dodging Prayer Times p164).

ISLAMIC CUSTOMS

History of the Wahhabis, by Louis Alexander Olivier De Corancez, can be hard to find but it's worth it for those with an interest in the theological foundations of Saudi Arabia.

Before Muslims pray, they must first wash their hands, arms, feet, head and neck in running water; all mosques have an area set aside for this purpose. If they're not in a mosque and there's no water available, clean sand ('wholesome dust' according to the Quran) suffices; where there's no sand, they must go through the motions of washing (sura 5:5). Then they must face Mecca – all mosques are oriented so that the mihrab (prayer niche) faces the holy city – and follow a set pattern of gestures.

In everyday life, Muslims are prohibited from drinking alcohol (sura 5:90-95) and eating carrion, blood products or pork which are considered unclean (sura 2:165), the meat of animals not killed in the prescribed manner (sura 5:1-5) and food over which has not been said the name of Allah (sura 6:115). Adultery (sura 18:30-35), theft (sura 5:40-45) and gambling (sura 5:90-95) are also prohibited.

Islam is not just about prohibitions but also marks the important events of a Muslim's life. When a baby is born, the first words uttered to it are the call to prayer. A week later there follows a ceremony in which the baby's head is shaved and an animal sacrificed in remembrance of Abraham's willingness to sacrifice his son to Allah. The major event of a boy's childhood is circumcision, which normally takes place between the ages of seven and 12. When a person dies, a burial service is held at the mosque and the body is buried with the feet facing Mecca.

SUNNIS & SHIITES

The Prophet Mohammed died leaving no sons, which lead to a major dispute over who would succeed as the Commander of the Faithful. Competing for power were Abu Bakr, the father of Mohammed's second wife Aisha, and Ali ibn Abi Talib (Ali), Mohammed's cousin and the husband of his daughter Fatima. Initially, power was vested in Abu Bakr, who became the first caliph.

Abu Bakr's lineage came to an abrupt halt when his successor was murdered. Ali reasserted his right to power and emerged victorious in the ensuing power struggle. He moved his capital to Kufa (later renamed Najaf, in Iraq), only to be assassinated himself in AD 661. The Umayyad dynasty, after defeating Ali's successor, Hussein, in AD 680 at Kerbala, rose to rule the vast majority of the Muslim World, marking the start of the Sunni sect, Islam's largest. Those who continued to support the claims of the descendants of Ali became known as Shiites.

Beyond this early dynastic rivalry, there is little doctrinal difference between Sunni and Shiite Islam, but the division remains Islam's greatest schism to this day. Sunnis comprise some 90% of the world's more than 800 million Muslims.

In Saudi Arabia, just 15% of the population are Shiites, and this is concentrated in the east of the country (the Qatif and Hasa Oases), close to the border with Bahrain. This Shiite minority has always been viewed with suspicion by the Saudi government who fear that the Shiites may harbour secret desires to follow the path of Islamic revolution as taken by their coreligionists in Iran. Many in the Al-Saud family also remember that the Saudi ruler Abdul Aziz was assassinated by a Shiite in 1803.

For their part, many Shiites remember with great anger the 1801 Al-Saud sacking of the holy Shiite cities of Najaf and Kerbala (p21), and the early 20th century annexation by Ibn Saud of predominantly Shiite territories (p23). There's also discontent that less than 4.5% of the Majlis ash-Shoura (Consultative Council) are Shiites.

Riots in eastern Shiite towns in December 1980 and clashes between Iranian pilgrims and the Saudi authorities in 1987 (p26) have ensured that the division is never far beneath the surface.

The Kingdom of Saudi Arabia, by David Long, discusses the country's oil wealth and its moves towards modernisation, but is particularly noteworthy for its sympathetic coverage of the haj pilgrimage and its importance in Saudi life.

ISLAMIC HOLIDAYS
The principal religious holidays in Muslim countries are tied to the lunar Hejira calendar (the year AD 622 is the year 1 AH). The calendar is about 11 days shorter than the Gregorian (Western) calendar, meaning that in Western terms the holidays fall at different times each year. See p168 for a table of dates of Islamic holidays. The principal religious holidays are:

Ras as-Sana New Year's day, celebrated on the first day of the Hejira calendar year, 1 Moharram.

Mawlid an-Nabi A lesser feast than that which follows Ramadam and the haj, celebrating the birth of the Prophet Mohammed on 12 Rabi' al-Awal.

Ramadan & Eid al-Fitr The month of fasting and the subsequent feast.

haj & Eid al-Adha The pilgrimage to Mecca in Zuul Hijja, the 12th month of the Muslim year (pilgrimage should be accomplished at least once at this time). The haj culminates in the ritual slaughter of a lamb (in commemoration of Ibrahim's sacrifice) at Mina. This marks the beginning of the Eid al-Adha, or Feast of the Sacrifice. For a personal account of the haj, see p62.

Women and Words in Saudi Arabia, by Saddeka Arebi, paints a fascinating and illuminating picture of life for women in Saudi Arabia by looking through the eyes of nine female Saudi writers; highly recommended.

WOMEN IN SAUDI ARABIA
In the opinion of many people, life for women in Saudi Arabia is more difficult than in any other country in the world, particularly with regard to freedom of movement (women are forbidden from driving and may not travel without being accompanied by a male relative), freedom of speech and freedom from dress restrictions. Many Saudis would argue vociferously for reforms, even as many would counter with the claim that women in Saudi Arabia live free from the fear of public sexual violence and dishonour under Islam.

Saudi Arabia recently signed the United Nations Convention to Eliminate Discrimination Against Women, although it has yet to enact this in any meaningful way. Female children enjoy the same rights to attend (single-sex) schools and universities as men, although families often place restrictions upon their daughters attending. Women are also active as teachers, doctors, nurses, social workers, journalists in the print media and business managers (Mohammed's first wife ran her own business), although their numbers are proportionally small and most women are employed to deal only with other women.

In recent decades a number of small, but potentially significant events have occurred in Saudi Arabia in relation to the involvement of women in public life:

'Being a Woman in Saudi Arabia', a thought-provoking and insightful essay, written by an American woman who has lived in Saudi Arabia for more than 30 years, can be found at www.saudi-american-forum.org/Newsletters/SAF_Essay_07.htm.

1991 Saudi women drive in Riyadh in protest against prohibition on female drivers.

October 1999 20 Saudi women attend a session of the Consultative Council as observers.

July 2003 A Saudi woman successfully sues her male relatives and wins back her inheritance.

Late 2003 Consultative Council appoints three women to serve on advisory council.

January 2004 Akbaria, an all-news Saudi station, features three unveiled female presenters.

Voices of Change: Short Stories by Saudi Arabian Women Writers, by Abu Bakr Bagader (ed), is a diverse exploration of social issues (divorce, alcohol and other seemingly taboo subjects) and their impact upon the lives of women and their families.

January 2004 At the Jeddah Economic Forum, four Saudi women (a CEO, journalist, doctor and college professor) share a platform with former US president Bill Clinton and Queen Rania of Jordan; one scarcely wore a headscarf and discussed women's education, employment and women's control over their financial assets.

Reformers insist that changes are coming in Saudi Arabia, but for every gain there is a conservative backlash and hence reforms take longer here than anywhere else.

All foreigners, particularly men, should *never* seek to make contact with a Saudi woman unless expressly invited to do so and with the full knowledge of her male relatives. Western women may enjoy the occasional chance encounter in a shopping centre or similar public place, but generally the same rules apply. Remember that breaking such a taboo would not just place you in a potentially dangerous position, but would put the woman in question also.

ARTS
Literature

The Sheltered Quarter: A Tale of a Boyhood in Mecca, by Hamza Bogary, is set in early 20th-century Mecca before the discovery of oil; it provides a fascinating window onto a forgotten world at the heart of Islam.

Bedouin poetry and storytelling are part of a rich oral tradition with desert and Islamic legends, often in poetic form, at their heart. However, little has been committed to written form and even less translated into English.

Modern Saudi Arabian poets include Hasan Faqi, Hasan al-Qurashi, Tahir Zamakhshari and Mahrum. Sadly, English translations of their work can be difficult to find. An exception is the highly imaginative Ghazi al-Gosaibi who writes in both Arabic and English.

Novelists who have chronicled the impact of oil money and modernisation on a deeply traditional desert kingdom include Hamza Bogary, Ahmed Abodehman and Abdelrahman Munif; the latter's citizenship was revoked and his books, thinly veiled parables of Saudi Arabia, banned in the Kingdom. Hamid al-Damanhuri's *Thaman al-Tadhiyah* (The Price of Sacrifice) and *Wa-Marrat al-Ayyam* (And the Days Went By) are two novels available in English.

The Belt, by Ahmed Abodehman, is a moving and fictitious portrayal of a rural family's attempts to come to terms with the complex interplay between rural Saudi life, tribal traditions and the encroachment of modernisation.

Recent translations of Saudi women writers offer a previously unavailable window into their world. Among the most rewarding are: Saddeka Arebi; Raja Alim (plays); Fowziyha Abu-Khalid (poetry exploring the relationship between literature and religion); Ruqayya Ash-Shabib (short stories about ordinary Saudi women); Sharifa As-Shamlan (short stories); Khayriyya As-Saggaf (short stories); and Najwa Hashim (short stories).

Cinema & Television

Saudi Arabia has no history of film-making and cinemas are banned in the Kingdom.

Spike Lee visited Saudi Arabia during the course of filming *Malcolm X*, in order to shoot authentic footage for the protagonist's 1964 pilgrimage to Mecca. *Lawrence of Arabia* also dealt with some very Saudi subjects, but was filmed in Jordan.

Music

Since the early 1980s, the Saudi government has made recordings of folk music traditions from supposedly every village of the Kingdom and some of these are shown on Saudi television in a show called 'Folk Arts'. In the Hejaz, the al-Sihba form of folk music blends Bedouin poetry with the songs of Arab Andalusia in medieval Spain. The most popular traditional instruments are the oud, the *tar*, and, in the Hejaz, *al-mizmar*, a wind instrument similar to the oboe.

Beyond that, the most musical thing that you'll hear is the melodic calls o prayer from the Kingdom's mosques. Under the dictates of Wahhabi, slam generally frowns upon nonreligious music for its potential to excite he senses and prompt good Muslims to commit un-Islamic acts.

Of the musicians whose music has found a listening audience in the wider Arab World, the most important are Tariq Abdul Hakim, Mohammed Abdou (more than 100 albums), Abadi al-Johar (a particularly fine oud player), Mohammed Aman (Arabic poetry put to music) and Abdou Majeed Abdullah (the secret favourite of young Saudi women and as close to a pop star as Saudi Arabia gets).

An extensive listing with links to websites with information pertaining to the Kingdom is on the web at www.searchbeat.com /saudiarabia.htm.

Architecture

Saudi Arabian architecture was traditionally functional in conception and style: high-walled homes to keep out prying eyes, built from mud, stone and palm products. Probably the best examples still in evidence today are at Al-Ula (p116) and Dir'aiyah (p91).

Mud fortress-style architecture found its most enchanting expression in Najran (p135) in southwestern Arabia. Further north, the merchants of Jeddah (see The Architecture of Al-Balad p101) built stunning homes from Red Sea coral and with lattice-work wooden balconies.

Wahhabi asceticism ensured that Islamic architecture developed an austere, unadorned style. Masjid (mosques) adhered to the layout of the Prophet Mohammed's house in Medina: an enclosed, oblong courtyard with huts along one side wall and a rough *zulla* (portico) providing shade at one end for poorer worshippers. A mosque's *sahn* is based on Mohammed's courtyard; the arcaded *riwaqs* (colonnades) on Mohammed's portico; and the haram (prayer hall) on the huts. The mihrab (a vaulted niche indicating the direction of Mecca) is at the centre of the *qibla* wall (also facing Mecca) and is also the site of the minbar (pulpit) from where the *khutba* (Friday sermon) is delivered. Almost every mosque has a minaret (from *menara*, meaning lighthouse) from where Muslims are called to prayer.

Modern Saudi architecture has taken a daring new turn, with stunning new buildings providing a much-needed counterpoint to the functionality of sprawling Saudi cities. The most stylish expressions of this new aesthetic are the Kingdom Tower (p87) and Al-Faisaliah Tower (p86).

Visual Arts

Undertake a search for painters in Saudi Arabia and you're more likely to find someone who can paint your villa rather than something to hang on its walls – the Quran forbids images or any form of representations of living figures.

Theatre & Dance

The mesmerising Bedouin *ardha*, with its roots in the Najd, is the national dance of Saudi Arabia and involves a pastiche of singers, dancers and a poet or narrator. Sword-bearing men, shoulder to shoulder, are set off by a singing poet – they begin to sway in unison to rhythmic drumbeats.

Another traditional dance is *al-mizmar* (particularly popular in the Hejaz) where men dancing in unison are accompanied by the instrument of the same name (p38).

Your best chance of seeing one of the more than 50 folklore dance and music groups in Saudi Arabia, is at the annual Jenadriyah Festival (p87).

Environment

THE LAND

Saudi Arabia takes up 80% of the Arabian peninsula, its territory consisting of 2,149,690 sq km (829,780 sq miles). It is four times the size of France, roughly comparable to the size of Western Europe and is approximately a quarter the size of Australia.

Over 95% of Saudi Arabia is desert or semidesert and is occupied by the central desert plateau, known as the Najd plateau. The country is also home to some of the largest desert areas in the world, including the Al-Nafud desert in the north and the Rub al-Khali (Empty Quarter) in the south and southeast. In keeping with its arid climate and high levels of evaporation, the east and northeast of the country have a large number of salt flats, particularly in the east and northeast. Many of these salt flats are criss-crossed by wadis (dry riverbeds). Just 0.5% of Saudi territory is considered to be suitable for agriculture and less than 2% of the land is covered by forest.

A different world awaits along the Red Sea coastline, particularly in the south, where you'll even find forests and mountains shrouded in fog. Saudi Arabia's most elevated regions run like a spine down the west coast, from 1500m (4921 feet) in the north up to Jebel Soudah (2910m) in the southwestern Asir highlands. In geological terms the Asir ranges are part of the same geological fault line as Africa's Great Rift Valley.

WILDLIFE

The animal and plant life of Saudi Arabia is surprisingly diverse given the proportion of the Kingdom which is covered by desert. For more information on the Kingdom's wildlife, contact the **National Commission for Wildlife Conservation and Development** (NCWCD; ☎ 01-441 8700; ncwcd@zajil.net). You can also visit the National Wildlife Research Centre (NWRC) near Taif (p110) by appointment.

Animals

Among the creatures you might see on your travels across the Kingdom are desert mice, *idmi* (mountain gazelle), *reem* (sand gazelle) and *afri* (Saudi dorcas gazelle). Indeed, the rare sight of a gazelle racing across the Rub al-Khali is among the most exhilarating in nature. More likely, you'll come across the Arabian hamadryas (baboons) which are proliferating along the mountain roads of southwestern Arabia, largely because their former predators, the leopard (p41) and striped hyena, are either dying out or extinct; travellers along the roads frequently feed the baboons, which inhibits their long-term ability to survive in the wild. Other species in the Kingdom include honey badgers, foxes, gerbils, hedgehogs, hyenas, jackals, jerboas, mongooses, porcupines and wolves.

No matter what any Saudi tells you, there's no such thing as a wild camel; all are privately owned.

The waters surrounding Saudi Arabia are also rich in wildlife (see Red Sea Diving p107), including five species of marine turtles; green and hawksbill turtles sometimes breed on Saudi Arabia's Red Sea beaches. Whales and dolphins are also present in both the Red Sea and Arabian Gulf.

Many expats living in the Kingdom find themselves distressed by the treatment of animals in Saudi Arabia. As one told us:

DID YOU KNOW?

The Al-Hasa oasis, near the town of Al-Hofuf in eastern Saudi Arabia, is considered by many geographers to be the largest oasis in the world. It covers 2500 sq km and boasts at least two million palm trees.

The Wildlife of Saudi Arabia and Its Neighbours, by Wilhelm Buttiker, is a comprehensive study of the Kingdom's wildlife, although its 1992 publication date ensures that important recent developments are missing.

One of the big things I had to endure was the appalling attitude that the Saudis have in regard to animals. Cats everywhere, in health conditions that I would rather not remember. It is Haram (not allowed) to practise euthanasia but ok to run them down in the car…The zoos and pet stores are another issue altogether, along with the illegal trade of exotic animals from chimpanzees, hyenas, [to] alligators etc.

Alanna Lee, Jeddah

BIRDS

Saudi Arabia is home to almost 450 species of birds, most of which are migratory species; Saudi Arabia is an important staging post on migratory routes between Africa and Asia.

Southwestern Saudi Arabia has the Kingdom's widest variety of birdlife which includes bustards, eagles, goshawks, linnets, magpies, partridges, thrushes and woodpeckers. Central and northern Saudi Arabia are home to eight species of lark, including the breeding grounds of Dunn's lark, the thick-billed lark and Temminck's horned lark. Sand grouse and various wheatear species are also present in the area.

Coastal regions are also rich in bird life and the tidal flats of the Arabian Gulf in winter host up to two million waders belonging to almost 125 species. Also present in the gulf are the Socotra Cormorant, lesser crested tern, and bridled tern. At least 14 species of sea birds breed along Saudi Arabia's western Red Sea coast where the brown booby, pink-backed pelican, sooty gull, white-eyed gull and crab plover are all present.

ENDANGERED SPECIES

Seven species were threatened with extinction in Saudi Arabia in 2000, among them the Syrian wild ass, Arabian gazelle, Saudi Gazelle, Arabian *jird*, Arabian oryx and Nubian ibex. Efforts such as captive breeding and reintroduction programmes are at the forefront of the government's efforts to arrest the slide (see the Return of the Arabian Oryx below).

Also highly endangered is the Arabian leopard (*nimr* in Arabic) which once ranged across the Arabian peninsula. The last of Arabia's big cats, the leopard is particularly vulnerable because it is present only in small and isolated populations. The most recent estimate is that between just 80

THE RETURN OF THE ARABIAN ORYX

Just two hundred years ago, the Arabian oryx (Oryx leucoryx), with its distinctive white coat and curved horns, once roamed across much of the Arabian peninsula, with the greatest concentrations present in the Al-Nafud desert in northern Arabia and the Rub al-Khali (Empty Quarter; see p141) in the south. Hunting devastated the population and the last wild oryx was killed in the Dhofar foothills of Oman in 1972.

Fortunately, a captive breeding programme had begun in the early 1960s and in 1964 nine Arabian oryx (gifts from Gulf sheikhs) were taken to the Phoenix Zoo in the United States. By 1977 the 'World Oryx Herd' in America had grown to almost 100. Between 1978 and 1992, members of the herd were transported back to the Middle East, including 55 oryx to Saudi Arabia.

Arabian oryx from the breeding programme of the National Wildlife Research Centre (NWRC; p110) near Taif were released into the fenced Mahazat as-Sayd protected area (2244 sq km). And since 1995, 149 oryx have been released into the 'Uruq Bani Ma'arid protected area (p146) in Rub al-Khali near Sulayyil. Their territory now measures 12,000 sq km and, despite the challenges of poaching and drought from 1997 to 2000, the remaining animals (estimated to number between 160 and 500) are the only viable herd of Arabian oryx left in the wild, 30 years after they disappeared from the peninsula.

and 250 leopards survive, spread across Oman, Yemen and Saudi Arabia. No longer present in the deserts of the Rub al-Khali, the leopard's last strongholds are the mountains and coastal hills, even up to an altitude of 2600m. At last count, captive breeding programmes consisted of just 16 animals spread across four of the Gulf States, including Saudi Arabia.

Also vulnerable are Geoffroy's bat, the lesser horseshoe bat and Sind bat. The Kingdom's waters are among the last remaining habitats for the dugong.

Endangered bird species include the Arabian bustard (found on the Tihamah coastal plain). The ostrich and Houbara bustard are being bred in captivity and the latter has been successfully reintroduced into the wild. Also under close observation is the lappet-faced vulture which is subject to a captive breeding population in the Mahazat as-Sayd Protected Area.

A good site dedicated to programmes preserving the endangered species of the peninsula is at www.breedingcentres harjah.com/.

Plants

Saudi Arabia is home to almost 3500 plant species, which are most heavily concentrated in the southwest of the country where up to 1000 types of plants with Mediterranean characteristics are present. In more arid desert regions, only the most hardy of plants survive: tamarind and acacia trees, desert shrubs, salt bushes, tussock grass, and cacti. In the oases and other regions where water is more plentiful, date palms abound, providing ample shade for gardens of apricot, lime and quince trees as well as grape vines and vegetables to thrive.

For where to watch birds and other wildlife in Saudi Arabia, and a good listing for most of Saudi Arabia's protected areas, go to www.arabian wildlife.com/archive /vol2.2/sauwhe.htm.

Saudi Arabian territory is covered by just 20,000 sq km of forest (see p128 for more details).

NATIONAL PARKS

The system of national parks in Saudi Arabia seems quite haphazard, and information pertaining to them somewhat elusive. At the time of writing, the Saudi authorities had designated 11 wildlife reserves (which amount to over 5000 sq km). Only the Asir National Park, however, was really operational (or discernible) for visitors.

When Saudi authorities set up the Asir National Park, they reassured the population that 'planners expect these projects can be implemented with a minimum of impact on the country's social values'. This must have been a success because the Saudi government has ambitious plans for setting aside many more protected zones where wildlife can flourish; 100 protected areas such as the 11 already in place have been planned. To visit any of these places, apart from the Asir National Park, you'll first need to contact the NCWCD (p40).

Some of Saudi Arabia's national parks:

Asir National Park Saudi Arabia's largest national park covering 4500 sq km in the Asir highlands; one of last homes of the Arabian leopard (p132).

Al-Hasa National Park A 45 sq km reserve centred on the Al-Hasa oasis.

Sa'ad National Park 300 hectares under development as a national park, east of Riyadh along the highway to Dammam.

Harrat al-Harrah First National Park Northern breeding ground for larks and the endangered Houbara bustard, as well as the Golden Eagle.

'Uruq Bani Ma'arid Protected Area 12,000 sq km site for the reintroduction of the Arabian oryx (p146).

Other areas earmarked for protection:

Abu-Ali Islands connected to the mainland by a causeway north of Jubail and a stopping point for migratory birds.

Al-Ha'ir Special Nature Reserve Man-made river near Riyadh, home to teals, herons, stilts and egrets.

At-Tubayq Nature Reserve Rough sandstone terrain providing one of last habitats for Nubian ibex.
Farasan Islands Special Nature Reserve Red Sea island reserve where the Farasan gazelle, turtle and seabird breeding colonies are present.
Hawat Bani Tamin Special Nature Reserve 900 sq km ibex reserve 200km south of Riyadh; also home to Houbara bustard and Griffon vulture.
Hima al-Figrah Mountainous juniper forest west of Medina and an important site for leopard, wolf and ibex.
Jebel al-Jawz Northern mountainous region near Tabuk, home to Egyptian vulture and chuker.
Mahazat as-Sayd Special Nature Reserve Enclosed area 175km northeast of Taif; refuge of the sand cat, the Rueppell's fox, the reintroduced Arabian oryx, and the Houbara Bustard as well as 115 bird species.

A UN-generated site with comprehensive analysis of Saudi Arabia's moves towards sustainable development can be found at www.un.org /esa/agenda21/natlinfo /countr/saudi/natur.htm.

ENVIRONMENTAL ISSUES

Saudi Arabia's environmental problems are legion, and include (but are not limited to): desertification; critical depletion of underground water; pollution from oil industry spills and fertilizers; underwater damage caused by oil extraction; and the fate of endangered species.

The most serious environmental crisis for the Kingdom came during the 1991 Gulf War when up to eight billion barrels of oil were released into the Arabian Gulf by retreating Iraqi forces and 616 Kuwaiti oil wells were set on fire. As a direct result of this environmental vandalism, up to 30,000 birds and countless marine mammals died. Although billions were spent on the largely successful clean-up, Saudi Arabia remains vulnerable to such environmental catastrophes.

Everything you wanted to know about the Arabian Oryx and the fight to protect it against extinction is on this website: http://arabian -oryx.com.

The NCWCD (p40) is responsible for formulating regulations governing water and land use and oil-spill response programmes. They also oversee wildlife rescue centres, the creation of national parks, animal welfare education programmes, and reforestation and soil stabilisation programmes.

Captive breeding programmes and the subsequent reintroduction of species formerly extinct in the wild (see p41) are considered to be among the most successful in the world, and the Kingdom's water shortages are being partially addressed through the development of costly seawater desalination facilities.

However, serious problems remain. Illegal hunting remains widespread and punishment by Saudi authorities is thought to be nonexistent. Apart from poaching, the greatest threat to the survival of the leopard (p41) and other endangered species is the expansion of human settlements to accommodate Saudi Arabia's rapid population growth and the decline in numbers of ungulate (hoofed mammal) species. This latter problem has resulted in leopards killing domestic stock. Hunting for prized leopard skins also continues.

Saudi Arabia has signed many international agreements protecting the environment, but few have been ratified by the government and they are yet to be incorporated into domestic law.

Food & Drink

Saudi food shares many characteristics with the cuisines of other Gulf states. When this is combined with the varied diet carried here by millions of expatriates from across Asia and further afield, the result is some of the most diverse dining in the Middle East.

DID YOU KNOW?

The *truh* is a long, thin and dark cucumber with grooved skin. Gulf legends state that, when the moon is full, you can hear these cucumbers moaning as they twist themselves into the most improbable shapes.

Great feasts mark the momentous events of Saudi society: the daily breaking of the fast during Ramadan (see Ramadan in Saudi Arabia p47); Eid al-Adha, the joyous celebration for carnivores after the completion of the haj (see A Bedouin Feast p46); and a whole host of family landmarks such as weddings and births. You may not encounter these very often, but they're the essential context within which Saudi food must be viewed.

In between such feasts, there's a bounty of international dishes to enjoy in the larger cities of Saudi Arabia. Indian, Filipino, Thai, Chinese and Italian restaurants abound, so you're unlikely to ever be too far away from a great meal.

STAPLES AND SPECIALITIES
Starters

If you're counting your riyals and eating in predominantly cheap restaurants, the closest you'll come to an appetizer is a fresh salad, which could include lettuce, cucumbers, tomatoes, sweet peppers, radishes and/or herbs. Whatever the ingredients, they'll almost certainly be fresh swimming in a vinegar dressing and be accompanied by a bag of *khobz* (flat bread), yogurt and perhaps a small bowl of pickled vegetables.

In better restaurants, the menu may include mezze, truly one of the joys of Arab cooking. Similar in conception to Italian antipasto or Spanish tapas, the possibilities for mezze are almost infinite, but can include dips such as hummus (chick peas), a variety of nuts, *lahm bi-ajin* (small lamb pies), *kofta* (meat balls), *waraq aynab* (stuffed vine leaves) and other savoury pastries.

SAUDI ARABIA'S TOP FIVE RESTAURANTS

The following are our picks for the best five restaurants in the Kingdom, based on the quality of the food and the setting:

- **Al-Nakheel** (p89) Perhaps the Kingdom's highest quality restaurant for Arabic food, located in the capital.
- **Al-Sanbok** (p155) Best seafood in Al-Khobar, beautifully cooked and presented in lavish surrounds.
- **Globe** (p89) Located in a glass globe, nearly 250m above Riyadh; quality European dishes with exceptional views.
- **Green Island Restaurant** (p105) Romantic restaurant in Jeddah; wooden chalets branch out over the Red Sea.
- **La Gondola** (p155) Best and most creative Italian restaurant in Saudi Arabia, also located in Al-Khobar.

Other honourable mentions include **Al-Alawi Traditional Restaurant** (p104) in Jeddah, **New Chiang-mai Seafood Restaurant** (p154) in Al-Khobar and **Il Terrazo** (p89) in Riyadh.

Main Dishes

Grilled chicken, *fool* (fava bean paste) and *shwarma* (beef or chicken in pita bread) are the ubiquitous cheap dishes. You'll find restaurants specialising in nothing else on seemingly every street in every town in the Kingdom. At all such places, your chicken will be served with rice and salad.

At more expensive restaurants, the rice (hard-grain basmati) will itself be a highlight. It's aromatic and enlivened by a spice mix known as *baharat* which can include include any or all of cardamom, coriander, cumin, cinnamon, nutmeg, chilli, ginger, pepper, with (occasionally) turmeric and saffron added for colour. Rose water (or orange-blossom water), pine nut, tomato and *samneh* (ghee; clarified butter) are also sometimes used in the cooking. The *baharat* spice concoction, is also sometimes used in preparing soups, fish and other meat dishes. Another enduring favourite Gulf palates is kebab *mashwi* (grilled meat on skewers).

Upmarket restaurants serve a variety of international cuisines. Seafood is a widely available Saudi Arabian highlight, with more expensive restaurants offering prawns, mussels, lobster and fish (best when slow-cooked over coals or baked in the oven). At cheaper places, fish is usually fried.

Desserts

The Arabs love their sweets, particularly fruit (water melons, pomegranates, bananas, grapes and apricots). Of the super-sweet desserts which you may come across, baklava and rice pudding served with cinnamon and almonds are popular, while pastries of every imaginable variety are widely available.

DRINKS

Coffee, and the long-spouted brass coffee-pots from which coffee is served, are the great symbols of Bedouin hospitality and still used in more modern settings to seal a business deal. Traditionally, only a third of a very small, handle-less cup is poured each time and the unsweetened coffee is flavoured with cardamom.

Tea is also popular and usually served with copious amounts of sugar and sometimes with mint. Only a few traditional coffeehouses, in which everyone drinks tea, remain in Jeddah (p105), Taif (p110) and some provincial towns, but most have yielded to Western-style cafés (eg Starbucks) situated in shopping malls.

Of course, alcohol is banned, so cold drinks don't extend much beyond soft drinks, mineral water and fruit juice. Nonalcoholic beers are available in restaurants and supermarkets, while the only thing risqué about Saudi 'champagne' (apple juice mixed with Perrier) is the name.

DID YOU KNOW?

Spices have been used here since the days of the spice caravans which once crossed Arabia, connecting Asia and India to the Mediterranean.

DID YOU KNOW?

Bedouin hospitality demands that the most honoured guest is seated next to the host, who chooses the most succulent parts and places them before his guest – reserved for this are the lamb's eyes, considered a great delicacy. Don't even think of refusing.

TRAVEL YOUR TASTEBUDS

You might think that there are only so many ways to cook meat or fish. Think again. Some of our Saudi favourites (including one meatless option):

- **camel steak** – most commonly grilled or stewed with onions and spices
- **kabbza** – lamb or chicken cooked with onion, tomato, cucumber, grated carrot and fruit
- **khouzi** – whole lamb on top of chicken and rice stuffing, see A Bedouin Feast p46
- **labneh makbus** – yogurt cheese balls, sometimes made into a frittata-like creation or rolled in paprika; a treat for sweet tooths
- **mihammar** – lamb cooked in yogurt sauce and stuffed with nuts, raisins and other dried fruit
- **samak mashwi** – fish basted in a date purée and barbecued over hot coals

CELEBRATIONS

The great of events of family life are celebrated with great ceremony and always centre around a feast of some sort. Homes of even moderately wealthy Saudis usually have a living room custom-built for receiving guests and hosting important gatherings.

Before meals, endless rounds of coffee and tea are served, while the ceremonial offering of dates (highly valued by Saudis for their nutritional value) is a sign of welcome. Guests sit on the floor and eat with their hands from the communal platter. After the meal, sweetmeats may be served before all retire to another room for more coffee, conversation and the smoking of the *sheesha* (water pipe).

Of course, men and women eat separately.

The most famous ceremonial dish for important Saudi or Bedouin feasts is *khouzi* (see A Bedouin Feast below), and the Saudi version of *khouzi* is considered the best of all the Gulf States.

Another important dish is *thurid* (chicken in a cream sauce served on leaves of dough) which is served during New Year celebrations in Mecca, while *shurba* (a soup) and *sambusik* (triangular wafers with spicy meat and onion filling fried in oil) are the food of choice for breaking the Ramadan fast.

WHERE TO EAT & DRINK

Saudi Arabia's multiplicity of restaurants is enjoyed as much by Saudi families as expats; well-to-do Saudi families eat out regularly (especially on Thursday or Friday nights). Riyadh (p88), Jeddah (p104), Al-Khobar (p154) and, to a lesser extent, Dammam (p153) have excellent restaurants with a variety of international cuisines; outside these places, you're unlikely to have much choice.

Saudis also love to dine alfresco, especially on weekends when large family groups gather in parks, at beaches and even in the most unappealing places by the roadside. We suggest something more picturesque than dining under overpasses along the highways.

A BEDOUIN FEAST *Anthony Ham*

In a village in the northern Najd region of central Arabia, I was invited to the annual Eid al-Adha feast as a guest of the local village sheikh. When we entered the room together, the waiting men of the village greeted the sheikh with great respect. Around the walls of the room, lounging on cushions, were the (all-male) great and good of the village. Coffee and tea appeared every few minutes, while plates of dates were spread liberally around the room. Then came smoking incense to inhale.

In another room, on the floor, lay three enormous platters with great mounds of steaming rice, on top of which sat a lamb, head and all. This was the *khouzi*, a dish renowned throughout Arabia. To make it, a stuffing of rice, nuts, onions, sultanas and spices had been prepared and packed into a chicken along with hard-boiled eggs. Thus filled, the chicken had been placed inside the cavity of the lamb with the remainder of the stuffing. The whole hybrid animal had then been placed in a large cooking tray and baked until the lamb came easily away from the bone. The stuffing had then been removed and spread, ready for eating, and the lamb placed on top.

Around the perimeter of this were salad, grapes and yogurt. After finishing their tea and coffee, the Bedouin men formed a seated circle around this offering, and quietly and discreetly partook of it with their hands. All the while, my host broke off the choice pieces and forced them upon me. Reluctantly, I accepted.

The meal completed, we washed our hands in perfume and then retired to the living room for postprandial repose, conversation, the distribution of sugar cane (for cleaning the teeth) and gifts (prayer beads).

RAMADAN IN SAUDI ARABIA

Oh believers, prescribed for you is the Fast, even as it was prescribed for those that were before you…the month of Ramadan, wherein the Quran was sent down to be a guidance to the people, and as clear signs of the Guidance and the Salvation. So let those of you, who are present at the month, fast it.

The Quran, sura 2: 175-185

In Saudi Arabia, the invocation to fast during the holy month of Ramadan is taken very seriously. Commencing with the new moon for the month of Ramadan (cash prizes are often awarded to those who make the first recorded sighting), the fast is universally observed and enforced by the mutawwa (religious police). Ramadan can be a difficult time for the non-Muslim in the Kingdom. Shops and other businesses are open shorter hours and those supposedly at your service can be decidedly short-tempered; this is especially so in summer. The streets of even large cities can be eerily deserted.

That said, the Ramadan celebratory aspects almost compensate for the hardships of the day just passed. *Iftar* or *ftur*, the breaking of the day's fast, is a time of great and clamorous activity, when people come together to eat, drink and pray.

During Ramadan, it can feel as if night and day have been reversed, with evenings given over to crowds of people shopping, sitting in traffic jams and, above all, eating long into the night. Many restaurants shelve their menus and offer night-time buffets which are hugely popular.

The end of Ramadan marks the Eid al-Fitr, the Festival of Breaking of the Fast, which lasts for up to five days. It can be a great experience if you're invited to share in the festivities with locals.

Non-Muslims are not expected to participate in the fasting, even if more pious Muslims suggest that you do. However, restaurants that are open during the day can be very hard to find (your best chances are top-end hotels). Avoid openly flouting the fast – there's nothing worse for the hungry smoker than seeing a non-Muslim cheerfully wandering, cigarette in hand or munching away – unless you want an unpleasant encounter with a mutawwa.

Roadside restaurants have little variety on the menu, but you can eat Bedouin-style, seated cross-legged on slightly raised platforms.

Quick Eats

You're never far from a cheap restaurant serving *shwarma*, *fool*, burgers and/or chicken and rice.

Saudi Arabia is the biggest per-capita consumer of American junk food in the world outside the US, and there has been a worrying increase in obesity among Saudi teenagers; there are outlets of the usual suspects in all the main cities.

VEGETARIANS & VEGANS

Many Saudis consider vegetarianism either as an incomprehensible Western affectation or something bordering on culinary apostasy. In smaller towns, you'll have to make do with rice and salad. However, the large number of expatriates (and restaurants) from Asia and the Indian subcontinent mean that vegetable dishes are quite widely available. Obviously, the greatest choice is available in the large cities, while top-end hotels and upmarket restaurants are always willing to cook a vegetarian meal (without the head-shakes of bewilderment that you'll encounter in cheaper Saudi restaurants).

WHINING & DINING

Eating out as a family is a common pastime among Saudis, so it's rare for a waiter to bat an eyelid as he almost trips over a running child. Restaurants

DID YOU KNOW?

The spouts of Arabian coffee pots are sometimes lined with fibre to strain the liquid of impurities.

DOS & DON'TS

■ Don't (ever) eat, pass or receive food with your left hand.

■ Don't hesitate to ask for cutlery if you're experiencing difficulties getting rice from hand to mouth.

■ Don't point the soles of your feet at other diners when seated on the floor.

■ Don't noisily slurp your tea or coffee unless you're sure of your company; once a sign of appreciation, it's not the done thing in modern, well-mannered Saudi society.

■ Do jiggle your cup from side to side to indicate you've drunk enough coffee or tea; otherwise they'll keep pouring thinking you're thirsty.

■ Do accept the first three cups of coffee offered by your host; it can be an insult not to.

■ Do remove your shoes before entering the dining area if eating in a private home.

The Complete Middle Eastern Cookbook, by Tess Mallos, is an excellent cookbook but is also excellent for background on the food and social context of the region, with a section on Saudi Arabia and the Gulf.

are also accustomed to making special arrangements (ie smaller portions) for children. In cheaper places, this usually amounts to nothing more complicated than serving a quarter (rather than a half) chicken to a child, while many mid-range and top-end restaurants have children's menus and are always happy to improvise. Indeed, many restaurants in the Kingdom are more child-friendly than those in Western countries.

HABITS & CUSTOMS

As you'll almost always eat in restaurants not that dissimilar from those at home, local customs rarely come into play. See Dos & Don'ts above.

EAT YOUR WORDS

If you're tired of conversations in Arabic passing you by, learning the words for food will simplify your life and may even win you a few smiles from hassled waiters. For pronunciation guidelines see p193.

Useful Phrases

Do you have ...?	*haal indaak ...?*
I'd like ...	*ana areed ...*
Does anyone here speak English?	*Haal yoogaad ahad yatakaallam ingleezi?*
What do you recommend?	*bi maza tinsahnee*
May I have the menu?	*ana areed al-kaart?*
Do you have vegetarian dishes?	*haal indaak akl nabati laahm?*
Nothing more, thanks.	*yaakfee shukran*
Just a small portion.	*miqdar sageer*
I'd like the bill please.	*ana areed al-hisaab min fadhlach*
That was delicious.	*kan al-aakl lazeez*
It's to take away.	*sa 'aakhodho maa'ee*

Menu Decoder

beya – mullet

chanad – mackerel

fool – fava bean paste, often eaten at breakfast

kebab mashwi – meat paste moulded onto flat skewers and grilled

khobz – flat bread

kofta – meat balls

laban – a refreshing drink of yogurt, water, salt and crushed mint

mashboos – grilled meat (usually chicken or lamb) and spiced rice

mashkul – rice with onions

mezze – assorted appetizers

muaddas – rice and lentils
muhammar – sweet rice
hehen – bream-like fish
hwarma – beef or chicken carved from a spit and rolled in pita bread with lettuce, tomatoes,
  ummus and hot sauce
wahar – flathead
waraq aynab – vine leaves stuffed with rice and meat
ubaydi – pomfret

Arabic-English Glossary

ashaa	dinner	makoolat baHreeya	seafood
asir	juice	maqlee	fried
aalah/tamr	dates	mashrubaat	drinks
ed	eggs	mashwi	grilled
awaakih	fruit	mashwi 'aalal fahm	barbecued
l forn	baked	masluq	boiled
tar	breakfast	mooghabilat	appetizer
hadhe	lunch	qahwa	coffee
alawiyyaat	pastry	roz	rice
aj	chicken	salatat	salad
bna	cheese	samak	fish
hobz	bread	shorba	soup
hodrawat	vegetables	shay	tea
aahm	meat	tahaali	dessert

Expats

For the decades of Saudi Arabia's oil boom, life in the Kingdom for expatriate workers has been a constant trade-off between a number of factors: money; the restrictions of living in a strictly Muslim country; the opportunity to experience first-hand the fascinating social and geographical landscape of Saudi Arabia; and, more recently, the all important question of security. Deciding whether to live in Saudi Arabia is not a decision to be taken lightly and it's certainly not for everyone, but for many it's the best decision they ever made.

PROS & CONS
The Pros

Let's face it, you didn't come to Saudi Arabia for the nightlife, but there are nonetheless many reasons why the Kingdom has proven such a popular destination for expats over recent decades.

MONEY

The strongest motivation for many people in choosing whether to live and work in Saudi Arabia is the opportunity to earn incomes far in excess of those available at home.

For many expats, the 1980s were the decade of exceedingly generous wages. In more recent times, particularly as a result of the debilitating costs of the Gulf War, base annual salaries have fallen and are now only slightly higher than in the West. Teachers, for example, earn between US$24,000 and US$34,000, and registered nurses earn an average of US$35,200 (though this can go up to US$50,000). This is offset by the various 'perks' that are still considered to be standard in most expat contracts (see Working Conditions p55).

ACCOMMODATION

This is one facet of expat living that receives very few complaints. In these days of elevated security concerns, most expats live in compounds (see below) which consist of high quality and spacious Western-style houses custom-built for Western expatriates; you'll be hard pressed to find anything that's more than 25 years old. Expect air-conditioning and full-time security to be standard. Single female expats, who are generally employed as nurses, may find themselves sharing flats with other women.

The other form of accommodation offered to expats, although it is becoming quite rare, is in high-rise apartments which seem to have been designed to Arabic taste. *Majlis*-style reception or sitting rooms are often accompanied by washrooms for ablutions before prayer. In practical terms, this means that living areas are generally large and often kitted out with multiple bedrooms and bathrooms.

LIVING IN A COMPOUND

The concept of compound living can appear just as foreign to newly arrived expats as the country itself. For many, this is the first experience of living within a walled enclosure, and it comes with its share of positives and negatives.

In some ways, the compound offers a world-within-a-world, a self-contained place to retreat when the idiosyncrasies of life in Saudi Arabia

Professional Systems & Services website discusses 'Why Saudi Arabia?' then moves on to job opportunities and other useful things to consider when moving to Saudi Arabia, see www.sais.8k.com /why.html.

Saudi Customs & Etiquette, by Kathy Cuddihy, is the ideal guide to avoiding the pitfalls of Saudi society, impressing your Saudi friends and understanding the quirks of Saudi living.

ecome too difficult. The strong sense of community felt in many of the ompounds, coupled with the other residents' wealth of local knowledge an provide the soft landing many new expats need, especially when ntering the Kingdom for the first time and surrounded by a country that an be quite alienating. The compound is also a great place to pick up tips bout excursions from the city and the latest news (eg when the mutawwa uddenly become active in your area). Swimming pools, supermarkets, eauty salons, coffee shops, restaurants, BBQs, sports fields, gyms and the ccasional band and disco all help to ease the transition, as well as break sometimes-monotonous routine.

Illegal bars within compounds have existed for many years and, despite aids and closures, continue to reappear and prove popular with many in he expatriate community. Alcohol is strictly forbidden in the Kingdom, ut some supermarkets stock (even on a single shelf) all of the raw ngredients needed to make a brew and there remains a constant demand or the product. Whether or not you decide to indulge, remember that the onsequences if you are caught are extremely harsh (see p168).

An A-Z of Places and Things Saudi, by Kathy Cuddihy, should be in every expat home; it contains everything from the abaya (a black robe that covers the body) and Islamic banking to an overview of key places around the Kingdom.

CHILDREN

The large scale of most compounds and the high levels of security ensure hat children can often roam safely and at will throughout the compound vithout the fears and dangers associated with living in many Western ities. The experience of growing up in a foreign culture is also something hat they'll never forget.

For more details, see p61 and p164.

LIVING IN A FOREIGN CULTURE

Apart from money, the other defining motivation for many expats who ome to Saudi Arabia is the opportunity to live within, and learn about, nother culture. For many expats, living and working in Saudi Arabia is a ositive, once-in-a-lifetime experience. Indeed, for many, the opportunity o live in a country which is all-but-closed to tourism carries long-term ewards which ultimately outweigh the financial factor.

This is an extraordinary country to visit with a host of fascinating ights which are covered throughout this book, while the Kingdom's geographic location (along with more disposable income and leisure ime) also makes it an excellent base for anyone wishing to travel to Asia, Africa and Europe, all of which are within close reach.

Islam, Arabs and Saudi Arabia itself are all currently the subjects of unprecedented Western media coverage, most of which is negative in ocus. Living here allows you to make up your own mind, to confirm or deny the stereotypes with unusual access to first-hand experience. If ou're prepared to learn a little about Arab culture, and enter the country vith an open mind, the prospect of enjoying the hospitality of Arabs and Muslims can be a rare privilege.

This is also a critical period for Saudi Arabia and the Middle East. By iving in the Kingdom, you'll enjoy a front-row seat from which to watch history unfold.

LOW LEVELS OF CRIME

Crime continues to be all-but-unknown, other than some petty theft. Compounds, particularly in these days of terrorist threats, have high evels of security, while street crime is also extremely rare. Strangely, stealing the spare wheels off the back of 4WDs seems to be the most prolific.

The Cons

Living and Working in the Gulf States & Saudi Arabia, by Robert Hughes et al, was published in 2003 and should be read by anyone thinking of a move to the Kingdom; it contains a sanguine analysis and loads of helpful tips.

For every expat enamoured with his or her new home and all of the benefits it brings, there seem to be just as many for whom it is a time to be endured, the days counted until the end of the contract, offset only by the money saved while in the Kingdom.

BOREDOM

Apart from travelling and eating out, there's not a lot else to occupy your time with. During the summer months (and at other times), the fierce heat forces many expats to retreat indoors to the relative sanctuary of air conditioning, DVDs and satellite television. Saudi Arabian downtime is a great opportunity to learn Arabic, an opportunity which sadly, as many expats readily admit, few take. You're unlikely to be woken in the middle of the night by loud, drunken parties, but you will hear the sunrise call to prayer (something you're probably less inclined to join) over loudspeakers.

LACK OF RELIGIOUS FREEDOM

The practice of any religion other than Islam is strictly prohibited, whether in public or private. This extends to bringing into the country printed religious material or other symbols. Although bag searches upon arrival have diminished in recent years, the authorities are very serious about enforcing this.

LEGAL PERILS

The possibility of transgressing some seemingly obscure local law is a constant concern in the Kingdom. The agency or employer who recruited you should provide you with an information pack that addresses most of the laws and customs. One area of common anxiety to all expats is surrendering your passport upon arrival. While you're in Saudi Arabia, your employer safeguards your passport, and you are issued with an *iqama* (identity booklet) that you *must* carry at all times. This prevents you from leaving the country if you've decided you've had enough, and is returned one day prior to travelling overseas.

For more information on legal issues and prohibitions, see p168.

LIVING IN A COMPOUND

Many expats told us that their greatest frustration was the limited opportunities for meeting Saudis outside the work context. Strictly segregated Saudi society is certainly a major factor responsible for this and many compounds won't allow Saudis to enter, even with an invitation from a resident.

It's also the case that living within a compound can foster a tendency to fall back into the familiarity of a Western lifestyle. If you don't think this will happen to you, remember that retreating to the relative comfort and security of the compound (away from the security fears and potential hassles which lie beyond the compound walls) can be attractive in those early days of culture shock and, before you know it, it has become a way of life. The situation is not helped by the fact that many of the larger compounds are on the edge of cities, where you could be relatively isolated from the local population.

SAUDI BUREAUCRACY

Negotiating the arcane workings of Saudi bureaucracy could test the patience of Mother Theresa. The queues upon arrivals at airports (see p176) are a good introduction to this phenomenon, and things don't mprove from there. Long arduous lines at government offices, and the feeling of being ushered from one place to the next, are only compounded by the frequent lack of interest or courtesy shown by officials. The only advice is to be patient; losing your temper only creates a confrontation which you cannot win and certainly will not defuse the situation, even if it does make you feel better at the time.

SECURITY

One of the most enduring reasons given by Al-Qaeda for its terrorist attacks is the presence of non-Muslims in Saudi Arabia, the land of the holy cities of Mecca and Medina. Always keep abreast of the latest travel and security warnings issued by Western governments (see p166) and always keep your embassy advised of your presence (and contact details). Security at Western compounds and places of work is generally excellent and the Saudi authorities are cracking down hard on any terrorist activity. But always having to nervously watch the security situation and, during times of heightened alert (eg the war in Iraq), be willing to pack up and leave at a moment's notice, can be wearing and nerve-wracking in the extreme. After a while you may no longer even notice the fortifications – boom gates, two- to three-metre-high concrete wall and barbed wire – which surround you.

Some expats go to the extreme of welding steel plates across the underbelly of their cars to aid detection of any attached devices (ie bombs), but you should definitely always check your car (the engine, boot, wheel arches, underneath) before starting the engine.

SOCIAL RESTRICTIONS

If you simply can't live without Western forms of entertainment, Saudi Arabia is not for you. Entertainment in general is very thin on the ground; there are neither cinemas nor bars in Saudi Arabia. While that can even appeal to some people, it can wear you down after a while. Don't for a second imagine that the absence of some aspects of Western culture means an escape from the worst of Western commercialism, which the Saudis have embraced at full-speed.

Live & Work in Saudi & the Gulf, by Louise Whetter, is a bit dated (2000) but is an excellent overview for all expats of living in the Gulf, with a detailed section on Saudi Arabia and a focus of the UK market.

WOMEN

Women living in Saudi Arabia undoubtedly have the most difficult time. Segregation between male and female is the norm and anger is a common emotion when women discover that Saudi Arabia in public is an uncompromisingly male domain which they cannot freely enter. Apart from the indignity of such treatment, this can seriously inhibit the freedom of movement. However, women are allowed to travel alone in taxis and long-term expats always have their regulars who can be relied upon.

Within the compounds (and in some workplaces), you're generally free to do as you like, but the Saudi authorities are very serious about enforcing social segregation outside the compounds, and if you're caught, there's a high probability of spending time in jail.

It must also be remembered that, in spite of the limitations and although it's not for everyone, many Western women do enjoy their time in Saudi Arabia. For more details of what to expect, see p174 and Advice from Expat Women p54.

Finding Out More

Ultimately, talking with someone who has already worked (or is currently working) in the Kingdom will provide the most accurate account of life there and enable you to ask questions about particular concerns you may have.

A WOMAN'S PERSPECTIVE

It may be hard to imagine living with the rules and regulations that govern the life of women in Saudi Arabia. The following show different perspectives of women who have lived and worked here.

Expat women can easily find a job. Many work privately as tutors for different subjects or start little businesses in compounds, like teaching ballet, martial arts, arts & crafts, art, some teach special handicrafts and sell things there, some work as secretaries and even lawyers for big companies. You always have to know someone who knows someone who knows someone. It's all about *wasta* (connections)… The American schools always love to have volunteer mothers for minor works or helping out for performances. It is a great opportunity to meet people…

Anonymous, Jeddah

What's it like? Hard, even harder being a female. We are treated as third-class citizens behind the men and their cars. But in saying that, if you have a good network of friends and a male with a car, life can be very comfortable. There are many things to endure. Most are small…dealing with the crazy driving…men pushing in for service ahead of you…being stared at…Being followed, approached and hit-on.

…After all that you think that I have no [positive things to say], but I do. I had wonderful travelling experiences in the Kingdom, [visiting] ancient sites, meeting people in small communities away from the cities. The history I learned, the friends I made, and the diving I did. And as a photographer it was fantastic for me, though you do have to take caution where you point your camera. On the whole my time in Saudi Arabia was truly an adventure for me…The best thing about being an expat in Saudi is the adventure. And the fact you can go home.

Anonymous, Jeddah

Don't listen to all the horror stories about Saudi before you come: it took me four weeks before I'd let my husband out of my sight, I was so scared!

Anonymous, Jeddah

Recruitment agencies (see opposite) and the employers themselves can often put you in touch with other expats, many of whom are willing to share their experiences. They will also sometimes send information packages dealing with life in Saudi Arabia, although keep in mind that it will probably be a highly polished account. Alternatively, there are websites containing message boards and discussion forums dedicated to expat living, many of whose contributors have lived and worked in Saudi Arabia. Some of the best ones include:

Going Global's website is mainly a selling point for its 'Saudi Arabia Mini Career Guide', which may just be reason enough to visit www.goinglobal.com /countries/saudiarabia /saudi_arabia.asp.

Expat Exchange (www.expatexchange.net)
Expat Forum (www.expatforum.com)
Expats in Saudi Arabia (www.expatsinsaudiarabia.com)
Survive Abroad (www.surviveabroad.com) Has a useful 110 FAQs section about Saudi Arabia.

GETTING STARTED
What Sort of Job?

Most Westerners who work in Saudi Arabia do so as engineers (particularly in the oil and construction industries), doctors, nurses or teachers.

Nurses and, to a lesser extent, doctors and other healthcare workers are highly sought-after in Saudi medical circles. The defence contractor BAE Systems (British Aerospace) has also been a major long-term employer of expats in the Kingdom and all types of engineers (civil, electrical, mechanical) continue to be in great demand. Financial services and IT companies have also actively recruited. Teaching remains another possibility, although a knowledge of spoken Arabic may be a prerequisite. Saudi Aramco is the dominant employer in the oil industry, but as oil exploration and production has been nationalised, this is one area that increasingly employs Saudis.

The Kingdom's recent and ongoing policy of 'Saudisation' (see p32) has meant that many positions previously held by foreigners are increasingly being undertaken by Saudis. The Saudi government's Manpower Council has even begun closing some professions to foreigners. However, the shortage of suitable Saudi graduates for highly skilled jobs (see p31) means that positions will continue to be available for some years to come.

Finding a Job

The simplest and most accessible method of finding work in Saudi Arabia has always been through employment agencies that recruit specifically for the Gulf region. Some companies in the Kingdom may also advertise positions directly, but agencies are a better option. These offer the possibility of face-to-face contact with the recruiters, the ease of correspondence, and the chance of dealing with someone who may have had first-hand experience in the Kingdom, and is thus more likely paint an honest picture of life there. Never forget, however, that agencies ultimately exist by their success in selling you the job.

Recruitment agencies sometimes advertise internationally in the employment sections of the print media, but there are dozens of recruitment agencies who specialise in matching available jobs in the Gulf with prospective employees. Try the following:

Alba (www.alba.net) Oil & gas.
Arabian Careers Ltd (www.arabiancareers.com) Healthcare.
Bayt Lifestyle Engineering (http://jobs2.bayt.com/app/gen/home.adp) Engineering.
Career Builder (www.careerbuilder.com/JobSeeker/) Extensive listings.
CCM Recruitment (www.ccmrecruitment.com) Engineering and healthcare.
International Hospital Recruitments (www.ihrcanada.com) Healthcare.
International Staffing Consultants (www.iscworld.com) Oil and gas.
Jobs of Arabia (http://users.aol.com/saudijobs/saudijob.htm) General.
TEFL (www.tefl.com) Teaching English.

For women, marital status may significantly limit work opportunities. Although married couples seeking employment should not experience difficulties, and married men in senior positions must register their wife as a dependant, the situation is not the same for married women. They may find it impossible to gain work unless their husband will also be employed, or they may be forced to enter the Kingdom on a single status contract, thus leaving their husband at home. This has been the policy in Saudi Arabia for many years, and seems unlikely to change in the near future.

WORKING CONDITIONS

Employment contracts tend to be of one- or two-year duration, with annual bonuses and opportunities to re-contract. That said, your employer retains the right to terminate your contract at any time, and often a three-month probation period will apply from the time you commence work. An early resignation would also have ramifications upon the various bonuses included in your contract. Clearly, the specific conditions will vary from job to job, and the best advice is to scrutinise the contract carefully.

A 40- to 48-hour week is the norm; often Thursdays and always Fridays are the days off, although that usually changes to just Fridays during Ramadan when daily working hours are fewer. The most unusual aspect of work in the Kingdom is the constant breaks. Because of the sheer heat, many offices take an early afternoon siesta (usually from 2pm

Maybe you'll decide that living and working in Saudi Arabia is not for you – there are plenty of other opportunities out there; check out www.expatexchange .com.

DID YOU KNOW?

A normal working day in Saudi Arabia varies little from 8am to 1pm and from 5pm to 8pm (plus prayer times).

THE GREAT DIVIDE

There's an open division (some would say a further layer of segregation) clearly at work in Saudi Arabia between expatriates of different nationalities. Westerners (mostly Europeans, North Americans and Australasians) work in highly skilled jobs for which most Saudis do not have the qualifications. Non-Western expats (primarily Pakistanis, Bangladeshis, Indians and Filipinos) perform mostly unskilled labour (taxi driving, construction work, domestic help) which many Saudis consider beneath them.

Although non-Western expats usually earn incomes (which average around SR1000 per month) which are simply not possible in their countries of nationality (hence the high demand for such positions), the conditions of employment and under which they live could not be more different from those enjoyed by Western expats. Most live in cramped, shared accommodation which is anything but luxurious and few are allowed to return home more than once every two years. Unlike Western expats, very few may bring their families with them, ensuring that workers must endure long years of separation from their partners and children. Many also work seven-day weeks, have little freedom of movement and spend their first few years in the Kingdom earning just enough to pay back debts to unscrupulous agents and middle-men in their home countries and Saudi Arabia. Women working as domestic servants are also particularly vulnerable in their isolated setting, as are any who commit offences in the Kingdom.

When this is added to the high degree of prejudice which non-Western expats experience at the hands of many Saudis, it's hard not to admire the endurance of many such workers and the lengths to which they go to provide for their families back home.

Off-Road in the Hejaz, by Patrick Peirard and Patrick Legros, is a must-have for expats living in Jeddah as it enables you to get the most from what should be considerable spare time.

to 4pm). This is augmented by the compulsory pauses for prayer, with each lasting for about 25 minutes. These enforced breaks will not usually affect healthcare workers who usually work 12-hour shifts. During the month of Ramadan, offices will probably run on skeleton staff, with many Muslims working short days (if at all). Occupational health and safety is all but unknown, and any injuries suffered that may affect your work performance are likely to mean an early termination of your contract.

With all working conditions (see also p55), the onus is always on you to make your contract as watertight as possible; if it's not in the contract, it's too late.

Getting a Visa

Visas are issued after an employment contract has been signed. The application process can be an epic (and utterly frustrating) adventure, involving endless passport photos, multiple forms riddled with intrusive questions, police checks in your home country and the mandatory medical examinations and blood tests (including an HIV test). Apart from filling in countless forms in triplicate and learning new heights of patience, be prepared for particularly long waiting periods during the application process. Your prospective employer, who will sponsor you during your stay in the Kingdom, or your recruitment agency handle the processes related to visa application (either directly or as a go-between) with the Saudi authorities.

American Citizens Abroad has a website dedicated to offering advice to American expats around the world, including unexciting (but important) issues such as US tax liability and health care cover at www.aca.ch.

One problem is that it can take anywhere from three months to three years for married family status (and hence visas for wives and children) to be issued; it's not possible at all unless your job is one which requires a university degree or other high-level expertise. It's also more difficult to obtain visas for children if they are over 18.

BEFORE YOU GO

There are a number of organisations whose role is to prepare expats for living and working abroad. Although these are usually general n nature (rather than specifically about Saudi Arabia), they can be extremely useful as part of your preparation and some can even tailor their briefings to your specific needs. Such courses can be expensive, so ask your prospective employer if they're willing to foot the bill. Some recommended organisations:

Centre for International Briefing (www.farnhamcastle.com) UK-based intercultural training with specific programmes for the Middle East.

Global Integration (www.global-integration.com) Training for senior business staff and upper level management.

Living Abroad (www.livingabroad.com) One of the few to offer Saudi-specific predeparture programmes which include assistance with visas, homes and schools, settling-in and support services.

Where to Settle

The decision of where to live and work in Saudi Arabia is usually determined by the job opportunities available. Healthcare workers will probably have the greatest choice, as work in this field is usually available in all of the large cities. The oil industry is generally limited to the Eastern Province, while administrative and management positions tend to be in Riyadh or Jeddah.

Jeddah has always been the most popular choice for expats. With its seaside setting and proximity to the sights of the Hejaz, Asir and Madain Saleh, it's an ideal base for weekend excursions, far more so than Riyadh and the Eastern Province. Diving in the Red Sea (see p107) is extremely popular among expats. Jeddah also has an international airport. The strict Islamic laws enforced elsewhere in the Kingdom are noticeably more relaxed in Jeddah, and the mutawwa (religious police) are largely (though not completely) absent. Jeddah's main drawback is that the summer combination of heat and humidity can be almost unbearable.

Riyadh has some wonderful sights, most of the embassies and great shopping, but its general conservatism, large concentration of mutawwa upholding strict Islamic codes and extreme summer heat (up to 50°C in August) mean that it can be a soulless place which wins few prizes among expats.

The Eastern Province (particularly Al-Khobar and Dhahran) is quite liberal by Saudi standards and, because of the oil industry, this is the region with the longest history of contact with Westerners. Summer humidity can also be a problem here, as is the question of what to do with your weekends if you're here for a while.

PRACTICAL MATTERS

The contract is ready and your departure date is set. Next come all those tasks which are difficult enough in your own country, let alone Saudi Arabia.

Finding a Home

Foreigners commencing work contracts in the Kingdom are routinely offered accommodation in a compound (p50) as part of their employment package (non-Gulf nationals are forbidden from owning homes in Saudi Arabia). Just because your accommodation is arranged by your employer doesn't mean it will be close to where you work, although free transport to and from your place of work should be provided. A general description of the type of accommodation that is available to employees of your company should be supplied by the recruitment agency during the application stage; if it isn't, ask why. Be aware that although the standard of accommodation on offer is generally very good, it is not

Desert Treks from Riyadh, by Ionis Thompson, is a guide aimed at expats living in the capital and wondering what to do with their weekends.

Desert Treks from Jeddah, by Patricia Barbor, is also good with a range of get-away ideas.

uncommon for recruiting agencies to show you somewhat outdated photos.

If when you arrive at your new home you find that not everything works, always be prepared to wait a frustratingly long period of time for a plumber, electrician or air-conditioner repairman to come; in most compounds, you'll have maintenance staff on site, but the extreme heat puts a lot of stress on these things, and imported parts are not always in supply.

Renting a Home

Some companies offer the option of a housing allowance. Because the employer bears the burden of maintaining accommodation, as well a paying utilities, it often works out cheaper (for the company) to simply pay the employee an annual housing allowance; the allowance is comparable to the cost of a cheaper one- or two-bedroom apartment in a compound This does give some freedom in choosing which area or compound you wish to live in, but it is highly unlikely that the allowance alone will cover the total cost of your rent (quite apart from utilities), which will probably mean dipping into your savings. Renting an apartment in a compound usually starts at SR30,000 per year, but the average for a furnished two bedroom apartment is around SR70,000, while a three-bedroom villa is normally SR125,000 (but can cost SR220,000). If that sounds high remember that you're probably also paying for the two armoured vehicles stationed outside.

Renting an apartment outside a compound is usually cheaper and generally costs between SR12,000 and SR60,000 per year, while a villa (usually between SR30,000 and SR200,000 per year) will usually come with a small private garden and often a pool. You'll also have to pay for all running costs, including maintenance, although the owner normally pays for any major work. A year's rent is usually payable in advance. The housing allowance was once commonly offered in the first month of arrival, but a scam developed whereby recently arrived expats would apply for it and, upon receiving the funds, would promptly go on holidays, never to be seen again. These days, it's generally offered three months after arrival.

Probably the greatest advantage to renting your own accommodation is the opportunity of mixing with Arab-speaking expats. Many companies tend to recruit from certain countries or regions, and this is reflected in the lack of population mix in company-owned compounds. Renting outside a compound is likely to place you in contact with nationals from Lebanon, Syria, Egypt, the Sudan, and the Horn of Africa.

If you do decide to rent, you won't be really in a position to make decisions until you arrive. However, you can start getting an idea of what's available before you go. Some examples include:

Arabian Homes (www.arabian-homes.com.sa) In Riyadh and Jeddah.
Canary Village (www.canaryvillage.com) In Dammam and Al-Khobar.
Sharbatly Village (www.sharbatlyvillage.com) In Jeddah.

There are three excellent annual guides published in English by the local chambers of commerce and which include guides to the compounds in their respective areas. They are: *Riyadh Today*, *Jeddah Today* and *Eastern Province Today*. Each costs SR20 and they're usually available from any Jarir Bookstore (see individual city entries).

Renting does carry the potential pitfalls of having to deal with leases. Always seek legal advice (ask other expats or ask for recommendations from your employer or embassy). Rental rates are sometimes negotiable.

Moving House

Because the Kingdom has accommodated expats for almost 70 years, numerous companies offer removal services from your home country to Saudi Arabia. The cost of relocating to the Kingdom should be included in your employment contract (always ask before signing) so the choice of which company to use may not be yours to make. Also remember that most homes in Saudi Arabia come fully furnished.

If it's left up to you, take your time to shop around for the most reliable (talk to other expats or the recruiting agencies) and cost-efficient companies. It's also essential that you take out full insurance (p59) in case anything goes wrong (or astray). Good places to start looking for international companies with services to Saudi Arabia include:

Association of Relocation Agents (www.relocationagents.com) Listing of UK and Ireland-based international removal companies.

Bishop's Move (www.bishops-move.co.uk) UK-based.

Continental Express Systems (www.ces-sa.com) Offices in Saudi Arabia.

Four Winds (www.fourwindsint.com.au) Offices in Saudi Arabia and worldwide.

Team Relocations (www.transeuro.com) European-based.

Vanpac International (www.vanpac.com) US-based.

Arguably the best of the discussion groups for expats working in Saudi Arabia can be found at www.expatforum.com.

When leaving Saudi Arabia, it's a good idea to send your goods before leaving the Kingdom; any problems at the Saudi end will be easier to solve if you're still there. One Saudi company which has been recommended by expats for getting everything back home is **Namma Cargo Services** (www.nammacargo.com).

For moving home within Saudi Arabia, your best bet is to get recommendations from other expats who've been through what can be a painful process; Saudi removal companies have a reputation for not being particularly conscientious with fragile items (notably electronic goods).

Changing Jobs

Although it is, in theory, possible to move to another city or change employers once you are in the Kingdom, you're more likely to be bound to your original employer for the period specified in your contract. Remember that these people wanted your expertise in the first place, and after investing much money on your flights, accommodation and utilities, will probably be reluctant to see you poached by another company. However if you're nearing the end of your contract and the possibility of employment elsewhere in the Kingdom arises, as a resident who is already living and working in Saudi Arabia, the application process should be free from much of the bureaucratic red tape of your initial application.

Insurance

The cost of insurance for moving your family, luggage and furniture to Saudi Arabia should be borne by your employer; again, always check your contract (employment and any removal contract) carefully. Medical insurance inside Saudi Arabia should also be covered by your employer. Keep handy a list of where the medical facilities are and make sure that you are clear how emergency transport can be arranged; if an emergency occurs, it's likely that someone who only speaks Arabic will be at the other end of the phone. If medical cover is not arranged by your company, or you're looking for better coverage, **Norwich Union** (www.norwichunion.com) and **John Wason Insurance Brokers** (www.johnwason.co.uk) both offer worldwide insurance plans.

TOP TIPS FOR SETTLING IN SAUDI ARABIA
The experience of living and working in Saudi Arabia is a very personal experience, as the following advice from expats testifies:

Being Prepared
The biggest tip I can give is to read/research anything and everything about the culture. What the culture was like before the country came into oil and the effects this industry has had on the culture. Knowing some of the basics of Islam and the teachings of the Prophet Mohammed will be beneficial in the understanding of how the Saudis think and work... On a personal note, take the time and have patience. Saudis rush for no one and, *inshallah* (God willing), it will get done. And stand your ground. You will be pushed around if you do not speak up.

Anonymous, Jeddah

Don't overfill your suitcase, you can find virtually everything you need here and most things are cheaper than, or the same price as, in Europe.

Anonymous, Jeddah

Taking the Kids
You meet people from all over the world. Children grow up in a multinational surrounding, they have a broader view of life, are more open minded and open to other opinions and are more tolerant and accepting of other cultures.

Anonymous, Jeddah

Making the Most of It
The positive side [of living in Saudi Arabia] is that there is often time and opportunity (and money) to pursue some leisure activity that pressures of living in the UK (and the weather) does not allow. Sports activities are popular, tennis, squash, sailing, diving, football among others...Many also follow study courses – I've had time to nearly complete a PhD while working. What else? Lots of sunshine! Oh yes, and a far better wage than an English language teacher could expect to get anywhere else.

Roderick Neilsen, Australia

As anywhere it's what you make of it; you can spend your time partying and going on desert treks, or if you don't do anything it can be a very depressing experience! Jeddah has hundreds of clubs and societies open to and run by expats ranging from patchwork to natural history, from rugby to the Caledonian society.

Rebecca Moreau, Jeddah

Buy a 4WD if you like to get away from it all; they're more expensive than 2WD but hold their value better and you'll get a totally different view of Saudi.

Anonymous, Jeddah

Living in a Compound
There are a few disadvantages – the cost, the lack of privacy (companies often put all their employees on the same compound as they can get a better deal, this means that you will live on very close terms with people your husband works with) [and] everyone knows everything!!

Rebecca Moreau, Jeddah

When you are new in the Kingdom it is much more comfortable to live in a compound where you find a lot of expats...Most compounds (Western compounds) don't require that women wear *abayas*, you can even walk around in shorts. In bigger compounds, women can even drive unofficially.

Anonymous, Jeddah

In the compounds there are noticeboards with ads from people leaving the Kingdom and selling either their car and/or household items. This is a good way to get set up at a discounted rate. There are also notices from diving instructors, dates for the latest play or musical performances or some social event and teachers advertising classes such as ballet or language.

Alanna Lee, Australia

Electrical Goods

For short stays in Saudi Arabia, renting electronic equipment can be infinitely preferable to buying. Electronic goods are not subject to import taxes, so can be very cheap, but many people forget that much of the country uses 110V (although that is changing); hence electronic goods are rendered useless when returning to a country with 220V. Installing satellite television can be expensive, and it may be difficult to sell before leaving. Again, renting is a better idea. White goods can also be rented, but company-supplied accommodation should include fridges, cookers and washing machines. Like many other services, finding rental outlets can prove difficult, and your best bet would be to ask experienced expats, or alternatively an Arabic speaker.

Desert Treks from Al-Khobar, by Jon Carter, allows expats to escape the oil wells and track-down many little-known sites in the Eastern Province.

Bringing Your Pet

The paperwork involved in bringing your pet to Saudi Arabia could consume a small forest and even then you may not be successful; a surprising number of pets are abandoned by expats when they leave the Kingdom and the Saudi authorities are understandably wary of allowing in any more. Cats may not be brought to the Kingdom; adopting a local stray may be an alternative. For information on bringing pets to Saudi Arabia, contact the Abu Dhabi-based **British Veterinary Centre** (www.britvet.com) who can offer advice or help with paperwork. One company which does move pets internationally is **Bishop's Move** (www.bishops-move.co.uk).

Schools

The standard of international schools in Saudi Arabia is excellent. There are three main types: American, British and French, some of which offer British, American *and* the International Baccalaureate. Other significant expat national groups also have their own schools which follow the curriculum in their home countries. International schools in Riyadh:

American International School (☎ 01-491 4270; www.aisr.org)
The British International School (☎ 01-463 0926)
The British School, Riyadh (☎ 01-248 2387; www.britishschoolriyadh.com)

International schools in Jeddah:

The British International School (☎ 02-699 0019; www.continentalschool.com)
French International School (☎ 02-238 0223)
Jeddah Preparatory & Grammar School (☎ 02-238 0223; www.jprepgramm.sch.sa)
Saudi Arabian International School (☎ 02-667 4513; www.sais.sch.sa) US curriculum.

A mine of information on visas, setting up home and finding a school in Saudi Arabia is available at www .livingabroad.com.

And in the Eastern Province:

British International School (☎ 03-882 5303; www.britishschool-ksa.com) Al-Khobar.
Ecole Française (☎ 03-887 1216) Al-Khobar.
The International Programs School (☎ 03-857 9780) Al-Khobar; US curriculum.
International Schools Group (☎ 03-330 0555; www.isgdh.org) Covers eight schools in the Eastern Province.

Some larger companies like Aramco and British Aerospace also operate their own schools, while some expats send their children to boarding schools in their home countries; your employer may contribute to the cost.

School fees are expensive (starting from SR12,000 per year for the young up to SR35,000 at some secondary schools). Most employers will pay for part or (rarely these days) all of your children's school fees if your family is mentioned in your employment contract; always check your contract.

For schooling after the age of 16, you'll need to send your child abroad.

The Haj <small>Martha Brekhus Shams</small>

Princes and paupers, rich and poor, haj pilgrims from the four corners of the earth have journeyed to Mecca for thousands of years. It is the ultimate traveller's tale – the haj remains the oldest and largest international gathering of people in the world.

The haj is an experience that millions of Muslims around the world look forward to with reverence. Over four thousand years ago, the Prophet Ibrahim (Abraham) originated the haj with rituals similar to those practiced today. Speaking many languages, pilgrims from over 70 countries travel to Saudi Arabia during the month of Dhu al-Hijjah (12th month of the Islamic calendar) to perform this obligation, which fulfils one of the five pillars of Islam.

> I pray that someday I can fulfil the haj obligation. For Muslims it is our dream destination.
>
> *Hazem Beti*

Martha Brekhus Shams has studied Middle Eastern culture for 25 years. She has worked with the Iranian Cultural Heritage Organization and for the Iranian film industry. As an American with Muslim credentials, she opens the doors to the haj with a Western perspective.

WHO SHOULD PERFORM THE HAJ?

The haj is an obligation for all who are able to perform it. It takes place on the eighth, ninth and tenth days of Dhu al-Hijjah, the last month of the Muslim year. Those who visit Mecca and complete the haj rituals at other times of the year undertake a different rite, the *umrah*.

Allah has no wish to burden anyone with an obligation that is too difficult to fulfil with happiness. Only these people are obliged to perform the haj:

Mature and stable-minded people Children should not perform the haj, or people who are mentally ill. The pilgrim should be mature enough to understand the significance of the haj. Some people may have their children accompany them to the haj, but there is not any significance in what they do; the children have not performed the ritual of haj.

The physically able The haj is physically demanding. People who are ill or severely disabled should not attempt to perform the haj.

The financially secure Pilgrims should be financially secure enough to support their trip to the haj, and support their family and dependents while they are away, with no additional hardship in the future. If a sponsor offers to send you to the haj, you are obliged to go.

Those who have the time Those who satisfy the requirements too late are not obliged to perform the haj; however, they should go the next year. In recent times, Saudi Arabia also maintains a quota system. If a prospective pilgrim cannot secure a visa, he may add his name to the list for the next possible opportunity.

> The haj is a very strenuous ceremony. Some elderly or infirm are carried on stretchers over the heads of the pilgrims. They are passed along from hand to hand. It is a deeply humbling thing to see. Children bring their elderly parents and carry them on their very backs.
>
> *Reyanna Sultana*

PLANNING YOUR HAJ

Many people dream of the haj for years before they are ready to set the date, but be sure to begin planning your haj at least a year before you expect to leave for Saudi Arabia. For this once in a lifetime experience you should be prepared mentally, spiritually, physically and financially.

Encountering problems because you are not prepared will disrupt your peace of mind and greatly affect your haj. It is very important that you alk to Muslims who have performed the haj. You will find that they enjoy sharing their experiences as much as you enjoy listening to them!

Long-Term Preparations

Spending some time doing research as you are preparing for your haj is invaluable. There are many books, CDs and sources of information on the Internet which are worth investigating as you are preparing.

From the very beginning, be sure that your intentions are *ikhlass* (pure). Write this recitation on a small card and use it as a bookmark to remind you of the meaning of haj: 'O Allah! I wish to fulfil your compulsory order of haj. I wish to gain your pleasure. I wish to gain the great rewards promised for haj.'

The haj should never be for shopping, show, business, touring, or any other purpose.

Be sure that your financial assets and earnings are *halal* (lawful or permitted in Islam). Your haj will not be acceptable if it is funded with questionable earnings. If you are in doubt, consult your local Islamic advisor.

Set your financial records straight. If you have borrowed money, repay it if possible. If any creditors are still due, make sure that they are satisfied with your arrangements before leaving. Return any borrowed items to their rightful owners.

Research and find a haj group. Do not plan to move with a large group because the chance of one lost or missing person can cause delays or make you miss a ritual. See below for more on agents.

Ensure that your relationships are open and honest well before you leave. Tie up loose ends and ask for forgiveness from people who perceive you have wronged them, even if you think you have not. If you are not on speaking terms with anyone, make amends before you leave.

Have a general health check-up. The rites of the haj are taxing. The physical proximity and crush of the masses at the haj, as well as the hot weather and possibly unfamiliar food, will test your strength to the limit. Although you may feel healthy, some asymptomatic illnesses may surface because of the conditions in Saudi.

Start exercising and get into good physical shape. If you do not already have a set exercise regimen, increase your activity every week. You will be glad you did after an arduous day of walking in the Saudi Arabian sun!

Renew your passport if necessary. The Saudi government requires your passport to be valid at least six months after the haj date. See p172 and p66 for more on visa requirements.

The Hajj, by FE Peters, gives firsthand accounts of travellers to the haj, together with a history and detailed steps of the ritual.

Haj Agents & Caravans

Choosing the right 'caravan' or agent is especially important, as he will be your guide along the way. Look for someone who offers a wide selection of haj programmes. The best way to find out about value for money is to talk with people who have been there before. You can also contact the Saudi Arabian embassy in your country – they have a list of reputable agents.

You should inquire whether your guide will be accompanying you to Saudi Arabia, and whether that includes accompanying you to Arafat and Mina. Also ask how experienced and familiar with the rules and procedures of customs and immigration your guide is. Determine if he will be staying with you until the end of your trip as you don't want to be stuck in Saudi without someone who can help you; procedures there can be difficult and frustrating. It's also important that your guide is either fluent in Arabic or will provide an interpreter.

THE STORY OF MECCA & THE HAJ

The tradition of the haj extends back to Ibrahim (Abraham), a prophet for Muslims, Christians and Jews, who is the patriarch of belief in Allah (the one God).

During his lifetime, Ibrahim survived many tests of his faith in Allah. One of the most important trials was when he took his wife Hajar and infant son Ismail (Ishmael) to Arabia. Obeying Allah's command and assurance that he would provide for them, Ibrahim left Hajar and Ismail in a dry valley with few provisions. Soon, the provisions ran out. Hajar began to roam the valley in a frantic search for food and eventually collapsed in despair. Pilgrims today commemorate that search for water by performing the sa'ee, walking seven times between the two hills of Safa and Marwah.

She prayed for Allah to help her – the baby Ismail was crying from hunger and thirst. As Ismail cried, he struck his foot upon the ground, and up gushed a spring of water. They named the spring Zamzam. In time, trading caravans and nomads began stopping in the valley to water their camels. A desert city sprang up around the well of Zamzam. That city was Mecca, and Zamzam remains the only natural source of water in the city.

One of Ibrahim's greatest trials was when Allah commanded him to take his son Ismail to the mountains and slay him. Ibrahim left Mecca with his son and sorrow in his heart, but his faith was stronger than his despair. On the way to the mountains, Shaitan (the Devil) tempted the Prophet and told him not to kill his son. He harried Ibrahim along the way, cajoling and taunting. Finally, Ibrahim began to throw stones at Shaitan – an act which is commemorated by the stoning of the jamrah (pillars) in Mina.

When Ibrahim arrived at the appointed place, Allah commanded him to let Ismail live and sacrifice a ram in his place. This is remembered at Eid al-Adha, or Festival of Sacrifice, when pilgrims at the haj and Muslims all over the world sacrifice an animal.

Ibrahim continued to visit Mecca occasionally, and Allah commanded him to build a house of worship and call all who believed in Him to make a pilgrimage there. Ibrahim and Ismail constructed the Kaaba, an empty cube-shaped building, for worship. This is the building which the pilgrims circle when performing the tawaf (circling).

After the death of Ibrahim, Ismail maintained the Kaaba and continued the pilgrimage every year. However, over the centuries, worship at the Kaaba descended into paganism; idolatry spread throughout Arabia, and the people began to worship many gods. People circled the Kaaba naked arguing that they should worship in the same form that they were born in. Instead of prayers in remembrance of Allah, they clapped, sang, and blew horns. The people had completely abandoned the teachings of their Prophet Ibrahim, and this continued for nearly 2500 years.

Eating and sleeping arrangements are of primary importance also. You should inquire how far away from the haram (prayer hall), in both Mecca and Medina, you will stay. If it is not within walking distance, will the agent provide transportation? You would be surprised how many guides try to get out of arranging for your breakfast. Find out which meals are taken care of for the duration of your trip.

Arrangements should also be made for your sacrifice on the 10th of Dhu al-Hijjah. This is a usual service but inquire if the cost is included in your fee. Your agent should also inform you when the sacrifice is made so that you can complete the rituals accordingly.

Ascertain how long you will stay in Mecca and Medina and whether the agency will cover your travel expenses in Medina. It's better to go to Medina before you start the haj rituals in Mecca, because it's less crowded at that time. Inquire if their programmes are flexible and if there are costs for any changes.

Finally, it's important to find out if you can fly from Medina to Jeddah on your return trip, rather than taking a long bus journey, and if this will involve extra charges.

Haj agencies in Canada, the Netherlands and South Africa:

In his lifetime, Ismail had once prayed, 'Our Lord! Send amongst them a messenger of their own, who shall recite unto them your *aayaat* (verses) and instruct them in the book and the Wisdom and sanctify them. Verily you are the 'Azezul-Hakeem' [the All-Mighty, All-Wise].'

Surah Al-Baqarah 2:129

Many prophets were sent throughout the years. Then, in AD 570, a man by the name of Mohammed ibn Abdullah (peace be upon him; pbuh) was born in Mecca. For 23 years, the Prophet Mohammed (pbuh) spread a message of obedience to Allah and a law of peace and order in Arabia.

At the time of the birth of Mohammed (pbuh), Mecca was a centre of commerce ruled by powerful merchant families from the Quraysh tribe. Initially, the Meccans objected to the rise of Islam as the new religion jeopardised profits and revenues collected from visiting pilgrims.

Mohammed (pbuh) was forced into exile in Medina in 622 where he established a model Islamic community. Six years later, he returned to Mecca from exile with thousands of followers. He destroyed idols, purified the Kaaba, and rededicated the House for the worship of Allah alone.

Thousands of followers gathered to hear the sermon of Prophet Mohammed (pbuh) at the haj where he envisioned equality; belief in one God; the sanctity of life, property, and honour; women's rights; and the concept of a united Muslim community. The Kaaba was once again a centre for the worshippers of the One True God.

Mohammed (pbuh) returned the haj rituals to their original purity and instructed his followers in two ways: by example and by approving the practices of his companions. For the benefit of all pilgrims, he also added some complexity and flexibility to the rituals.

At first, Muslim pilgrims travelled by foot, camel, horseback and ship to fulfil their obligation. The haj journey took months, and pilgrims carried with them all the necessities that they would need on their trip. Caravans were elaborately supplied and hired security if the travellers happened to be wealthy, but poorer pilgrims would run short on money along the way and would have to find work to fund their travel. This resulted in long journeys which in some cases took years.

Later, caravans set off for Mecca from important cities in the Islamic world such as Cairo, Baghdad, Istanbul and Damascus.

The road held peril and adventure – bandits, thieves, tricksters and slave traders The threat of feuding local tribes and highwaymen was constant. Many Bedouin tribes survived on tolls levied on pilgrims. Surviving the journey became a larger test of endurance than the pilgrimage itself.

Today, each year up to two million pilgrims from all over the world arrive in Saudi Arabia by every mode of transportation, completing a journey which is much shorter and less arduous than in the past.

Bali Indah Travel (☎ 011 60-31-70-380 00 13 13; fax 011 60-31-70-388 99 69; www.indah.nl/uk/; Ferdinand Bolstraat 40, 2525 XH Den Haag, Holland)
Hajj Assistance Committee North America (☎ 905-737-4401; fax 905-737-0848; www.hajj.org/; 10520 Yonge Street, Unit 35B, Ste 209, Richmond Hill, Ontario, Canada L4C 3C7)
Mustafa Hajj & Pilgrimage (☎ 64-3-954 5454; fax 954 5656; www.mustafa.com.de; 63 Smith St, Cape Town, South Africa)

Haj agencies in the UK:
21st Century Haj & Umra Services (☎ 0208-551 0786; fax 0208-551-0786; www.haj-umra.co.uk/; 20 Rosemary Drive, Redbridge, Ilford, Essex, IG4 5JD, UK)
Al-Hidaayah Hajj & Umrah Tours (☎ 0121-753-1889; fax 0121-753-2422; www.al-hidaayah.co.uk/; 522 Coventry Road, Birmingham, B10 0UN)
Al Muntada Al Islami Trust (☎ 0171-736-9060; fax 0171-736-4255; www.almuntada.org.uk/; 7 Bridges Place, Parsons Green, London, SW6 4HW, England)

Haj agencies in the USA:
Dar El Eiman (☎ 703-534-0044; fax 703-237-0561; www.dareleiman.com/Travel/index.asp; 360 S. Washington St. Ste 101, Fallas Church, VA 22046)
Dar El Salam Travel (☎ 212-725-2022, toll free 1-866-327-7252; fax 212-725-6581; www.darelsalam.com/; 280 Madison Avenue, Ste 905 New York, NY 10016)

Islamic Assembly of North America (☎ 734-975-9988; fax 734-975-9977; www.iananet.org/; 3060 Packard Rd. Ste E, Ann Arbor, MI 48108)

Visas & Documents

In all countries except the Gulf States you must contact a travel agent or haj delegation accredited by the government of Saudi Arabia to take care of flights, accommodation and travel inside Saudi Arabia. Many tour guides also act as a liaison with the Saudi embassy and assist you with your visa.

Journey of Discovery: A South African Hajj, by Na'eem Jeenah & Shamima Shaikh, is the true personal story of a South African couple who journey to Mecca together and include excellent details about Islam for non-Muslims.

A haj visa is valid according to the length of time contracted for your particular group during the month of Dhu al-Hijjah, including but not limited to the period from the 8th to the 10th of the month. It applies to Mecca, Medina, the extended haj area, and roads linking them to Jeddah or your point of entry. *Umrah* visas are usually valid for only one week in any month other than Dhu al-Hijjah, and permit your travel in Mecca, Medina, Jeddah and any roads linking them.

Visas are issued according to a quota system – one for every 1000 Muslims in a country's population. It is difficult if not impossible to get a visa in a country other than the one you reside in. Check with your local Saudi embassy to see if they will require photocopies of local documents such as identification cards, permanent residence cards, or student identification cards. The rules vary by host country.

To avoid any immigration problems, pilgrims are required to confirm their departure date from Saudi Arabia *before* the start of their pilgrimage. The departure date should not extend beyond the haj season.

Carry at least ten passport-sized photos for the ID cards which will be made for you in Saudi Arabia.

Female pilgrims under the age of 45 must be accompanied by their husband or *mahram* (a male member of the immediate family approved by Islamic law). This is not required of pilgrims from some Middle Eastern countries; check with your Saudi embassy. Women over 45 can travel without a *mahram* if travelling with a group and sponsored by a family within her group. She must, however, submit a notarised letter from her husband, son or brother authorising her to travel for haj with the named group.

If you have a non-Muslim name, you will be required to carry a certificate issued by an Islamic authority (the imam of your local mosque) stating that you are a Muslim. This is very important and you must carry it with you at all times in Saudi Arabia.

If you should lose your passport, immediately report the loss to your guide or the group representative who is taking care of you during the haj. He must obtain a certificate from the office of the Unified Agents, in which the loss of the passport is mentioned. A pilgrim will not be able to depart from Saudi Arabia without this certificate.

What to Bring

Many everyday items are available in Saudi, but you don't want to spend your time shopping for mundane things. Your exact requirements will vary according to your own desires and circumstances, however, it is worth considering bringing the following things with you: your prayer rug, Quran (a pocket edition is ideal), *tasbeeh* (prayer beads), and a container for stones and pebbles at Muzdalifah. Following are suggested items which will make your trip more comfortable and convenient.

CLOTHING

Saudi Arabia is a hot, arid country. Your health, comfort and stamina will benefit from wearing loose-fitting clothing, allowing air to

HAJ VISA REQUIREMENTS

Haj visa requirements listed by the Saudi Arabian authorities are as follows (much of this information is directly quoted from the representatives of the Kingdom of Saudi Arabia):

- A passport valid at least six months past the date of departure.
- One passport-sized photograph.
- A confirmed airline ticket for arrival and departure from Saudi Arabia.
- A quadrivalent meningitis vaccine protecting against ACYW is required from all pilgrims, with validity not less than three years. (Pilgrims must have their immunisation at least ten days before travelling.)
- All foreign passport holders must have permanent residency in the host country.
- Applications for haj must be submitted through agencies, tourist companies, or charitable organisations certified in the host country.
- An approval letter issued by the Saudi Ministry of Haj confirming that the authorised agent, tour company or haj group has completed the necessary requirements regarding their pilgrims.
- Relevant cheques for service fees and transportation fees inside Saudi Arabia; check with your Saudi Arabian embassy for current amounts.

circulate. Natural fabrics like light cotton with an open weave will absorb perspiration.

Many men choose to wear the Saudi *thobe*, which is a comfortable, practical full-length garment. Women must wear the *hijab* (conservative mode of dress) at all times.

Both men and women wear sandals or flip-flops. If you do not have sandals, you do not have to walk barefoot. Wear what you have until you find a place to get sandals.

If you will be travelling in the winter months, pack a light sweater for the early morning when it may be cooler.

Ihram

This is the required garment for men while on the haj. *Ihram* (which also refers to the sacred state) consists of two pieces of white unsewn cotton cloth (or light towelling), secured by safety pins, a belt or a strip of cloth torn from the *ihram*. The bottom piece of your *ihram* should measure 1.15m (45 inches) by 3m (120 inches), and the upper piece should measure 1.15m (45 inches) by 1.8m (72 inches). It may be worth practicing putting on your *ihram* at home to avoid any embarrassment when you arrive in Saudi Arabia. It's a good idea to wear it around the house to get accustomed to the feeling of the garment.

MONEY

The amount of money you bring is entirely up to you and will depend on what is covered in your particular contract with the haj agency. It's best to bring a combination of cash (US dollars or euros are recommended) and travellers cheques to the haj. You may also bring a credit card for telephone calls and unexpected expenses.

If any of your valuables go missing report the loss immediately to your guide – he will help you report the loss to the proper authorities.

Wired bank transfers to be picked up at a bank in Saudi are *not* recommended. Saudi banks have variable business hours, and you don't want to interrupt your haj by visiting a bank which may be closed.

IMMUNISATION CERTIFICATE

Disease and illness spread quickly and easily in the haj environment where multitudes of people from all over the world move in extremely close conditions. Inoculations are required for illnesses such as meningitis, polio, typhoid fever, pneumonia, diphtheria and tetanus. Carry your immunisation certificate with you to the haj and present it to Saudi authorities on arrival. See the Health chapter for more information.

Before You Leave

The night before your departure should be spent in sincere spiritual cleansing so that you leave home not just with a bag of clean clothes, but a clean and pure heart, which is much more important.

It is important to leave according to ritual. Make two *rakat* (prayers) before you leave, asking for Allah's forgiveness, protection and ease along the journey, an accepted haj and safe return. Make *du'a* (personal prayer, supplication) for the safety of your family members. Give an amount of money to the poor and needy for safety and protection along the journey, and plan to give a small beneficial amount along your entire journey.

Be well informed of the rituals you want to perform. There are many forms of Islam, and another pilgrim may not be able to advise you. Although your guide is there to help you, do not expect him to be your personal Islamic advisor.

Look forward to the opportunity of humbly helping others. Assist the elderly or weak, make a vow to behave politely and patiently to all. Leave behind all anger, expectation of comfort, and panic. Some excitement is natural, so bring a small measure of that with you – you will have a wonderful haj, *Inshallah* (God willing).

On the flight, make a mental list of the *du'as* you would like to make upon first seeing the Kaaba. Keep the list in your mind at all times, especially on the going and returning journey.

When you arrive, be extremely patient. You will be spending hours waiting in lines so recognise that this is also a part of the haj. If you see someone who does not respect others, move to a different spot. Do not hesitate to check with your haj guide at any time.

On Arrival

If you are landing in Jeddah and going to Mecca to perform haj directly, you must be in a state of *ihram* before you land, as the plane shall enter the *miqat* (place where Muslims declare their intention to make haj). Women in their menses must be in a state of *ihram* when they pass the *miqat*. They should shower and do *talbiyah* like everyone else.

While one would expect that all people at the haj would be there for one single purpose, unfortunately some go to take advantage of the atmosphere of trust. Pickpockets and thieves know that many pilgrims are so caught up in the atmosphere that they forget to guard their valuables. Use adequate safety measures to ensure that your passport and funds remain intact.

THE HAJ STEP BY STEP

This is a step-by-step example of the rituals of Umrah Tamattu, the haj which is performed from the 8th to the 10th of Dhu al-Hijjah. This is a generalised account of the haj; as there are many forms of Islam, some rites described here may differ from your individual teachings. The Prophet Mohammed (pbuh), in his wisdom, added flexibility to many rituals of the haj for our benefit and it would be impossible to explain all of them here.

Talbiyah & Miqat

The rites of pilgrimage begin by donning the *ihram*, in both dress and attitude; and reciting the *talbiyah*.

> *Labbeik Allahomma Labbbeik, Labbeik La Sharika Laka Labbeik,*
> *Innal hamda Wal Nimata Laka Wal Mulk, Laa Sharika Lak*

> Here I am, O God, at Thy Command! Here I am at Thy Command!
> Thou art without associate; Here I am at Thy Command! Thine are
> grace and dominion! Thou art without associate.

This is done in preparation for the haj, before the 8th of Dhu al-Hijjah. Those already in Mecca start their haj by putting on the *ihram* and declaring their individual intention of performing the haj. Many pilgrims travel already clothed in their *ihram* and start reciting the *talbiyah* before they land.

If you do not arrive in Mecca clothed in your *ihram*, your guide will direct you to the location of your *miqat*. There, you will shower if possible and take care of personal hygiene before donning the *ihram*.

The *miqat* marks the boundary of the sacred haj territory; the boundaries are denoted by Thul-Halaifa in the north, Al-Juhfah in the northwest, That 'Irq in the northeast, Yalamlam in the southeast, and Qarn al-Manazil in the east.

Be careful not to utter the *niyyah* (intention of *ihram*) until you are sure that you are at the point of *miqat*. When you are clothed in your *ihram*, recite the *talbiyah*, and declare the *niyyah*, you will be *muhrim* – consecrated and ready to perform the haj.

One Thousand Roads to Mecca: Ten Centuries of Travelers Writing About the Muslim Pilgrimage, by Michael Wolfe, relates twenty accounts of the haj, spanning 10 centuries, through the eyes of people who have undertaken the journey.

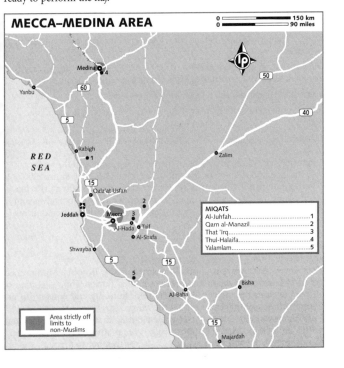

MECCA–MEDINA AREA

0 — 150 km
0 — 90 miles

Medina
Yanbu
60
50
40
5

RED SEA

Rabigh ●1
Zalim
15
Qala'at Usfan
Jeddah
Mecca 3
2
Al-Hada
Taif
Al-Shafa
Shwayba
5
15
5

Bisha
Al-Baha

MIQATS	
Al-Juhfah	1
Qarn al-Manazil	2
That 'Irq	3
Thul-Halaifa	4
Yalamlam	5

Area strictly off limits to non-Muslims

15
Majardah

FORBIDDEN ACTIONS DURING IHRAM

The rules of the *ihram* should be followed whenever you are in a state of *muhrim*. There are 24 deeds that break your *ihram*; four of them are prohibited for men, four are prohibited for women, and the rest are forbidden for both men and women.

For Both Men & Women

- Hunting desert animals.
- Any type of intercourse or sexual foreplay.
- Marriage.
- Masturbation.
- Using perfume and eating anything that is perfumed.
- Using makeup.
- Looking in the mirror (although you are allowed to look at other smooth surfaces and into the water).
- Behaviour such as lying, speaking loudly to attract attention, or showing off.
- Swearing.
- Killing animals, including small insects.
- Wearing rings for beauty (you are allowed to wear a ring for religious purposes).
- Using henna (it is okay to have Henna on from before *ihram* even it the colour remains during *ihram*, but it is better not to use henna before *ihram*).
- Rubbing any type of oil upon the body. If you used any kind of lotion or oil before *ihram* and the smell is still on your body, you must wash it off. If you must use oil or lotion (eg for medical reasons) you may do so, but you will have to pay the *kaffarah* (see p71).
- Any kind of intentional removal of hair from the body. If some hair naturally comes off during washing, it is permitted.
- Causing the body to bleed, eg harming yourself by scratching roughly or brushing your teeth so hard that your gums bleed. It is permitted to extract blood for medical reasons.
- Trimming your nails (both fingernails and toenails) with any implement.
- Pulling teeth. You may not pull a tooth even if it does not bleed. If you have to do so, you must pay the *kaffarah*.

During haj, all the problems of the world fall away and the soul cries with love and thanks for the gift of life. One feels their humanity as never before and one learns how temporary this life really is. It is like all of our defences are stripped away and we can see ourselves and our cosmic place so clearly but instead of being painful it is soothing and pure contentment.

A. Osman

DURING IHRAM

The *ihram* was worn by both Ibrahim and the Prophet Mohammed (pbuh). The whiteness of the *ihram* signifies purity while the state of *ihram* envelops the pilgrim with a sense of humility and equality in the eyes of Allah. See p66 for more on the *ihram*.

Women wear the same conservative clothing that they wear every day, with a light headcovering but not a veil. Women must keep their face and hands uncovered and may wear intimate apparel, but not gloves.

- Removing any kind of plant in the area of the haram, although the fruit of date trees and fruit trees may be removed.
- Carrying weapons.

For Men

- Wearing sewn clothes. Any clothes that have been sewn or with seams are forbidden. The exception is a moneybelt, which may be worn even if it is sewn.
- Wearing anything that covers the whole of the top of the foot. This includes socks, shoes or any other thing that covers the foot. You are allowed to wear slippers, but they must not cover the whole of the foot.
- Covering the head. You may not cover your head or carry anything upon your head. You are allowed to tie a headband for a headache, to go under the tent, and to put your head upon a pillow to sleep.
- Holding a shade over the head (such as an umbrella). You may not use any kind of shade or go under the shade while walking in between destinations. You are also not allowed to ride a car, ship, or plane with a roof. It is okay to walk under bridges or into restaurants or shops.

For Women

- Wearing jewellery for beauty. You may wear jewellery that is not publicly visible, that you are accustomed to and wear all the time, but you are not allowed to show it to any man, even your husband.
- Covering the face. As a woman, you are not allowed to cover your face with any kind of veil. You are allowed to put your face on a pillow to sleep and to cover your face with your *chador* or clothing to turn away from *namahram* (a man who is not related to you as *mahram* under the rules of Islam).

KAFFARAH

If you break one of the rules, you will be required to pay a *kaffarah*. The *kaffarah* is not a form of punishment! It is simply to remind you of the obligations while in your state of *ihram*, and is an opportunity to renew your haj commitment. Depending on which rule you have violated there are three ways to submit the *kaffarah*: by offering a sacrifice; by feeding six indigent and poor people; by fasting for three days.

You may wear a watch, eyeglasses, a belt, use unscented soap and a pillow. You may cover yourself with a blanket in cold weather but be sure to leave your head and face uncovered.

Both men and women may shower with unscented soap. Women and men may also comb their hair, as the Prophet's wives did when they were in *ihram*. See Forbidden Actions During Ihram above.

Note: do not uncover your right shoulder until you reach the Kaaba and begin *tawaf*. This is the time that the Messenger uncovered his shoulder and it is an act of haj, so we must follow when the Prophet did it.

Beginning Your Haj

Once you are clothed in your *ihram*, pray two *rakat* (leaning forward and putting your hands on the knees), pronounce your *niyyah* (intention) to perform the haj, and begin reciting the first invocation of the haj, the *talbiyah*. All acts of worship are preceded by a *niyyah*. A suggested *niyyah* is:

O Allah! I intend to perform the haj. Make it easy for me and accept it from me. I make the *niyyah* for haj and enter into the state of *ihram* for the sake of Allah alone, the Most high.

Tawaf al-Qudum

As you recite the *talbiyah*, you begin to move towards the Al-Masjid al-Haram, which encircles the Kaaba, in order to perform the Tawaf al Qudum (the *tawaf* of arrival). You enter into the Al-Masjid al-Haram with your right foot first. As you do so you say three times '*Allahu akbar* (God is great) and then say three times '*la Ilaha Illallah*' (there is no God but God). The idea is to praise and glorify your Creator before making *du'a* and supplications. Therefore, in lieu of '*Allahu akbar*' and '*la ilahe Illallah*', you may recite some other similar holy verses if you so desire.

Proclaim *du'a* on the beloved Prophet (peace be upon him) and very humbly supplicate to Allah for whatever you wish. This is a special time for the acceptance of prayers.

Upon sight of the Kaaba, move forward to perform *tawaf* of Kaaba, see the Tawaf p74. Move with the crowds and begin to circle the Kaaba in a anticlockwise direction starting at the line of the *Hajar-e-Aswad* (Black Stone; see the Black Stone p75). The black stripe on the floor should be on your right side. As you walk, you will join the masses in prayer, circling the Kaaba seven times. You have begun your haj.

Sa'ee Between Safa & Marwah

Some pilgrims choose to perform the *sa'ee* between Safa and Marwah after the Tawaf al-Qudum, and some complete the *sa'ee* later in their pilgrimage after the Tawaf al-Ifadha. The *sa'ee*, also known as the 'running', symbolise Hagar's frantic search for water to quench the thirst of her son Ismail. Hajar ran seven times between the knolls of Safa and Marwah. The haram has been extended to surround the distance between the two hills.

There is no specific *du'a* to say between Safa and Marwah. Do not miss the *du'a* that the Prophet said when he stood on Safa. Raise your hand and pray as he did, '*Sal Allahu alayhi wa Sallam*' (Peace be upon him).

Women walk the distance of the *sa'ee* (a total distance of around 3km) men run or jog. Start at the hill of Safa and head towards Marwah. When you

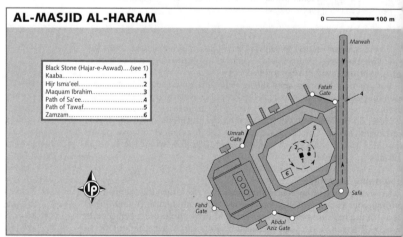

AL-MASJID AL-HARAM

0 ⊏▬▬▬■ 100 m

Black Stone (Hajar-e-Aswad)....(see 1)	
Kaaba	1
Hijr Isma'eel	2
Maquam Ibrahim	3
Path of Sa'ee	4
Path of Tawaf	5
Zamzam	6

Marwah

Fatah Gate

Umrah Gate

Safa

Fahd Gate

Abdul Aziz Gate

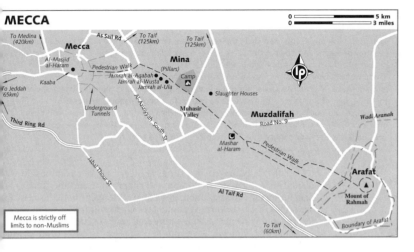

et to Marwah, return to Safa. When you reach Safa, you have performed two *shawt*. When seven *shawt* are complete, you will be at Marwah.

Note that you can take a break after *tawaf*, before *sa'ee*, and you can take breaks during *sa'ee* to drink water or rest.

The 8th of Dhu al-Hijjah

On the 8th of Dhu al-Hijjah, after *fajr* (dawn) prayers but before *zuhur* (noon) you will change into your *ihram*, pronounce your *niyyah*, and proceed to Mina. Mina is a small, uninhabited village in a desert location approximately three miles from Mecca. If you choose not to walk the three miles, roofless buses are provided so you can stay in *ihram*.

You will perform your daily prayers in Mina beginning with the *zuhur* prayer. Most pilgrims spend their day in Mina meditating and praying as the Prophet Mohammed (pbuh) did on his pilgrimage.

You will stay overnight in Mina, and a tent should be provided by your tour group. Each tent is identified by section number and colour, so be sure to remember yours because it is easy to get lost! This completes the first day of the haj, known as the Day of Tarwiyah.

The 9th of Dhu al-Hijjah

Rise early for the *fajr* prayers, and begin to move with the masses towards Arafat (Arafah). This is the day of rite simply known as the *wukuf* (standing) on the plain of Arafat. There will be huge crowds and if it is not your preference, you do not need to go all the way up on the Mount of Rahmah (The Mountain of Mercy). You can stay anywhere within the boundaries of Arafat. Here is a suggested prayer upon entrance to Arafat:

O Allah! Forgive my sins, help me to repent to you, and grant me all that I beseech of you. Whenever I turn, let me see goodness. Allah is praised! All praise is due to Allah! There is no deity except Allah! And Allah is the Most Great.

After settling in your tent, you may start your obligatory daily prayers. Most pilgrims combine their prayers as a Muslim traveller; refer to your individual beliefs for the form of your prayers.

Hajj: Reflection on Its Rituals, by Ali Shariati, is a masterpiece translated from the original Persian. The well-known Muslim writer talks about the importance behind each step of the haj.

THE TAWAF

To perform the *tawaf*, you must circle the Kaaba seven times, always in a anticlockwise direction. Each *tawaf* begins and ends at the Black Stone. A black line on the ground will guide you. The Kaaba should be on the side of your left shoulder at all times; it is not permissible to face the Kaaba while moving or walking backwards. Always walk around the Black Stone, never between it and the Kaaba. Litters are supplied for those with physical limitations; they may be hired close to the *sa'ee* door of the haram. The litters are carried by four people above the heads of the crowd. Women should not perform the *tawaf* while they are menstruating, or if they are still bleeding after childbirth. You may be pushed or elbowed during the *tawaf* and it will be easy to loose your patience. If you get angry, your haj is broken – so keep your cool!

After the daily prayers, it is time to reflect on your relationship with Allah. This is a day for reflection and submission, and the time to ask Allah for mercy and absolution. It is a time of cleansing both the heart and mind. This is also the turning point of the Great Pilgrimage, when you are cleansed and you emerge with a pure soul ready to start life anew.

After sunset, you will leave your tent and start to move towards Muzdalifah. Move quietly, reciting the *talbiyah* and other prayers. Muzdalifah is a desert location, between Mina and Arafat. You will spend the night there. Toilets and washing facilities are available but be especially conscious of courtesy because it will be crowded. No tents or lodging facilities are available, and you will sleep under the stars.

Pilgrims walk to the nearby foothills to collect pea-sized pebbles before turning in for the night.

Everyone who is able to stay should spend the night at Muzdalifah. Only sick, elderly, disabled, and women who cannot physically endure the night outside are considered to have a legitimate excuse for leaving before dawn.

The 10th of Dhu al-Hijjah

After *fajr* prayers, there will be a *khutba* (speech or sermon) in Muzdalifah. Depending on your individual school and custom, you may stay and hear the *khutba*, and the trip back to Mina may include a stop at Mashar al-Haram.

Many pilgrims travel through the Mashar al-Haram and make *du'a* at the shrine until the sun's brightness has spread through the sky, and speed up their walk while passing through the Muhasir valley on the way to Mina.

All pilgrims must be especially careful and courteous during this part of the haj. The day of the stoning of the *jamrah* (pillars) has seen many tragedies. The sheer size of the masses all moving in one direction will give you the impression of moving with a wave. It is especially important to be courteous here – help those for whom the Prophet Mohammed (pbuh) has provided some flexibility in this area. If you are elderly or disabled you may throw your pebbles at night when it's less crowded.

Throw seven pebbles at the Jamrah al-Aqabah (Jamrah al-Kubra), you will return later to stone the two remaining pillars. Your pebble should reach the inside of the *jamrah's* fence, and you may throw it from under the bridge or over it. Every time you throw a stone say, 'Allahu Akbar'.

The three pillars represent the powers of Shaitan. The seven stones indicate your wish to reject him not once, but seven times. The number seven also symbolises infinity. Note: The *jamrah* are not devils, and Shaitan himself is not tied up for stoning. *Hajis* who hold this misconception may end up cursing, swearing or throwing sandals.

CELEBRATING EID AL-ADHA

Eid al-Adha (The Festival of Sacrifice) is celebrated on the 10th day of Dhu al-Hijjah by Muslims around the world in commemoration of the Prophet Ibrahim's obedience to Allah. In Mina, the sacrifice of an animal is performed between the 10th and 13th of Dhu al-Hijjah but not after the 13th. It is usually a sheep or goat; or a cow or camel which may be shared with seven other people. You may perform the sacrifice yourself, but most *hajis* ask a professional butcher to do it. Part of the meat may be eaten, but most of it is given to the Saudi authorities who distribute it to the needy.

CUTTING HAIR

After Eid al-Adha, as a symbol of humility, men can trim their hair or shave their heads, starting from the right side. If you shave your head do not leave parts unshaved.

If you trim your hair, take from all sides of your head. Do not take off your *ihram* until you have shaved or trimmed. There will be people on the streets of Mina who will shave your head for a small price, but if you have concerns about hygiene bring a razor with you. Women cut a fingertip's length of hair.

TAHALUL AL-ASGHAR

You may now remove your *ihram*. All restrictions are lifted, except for those on conjugal relations that stay in place for most Muslims until after Tawaf al-Ifadha (circling the Kaaba) and *sa'ee* (walking between the two hills, Safa and Marwah) are completed. The state of partial lifting is called Tahalul al-Asghar, but there are still a few other ceremonies to be performed. You may now shower and change into everyday clothes.

STONING THE REMAINING JAMRAH

After Eid al-Adha most pilgrims prefer to return (while in Mina) and stone the other two *jamrah*. Follow the process described above for the stoning of the first pillar (see p74).

GOING TO MECCA & THE TAWAF AL-IFADHA

You will now travel back to Mecca for one of the most cherished rites of the haj, the Tawaf Al-Ifadha (Tawaf Ziarat) at the Al-Masjid al-Haram. This *tawaf* symbolises unity between Allah and man, and embodies the concept of Allah at the centre of humanity. You will move around the

---

THE BLACK STONE

While circling the Kaaba, many pilgrims stop to kiss or touch the Black Stone, emulating the Prophet Mohammed (pbuh). Some believe that they should not, so it's up to your particular belief as to whether you do this.

No-one knows where the oval stone came from; some say it is the only original piece of the structure built by Ibrahim and Ismail. Whatever the case, it was first mounted in a silver frame in the seventh century and is actually reddish-black in colour. The Prophet Mohammed (pbuh) is quoted as saying, 'The stone and the station of Ibrahim are two bequeathed from paradise, but Allah obliterated their light, otherwise they would have lit between east and west'. He also said, 'When the black stone was lowered from paradise, it was whiter than milk, but the sins of humans made it black'.

Be aware that the authorities often apply perfume to the Black Stone and the Rukn Al-Yamani (the corner of the Kaaba that faces Yemen). If so, do not touch them while in the state of *ihram*, otherwise a *kaffarah* will be required as a penalty. You do not have to touch the Black Stone for your *tawaf* to be accepted. If it is crowded, you may face your hand toward the stone and say '*Allahu akbar*'.

MECCA OR MAKKAH?

The term 'mecca' has come to be used in English to mean any place that draws a large number of people (in reference to the huge numbers that visit the Mecca during the haj). As Mecca is the holiest city of Islam, many Muslims find this use of the term offensive, and travellers should be sensitive to this. In the 1980s the Saudi government officially changed the spelling of Mecca to Makkah, or more correctly, Makkah Al-Mukkaramah (The Holy City of Makkah). In many senses, this is closer to the Arabic pronunciation.

This spelling has yet to be adopted world-wide – even many Muslims are unaware of the change. Throughout this book we have used Mecca as this spelling is more easily recognised by English speakers, but be aware that in Saudi Arabia you will see both.

Kaaba in a anticlockwise circle, completing seven revolutions beginnin and ending at the line of the Black Stone. As you walk, recite the *talbiya* and two *rakat*.

You have the option to choose the time of your *tawaf*. This is especiall convenient for women who should use this flexibility because they canno perform the *tawaf* while they are menstruating.

MAQUAM IBRAHIM

Islam: Religion, History, and Civilization, by Seyyed Hossein Nasr, is an introduction to the Islamic faith and discusses the diversity of 1.2 billion adherents in detail.

After completing the seven revolutions of the *tawaf*, many pilgrims as semble to pray behind the Maquam Ibrahim (Station of Abraham). It is th stepping-stone used by the Prophet Ibrahim during the original constructio of the Kaaba. The stone is in a glass case on the North side of the Kaaba, cir cled with silver, and impressions of footprints are clearly seen in the stone

DRINKING FROM ZAMZAM

After praying at Maquam Ibrahim, you may visit the well of Zamzam and drink the holy water of Mecca. The well is enclosed in a marbl chamber.

PERFORMING SA'EE BETWEEN SAFA AND MARWAH

Some pilgrims choose to perform *sa'ee* after the Tawaf al-Ifadha, an some complete the *sa'ee* earlier in their pilgrimage after the Tawaf a Qudum.

TAWAF AL-NISSA

This is an optional *tawaf*, performed by some schools of Islam. It is identi cal to the other *tawafs* and should be completed any time after the Tawa al-Ifadha but before the Tawaf al-Wada. Pilgrims cannot resume conjuga relations with their spouse until this *tawaf* is accomplished. If the pilgrin neglects this duty and leaves Mecca, he must return and fulfil the Tawa al-Nissa before any conjugal relations can be resumed.

TAWAF AL-WADA

This is the farewell *tawaf* adding closure to your haj. It should be con nected to your departure; if you are delayed, you should repeat it. Like th other *tawafs*, you will circle seven times around the Kaaba, starting an ending at the Black Stone, and pray at the Maquam Ibrahim.

Extended Haj

Some pilgrims choose to take an extended haj from the 11th to the 13th c Dhu al-Hijjah. This time is spent in Mina with friends and family enjoy ing companionship in Allah's holy land. The restrictions of the *ihram* ar

HAJ TAMATTU (UMRAH TAMATTU) & UMRAH

In general, the isolated form of *umrah* is a different sort of trip, for enjoyment and recreation. *Umrah* is a mini haj that can be done at any time of the year. It is said that '*Umrah* is in the stomach of Tamattu,' which means that all of the things done for *umrah* are also included in Haj Tamattu, hence the name of the combined 'Umrah Tamattu'.

If you will be visiting Mecca at any time other than from the 8th to the 10th of Dhu al-Hijjah, you will be performing the isolated form of *umrah*. Visiting Saudi for the purpose of *umrah* during the month of Ramadan is 'most commendable and equal to haj in merit and excellence'. However, *umrah* during Ramadan does not release one from the obligation of performing the Haj Tamattu at another time. The rituals for *umrah* are shortened; you will not throw stones at the *jamrah*, visit Mina, Arafat, and Muzdalifah, or perform a sacrifice. After completing these five actions, the *muhrim* is released from the obligations of *ihram*:

- *miqat*
- *ihram*
- *tawaf* prayer
- *sa'ee* between Safa and Marwah
- *taghsir*, which means clipping a part of the hair or fingernails.

lifted and spouses can have sensual pleasure at this time. Every day you visit the three *jamrah* and throw seven stones at each of them. You will return to Mecca on the 13th and make a final *tawaf* around the Kaaba.

Many pilgrims like to visit the tomb of the Prophet Mohammed (pbuh) in Medina when their haj obligations are complete. The Prophet lies in a simple grave under the green domed Mosque of the Prophet. This is the city that welcomed Mohammed (pbuh) after his flight from Mecca and it's full of interesting history and memories of him. It was once a collection of villages called Yathrib and for over thirteen hundred years, the city has been called Medina an-Nabi or 'The City of the Prophet'.

> Whoever goes to haj without obscenity he or she will be forgiven as a newborn. A Sound haj has no reward but paradise.
>
> *The Prophet Mohammed (peace be upon him)*

HAJ GLOSSARY

See also p200.

Black Stone (Hajar-e-Aswad) – a sacred stone in the Kaaba; it is from here that pilgrims begin the *tawaf*

du'a – personal prayer; supplication and communication with Allah

ihram – a sacred state of dedication in which pilgrims' simple, white attire is worn. Purity and human equality are represented in this state, and certain acts are banned.

ikhlass – pure intentions; seeking to do the haj for Allah's favour alone

jamrah – a pillar in Mina at which pilgrims throw pebbles. There are three Jamrah pillars (representing devils).

kaffarah – payment or sacrifice that must be offered if one knowingly breaks the rules or obligations of the *ihram*

miqat (meeqat) – the place around the Kaaba where the declaration of intention to make haj or *umrah* is made

muhrim – a person in *ihram*

niyyah – literally 'intention' to perform the pilgrimage

sa'ee (sa'yi) – a haj rite in which pilgrims run between the hills of Safa and Marwah in a re-enactment of Hagar's search for water and food

shawt – circuit around the Kaaba; seven of these are performed in a *tawaf*

talbiyah (talbeeya) – the supplication a Muslim recites once he is in *ihram*, declaring his intention to perform the haj

tawaf – a haj rite in which pilgrims move together in an anticlockwise direction around the Kaaba

wukuf – literally 'standing' – on the plain of Arafat, the central rite of the haj

Riyadh & the Najd
الرياض و نجد

CONTENTS

Riyadh is one of the most fascinating places in the Kingdom, the city where the innovation complexities and contradictions of modern Saudi Arabia are most evident.

Visiting the Saudi capital is like entering a constantly evolving museum where histo is not yet a thing of the past. It was on this soil that Wahhabi Islam was born and it w from neighbouring Dir'aiyah that the enduring hegemony of the Al-Sauds was launche (see p21). Yet it is also in Riyadh that the most breathtaking examples of the Al-Saud visic for modernising the Kingdom can be found. The juxtaposition of towering, super-mode skyscrapers in Riyadh with the mud-brick ruins of the Masmak Fortress and Dir'aiyah – tw hugely significant historical monuments – serves as an emblem for Saudi Arabia's fraug relationship between past and future colliding in an uncertain present. This relationship nowhere more on display (nor more harmonious) than in Riyadh's King Abdul Aziz Historic Area. Here, the mud fortress of Murabba Palace looks out across landscaped gardens towar the innovative and hugely impressive National Museum. When this is added to goc bookshops and excellent restaurants, Riyadh has much to be enjoyed.

The Najd region, which stretches deep into the desert north from Riyadh, forms the cultur bedrock of Saudi Arabia, the Kingdom's conservative Islamic heartland (particularly arour Buraydah). Najdis may consider themselves the purest Bedouin Arabs and the most faithf inheritors of the strictly orthodox Wahhabi legacy, yet they're nonetheless also the custodia of some of the finest and most sophisticated pre-Islamic rock art in the Kingdom at Jubba

This complex combination of past and present, of interesting cities and fascinating cultur encounters, make Riyadh and its surrounds unlike any place on earth and a great place start your Saudi journey.

HIGHLIGHTS

- ■ Spanning Arabian history in the exceptional **National Museum** (p85) in Riyadh
- ■ Stepping back in time at **Dir'aiyah** (p91) and the **Masmak Fortress** (p86) in Riyadh
- ■ Rising above Riyadh in the stylish **Kingdom tower** (p87) and **Al-Faisaliah tower** (p86)
- ■ Cheering on the camels at the **camel race track** (p91) on the northeastern outskirts of Riyadh
- ■ Tracking down pre-Islamic Arabia amid the rock carvings of **Jubba** (p95)

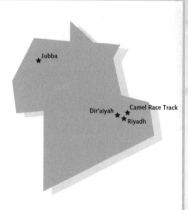

- ■ POPULATION: 6.9 MILLION
- ■ AREA: 565,000 SQ KM

RIYADH & THE NAJD

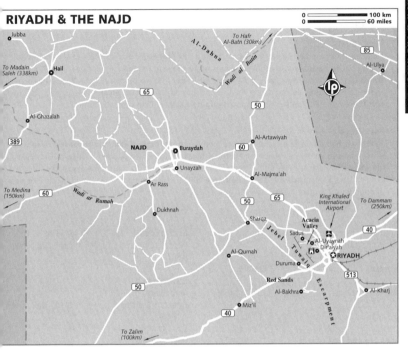

RIYADH   الرياض

☎ 01 / pop 3.3 million

Nowhere are the contradictions of modern Saudi Arabia more evident than in Riyadh, a burgeoning, fast-moving city surrounded by the deserts of central Arabia. Parts of the city seem to rise up from the desert as high-tech oases of glass-and-steel buildings and modern shopping malls, while not far away, remnants of Old Riyadh offer reminders that the growth of this city has been exponential. Wherever you go, you'll find the uneasy cohabitation of old and new, finding human expression in the uneasy clash between the guardians of Riyadh's conservative past – the mutawwa – and those who would shape its future – Riyadh's increasingly disaffected youth.

HISTORY

Riyadh was a small and insignificant watering hole for nomads until 1746 when a wall was built around the settlement. Riyadh became the Al-Saud capital in 1818 when they were driven from Dir'aiyah by soldiers loyal to the Ottoman sultan. Riyadh fell to the Al-Rashids in the 1890s and it was not until the dramatic recapture of the city in 1902 (p85) that Riyadh became the Al-Sauds' undisputed capital.

Despite its historical status as capital, Riyadh is a very new city; it was not until the 1970s (when most of the embassies moved from Jeddah) that it began to grow at a seemingly unstoppable rate.

ORIENTATION

Riyadh is a sprawling mess with most street signs only in Arabic. The first thing you should do is learn the names of the main districts and major landmarks as these are necessary for getting directions.

Al-Bathaa is the central, older portion of town. Most of what you'll need in Riyadh lies north of here, especially Olaya and Sulaimania, the main business and shopping areas. The main north–south thoroughfares are Olaya St and King Fahd Rd, while Makkah Rd is the main east–west artery.

Residents of Riyadh have stubbornly stuck to using the old or informal street

RIYADH IN...

Two days

For a leisurely two days seeing the sights, start at the **Masmak Fortress** (p86) to see the humble origins of Old Riyadh and then make your way to the very modern Sky Bridge of the **Kingdom Tower** (p87) or the viewing deck of **Al-Faisaliah Tower** (p86) to see just how far Riyadh has come. Spend as much time as you can in the crumbling mud ruins of **Dir'aiyah** (p91), just outside the city. There are plenty of high quality **restaurants** (p88) to fill in any extra time.

Four days

Follow the two-day itinerary, but spend a morning at the **King Abdul Aziz Historical Area** (p86) where you can enjoy the wonderful **National Museum** (p86) and another vestige of Old Riyadh, the **Murabba Palace** (p86). If it's Thursday, head out of town to the **Camel Races** (p91). In the evening, thank Allah for the **Jarir Bookstore** (p82), which should have something to see you through Riyadh's quiet nights.

names. The more important ones include (formal name first):

Formal	Informal
King Abdul Aziz Rd	Old Airport Rd
King Faisal St	Al-Wazir St
Prince Sultan ibn Abdul Aziz St	Tallateen St
Salah Al-Din Al-Ayoubi Rd	Sitteen St
Imam Faisal ibn Turki ibn Abdullah St	Al-Khazan St
Al-Ahsa St	Pepsi Cola St
Prince Mohammad ibn Abdul Aziz St	Tahlia St

Maps

The Farsi *Map & Guide of Riyadh* (SR20) is essential to finding your way around Riyadh. It's very detailed and contains an extensive index of street names and points of interest. *Riyadh Today* (SR20) is a yearly directory for just about everything you'll need in Riyadh. Both are available from the Jarir Bookstore (see following).

INFORMATION
Bookshops

Jarir Bookstore (☺ 9am-2pm & 4-11pm Sat-Thu, 4-11pm Fri) Al-Ihsa St (Map p83; ☎ 477 3140); Olaya St (Map p83; ☎ 462 6000) If you can't find it in one of the branches of the Jarir, then it's probably not available in Saudi Arabia. Branches are just south of the intersection with Mosa Ibn Nosayr St, and south of Makkah Rd in the Ar-Rabwah district.

Cultural Centres

Alliance Française (Map p83; ☎ 476 6436; Al-Dhobbat) Annual library membership is SR50. It's behind the Hyatt Regency Hotel.

British Council (Map p83; ☎ 462 1818; 1st fl, Al-Musa Bldg, Olaya St) Six-monthly library membership is SR175.

Emergency

Ambulance (☎ 997)
Directory Assistance (domestic ☎ 905, international ☎ 900)
Fire (☎ 998)
Police (☎ 999)
Traffic Accidents (☎ 993)

Internet Access

There are loads of Internet cafés. Try:
Blizma Internet Café (Map p83; ☎ 473 6843; Makkah Rd; per hr SR10; ☺ 24hr)
Galaxy Internet (Map p83; ☎ 473 7355; Salah ad-Din al-Ayubi Rd; per hr/6hr SR8/25; ☺ 4pm-7am)
Sky2PC Internet Center (Map p84; ☎ 405 7085; 3rd fl, Al-Rajhi Center; ☺ 9am-10pm Sat-Thu, 4-10pm Fri) Off Al-Bathaa St.
Zinc Internet Café (Map p83; ☎ 465 7993; Prince Mohammad ibn Abdul Aziz St; per hr SR10; ☺ 5.30-1am)

Internet Resources

There's not much on the net about Riyadh. www.riyadhvision.com/english/placetovisit .htm gives an overview of its sights, including some lesser-known attractions.

Medical Services

Embassies can usually steer their national toward doctors in emergencies. Expats will have a company doctor.
Dallah Hospital (☎ 454 5277; cnr King Fahd Rd & Al-Imam Saud Ibn Abdul Aziz Ibn Mohammad Rd) Takes emergency cases on a walk-in basis.

RIYADH

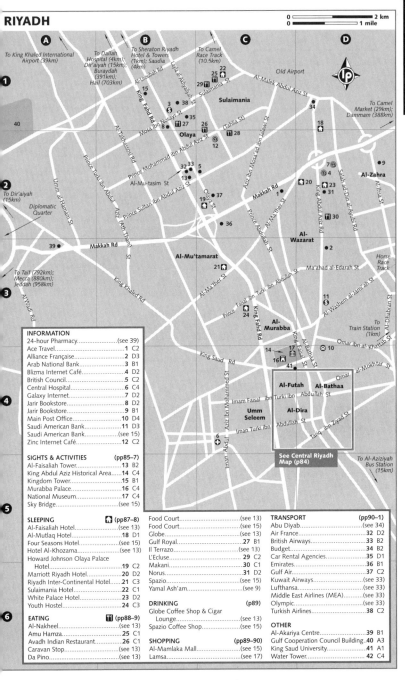

0 — 2 km
0 — 1 mile

To King Khaled International Airport (39km)

To Dallah Hospital (4km); Dir'aiyah (15km); Buraydah (391km); Hail (703km)

To Sheraton Riyadh Hotel & Towers (1km); Saudia (4km)

To Camel Race Track (10.5km)

Old Airport

To Camel Market (29km); Dammam (388km)

Sulaimania

Olaya

Al-Zahra

To Dir'aiyah (15km)

Diplomatic Quarter

Makkah Rd

Al-Wazarat

Horse Race Track

Makkah Rd

To Taif (792km); Mecca (880km); Jeddah (958km)

Al-Mu'tamarat

Ma'ahad al-Edarah St

Al-Murabba

To Train Station (1km)

Al-Futah   Al-Bathaa

Umm Seleem

Al-Dira

See Central Riyadh Map (p84)

To Al-Aziziyah Bus Station (15km)

INFORMATION	
24-hour Pharmacy	(see 39)
Ace Travel	1 C2
Alliance Française	2 D3
Arab National Bank	3 B1
Blizma Internet Café	4 D2
British Council	5 C2
Central Hospital	6 C4
Galaxy Internet	7 D2
Jarir Bookstore	8 D2
Jarir Bookstore	9 B1
Main Post Office	10 D4
Saudi American Bank	11 D3
Saudi American Bank	(see 15)
Zinc Internet Café	12 C2

SIGHTS & ACTIVITIES	(pp85–7)
Al-Faisaliah Tower	13 B2
King Abdul Aziz Historical Area	14 C4
Kingdom Tower	15 B1
Murabba Palace	16 C4
National Museum	17 C4
Sky Bridge	(see 15)

SLEEPING	(pp87–8)
Al-Faisaliah Hotel	(see 13)
Al-Mutlaq Hotel	18 D1
Four Seasons Hotel	(see 15)
Hotel Al-Khozama	(see 13)
Howard Johnson Olaya Palace Hotel	19 C2
Marriott Riyadh Hotel	20 D2
Riyadh Inter-Continental Hotel	21 C3
Sulaimania Hotel	22 C1
White Palace Hotel	23 D2
Youth Hostel	24 C3

EATING	(pp88–9)
Al-Nakheel	(see 13)
Amu Hamza	25 C1
Avadh Indian Restaurant	26 C1
Caravan Stop	(see 13)
Da Pino	(see 13)

Food Court	(see 13)
Food Court	(see 15)
Globe	(see 13)
Gulf Royal	27 B1
Il Terrazo	(see 13)
L'Ecluse	29 C2
Makani	30 C1
Norus	31 D2
Spazio	(see 15)
Yamal Ash'am	(see 9)

DRINKING	(p89)
Globe Coffee Shop & Cigar Lounge	(see 15)
Spazio Coffee Shop	(see 15)

SHOPPING	(pp89–90)
Al-Mamlaka Mall	(see 15)
Lamsa	(see 17)

TRANSPORT	(pp90–1)
Abu Diyab	(see 34)
Air France	32 D2
British Airways	33 B2
Budget	34 D1
Car Rental Agencies	35 D1
Emirates	36 B1
Gulf Air	37 C2
Kuwait Airways	(see 33)
Lufthansa	(see 33)
Middle East Airlines (MEA)	(see 33)
Olympic	(see 33)
Turkish Airlines	38 C2

OTHER	
Al-Akariya Centre	39 B1
Gulf Cooperation Council Building	40 A3
King Saud University	41 A1
Water Tower	42 C4

RIYADH & THE NAJD

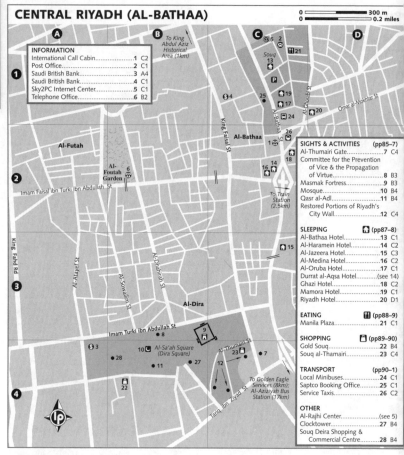

CENTRAL RIYADH (AL-BATHAA)

0 — 300 m
0 — 0.2 miles

Pharmacy (Map p83; Mosa ibn Nosayr St; ☽ 24hr) In the Al-Akhariyah Centre.

Money

Riyadh is awash with banks, drive-thru ATMs and moneychangers; many of these are marked on the maps. A good place to look is along Olaya St between the Al-Khozama Hotel and Makkah Rd, but there are also plenty of banks in Al-Bathaa, and the Kingdom and Faisaliah towers. AmEx is represented by **Ace Travel** (Map p83; ☎ 464 8810; Makkah Rd; ☽ 9am-1.30pm & 4.30-8pm Sat-Thu).

Post

Main post office (Map p83; Prince Abdul Aziz St; ☽ 7.30am-2.30pm & 4-10pm Sat-Wed) Near the inter-section with Al-Bathaa St. The express mail window is open from 7.30am to 1pm Thursday.

Telephone

You're never far from an international call cabin in Riyadh; there are dozens in the streets surrounding Al-Bathaa Hotel. Prepaid phonecards are available from any grocery in various denominations, and can be used with any private or public phone.

Travel Agencies

Ace Travel (Map p83; ☎ 464 8810; Makkah Rd; ☽ 9am-1.30pm & 4.30-8pm Sat-Thu) One of the most reliable among Riyadh's hundreds of air ticket sellers.
Bin Zaid Travel (☎ 419 4688; www.binzaidtravel .com.sa)

olden Eagle Services (Map p83; ☎ /fax 492 2550; ldeneagletours@hotmail.com; Manar District)

ehlat Travel (☎ 466 0726; www.rehlat.com; -Dugaither Commercial Center, Tahlia Rd)

ANGERS & ANNOYANCES

iyadh has a higher concentration of ctive mutawwa (religious police, p165) than ny other large city in the Kingdom. Women ill frequently be asked here to cover their ead. Their other preoccupations include nforcing the prayer times and preventing eople from smoking or eating in public reas during Ramadan. The mutawwa are t their most threatening when they are ccompanied by police.

Riyadh has been a particular target of xtremists and it always pays to be vigilant, specially around compounds and other laces frequented primarily by Westerners. ee p166 for further information.

Riyadh's reputation for dangerous drivers s rapidly catching up to Jeddah's. As a driver, : can be a harrowing experience, particularly he combination of speed and unpredictable hanges of direction; as a pedestrian it can be ownright frightening.

IGHTS

King Abdul Aziz Historical Area

This impressive **complex** (Map p83) covers lmost 360 sq km of landscaped paths, pen-air exhibitions, running water and pen lawns. Ask any taxi for *Abdul Aziz*

tarikhi (King Abdul Aziz Historical Area) as most haven't yet cottoned on to the fact that the museum has moved here.

NATIONAL MUSEUM

On no account should you miss the exceptional, state-of-the-art **National Museum** (Map p83; ☎ 402 9500, ext 1082; adult/child/student SR15/10/5; ☺ men & school groups 9am-noon Sun-Wed, families 4.30-9pm Sun-Fri). The eight galleries provide an epochal sweep of Arabia's history and include: the creation of the universe; the earliest Arabian civilisations and kingdoms; the *jahiliyah*, literally 'period of ignorance,' immediately before the arrival of Islam; the Prophet's Mission, Islamic Arabia; the early Saudi states; the Unification of Saudi Arabia and the haj. There are reconstructed Dilmun tombs, fragments of rock art, and models of old Dir'aiyah, Jeddah and the holy mosques in Mecca and Medina. But what makes this museum stand out are the push button prompts, virtual visits to ancient sites, small-screen cinemas and audio commentary in English and Arabic at many points.

Some archaeologists argue that relatively few original archaeological fragments are on display. Those with a specialist interest in ancient civilisations may indeed leave a little frustrated as the museum follows the broad brushstroke approach to history. However, there is no better place to get an overview of Arabian history in an engaging way that will appeal to children and adults alike.

THE RECAPTURE OF RIYADH

Saudi Arabia almost never happened. In the late 19th century, the Al-Sauds were in retreat from Ottoman armies eager to reassert their hegemony over Arabia. In the Al-Rashids, particularly the Shammar tribe whose homeland centred on Hail, the Ottomans found a willing ally with a history of tribal opposition to the Al-Sauds. When added to the fact that the Al-Sauds had become embroiled in squabbles over succession since the death of the iconic Faisal in 1865, the years of Al-Saud rule over central Arabia seemed to be numbered. By 1893, Riyadh was in Rashidi hands, the Saudi leader, Abdul Rahman, was in exile in Kuwait and many Al-Saud notables were hostages in Hail.

However, the Al-Rashids were aligned with the Ottomans whose power was decidedly on the wane and who had few resources left for defending desert outposts such as Riyadh. The Al-Sauds were under the protection of the Al-Sabah royal family of Kuwait, who in turn had signed treaties of co-operation with the British and were deeply concerned about further Ottoman expansion.

With its eyes on expansion elsewhere in Arabia, the Al-Rashids failed to notice the clandestine approach from the south of Ibn Saud (the son of Abdul Rahman) and a handful of his followers who had spent 50 days in the sands of the Empty Quarter, all the while covering their tracks. Masmak Fortress stood on the outskirts of old Riyadh and, on 15 January 1902, the raid was launched, the Rashidi governor of Riyadh was killed and Riyadh fell almost immediately to the Al-Sauds. It has been unchallenged as the Al-Saud stronghold ever since.

MURABBA PALACE

This combination of a fortress and a **palace** (Qasr al-Murabba; map p83; ☎ 401 1999; admission free; ☺ 8am-2pm Sat-Wed) provides an attractive counterpart to the sweeping, modern lines of the National Museum. Built by King Abdul Aziz in 1946, the palace surrounds a ground-level courtyard with a date palm growing in its centre. The upper level has displays of traditional clothes and crafts (eg antique chairs, carpets, camel saddles and weapons). The aesthetic here is one of impregnability with high, square walls turned inward with few openings onto the outside world. The impressive *diwan* (reception room) suggests that while enemies were to be kept out by the formidable walls, the doors were always open to the king's subjects who came here to bring disputes for resolution and to petition favours.

A permit is required to visit the interior (p173).

Masmak Fortress

One of the few remaining buildings from Old Riyadh, the **Masmak Fortress** (Qasr al-Masmak; map p84; ☎ 411 0091; admission free; ☺ men 8am-noon & 4-9pm Sat, Mon & Wed; women & families 8am-noon & 4-9pm Sun & Tues, 9am-noon Thu) is Riyadh's single most significant historical monument and is not to be missed. Built around 1865 on the site of an earlier fortification and extensively renovated in the 1980s, it was converted into a museum in the early 1990s.

Masmak was the scene of Ibn Saud's daring 1902 raid on the Al-Rashid garrison to regain control of Riyadh (p85). During the raid, one of the future king's companions (some say Ibn Saud himself) hurled a spear at the main entrance door with such force that the head is still lodged in the doorway (just right of the centre panel). The small panel in the door, known as *al-khokha,* allowed only one person through at a time, thereby reinforcing Masmak's defensive capabilities.

Inside, the fort is a veritable warren of rooms and courtyards, reflecting the fact that it needed to be self-contained during times of siege. The mosque on the left, off the entrance passageway, has attractive pillars while almost next door is the nicely reconstructed traditional *diwan.* An open courtyard at the rear of the fortress has a well surrounded by painted doors. The four watch towers stand around 18m high and the walls are 1.25m thick, punctuated with openings for firing weapons from within. In the centre of the fortress, the square **Al-Murabba Tower** allowed the ruler to keep watch over the fort itself. The residential quarters are on the first floor.

Apart from the displays of weapons and costumes, there is a short re-enactment video of the retaking of the fortress by the Al-Sauds. The fascinating photographs from 1912 to 1937 show how the fortress stood at the northern boundary of Riyadh – hard to believe today. Also worth lingering over are Philby's sketch maps of the fortress and surrounding area.

Al-Sa'ah Square (Dira Square)

Macabrely known by most long-term Riyadh residents as 'Chop Chop Square', this is the site of Riyadh's infamous public beheadings and it was here that Turki ibn Abdullah was assassinated in 1834 (p23). Surrounding it are the modern sandstone **Great Mosque, Qasr al-Adl** (Palace of Justice) and the Committee for the Prevention of Vice and Propagation of Virtue (ie mutawwa) headquarters. Despite these somewhat grim functions, the square can be pleasant in the evening with lanterns and the Masmak Fortress nearby.

Al-Thumairi Gate

About 200m southeast of the Masmak Fortress, you'll find this impressive restoration of one of the nine gates that used to lead into the city before the walls were torn down in 1950. The gate itself is surprisingly ornate, even overdone alongside the austerity of the Masmak fortress and the other reconstructed mud-brick sections of the **city wall** which are scattered around the area.

Modern Riyadh
AL-FAISALIAH TOWER

The first of the stunning new structures to rise above the Riyadh skyline, **Al-Faisaliah Tower** (Map p83; ☎ 273 3000; Olaya St; admission SR35; ☺ 10am-midnight) was opened in March 2000. This wonderful glass-and-steel monument to modern engineering is rendered unique by the enormous glass globe (which is 24m in diameter and made of 655 glass panels) near the summit. The tower's needlepoint pinnacle (with a crescent on the tip) sits 267m above the ground.

Atop its limestone foundations sits one of the largest lobbies in the world, above which thirty floors of offices rise up. On the 31st floor is the entrance to the viewing deck and gift shop (at the time of research all visitors received a small souvenir of their visit – a stress ball which is perhaps for those with a fear of heights). Above the deck are three floors of exclusive restaurants (p88 and p89).

KINGDOM TOWER

Riyadh's newest landmark **tower** (Map p83) is a stunning piece of modern architecture. Despite bearing a remarkable resemblance to a bottle opener, it's an extraordinarily stylish structure rising up from the monotonous and functional architecture of the Riyadh sprawl. Cased in glass, the tower reflects the mood of the city by catching the sun's changing angle and is particularly beautiful at night when the upper sweep is lit with subtle but constantly changing coloured lights. Rising 302m above the ground, its most distinctive feature is the steel-and-glass, 300-tonne bridge connecting the two towers.

The first floor lobby areas are given over to shops (p90). To get a unique perspective on the Saudi capital, ride the high-speed elevators up to the 99th floor **Sky Bridge** (☎ 201 1888; admission SR35; ☻ 10am-midnight) which arches between the two towers. The views are breathtaking, but not for those who suffer from vertigo.

FESTIVALS & EVENTS

The annual two-week-long **Jenadriyah National Festival** takes place in late February or early March at a special site about 45km northeast of central Riyadh. The festival programme commences with an epic, and utterly improbable, **King's Cup** (see The Arabian Horse p31), Saudi Arabia's most prestigious camel race, which takes place over a 12-mile track and has up to 2000 participants. The programme includes the performance of traditional songs, poetry competitions and dances as well as demonstrations of traditional crafts, and falconry from around the Kingdom. It's hugely popular with Saudis and other Gulf Arabs, especially the camel and horse racing. This is also one of the few places where you'll be able to see a performance of the *ardha* (p39).

SLEEPING

In 1974, Riyadh had just one hotel, the Al-Yamana, where a bed in a shared room was obtained through bribery and the unlucky slept on the lobby floor. Now, Riyadh has everything from international standard five-star hotels to lucky-to-still-be-in-existence dives that you wouldn't be seen dead in.

Budget

Apart from the youth hostel, all the cheap options are in the noisy Al-Bathaa area.

Youth Hostel (Map p83; ☎ 405 5552; Shabab Al-Ghansani St; r per person SR10) This is one of the more central hostels in the Kingdom, but you'll still need a taxi to get anywhere.

Al-Medina Hotel (Map p84; ☎ 403 2255; Imam Faisal ibn Turki ibn Abdullah St; s with/without bathroom SR60/50, d SR95/80; ✖) These are the cheapest habitable beds in Riyadh; they're basic and the whole place has something of an Egyptian rooming-house ambience. The rooms at the back are quieter.

Al-Jazeera Hotel (Map p84; ☎ 412 3479; fax 412 4993; Al-Bathaa St; s/d SR60/100; ✖) The simple, clean rooms here are the best you'll get for the price.

Al-Haramein Hotel (Map p84; ☎ 404 3085; Al-Bathaa St; s/d SR60/100; ✖) This hotel has tidy (if soulless) rooms that are reasonably well maintained.

Mamora Hotel (Map p84; ☎ 401 2111; fax 401 0167; Al-Bathaa St; s/d SR70/100; ✖) The Mamora offers excellent value despite the building showing distinct signs of age. The rooms are spacious and some of the balconies have downtown views.

Mid-Range

Al-Bathaa Hotel (Map p84; ☎ 405 2000; Al-Bathaa St; s/d SR100/150; ✖) Don't be put off by the run-down lobby which could once (at a stretch) have been described as elegant. Rooms are huge, pleasant, carpeted and come with satellite TV, minibar and bathroom, making this by far the best option in the downtown area.

Al-Oruba Hotel (Map p84; ☎ 405 5959; fax 405 5619; Al-Bathaa St; s/d SR80/120; ✖) This place is actually very good value if you ignore the three stars on the door and the depressing reception area. Although get here before it ages any further.

Sulaimania Hotel (Map p83; ☎ 461 3500; fax 461 3800; Sulaimania St; s/d SR140/180; ✖) The rooms here are spacious, well-kept (if a little bit old) and come with a satellite TV. The area has plenty of restaurants and lively streets, at least for Riyadh.

White Palace Hotel (Map p83; ☎ /fax 478 7800; King Abdul Aziz Rd; s/d SR160/200; 🕅) The White Palace Hotel is worth the extra riyals for spacious, pleasant rooms that have balconies, satellite TV and more character than most in this price range.

Al-Mutlaq Hotel (Map p83; ☎ 476 0000; res@hotelal mutlaq.com; King Abdul Aziz Rd; s/d SR200/250; 🕅 🖳 🖳) In the upper mid-range category, the Al-Mutlaq is great with tastefully appointed rooms, good service and a business centre.

They don't get many Westerners at other places at the cheaper end of mid-range so expect to be a novelty. They include:

Ghazi Hotel (Map p84; ☎ 402 2287; fax 405 4001; s/d SR80/120; 🕅) Off Al-Bathaa St.

Durrat Al-Aqsa Hotel (Map p84; ☎ 276 0080; fax 276 0085; Al-Bathaa St; s/d SR80/120; 🕅) Slightly newer than Ghazi hotel.

Riyadh Hotel (Map p84; ☎ /fax 402 8777; Omar al-Mokhtar St; s/d SR80/120; 🕅) The oldest of these three options.

Top End

Hotel Al-Khozama (Map p83; ☎ 465 4650; www.rose woodhotels.com; Olaya St; s/d SR500/650; 🄿 🕅 🖳 🖳) In the shadow of the dramatic Al-Faisaliah Tower, the Al-Khozama is a tasteful choice, not least because it has some of the best restaurants in the capital. The quality of the service makes up for the smallish (though well-appointed) rooms.

Al-Faisaliah Hotel (Map p83; ☎ 273 2000; fax 273 2001; www.rosewoodhotels.com; s/d SR800/1000; 🄿 🖳 🖳) Even closer to the tower, this place is a step up in elegance and charm. It's the opulence and attention to detail which makes it stand out. The location is also good.

Howard Johnson Olaya Palace Hotel (Map p83; ☎ 462 5000; fax 462 4487; s/d SR250/300; 🄿 🕅 🖳 🖳) Don't be put off by the name. For top-end quality without the five-star price tag, this well-situated place, off Olaya St, is very good value and it's renowned for its excellent service.

Rack rates at the international chains vary little from single/double SR450/550, but discounts are readily available (ask for the corporate rate or book over the Internet); prices listed here don't include the 15% service charge:

Four Seasons Hotel (Map p83; ☎ 211 5000; www.four seasons.com; 15-24th fl, Kingdom Tower; d from SR650; 🄿 🕅 🖳 🖳)

Marriott Riyadh Hotel (Map p83; ☎ 477 9300; www .marriotthotels.com; Al-Ma'ther St; s/d from SR395/450; 🄿 🕅 🖳 🖳)

Riyadh Inter-Continental Hotel (Map p83; ☎ 465 5000; www.intercontinental.com; Al-Ma'ther St; d from SR300; 🄿 🕅 🖳 🖳)

Sheraton Riyadh Hotel & Towers (Map p83; ☎ 454 3300; www.sheraton.com; cnr Prince Abdullah St & King Fahd Hwy; d from SR320; 🄿 🕅 🖳 🖳)

EATING

Eating out is the Riyadhis' favourite pastim (they don't have many).

Budget & Mid-Range

Al-Bathaa is packed with small *shwarm* (meat in pita bread) stands and restaurant the latter mostly of the chicken, rice an kebab variety. Full meals cost around SR10.

Manila Plaza (Map p84; set meals SR10; 🕘 11am midnight) Behind Al-Bathaa Hotel, the third floor food court has a dozen or so Asian stall which are popular with Asian expats (always good sign); most offer set meals with a coupl of main dishes, rice and a drink.

Yamal Ash'am (Map p83; ☎ 461 3292; Olaya St; meal around SR10) Consistently popular for Arabi food, this place has good kebabs (from SR1 including salad and drink). The outdoo eating tables are a pleasant enough place t watch the world go by.

Amu Hamza (Map p83; ☎ 462 6761; Sulaimani St; starters SR5-20, mains SR20-75; 🕘 lunch & dinner Although not as pleasant as its namesake i Jeddah, this is one of the more affordabl seafood restaurants in Riyadh with a rea sonably extensive menu.

Makani (Map p83; ☎ 464 6401; Sulaimania St; starter SR6-12, mains SR10-28; 🕘 lunch & dinner) Makan is a good choice for affordable but nicel prepared Punjabi, Hyderabadi and Goar specialties. Highlights here include th prawn/chicken tandoori (SR28/15), and th Peshawari naan (SR6) is spectacular. Th men-only dining area is a drawback.

For cheap Lebanese and Turkish sit down food, head to King Abdul Aziz S (Old Airport Rd), south of the White Palac Hotel. **Norus** (Map p83) is particularly popula with locals and expats alike.

The food courts at the **Al-Faisaliah Towe** (p86) and **Kingdom Tower** (p87) have a wid selection of cuisines; the former is a better place to people-watch.

Top End

Gulf Royal (Map p83; ☎ 465 5368; Mosa ibn Nosayr St; starters from SR15, mains from SR30; ⊗ lunch & dinner) Riyadh's best Chinese restaurant is particularly good for seafood.

L'Ecluse (Map p83; ☎ 465 7648; Prince Mohammad ibn Abdul Aziz St; set menu SR100-150, starters from SR20, mains from SR40; ⊗ lunch & dinner) This high-class seafood restaurant has simple décor, but the food is superb, fusing French and Arabic cuisine. Among the many highlights are the stuffed mussels (SR40).

Avadh Indian Restaurant (Map p83; ☎ 465 4109; fax 462 0509; Prince Mohammad ibn Abdul Aziz St; starters SR12-35, mains SR25-115; ⊗ lunch & dinner) Home to Riyadh's finest North Indian cuisine, Avadh has attentive service and an extensive menu which caters to vegetarians, as well as lovers of seafood (from SR58 to SR115); it also does a special menus for kids (SR20).

Reservations for the following places are essential.

Il Terrazo (Map p83; ☎ 273 3000; fax 273 2590; Al-Faisaliah Tower; buffet SR150; ⊗ lunch & dinner) Located on the leafy 1st-floor balcony of the Al-Faisaliah Hotel, this is one of the best dining options in the capital. The food comes with a Brazilian twist, the service is classy and there is a buzzy, liberal atmosphere which can be lacking in other Riyadh restaurants. The buffets (available for dinner from May to October and for lunch from November to April) are well worth the money.

Globe (Map p83; ☎ 273 3000; fax 273 2590; Al-Faisaliah Tower complex; meals from SR200; ⊗ lunch & dinner) Located in the stunning glass globe, nearly 250m above Riyadh, this restaurant serves high quality European dishes with exceptional views. A great splurge.

Spazio (Map p83; ☎ 211 1888; fax 211 1182; Kingdom Tower; meals SR200; ⊗ 10am-3pm & 7.30pm-1am Sat-Thu, 1-4pm & 7.30pm-1am Fri) Another of Riyadh's high-above-the-ground fine dining experiences, Spazio has terrific views with a predominantly French and Italian menu, as well as a teppanyaki and sushi bar.

Riyadh's home of fine dining is **Hotel Al-Khozama** (p88). **Al-Nakheel** (☎ 464 1400) is widely regarded as the Kingdom's highest quality restaurant for Arabic food, while **Caravan Stop** (☎ 464 1400; ⊗ lunch & dinner) is also good for Arab and international dishes. **Da Pino** (☎ 464

1400; ⊗ lunch & dinner) also has a well-deserved reputation, this time for top quality Italian food. At all of these places, starters begin at SR20 and mains at SR40; don't expect much change from SR120 per person.

DRINKING

Globe Coffee Shop & Cigar Lounge (Map p83; ☎ 273 3000; fax 273 2590; Al-Faisaliah Tower; minimum charge SR100; ⊗ noon-2am) As high as you can go in Al-Faisaliah Tower, and hence high above the mutawwa, this is as close as Riyadh gets to hedonism. For your SR100, you'll get a coffee and an assortment of snacks and you pay nothing extra to see young Riyadhis mingling with members of the opposite sex. You do pay extra for cigars, however, of which there is an extensive selection.

Spazio Coffee Shop (Map p83; ☎ 211 1888; fax 211 1182; Kingdom Tower; minimum charge SR100; ⊗ 10am-3pm & 7.30pm-1am Sat-Thu, 1-4pm & 7.30pm-1am Fri) Although it's trying hard, this coffee shop hasn't yet garnered the cool reputation of the Globe. It's still a great place.

ENTERTAINMENT

Riyadh's nightlife is notoriously thin, even by Saudi standards. Dining out is a popular pastime, but you'll probably find yourself watching a lot of satellite TV or reading lots of books. Your best bet is to get plugged into expat and diplomatic networks because the embassies frequently organise cultural and social evenings as well as musical or theatrical performances; there are even a few amateur theatre groups for men and women.

SHOPPING

Riyadh has some of the best shopping in Saudi Arabia.

Lamsa (Map p83; ☎ 401 4731; lobby, National Museum; ⊗ 9am-noon & 4.30-9pm Sun-Thu, 4.30-9pm Fri) For handicrafts head here. It has a good (and expensive) selection (mostly silver jewellery, daggers and other decorative pieces), although not all of it is from Saudi Arabia.

Souq al-Thumairi (Al-Thumairi market; Map p84; Al-Thumairi St; ⊗ 9am-noon & 4-9pm Sat-Thu, 4-9pm Fri) For a more traditionally Arabian experience of picking your way through junk and fending off persistent salesmen, head to Souq al-Thumairi, immediately south of the Masmak Fortress. The shops in the small lanes offer everything from carpets to coffee pots, silver daggers to silver jewellery.

SHEBAB AND SHOPPING MALL CULTURE

If you think that it's difficult living in a city with possibly the least inspiring entertainment scene in the world, spare a thought for young Saudis. In a country where cinema is banned, singles are kept strictly away from members of the opposite sex and nightclubs are a thing which other countries have, young Saudis have resorted to novel means of making contact with people of the opposite sex. The least subtle of these are the *shebab* (teenage boys) with little else to do but terrorise other drivers with their speed. Most, however, have a hidden agenda, a target group which, in spite of appearances, you probably don't belong to. Some openly admit that they spend so much money on their cars in an attempt to attract young women. To this end, you can often see cars cruising up and down outside girls' schools. More often than not, they'll throw their phone numbers from the window in the hope of receiving a call on their mobile if their cars and driving techniques have proven sufficiently impressive. A similar process takes place in the shopping malls (particularly Al-Faisaliah and Kingdom Towers), but is not restricted to young men as women are also known to follow this approach. Known as 'numbering', it's the Saudi version of a casual encounter.

Gold Souq (Map p84) Located across the car park from the Palace of Justice.

The modern shopping area is centred on Olaya St and the surrounding streets, where there are dozens of malls selling international designer brand names and electronic goods. Your first stop should be the **Al-Mamlaka Mall** (Map p83 ; ☺ 10am-11pm Sat-Thu, 4-11pm Fri) or the mall under the **Al-Faisaliah Tower** (Map p83 ; ☺ 9.30am-noon & 4-10.30pm Sat-Tue, families 10am-11.30pm Wed-Thu & 4-10.30pm Fri).

GETTING THERE & AWAY
Air
King Khaled International Airport (☎ 222 1700) is nearly 40km north of Al-Bathaa. Of the four commercial terminals (there's also a royal terminal), No 1 is not in use, No 2 is used for domestic flights, No 3 for Saudia international flights and No 4 for foreign airlines.

Domestic destinations include:

Destination	Cost (SR)	No of daily departures
Abha	280	3
Al-Baha	290	1
Buraydah	140	2
Dammam	150	8
Hail	200	3
Jeddah	280	9
Jizan	320	2
Jouf	280	2
Medina	250	4
Najran	280	2
Sharurah	280	1
Tabuk	390	4
Taif	250	3

AIRLINE OFFICES
Airlines with offices in Riyadh:
Air France (Map p83 ; ☎ 476 9666; King Abdul Aziz Rd)
British Airways (Map p83; ☎ 465 0216; King Faisal Centre, Olaya, Al-Mutasim St)
Emirates (Map p83; ☎ 465 5485; Mosa Ibn Nosayr St)
Gulf Air (Map p83; ☎ 462 6666; Olaya St)
Kuwait Airways (Map p83; ☎ 463 1218; King Faisal Centre, Olaya)
Lufthansa (Map p83; ☎ 463 2004; King Faisal Centre, Olaya)
Middle East Airlines (MEA; Map p83; ☎ 465 6600; King Faisal Centre, Olaya)
Olympic (Map p83; ☎ 464 4596; King Faisal Centre, Olaya)
Saudia (Map p83; ☎ 488 4444; cnr Prince Turki ibn Abdul Aziz & Olaya Sts)
Turkish Airlines (Map p83; ☎ 463 1600, ext 5; Olaya St)

Car
Car-hire agencies based in Riyadh tend to congregate in the same areas, making comparisons between them easy. Head for Olaya St, near Hotel Al-Khozama, where choices include **Budget** (Map p83; ☎ 463 3546) and **Abu Diyab** (Map p83; ☎ 464 7657); the corner of King Abdul Aziz Rd and Prince Sultan ibn Abdul Aziz St; and the airport domestic arrivals hall.

Bus
Al-Aziziyah bus station (☎ 213 2318) is around 17km south of the centre. There's a **booking office** (☎ 222 1700) in Al-Bathaa. Services departing from Riyadh to various destinations are frequent, and include:

Destination	Duration (hr)	Cost (SR)	No of daily departures
Al-Ula	13	170	1
Buraydah	4	75	10
Dammam	4½	60	10
Hail	8	130	6
Hofuf	4	55	5
Jeddah	10-12	140	10
Khamis Mushayt	14	135	10
Najran	12	135	3
Sakaka	14	200	2
Tabuk	17	210	2
Taif	10	120	10

Muslim-only buses also leave for Mecca (SR130, 10 hours, six daily) and Medina (SR150, 12 hours, three daily).

Train

From the **train station** (☎ 473 1855; Prince Abdul Aziz ibn Abdullah ibn Turki St), 2.5km east of Al-Bathaa, trains run to Dammam (2nd/1st class SR50/70, four hours) via Hofuf (SR30/40, 2½ hours) and back again three times a day, except Thursday when there's only one train in each direction.

GETTING AROUND
To/From the Airport

Buses (SR15) run between Al-Aziziyah bus station and the airport. A taxi from the airport to the centre could cost SR70 on the meter depending on where you start and how heavy the traffic is.

Buses & Minibuses

Red Saptco buses and private orange-and-white minibuses (both SR3) cover most of the city and have their routes posted in the front window, although only in Arabic. Most start around the intersection of Al-Bathaa and Imam Faisal ibn Turki ibn Abdullah Sts; elsewhere, the key is to stand by the roadside and shout your destination in the window as the bus slows.

Taxi

Riyadh's white taxis are everywhere and, unusually for Saudi Arabia, most of them readily use their meters; flagfall is SR5. The level of English proficiency ranges from idiosyncratic-but-willing to virtually non-existent. Identifying landmarks close to where you want to go along with the name of the district (eg, Al-Bathaa) are essential to getting where you want to go without driving all over town. Expect to pay at least SR30 from the bus station.

AROUND RIYADH

Desert Treks from Riyadh (SR20) by Ionis Thompson is available from any branch of the Jarir Bookstore. It contains numerous weekend excursions from the capital, complete with rudimentary route maps.

Camel Market & Races

Riyadh's **Camel Market** (Souq al-Jamal) is one of the largest of its kind in the Middle East. Spread out north of the Dammam road 30km from the city centre (take the Thumamah exit), this is a fascinating place to wander around; late afternoon is when the traders really find voice. The semipermanent shelters, ramshackle pens and overpowering aroma of camel are as authentically traditional as any market in Arabia. There is, however, one exception: camels, when bought, are no longer led across the sand, but are instead loaded into pick-ups, the process of which is one of the more ungainly and rancorous procedures in the Kingdom.

Every Thursday from 4pm onwards, **camel races** (p31) take place at the camel race track along the extension of Al-Uroubah St in the Thumamah district. It's a popular excursion for locals and there is something wonderfully chaotic about seeing the humped beasts loping across the sand. In winter, there are often races also on Friday afternoons.

In some Middle Eastern countries, camel jockeys are young children who have been kidnapped and kept vitually as slaves. Saudi Arabia has strict laws concerning camel jockeys; apprentices must be at least 16 years of age.

Dir'aiyah   الدرعية

The ancestral home of the Al-Sauds and the birthplace of the Saudi-Wahhabi union (p22), **Old Dir'aiyah** (admission free; 🕒 7am-6pm Sat-Thu, 1-6pm Fri) is a wonderful escape from the clamour of Riyadh. This old, walled oasis town built of mud has a few restored buildings, but most is in ruins lending it an evocative, abandoned air. The ruins are among the most accessible (no permit is necessary) and extensive of the old cities in the Kingdom and should not be missed.

HISTORY

The site was settled in 1446 by an ancestor of the Al-Sauds. Dir'aiyah reached its peak in the late 18th and early 19th centuries during the First Saudi Empire, in particular under Saud the Great who ruled from 1803 to 1814. The Ottoman backlash to the growing Saudi-Wahhabi threat reached Dir'aiyah in 1818. After a six-month siege, Abdullah bin Saud, Saud's son and successor, surrendered and was eventually executed. Dir'aiyah was razed and what was left of the Al-Saud and their followers moved to Riyadh. For further information see p19.

DIR'AIYAH WALKING TOUR

As you climb up from the car park, the **Palace of Salwa (1)**, once a four-storey complex of palaces, residential and administrative buildings, towers above the **visitors centre (2)** on your left. It is believed that Mohammed ibn Abd al-Wahhab lived here. Directly opposite, the **Al-Saud Mosque (3)** was once connected to the palace by a bridge.

The main path continues south, then east, then south again to the **Palace of Fahd**

(4) and **Palace of Abdullah Bin Saud (5)**. Many of the buildings in this area are slowly returning to the earth and open spaces are slowly encroaching. Further south are the somewhat nondescript ruins of the **Palace of Thunayyan Bin Saud (6)**, who was the brother of Saud the Great. Behind this palace there are good views out over the palm groves with a water well clearly visible on the wadi floor.

Returning to the main path, walk west for around 250m, passing the ruined **Palace of Mishaari (7)** on the right and the newly restored **Al-Turaif Bath (8)** with its original decoratively painted doors. A further 100m on to the west and northwest respectively, you'll find the restored **Palace of Nasser (9)** and the **Palace of Saad bin Saud (10)**, which has turrets, wall and door decorations and an overall sense of impregnability. This is how much of Dir'aiyah must once have looked.

The main lane continues west from here before entering an open area where few houses remain. You can continue on to the restored sections of the wall (which

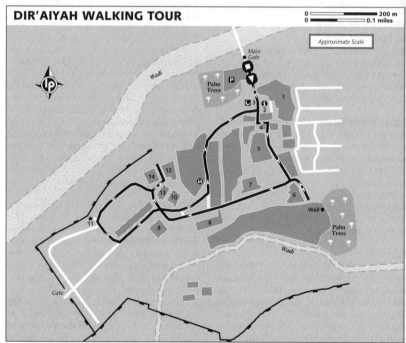

DIR'AIYAH WALKING TOUR

0 ▭▭▭▭▭ 200 m
0 ▭▭▭▭▭ 0.1 miles

Approximate Scale

once ran for 15km around the perimeter of Dir'aiyah) or branch off to the north to the **Tower of Faisal (11)**, the only restored tower in Dir'aiyah. A different path twists back to the Palace of Saad bin Saud, passing en route the ruined **Palace of Fahran bin Saud (12)** – note the rooms off the internal courtyard – and the **Saad bin Saad Mosque (13)**. Circle the Palace of Saad bin Saud from where a path heads north and then east back to the entry gate, passing some of the best preserved **houses (14)** along the way; watch for decoratively painted doors hanging forlornly from their hinges.

GETTING THERE & AWAY

The best way to reach Dir'aiyah, around 25km northwest of Al-Bathaa, is with your own car; take King Fahd Rd north and follow the signs off to the west after passing the Dallah Hospital.

A return trip in a taxi will cost at least SR120, including waiting time.

Northwest of Riyadh

Around 28km north of Dir'aiyah along the Route 535, there is a turn-off (west) to **Al-Uyaynah**, the birthplace of Mohammed ibn Abd al-Wahhab, the founder of Wahhabi Islam. Northwest from Al-Uyaynah is **Sadus** (21km), a much prettier oasis village with the remnants of 300-year-old walls, towers and fortifications. On your way back (preferably close to sunset), take the track (about halfway between Al-Uyaynah and Sadus) leading west towards the **Jebel Tuwaiq Escarpment** which cuts like a spine across Arabia from near the Yemeni border to the Al-Nafud desert in the north. The track leads through **Acacia Valley** before turning northwest (after nearly 9km) up onto the escarpment from where, after around 21km, you'll have stunning **views** down onto the desert plains and the old pilgrims' road to Mecca.

Sand Dunes

For true deep desert immersion, you'll need to head to Sharurah (p146).

Closer to Riyadh, there are numerous stretches of sand dunes just off the Riyadh–Mecca Hwy; the **Red Sands**, just west of the turn-off to Duruma, around 40km west of Riyadh, are probably the best because they have as their backdrop the cliffs of the Jebel Tuwaiq Escarpment.

THE NAJD نجد

Najd is Saudi Arabia's conservative heartland; here, fundamentalist Islam finds its most fertile ground. The pre-Islamic rock carvings near Jubba and some fine stretches of desert are the main reasons to come.

BURAYDAH بريدة

☎ 06 / pop 345,000

Buraydah has the unenviable reputation of being the least hospitable and most conservative city in Saudi Arabia. The old central square has a **covered souq**, and the residential areas two blocks either side of Khobib St (the main north–south road through town), near the communications tower, has a few good examples of traditional **Najdi mud-brick houses**. Other than that, you may wish to retreat to the **Jarir Bookstore** (☎ 381 0026; Uthman bin Affan Rd; 9am-2pm & 4-11pm Sat-Thu, 4-11pm Fri) until your transport leaves for elsewhere.

Al-Gassim Hotel (☎ 324 1858; fax 325 1854; Khobib St; s/d SR90/140) is the only place to stay in the town itself. It's simple, tidy and spacious, and some of the bathrooms have squat toilets.

Al-Salman Hotel (☎ 323 5984; fax 324 0373; s/d SR240/350), the only upmarket hotel, is almost impossible to find on your own; call from the airport or bus station and the staff will send a car to get you.

Khobib St has a number of small Turkish and Indian restaurants. These include the **Middle East Restaurant** (snack SR3, sit-down meal SR10) and **Madina Restaurant** (snack SR3, sit-down meal SR10) by the bus station.

Getting There & Away

Saudia (☎ 381 3333) flies to Buraydah (Gassim) several times a day from Riyadh (SR140) and Jeddah (SR270) with less regular flights to Dammam (SR280), Medina (SR180), Hail (SR110), Sakaka (Jouf; SR200) and Tabuk (SR310).

Saptco (☎ 324 3806) has buses to Riyadh (SR75, four hours, 10 daily) and Hail (SR50, four hours, three daily).

HAIL حائل

☎ 06 / pop 245,000

Hail (hay-el), a former trade crossroads and in Saudi Arabia's agricultural heartland, has played a somewhat inglorious role in Saudi history. This is the homeland of the Al-Rashid tribe, historical rivals to the Al-Sauds (p23), although it is now firmly under Al-Saud rule; carefully choreographed inter-tribal marriages have won more hearts and minds than military campaigns ever could. Hail has two forts here and makes a good base from which to visit the rock carvings at Jubba.

Orientation & Information

Hail's main north–south street centres on Commercial District Square by the Saudi Hollandi Bank building. Other banks, the bus station and most other services are all close to the square.

Sights

AL-QASHALAH FORTRESS

This mud fortress, which rises up from the centre of town, was closed for restoration when we visited. Built in the 1930s and used mostly as a barracks for Abdul Aziz's troops in Hail, the new king diplomatically chose the site, rather than existing Rashidi properties, to avoid alienating the Al-Rashid sheikhs.

Once the fort reopens, you'll need a permit (p173) to enter.

AIRIF FORT

On a hill just outside the centre of town, this fort was built around 200 years ago as a combined observation post and stronghold

and was sketched by Lady Anne Blunt when she and her husband Wilfred visited Hail in 1889. After climbing the hill and going through the main gate, look to your right for an open hall filled with low pillars. At one end of the large main courtyard of the fort is a doorway leading to a smaller inner court which gives you access to Airif's main watchtower.

Sleeping & Eating

Hail Hotel (☎ 532 0180; fax 532 7104; King Khaled St; s/d SR120/160) Hail Hotel is not located in one of Hail's finest buildings, but don't be put off by the exterior; the rooms are clean and quite good value.

Al-Jabalain Hotel (☎ 533 2294; fax 532 1166; s/d SR210/280) This is the best place to stay in Hail. It's not luxury but it's very comfortable and surprisingly good value for money.

Lahore Restaurant, opposite the Hail Hotel, is a decent choice for, you guessed it, chicken dishes, but it also has curries that are not as spicy as you might hope for. Another good bet is **Ababa Sera's**, a small Indian place offering cheap *samosas* (50 halalas). For *shwarma* and fresh juice try **Fast Food** (Main Rd). Near Al-Jabalain Hotel, try **Mishwar** (☎ 532 5455; meals SR10-15) for good barbecued meats.

Shopping

The **souq** is one of the best places in the Kingdom to find that black Bedouin goat's-hair tent that you've always wanted.

THE ROCK ART OF ARABIA

Saudi Arabia has almost 2000 rock art sites, making it one of the richest open-air museums in the world. Much of the country's rock art is on ancient sandstone. Over long periods of time, the rock surface has been covered with a wind-smoothed accretion of manganese and iron salts, a patina called 'desert varnish'. Where successive cultures over millennia have pecked and incised images onto the same rock panel, this varnish can help determine the relative chronology of the different works of art.

The major rock art periods are divided into discrete eras: Outline Abstract (11,000–9000 BC; characterised by large wild beasts); Early Naturalistic (9000–5000 BC; full-sized human figures, cattle and oryx); Neolithic (5000–3000 BC; schematic animal and human representations); Symbolic (5000–3000 BC; stick figures, cattle replaced by camels and ostriches); and the Literate Period (from 1000 BC). The general rule is that the earlier carvings display a higher degree of sophistication, while later carvings are simpler, even crudely child-like. The most impressive examples you'll come across in Saudi Arabia date from around 5500 BC and mark the transition from hunter-gatherer communities to sedentary agricultural ones, as reflected in the images of domesticated cattle.

The most impressive and accessible sites are those at **Jubba** (opposite), **Bir Hima** (p146); **Al-Ula** (p115) and **Sakaka** (p123).

Getting There & Away

There are daily **Saudia** (☎ 532 2222; Main Rd) flights to/from Riyadh (SR200, three daily), and Jeddah (SR250, one daily) and less frequent departures to Dammam (SR360), Buraydah (Gassim; SR110), Medina (SR160), Sakaka (Jouf; SR110) and Tabuk (SR230).

Saptco (☎ 531 0101) has buses to Riyadh (SR130, eight hours) via Buraydah (SR50, four hours), Al-Ula (SR70, 4½ hours) and Tabuk (SR125, 8½ hours).

Getting Around

Hail has metered taxis (flagfall SR5) although there aren't many of them.

JUBBA   جبة

Jubba, 100km northwest of Hail, is the only town of any size in the Nafud Desert, and it has a suitably sleepy, frontier feel about it.

Jubba's impressive **rock carvings** reveal a level of sophistication remarkable for their era, and include a wonderful long-horned buffalo, domesticated dogs and several sets of elegant and elongated human figures; they are believed to date from 5500 BC when much of the area was covered with water. There are also cruder carvings of camels and other domesticated animals dating from around AD 300; they stand in stark contrast to the graceful, well-executed lines of the older carvings.

A permit (p173) is necessary to visit the site. At the time of writing, it was no longer necessary to have the permit validated by the antiquities office in Hail, but always check before you make the long trek out here. The custodian of the keys and local guide in charge of the site is the genial **Atiq al-Shamali** (☎ 057 494 877). To find him, follow the signs to **Naif's Palace of Heritage** (museum admission SR20), which is just off the main street and something of an attraction in itself; it's the house in which the Blunts stayed in 1889 and it has been converted into a museum with a chaotic jumble of local artefacts, Lady Blunt's personal effects and an attractive **diwan**. Atiq speaks no English, so it can be worth contacting **Hadi Abdullah** (hadi1500@yahoo.com), a genial and helpful local English teacher. These are also the people to speak to if you want to arrange a journey into the **Al-Nafud desert** north of Jubba where you'll find some beautiful desert scenery.

You'll need your own transport to get to Jubba.

Hejaz الحجاز

CONTENTS

HEJAZ

The Hejaz region is one of Saudi Arabia's most diverse and rewarding regions. Strung out along the Kingdom's Red Sea coastline and with a mountainous hinterland (Hejaz means 'barrier'), it has a wealth of sights, not to mention a unique history of interacting with people from all over the world.

Jeddah, with its enchanting old city, is a microcosm of the Islamic world, a place to take the pulse of modern Saudi Arabia. One of the most liberal cities in Saudi Arabia, the fast-moving, modern commercial capital has also been the historical gateway to the holy Islamic cities of Mecca and Medina for almost fifteen centuries. Jeddah's heart is its Al-Balad district, with enchanting buildings made of coral. Their wooden latticework balconies overlook the narrow lanes of the souqs which have changed little in centuries and throng with pilgrims and traders from all over the world. Not far away, the waterfront corniche is home to an eclectic promenade of sculptures which speak of the city's vibrancy in embracing the modern.

The climate of the Hejaz can be oppressive – the summer heat is fierce and the humidity almost unbearable. Fortunately, there are ample excursions which enable you to escape the worst of it. From Yanbu in the north to Shwayba in the south, the coral-rich waters of the Red Sea offer world class diving opportunities. If you prefer a mountain retreat, the area around Taif, itself an attractive and liberal enclave in the mountains, offers exceptional scenery and a mild summer climate.

With the holy cities of Mecca (p73) and Medina (p69) not far away, the Hejaz is also as close as a non-Muslim can come to witnessing the grand epic of the haj pilgrimage, particularly in Jeddah.

HEJAZ

HIGHLIGHTS

- Joining the pilgrims in Jeddah's enchanting **Souq al-Alawi** (p100) with its houses of coral and wood
- Strolling along the **corniche** (p102) in Jeddah to catch a Red Sea breeze amid the sculptures
- Diving in the **Red Sea** (p107) between Jeddah and Yanbu
- Escaping the summer heat to **Taif** (p107) and the surrounding mountains
- Wondering through the **souq** (market; p109) in Taif

- POPULATION: 7.5 MILLION
- AREA: 305,000 SQ KM

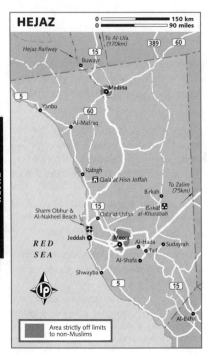

HEJAZ

0 — 150 km
0 — 90 miles

To Al-Ula (170km)
Hejaz Railway
Buwayr
389 60
15
Medina
5
Yanbu
60
Al-Mafraq
Rabigh
Qala'at Hisn Joffah
To Zalim (75km)
Birkah
Birkat al-Khurabah
15
Sharm Obhur & Al-Nakheel Beach
Qala'at Usfan
Jeddah Mecca
Al-Hada Sudayrah
RED Taif
SEA Al-Shafa
Shwayba
5 15
Al-Baha

Area strictly off limits to non-Muslims

JEDDAH

جدة

☎ 02 / pop 2.82 million

> The white town hung between the blazing sky and its reflection in the mirage which swept and rolled over the wide lagoon.
>
> *TE Lawrence*

Jeddah, a historical crossroads of pilgrims and traders, is the most fascinating of Saudi Arabia's big cities. The traditional gateway to Mecca, Jeddah has a decidedly cosmopolitan atmosphere and is the undisputed commercial capital of Saudi Arabia. At 1000 times the size of the original city, Jeddah is a modern, fast-moving city which is a bit ragged around the edges and an unwieldy symbol for the modernisation that has transformed the Kingdom. But look a little closer and you'll find that Jeddah is rare among Saudi cities in that significant vestiges of its heritage remain in full view. The Al-Balad district, the heart of Jeddah, is a treat with splendid coral architecture overlooking bustling souqs (markets).

History

Jeddah's history is the stuff of legend. It is believed that Eve died and was buried here: the name 'Jeddah' means 'grandmother'. Islamic tradition also claims that Jeddah was settled in the 3rd century BC by an ancestor of the Prophet Mohammed.

Since AD 646, when the Caliph Uthman officially established Jeddah as the gateway to Mecca, Jeddah's fortunes have been dominated by Islam's holiest city which lies to Jeddah's east. The spread of Islam drew pilgrims to Mecca from the four corners of the earth and, over the centuries, hundreds of thousands of people would land each year at Jeddah and make the two-day overland journey to Mecca.

In approximately AD 1080, Jeddah was destroyed after the city's leaders incurred the wrath of their overlords in Mecca. The entire Hejaz came under nominal Turkish control in the 16th century, though the local rulers retained a great deal of autonomy.

The Wahhabis, under Abdul Aziz, took control of the city in 1925.

Orientation

Al-Balad, the historic downtown district, loosely represents the centre of Jeddah; King Abdul Aziz St is its main north–south thoroughfare and has a host of restaurants, banks and shops.

Jeddah long ago expanded beyond these narrow confines and the bulk of the urban sprawl is north of Al-Balad. Medina Rd is the principal street running north from the centre, flanked to the west by Al-Andalus St.

The corniche (Al-Kournaish Rd) runs the length of Jeddah's coastline from Jeddah Islamic Port to the south to the city's northern outskirts.

MAPS

The best map is the Farsi *Map & Guide of Jeddah* (SR20) which is available from any Jarir Bookstore.

Information

BOOKSHOPS

Al-Mamoun Bookshop (Map p102; ☎ 644 6614; 1st fl, Corniche Commercial Centre, King Abdul Aziz St; ✆ 10am-1.30pm & 5-10pm Sat-Thu, 5-10pm Fri) Stocks a small range of books in English.

Jarir Bookstore (Map p100; ☎ 673 2727; www.jarirbookstore.com; Falasteen St; ✆ 9am-2pm & 4-11pm Sat-Thu,

4-11pm Fri) Jeddah's best bookshop. Has foreign newspapers, magazines and an excellent range of books in English.
Jarir Bookstore (Map p100; ☎ 682 7666; www.jarirbookstore.com; Sary St; ☺ 9am-2pm & 4-11pm Sat-Thu, 4-11pm Fri)

EMERGENCY
Ambulance (☎ 997)
Directory Assistance (domestic ☎ 905, international ☎ 900)
Fire (☎ 998)
Police (☎ 999)
Traffic Accidents (☎ 993)

INTERNET ACCESS
Jeddah has numerous Internet cafés where one hour's surfing costs SR10.
Divan Internet Cafe (Map p100; Gulf Plaza Bldg, Medina Rd; ☺ 9am-10pm Sat-Thu)
Magha.Net Internet Cafe (Map p100; Khalid bin Walid St; ☺ 24hr 4.30pm Fri to midnight Thu)
Millennium Internet Cafe (Map p100; ☎ 661 4664; Al-Rahman al-Tubajoti St; ☺ 9am-11pm Sat-Thu, 4-11pm Fri)

MEDICAL SERVICES
Dr Soliman Fakeeh Hospital (Map p100; ☎ 665 5000, 660 3000; Falasteen St) Near the US consulate; there's a good accident-and-emergency department.

MONEY
As you'd expect in Saudi Arabia's commercial capital, there are banks (with ATMs) on just about every corner, especially in Al-Balad; many of these are marked on the maps.
Ace Travel (☎ 665 660 5120; abe@goacetravel.com; Falasteen St; ☺ 9am-1.30pm & 4.30-8pm Sat-Wed, 9am-1.30pm Thu) The AmEx representative.

POST
Main post office (Map p102; Al-Bareed St; ☺ 7.30am-9.30pm Sat-Wed, Mumtaz Post express mail windows 7.30am-2pm Thu) Opposite the bus station; the entrance is from Al-Bareed St.
Post office (Map p100) There's a smaller post office in Hamra'a district, just off Medina Rd.

TELEPHONE
There are international call cabins all over the city; prepaid phonecards (which can be used from any phone) are sold in all grocery shops and bookshops.

TOURIST OFFICES
Located in the lane running along the west wall of Naseef House, the **Jeddah Historic Area**

Preservation Department (Map p102; ☎ 647 2280; off Souq al-Alawi) is the best place for information about Al-Balad. Lecture tours of the area, and entry to the museums and old houses around Al-Balad can be arranged from here. Opening hours are, however, elusive.

TRAVEL AGENCIES
Your best bet for airline tickets is **Ace Travel** (Map p100; ☎ 660 5120; abe@goacetravel.com; Falasteen St; ☺ 9am-1.30pm & 4.30-8pm Sat-Wed, 9am-1.30pm Thu). For tours around the Kingdom, particularly Madain Saleh, try:
Explorer Tours (☎ 667 5669)
Reeman Travel Agency (☎ 651 3905; fax 653 4649)
Samal Lagi (☎ 664 0638; ops@samallaghi.com, mostafaaa@zajil.net)

Dangers & Annoyances
Jeddah is noticeably more relaxed than Riyadh, so you're unlikely to have problems with the mutawwa (religious police) for minor indiscretions.

The most obvious danger is the reckless driving habits you'll encounter on the roads – some of the driving has to be seen to be believed. As one exasperated Jeddah resident wrote to the Arab News newspaper while we were there:

> It is only in Jeddah that you can make a right turn from any lane, including the third lane on the left. A red traffic light does not mean stop…The residents of Jeddah come from some 70 countries, if not more. They may not speak the same language, but they have a common medium of expression – their different and dangerous driving skills.

Tours
Red Sea Palace Hotel (Map p102; ☎ 642 8555, 051 855 609; King Abdul Aziz St) organises two-hour city tours (SR35) at 10am every Friday. It's a bit rushed but a good way to get an overview of this sprawling metropolis; you don't have to be staying in the hotel to take the tour.

An alternative is the 'lecture tour' run by the **Jeddah Historic Area Preservation Department** (see opposite).

Sights
AL-BALAD (OLD JEDDAH)
The old city of Jeddah is one of the most enchanting places in the Kingdom. The

JEDDAH

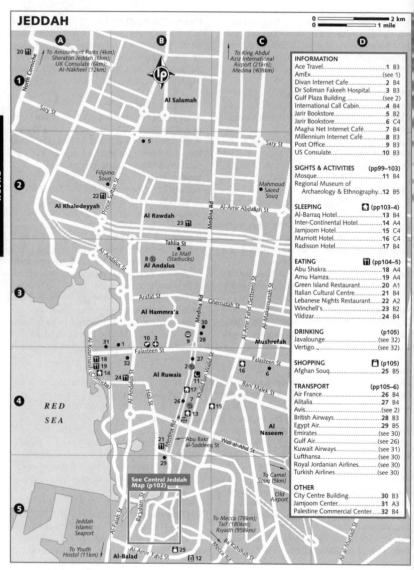

0 ————— 2 km
0 ————— 1 mile

To Amusement Parks (4km);
Sheraton Jeddah (6km);
UK Consulate (6km);
Al-Nakheel (12km)

To King Abdul
Aziz International
Airport (21km);
Medina (408km)

Al Salamah

North Corniche

Sary St

Sary St

Filipino
Souq

Mahmoud
Saeed
Souq

Al Khaledeyyah

Al-Amir Abdallah St

Prince Sultan St

Medina Rd

Al Rawdah

Tahlia St

Le Mall
(Starbucks)
Al Andalus

Al-Andalus St

Arafat St

Al Hammra'a

Ghernatah St

Medina Rd

Al-Amir Fahd (Setteen) St

Al-Makarounah St

Mushrefah

Falasteen St

Falasteen St

Al-Kournash (Corniche)

Al-Andalus St

Hail St

Khalid bin Walid St

Al Ruwais

Bani Malek St

Al
Naseem

Abu Bakr
al-Saddeeq St

Medina Rd

Wali al-Ahd St

RED
SEA

See Central Jeddah
Map (p102)

To Camel
Souq (5km)

Old
Airport

Jeddah
Islamic
Seaport

Al-Falah St

Baraim St

To Mecca (78km);
Taif (180km);
Riyadh (958km)

Ba Kahshab St

Mecca Rd

Al-Murtadi St

To Youth
Hostel (11km)

Al-Amir
Fahd St

Al-Balad

INFORMATION

Ace Travel...................................**1**	B3
AmEx..................................(see 1)	
Divin Internet Cafe......................**2**	B4
Dr Soliman Fakeeh Hospital.........**3**	B3
Gulf Plaza Building..................(see 2)	
International Call Cabin...............**4**	B4
Jarir Bookstore...........................**5**	B2
Jarir Bookstore...........................**6**	C4
Magha Net Internet Café.............**7**	B4
Millennium Internet Café.............**8**	B3
Post Office.................................**9**	B3
US Consulate...........................**10**	B3

SIGHTS & ACTIVITIES   (pp99–103)

Mosque...................................**11**	B4
Regional Museum of	
Archaeology & Ethnography...**12**	B5

SLEEPING   (pp103–4)

Al-Barraq Hotel.......................**13**	B4
Inter-Continental Hotel.............**14**	A4
Jamjoom Hotel.........................**15**	C4
Marriott Hotel..........................**16**	C4
Radisson Hotel.........................**17**	B4

EATING   (pp104–5)

Abu Shakra.............................**18**	A4
Amu Hamza.............................**19**	A4
Green Island Restaurant............**20**	A1
Italian Cultural Centre...............**21**	B4
Lebanese Nights Restaurant......**22**	A2
Winchell's...............................**23**	B2
Yildizar..................................**24**	B4

DRINKING   (p105)

Javalounge.........................(see 32)	
Vertigo..............................(see 32)	

SHOPPING   (p105)

Afghan Souq...........................**25**	B5

TRANSPORT   (pp105–6)

Air France................................**26**	B4
Alitalia....................................**27**	B4
Avis....................................(see 2)	
British Airways.........................**28**	B3
Egypt Air.................................**29**	B5
Emirates.............................(see 30)	
Gulf Air.............................(see 26)	
Kuwait Airways...................(see 31)	
Lufthansa...........................(see 30)	
Royal Jordanian Airlines.........(see 30)	
Turkish Airlines..................(see 30)	

OTHER

City Centre Building.................**30**	B3
Jamjoom Center.......................**31**	A3
Palestine Commercial Center.....**32**	B4

narrow lanes are lined with charming and decaying **merchants' houses**, which belong to wealthy local families.

Souq al-Alawi

In an architectural sense, **Souq al-Alawi** (Map p102) runs east off Al-Dahab St and is the most extensive traditional souq in the King-

dom, with wonderful old houses towering above. The stalls cut into the heart of the old city buzz with the activity of traders and pilgrims from across the sea and desert in much the same way as the souq has done for more than a millennia. The atmosphere is especially cosmopolitan during the haj season. Try to be here at sunset when the

---

THE ARCHITECTURE OF AL-BALAD

Al-Balad (Old Jeddah) is a delight with architecture that you're unlikely to see anywhere else in the world. Many of the old houses are built from Red Sea coral (faced with limestone wash) and climb more than five storeys high; because of the fragility of the building materials used, most houses date from the early 20th century although the style has changed little in centuries. Most distinctive of all are the intricate brown or (less common) green *rawashan* (wooden balconies) with busy latticework enabling the breeze to penetrate the upper rooms while concealing the women of the houses from view. The most extensive examples of these are along or just off **Souq al-Alawi** (including the restored **Naseef House**) and in the lanes to the south and west of **Shorbatly House**. One of the most exceptional buildings is next to the North City Gate. The multitude of balconies overshadow the modern brick supports holding it together and it looks out over the Al-Arbaeen Lagoon as a forlorn but stunning symbol of Jeddah's past. Another well-restored structure is the **Municipality Museum**.

Al-Balad was once surrounded by city walls which ran along what are now King Abdul Aziz St, Mecca Rd and Ba'najah St until they were torn down in the 1940s, but three city gates have been rebuilt in a style approximating their original form – **North City Gate** (Map p102; Maydan Al-Bayal), **Bab Makkah** (Mecca Gate; cnr Mecca Rd & Ba'najah St) and **Bab Sharif** (Map p102; Ba'najah St).

The old city is now a protected urban area. Buildings there cannot be torn down unless they are dilapidated beyond repair, in which case they must be replaced with something of a similar size and architectural style.

---

call to prayer fills the lanes – this is Arabia at its best.

Naseef House

Not far into the souq stands the delightful **Naseef House** (Map p102; ☎ 647 2280; fax 627 2191; admission SR20; ☼ 5-9pm), which belonged to one of Jeddah's most powerful trading families. Although the house now stands out as much for its restored façade in a sea of dilapidation, its location at the heart of the souq is an indicator of its owners' former status. So too is the expansive tree to the left of the house's front door; as recently as the 1920s, this was the only tree in all of Jeddah and messengers were once directed to 'the House of the Tree'.

After conquering the city in 1925 King Abdul Aziz (Ibn Saud) expropriated the house for his own use until a palace fit for a king could be built. He left his mark, building wide ramps in place of staircases so that camel-mounted messengers could rise all the way to the upper terrace in order to deliver messages. If it's open, the rooftop terrace has unparalleled views over Al-Balad.

Al-Shafee Mosque

Near the centre of Al-Balad, the **Al-Shafee Mosque** (Map p102), off Souq al-Alawi, is one of the oldest in the city. It is believed to date from the 16th century, although it has been much modified over the centuries. It can

only be admired from the outside; the green dome and white minaret with brown trim are highlights, as is the wooden balcony (a typical Hejazi flourish) near the summit.

Shorbatly House

If Naseef House is a symbol of what can be done to preserve Jeddah's architectural heritage, **Shorbatly House** (Map p102; Maydan al-Bayal) is a sad reminder of how much remains in ruins. The house was restored to something approaching its original state in the 1980s, but has since been allowed to deteriorate once again. Admire the peeling façade and attractive balconies before the whole place falls apart.

Municipality Museum

A 200-year-old restored traditional house built of Red Sea coral, and the only surviving building of the WWI-era British Legation in Jeddah, houses the **Municipality Museum** (Map p102; Beit al-Balad; ☎ 642 4922, 636 4271; King Abdul Aziz St; admission free & by appointment; ☼ 7.30am-1.30pm Sat-Wed). TE Lawrence stayed at the Legation when he visited in 1917.

The old photographs at the far end of the entrance hall include an aerial sequence from 1948, 1964 and 1988, dramatically illustrating Jeddah's astonishing growth. The room to the left of the entry hall has a large photograph of King Abdul Aziz surrounded by his family. The present king (Fahd) can be seen standing

HEJAZ

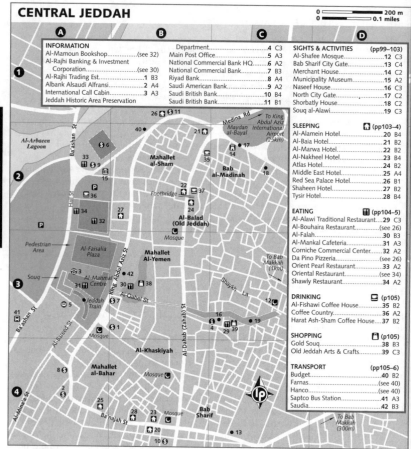

CENTRAL JEDDAH

0 _____ 200 m
0 _____ 0.1 miles

INFORMATION
Al-Mamoun Bookshop.................(see 32)
Al-Rajhi Banking & Investment
  Corporation..........................(see 30)
Al-Rajhi Trading Est.....................**1** B3
Albank Alsaudi Alfransi.................**2** A4
International Call Cabin.................**3** A3
Jeddah Historic Area Preservation

Department.....................................**4** C3
Main Post Office..........................**5** A3
National Commercial Bank HQ........**6** A2
National Commercial Bank..............**7** B3
Riyad Bank...................................**8** A4
Saudi American Bank.....................**9** A2
Saudi British Bank.......................**10** B4
Saudi British Bank.......................**11** B1

SIGHTS & ACTIVITIES   (pp99–103)
Al-Shafee Mosque.........................**12** C3
Bab Sharif City Gate.....................**13** C4
Merchant House...........................**14** C2
Municipality Museum....................**15** A2
Naseef House..............................**16** C3
North City Gate...........................**17** C2
Shorbatly House...........................**18** C3
Souq al-Alawi.............................**19** C3

SLEEPING   (pp103–4)
Al-Alamein Hotel.........................**20** B4
Al-Baia Hotel..............................**21** B2
Al-Marwa Hotel...........................**22** B2
Al-Nakheel Hotel.........................**23** B4
Atlas Hotel.................................**24** B2
Middle East Hotel........................**25** A4
Red Sea Palace Hotel....................**26** B1
Shaheen Hotel.............................**27** B4
Tysir Hotel.................................**28** B4

EATING   (pp104–5)
Al-Alawi Traditional Restaurant.......**29** C3
Al-Bouhaira Restaurant................(see 26)
Al-Falah....................................**30** B3
Al-Mankal Cafeteria.....................**31** A3
Corniche Commercial Center...........**32** A2
Da Pino Pizzeria........................(see 26)
Orient Pearl Restaurant.................**33** A2
Oriental Restaurant....................(see 34)
Shawly Restaurant.......................**34** A2

DRINKING   (p105)
Al-Fishawi Coffee House................**35** A2
Coffee Country............................**36** B2
Harat Ash-Sham Coffee House.........**37** B2

SHOPPING   (p105)
Gold Souq...................................**38** B3
Old Jeddah Arts & Crafts................**39** C3

TRANSPORT   (pp105–6)
Budget......................................**40** B2
Farnas.....................................(see 40)
Hanco......................................(see 40)
Saptco Bus Station.......................**41** A3
Saudia......................................**42** B3

---

in the back row to the right of his father. The other exhibits include Qurans, Persian astrolabes, pottery, silver jewellery and the sword presented by Britain's King George V.

Jeddah Museum
Jeddah's **Regional Museum of Archaeology & Ethnography** (Map p100; King Fahd St; admission free; ⏰ 8am-noon Sat-Wed) is similar in scope if not as impressive as Riyadh's museum. Most notable are the sections on Darb Zubaydah (p111), and local architecture, including a large-scale model of the Naseef House.

NEW JEDDAH
Jeddah's modern architecture lacks the audacity of Riyadh's signature skyscrapers, but

there are a couple of minor buildings worth seeking out.

The **Radisson Hotel** (Map p100) is a modern adaptation of traditional Hejazi architecture. The most beautiful modern **mosque** in Jeddah is nearby along Abu Bakr Al-Saddeeq St, around 750m south of Falasteen St. Its elegant white domes and minaret are attractively lit at night. The stucco work above the main entrance is superb, as are the wooden balconies along the west wall.

Corniche Sculptures
The 35km-long **corniche** (Al-Kournaish Rd) is a good place to promenade and catch a sea breeze on a balmy summer's evening. Sculptures line the wide pedestrian areas for 30km

north from the port. Subjects range from the mundane to the abstract, from anchors and dhows to pairs of hands and giant feathers, from flying seagulls to the curvaceous Henry Moore. It's difficult to escape the conclusion, however, that the most disconcertingly suitable sculpture for Jeddah is the one depicting concrete-encased cars protruding at bizarre angles. At the corniche's northern end, particularly in the Sharm Obhur area where the city starts to give way to less developed stretches of coastline, you'll find a number of amusement parks which are great for kids and for the young at heart. Admission is usually adult/child SR5/2.

Activities

BEACHES

There's a reason why many rich and royal Saudis have villas on the Costa del Sol. Jeddah's beaches are pretty ordinary and often given over to young Jeddah boys driving sand buggies and practising their reckless future on the city's roads. That said, most of the five-star hotels have their own private beaches where women will feel much more comfortable, although entry for nonguests can cost SR40 (more on weekends).

DIVING

For details of diving in the Jeddah area, see p107.

Sleeping

Jeddah has hotels to suit every budget. The less expensive hotels are in Al-Balad.

BUDGET

Shaheen Hotel (Map p102; ☎ 642 6582; fax 644 6302; s/d SR60/70) This hotel, off King Abdul Aziz St, is one of the better budget hotels in the Kingdom, although less so with the dropping of prices by mid-range places. The rooms are fine and clean, if a bit cell-like; most of the shared bathrooms sparkle.

Middle East Hotel (Map p102; ☎ 648 3330; fax 647 5509; Ba'najah St; s/d SR80/130) The rooms here are, depending on your perspective, clean and bright or clinical and stark. There's not much character and the bathrooms are tiny but they're still good value.

Al-Marwa Hotel (Map p102; ☎ 643 2650; fax 644 4273; Al-Dahab St; s/d SR80/100) Al-Marwa Hotel, in the heart of the old city, offers small rooms which are also decent value. The staff are quite friendly once they get warmed up.

Tysir Hotel (Map p102; ☎ 647 7777; Ba'najah St; s/d SR55/100) Drab but generally clean rooms are the order of the day here, but the singles are great value for your riyal.

MID-RANGE

All of the hotels listed here have foreign-language satellite TV unless otherwise stated.

Al-Baia Hotel (Map p102; ☎ 644 4446; King Abdul Aziz St; s/d SR140/180) Situated overlooking the Al-Arbaeen Lagoon at the northern end of the old city, Al-Baia Hotel is outstanding. The recently renovated rooms are well-appointed and attractive, and those on the upper floors have great views out over the water. Highly recommended.

IDI AMIN IN JEDDAH

Idi Amin, dictator-president of Uganda from 1971 until 1979, died in Jeddah in August 2003. Saudi authorities claimed in 1980 that they were offering sanctuary to a fellow Muslim who, as President of Uganda, had converted to Islam and constructed hundreds of mosques across the country. The only condition of his stay was that he keep a low profile and desist from all political activity.

For a larger-than-life figure such as Amin, keeping a low profile proved difficult. He was often seen strolling along the corniche, attending Friday prayers, cruising around Jeddah in his expensive cars or shopping in the city's supermarkets. At one time in the 1990s, he even tried his hand as a taxi driver before the Saudi authorities reined him in. By all accounts, his was a comfortable exile surrounded by an entourage of around 30 children, numerous wives and luxurious living arrangements (cars, drivers, cooks, maids and all expenses) paid for in full by the Saudi royal family.

But this was not Amin's first visit to Saudi Arabia. When he made a state visit to Saudi Arabia during his presidency, he appeared from the plane dressed in what he considered traditional Saudi clothes: a tight shirt stretching below his knees with splits every six inches and a white handkerchief tied in knots on each corner on his head. The Saudi officials there to welcome him could, by all accounts, scarcely conceal their mirth.

Al-Barraq Hotel (Map p100; ☎ 650 3366; fax 651 1322; htl_barraq@hotmail.com; Khalid bin Walid St; s/d SR125/170) One of the better mid-range choices, the Al-Barraq's rooms are spacious, carpeted and attractively furnished.

Jamjoon Hotel (Map p100; ☎ /fax 651 4300; Al-Tawbah St; singles/doubles SR140/190) Not far away, the Jamjoon is clean, carpeted and nicely furnished.

Al-Nakheel Hotel (Map p102; ☎ 647 5127; fax 647 1190; alnakhil@icc.net.sa; Ba'najah St; s/d SR100/150) If you like your beds huge, head to the Al-Nakheel, although understand that the rooms aren't correspondingly large. They do have a hint more character than most, which is just as well as some of the back rooms look out onto a wall.

Al-Alamein Hotel (Map p102; ☎ 648 3953; fax 648 2621; Ba'najah St; s/d SR100/150) The rooms here are simple and tidy, and the place is well-run which sets it above some of the others in the area.

Atlas Hotel (Map p102; ☎ 643 8520; fax 644 8454; Al-Dahab St; s/d SR100/150) Guests can sometimes feel like something of an inconvenience here; don't expect the satellite dish to pick up foreign-language channels but do expect rooms which are comfortable and tidy if uninspiring.

TOP END

Red Sea Palace Hotel (Map p102; ☎ 642 8555; fax 642 2395; King Abdel Aziz St; s/d SR270/351; P 🅿 💺) The only top-end hotel in the centre is a touch more personal and most rooms offer views over the Al-Arbaeen Lagoon. Ask about its weekend and diving packages (single/double SR460/590), which include two nights accommodation, all meals and transfers.

There's not much to choose between the international chains in terms of quality (all are luxurious), service (attentive) or amenities (fitness centres, restaurants, business centres and travel desks). Standard rack rates start at around singles/doubles SR450/550, but discounts are usually available (ask for the corporate rate or book over the Internet); prices don't include the 15% service charge. Some options are:

Inter-Continental Hotel (Map p100; ☎ 661 1800; www.intercontinental.com; Al-Kournaish Rd (corniche); s/d from SR395/525; P 🅿 🖥 💺) Has the advantage of overlooking the water.

Marriott Hotel (Map p100; ☎ 671 4000; www.marriott hotels.com; s/d from SR325/425; P 🅿 🖥 💺)

Radisson Hotel (Map p100; ☎ 652 1234; www.radisson .com; Medina Rd; s/d from SR350/425; P 🅿 🖥 💺)

Sheraton Jeddah Hotel (☎ 699 2212; www.sheraton .com; Al-Kournaish Rd (corniche); s/d from SR350/420; P 🅿 🖥 💺) Fairly close to the airport but 19km north of the centre.

Eating
BUDGET

Fast-food outlets (Western and local) and cheap eateries are on just about every street corner across the city. There's a concentration of cheap eateries on the eastern side of the Corniche Commercial Center (Map p102).

Al-Falah (Map p102; off King Abdul Aziz St; starters from SR5, mains SR10-15) This cafeteria stands out from the rest with a varied menu, including Arab staples, Chinese and Filipino dishes, burgers and pizza. The clientele is as varied as Jeddah's population and the food is always good. Highly recommended.

Lebanese Nights Restaurant (Map p100; ☎ 639 5069; cnr Prince Abdullah & Prince Sultan Sts; set meals SR22) Outrageously good value and popular with local families.

Shawly Restaurant (Map p102; ☎ 644 7867) It's hard to go past this Filipino-run place, where soup, rice, two meat/vegetable dishes and soft drink cost SR12.

Oriental Restaurant (Map p102; ☎ 644 6263) This Thai establishment, next door to the Shawly Restaurant, is another decent choice.

Level four of the Al-Mahmal Centre has a collection of places covering a wide range of cuisines, including Chinese/Filipino, Arab, burgers and fried chicken. The **Al-Mankal Cafeteria** (Map p102; Al-Mahmal Centre) does a good chicken *tikka* (SR14) and *fool* (fava bean paste) sandwiches for (SR3).

MID-RANGE & TOP END

The more expensive dining options tend to be in North Jeddah. All of the following places are open for lunch and dinner unless otherwise stated.

Al-Alawi Traditional Restaurant (Map p102; ☎ 644 7423; starters from SR10, mains SR30-40) One of the few upmarket restaurants in the old city, Al-Alawi, situated off Souq Al-Alawi, serves good Moroccan food in traditional surroundings. There's also a pleasant garden. Highlights include the *harira* (a thick beef and vegetable soup; SR10) and the lamb tagine (SR35).

Al-Bouhaira Restaurant (Map p102; ☎ 642 8555; fax 642 2395; King Abdel Aziz St; buffet from SR80) Also in the centre, the Red Sea Palace Hotel's restaurant has a good daily buffet for lunch and dinner, and an especially good seafood buffet (SR99) on Thursday evenings.

Orient Pearl Restaurant (Map p102; ☎ 644 2231; 2nd fl, Corniche Markets Bldg, Hail St; starters from SR10, mains SR25-40) The Orient Pearl serves upmarket Thai, Chinese and Filipino food. The seafood is especially good if expensive (from SR40 to SR70).

Italian Cultural Centre (Map p100; ☎ 643 0134; Al-Lazegeyah St; pasta dishes from SR35; ☻noon-3pm) Something of an oasis in Jeddah, you certainly won't find better (or more authentic) Italian food in Saudi Arabia. The menu changes with the (Italian) seasons.

Da Pino Pizzeria (Map p102; ☎ 642 8555; Red Sea Palace Hotel; meals from SR60) This place also serves high-quality Italian food.

Yildizar (Map p100; ☎ 653 1150; starters from SR15, mains SR40-60) Probably Jeddah's premier Lebanese restaurant, located off Al-Andalus St. Yildizar has an air of sophistication and its consistently high standards ensure that reservations are recommended for dinner.

Abu Shakra (Map p100; ☎ 660 4049; Falasteen St; starters from SR10, mains from SR25) Just across from the waterfront, this Egyptian institution serves pricey kebabs and the excellent *makaronah* (macaroni cooked with eggs and butter with a tomato sauce; SR20).

Amu Hamza (Map p100; ☎ 667 7070; Al-Kournaish Rd (corniche); starters SR5-20, mains SR20-75) A few doors south of Abu Shakra, this is a classy seafood restaurant with a good menu. Highlights include lobster soup (SR20), claypot shrimps (SR30) and fried lobster (SR65).

Green Island Restaurant (Map p100; ☎ 694 0999; Al-Kournaish Rd (corniche); buffet SR120) If money is no object, don't miss this place. The food can be patchy, but the wooden chalets that branch out into the Red Sea are possibly the most romantic place in Jeddah. Watch the sun set as the waves break under your feet and the corniche buzzes into life.

Drinking

Central Jeddah has several traditional coffee houses, where men sit on high couches, smoke water pipes and drink tea.

Coffee Country (Map p102; coffee SR3-6) Outside the northern end of the Corniche Commercial Centre in Al-Balad, Coffee Country has pleasant outdoor tables and serves cappuccino (SR6) and espresso coffee (SR3).

Traditional coffee houses in Jeddah:

Harat Ash-Sham Coffee House (Map p102; Al-Dahab St)

Al-Fishawi Coffee House (Map p102; Al-Dahab St)

Good places for watching young Saudis gently pushing the boundaries of Wahhabi propriety are **Vertigo** (Map p100; Falasteen St) and **Javalounge** (Map p100; Falasteen St), both in the Palestine Commercial Centre, or **Winchell's** (☎ 660 8923; Mosadia Centre, Medina Rd).

Entertainment

Make your own. The **Italian Cultural Centre** (Map p100; ☎ 643 0134; Al-Lazegeyah St) has a make-shift cinema, which sometimes screens both classics and the latest blockbusters.

Shopping

Jeddah is not Saudi Arabia's best spot for antiques and traditional souvenirs but it's a good place for almost everything else.

Old Jeddah Arts & Crafts (Map p102; ☎ 642 2435, 642 2433) This shop, off Souq al-Alawi, is the exception. It sells silver jewellery and copper and brass work, some old and some new. The Syrian owners have more pieces from their home country than Saudi and they're friendly and knowledgeable and the merchandise is definitely worth picking through.

Afghan souq (Map p100; Al-Bokharia St; ☻10am-11pm) Located to the east of Bab Mecca, this market is a must-see. The shops – in a narrow, dusty street – are managed by Afghans, and on breezy days the aroma of freshly baked Afghan bread fills the air. There are old and new carpets from Iran and Central Asia.

Gold souq (Map p102) Located in Al-Balad, 24-carat gold is the norm here. It has an extensive range of traditional Arabic jewellery and ornaments, although most of it will be a little overdone for Western tastes.

Getting There & Away

AIR

Both domestic and international **Saudia** (Map p102; ☎ 632 3333; King Abdul Aziz St) flights leave from the south terminal. Foreign airlines use the north terminal. Domestic departures are listed on p106.

AIRLINE OFFICES

Air France (Map p100; ☎ 651 2000; Medina Rd)
Alitalia (Map p100; ☎ 660 0640; City Centre Bldg, Medina Rd)
British Airways (Map p100; ☎ 669 3464; Al-Amoudi Centre, Medina Rd)
EgyptAir (Map p100; ☎ 644 1515; Cnr Medina Rd & King Khaled St)
Emirates (Map p100; ☎ 665 9405; City Centre Bldg, Medina Rd)
Gulf Air (Map p100; ☎ 653 3335; Abu Bakr Al-Saddeeq St)
Kuwait Airways (Map p100; ☎ 669 4111; Al-Jamjoom Center, Falasteen St)
Lufthansa (Map p100; ☎ 665 0000; City Centre Bldg, Medina Rd)
Royal Jordanian Airlines (Map p100; ☎ 667 4243; City Centre Bldg, Medina Rd)
Saudia (Map p102; ☎ 632 3333; King Abdul Aziz St)
Turkish Airlines (Map p100; ☎ 660 0127; City Centre Bldg, Medina Rd)

Destination	Cost (SR)	No of daily departures
Abha	190	4
Al-Baha	120	1
Dammam	390	3
Gassim/Buraydah	270	2
Hail	250	2
Jizan	200	4
Medina	140	5
Najran	250	1
Riyadh	280	9
Sakaka (Jouf)	300	1
Sharurah	320	1
Tabuk	280	3
Taif	110	1
Yanbu	110	2

There are less regular departures for Taif (SR100), Jouf (Sakaka; SR305) and Sharurah (SR330).

BOAT
For details of international boat services from Jeddah, see p179. For current schedules and prices, contact **Ace Travel** (Map p100; ☎ 665 1254; Falasteen St).

BUS
The chaotic **Saptco bus station** (Map p102; ☎ 647 8500; Ba'ashan St) is one of the busiest bus stations in the country. Daily departures from here include:

Destination	Cost (SR)	Duration (hr)	No of daily departures
Abha	120	12	6
Al-Baha	70	7	5
Dammam	205	17	3
Jizan	105	10	5
Khamis Mushayt	120	12	6
Najran	130	14	2
Riyadh	140	10-12	10
Taif	30	3	10
Yanbu	65	5	4
Tabuk	140	13	3

Check before boarding a bus that it doesn't go via Mecca (SR20, 1¼ hours) or Medina (SR60, five hours).

CAR
Unless you're experienced at driving in the Kingdom, Jeddah is not a good place to start – just getting out of the city can be as dangerous as pointing a camera at the US Consulate.

Car-hire agencies abound in the arrivals hall of the airport. **Budget** Wali al-Ahd St (Map p102; ☎ 651 3714); King Abdul Aziz St (Map p102; ☎ 642 9886) and **Avis** (Map p100; ☎ 667 2761; Gulf Plaza Bldg, Abu Bakr al-Sadeeq St) have offices in the centre. Local agencies in the centre include **Farnas** (Map p102; ☎ 645 2295; King Abdul Aziz St) and **Hanco** (Map p102; ☎ 642 7295; King Abdul Aziz St).

Getting Around
TO/FROM THE AIRPORT
King Abdul Aziz International Airport (☎ 684 1707, 688 5526; Medina Rd) is 25km north of the city. To get between the two terminals, you'll need a taxi (SR30). A taxi to either terminal from the centre costs around SR50 on the meter.

TAXI
Metered taxis are everywhere in Jeddah, but you'll invariably have to remind the driver to turn on the meter; flagfall is SR5.

AROUND JEDDAH
Al-Nakheel
The resort at **Al-Nakheel Beach** (☎ 656 1177; www.alnakheelbeach.com; admission SR50), 25km north of the city centre, is very well-run with a relaxed atmosphere that's popular with expats. It's also a good place for diving, with a well-stocked dive shop, medical clinic and team of dive instructors. Windsurfing is

RED SEA DIVING

Saudi Arabia rarely figures among the great dive destinations of the world, but that's only because no-one can get here. There is a surprisingly well-developed diving industry and the diving opportunities along the Red Sea Coast are world class. The marine life around the reefs is exceptional, including reef sharks, many species of rays, the Hawksbill Turtle and an astonishing array of weird and wonderful fish (including the Arabian Angelfish, Bearded Scorpionfish, Ghost Pipefish and barracuda).

The most popular sites are those within easy reach of Jeddah; there are at least 40 dive sites in the immediate vicinity, including off Jeddah's **South Corniche** and **North Corniche**, particularly off the waters north of **Sharm Obhur**, around 30km north of Al-Balad. Also within easy reach of Jeddah are very good sites at **Shwayba** (around 110km south of Jeddah), where the shore diving is preferable to that of Jeddah, and **Rabigh** (around 125km north of Jeddah). Further afield, both the **Farasan Islands** (p140) and **Yanbu** (p111) are excellent; the visibility is especially good at the latter. Along the coast there are at least a dozen sunken **wrecks**.

Before setting out, visit www.saudidiving.com. This comprehensive website covers everything from dive sites and a full listing of dive centres to good site maps and general information about the region.

In choosing a dive operator, you should try to get a recommendation from other foreigners and discuss with the centre your experience and requirements. Among the larger dive centres with offices in Jeddah which have been recommended to us are:

Al-Khorayf Marine (☎ 691 1585; divewithsharks_sa@yahoo.com)
Desert Sea Divers (☎ 656 1807; www.desertseadivers.ws)
Durrah Dive Center (☎ 221-2707)
Red Sea Divers (☎ 660 6368; redseadivers@arab.net.sa)

also possible and there are plenty of swimming pools.

Turkish Forts

The Ottoman Turks built numerous defensive forts to maintain control over pilgrimage routes from the north. The most accessible of these is **Qala'at Usfan**, 65km northeast of Jeddah and traditionally the penultimate stop on the pilgrim caravan route from Damascus to Mecca. The west and south walls of the fort, built from black lava stone, are the most well preserved, along with the circular guard towers. In spite of the nearby expressways, try to imagine the huge caravan of pilgrims from Egypt and Syria encamped around this small hill, stopping to rest for a few days before making the final push to Mecca. A permit is needed to visit the fort (p173).

Less accessible, but definitely worth seeking out is the well-preserved **Qala'at Hisn Joffah** with a largish inner courtyard and arches along the southern wall. Hisn Joffah's location amid low sand dunes and away from busy roads makes it easier to imagine the fort's original atmosphere. Take the road to Yanbu and then the turn-off east to Joffah Meegat, just before Rabigh.

TAIF
الطائف

☎ 02 / pop 690,000

Taif (Al-Ta'if), the summer capital of Saudi Arabia, is one of the more pleasant towns in the Kingdom. There's not a lot to see in the town itself, but its location 1700m above the baking coastal plain ensures a mild summer climate. With its wide, tree-lined streets, remnants of old Taif, one of the most extensive souqs in the Kingdom, beautiful surrounding scenery and relaxed atmosphere, you'll perhaps understand why the king and the government move to Taif for the duration of summer.

History

As the historical gateway to Mecca from the Arabian interior, Taif has always been a town of great strategic importance. In 1802 the warriors of the First Saudi Empire massacred the entire male population of the town as a means of frightening Meccans into submission. In 1916, Taif was seized by forces loyal to Sherif Hussein, as part of the Arab Revolt.

In 1924, the army of Sherif Hussein's son, Ali, slunk away under cover of darkness. King Abdul Aziz's *ikhwan* army entered the city and killed at least 300 people. Word

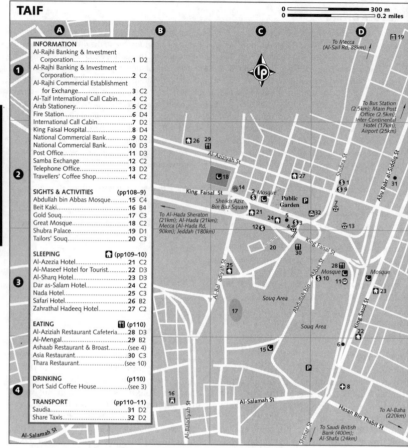

TAIF

0 — 300 m
0 — 0.2 miles

---

spread rapidly and, a month later, Sherif Hussein abdicated under pressure from Mecca's scholars and Jeddah's merchants.

In recent years Taif has also become something of a minor diplomatic centre. In 1989, the town hosted the critical peace conference that helped to end Lebanon's civil wars. From August 1990 until March 1991 Taif was the seat of Kuwait's government-in-exile.

Orientation

Taif is a rare Saudi phenomenon – not only do the streets have names but most of the signs are in Arabic *and* English. The centre of town stretches out from the southern end of Shubra St, south of King Faisal St.

Information

Arab Stationery (☎ 736 0400; King Faisal St) If you want to connect your computer to the Internet, talk to Asif Ali here; it also sells international magazines and English-language newspapers.

Main Post Office (Abu Bakr al-Siddiq St) Just south of King Faisal St.

Travellers' Coffee Shop (King Faisal St; per hr SR10; ⏰ 9am-10pm) Good internet connections.

Sights

ABDULLAH BIN ABBAS MOSQUE

This **mosque** (Abdullah bin Abbas St) is a good example of simple, refined Islamic architecture. Note the earth-coloured minaret with brown-and-white trim and dome. The mosque is named after a cousin of the

Prophet who was also the grandfather of the founder of the Abbasid dynasty and many pilgrims come here after the haj. Abdullah Bin Abbas died in Taif in AD 687.

GREAT MOSQUE

There's little that's remarkable about the exterior of the expansive Great Mosque, northwest of Sheikh Aziz Bin Baz Square, but the huge glass doors along Al-Aziziyah St offer excellent views of the interior, with its huge chandeliers and massive marble pillars.

SOUQS

Taif's **souq** spreads over a few square kilometres, with a range of pots, pans, electrical goods, clothes (from Real Madrid shirts to *abayas* and embroidered dresses), tents and spices. The architecture and merchandise may have changed over the years, but the sense of an Arabian bazaar remains, and really comes to life on summers' evenings.

Next to a Turkish restaurant and several small grocery stores is an old archway of sand-coloured stone. The short alleyway beyond this arch is part of the atmospheric **Tailors' Souq** (9am-noon & 5-11pm).

The **Gold Souq** is on the western side of the labyrinth.

SHUBRA PALACE

The city's **museum** (Admission free; 7.30am-2.30pm Sat-Wed) is housed in a beautiful early-20th-century house, which is the most impressive vestige of old Taif. The exterior is stunning with latticework windows and balconies made from imported Turkish timber, offset against the pristine white walls. The interior marble was imported from Carrara in Italy. The whole effect is lavish without being garish. King Abdul Aziz used to stay here when he visited Taif and it was later the residence of King Faisal. The exhibits include a good section on the Zubaydah Road; see p111).

BEIT KAKI

Another traditional house, now rather forlorn with its windows boarded up and its painted façade peeling, is **Beit Kaki** (Al-Salamah St). It still retains a decaying charm, however. Built in 1943 as a summer residence for the Kaki family, still one of Mecca's most important merchant families, it is one of Taif's oldest surviving buildings. Of particular interest

are the carved window and door frames and the intricately carved balconies.

Sleeping

Taif is transformed during summer into a boom town, particularly on weekends (Wednesday afternoon until Friday afternoon); don't turn up without a reservation. Summer rates listed here are for the period from 1 June to 30 September.

BUDGET & MID-RANGE

These hotels (bar Dar as-Salam) have air-conditioning, telephone, fridge and TVs with Arabic-language channels.

Dar as-Salam Hotel (736 0124; s/d SR40/60, summer SR50/70) In a small lane just off King Faisal St, this place has the cheapest beds in the centre. The rooms are basic but have ceiling fans.

Safari Hotel (734 6660; Al-Aziziyah St; s/d SR100/150, summer SR200/300;) Arguably Taif's best mid-range rooms are at the Safari, where its former grandeur is still just about visible. The rooms are spacious and pleasant and excellent value for money. Don't confuse this hotel with its thoroughly depressing namesake on Shubra St.

Al-Azezia Hotel (732 1666; Sheikh Aziz Bin Baz Sq; s/d SR100/150, summer SR200/300;) Another good choice, Al-Azezia is becoming run down, but the staff are friendly, the rooms are comfortable and some have great views over the Great Mosque and mountains. When things are quiet, it routinely offers suites (more an expression of size than sophistication) for the standard room rate. CNN occasionally makes a brief appearance on the satellite dish, then disappears with impeccably bad timing.

Zahrathal Hadeeq Hotel (727 6771; Al-Afghor St; s/d SR60/90, summer SR120/160;) This friendly spot doesn't get many tourists but it's the best place in this price range. The corridors may be glaringly bright and the rooms stark, but they're clean and spacious.

Nada Hotel (732 2516; Al-Baladiyah St; s/d SR70/100, summer SR150/200;) Opposite the entrance to the Gold Souq, this good choice has simply furnished rooms with decent bathrooms. The rates listed here are the discount rates which everyone who walks through the door seems to qualify for.

Al-Maseef Hotel for Tourist (Al-Maseef al-Siyahe Hotel; 732 4786; King Saud St; s/d without bath SR70/80, s/d with bath SR80/100; summer without bath SR110/130, with bath SR130/150; ☒) One of those Arab hotels which seems to love huge photos of the European Alps on the walls. It's a friendly, good-value place with slightly run-down but pleasant enough rooms.

Al-Sharq Hotel (☎ 732 3651; fax 732 5093; King Saud St; s/d SR80/100, summer SR150/200; ☒) Al-Sharq offers excellent value (the rooms are large and good). The staff don't speak English, but are patient and encouraging while you practise your Arabic. Most of the bathrooms have squat toilets.

TOP END

Both of Taif's top-end hotels are a considerable distance outside town.

Inter-Continental Hotel (☎ 750 5050; fax 750 5040; taif@interconti.com; s/d from SR360/450, summer from SR450/550; Ⓟ ☒ ▯ ▮) The Inter-Continental is something of an oasis 13km north of Taif's centre. Luxurious rooms are in a setting of palm trees and tinkling fountains. The hotel can arrange excursions to the surrounding sights.

Al-Hada Sheraton (☎ 754 1400; fax 754 4831; s/d summer only from SR450/550; ☒) Some 20km northwest from Taif, the Sheraton is suitably luxurious in a nice village setting.

Eating

Taif's centre is awash with cheap Turkish restaurants; upmarket options aren't really in evidence.

Al-Aziziah Restaurant Cafeteria (King Faisal St; meals from SR10) Al-Aziziyah is much bigger and nicer inside than it looks and the kebabs are excellent. It does the cheap Saudi staples (grilled chicken or a kebab with rice, bread and salad) better than most.

Ashaab Restaurant & Broast (King Faisal St; meals from SR10) This place is popular with locals and expats, and offers a decent alternative to the Al-Aziziah with good standard meals.

Asia Restaurant (King Faisal St; meals SR10-SR15) Not the friendliest place in town, Asia Restaurant has a very clean dining room and reasonable food that you won't be writing home about.

Al-Mengal (Al-Aziziyah St; meals SR10-15) Quieter than the restaurants in the city centre, Al-Mengal doesn't get many tourists but is friendly and the food is fine.

Thara Restaurant (Abdullah bin Abbas St; meals SR10) The Indian and Pakistani food here makes a welcome break from the ubiquitous grilled chicken and rice. The food isn't brilliant but variety is the key.

Drinking

Port Said Coffee House (King Faisal St) Above the Al-Rajhi Commercial Establishment for Exchange office, this Egyptian-inspired traditional coffee house has backgammon, *sheeshas* (water pipes), TV and lots of smoke.

Travellers' Coffee Shop (King Faisal St) Below the Internet café, the coffee shop has a touch of charm and does cappuccino and espresso coffee for SR5.

Getting There & Away

AIR

The **airport** (☎ 685 5527) is 25km north of the town. Daily flights go to Riyadh (SR250), Dammam (SR360) and Jeddah (SR110). Less frequent flights go to Abha (SR150), Medina (SR250), Tabuk (SR380) and Sharurah (SR310). **Saudia** (☎ 733 3333; Abu Bakr al-Siddiq St) is just northwest of the centre.

NATIONAL WILDLIFE RESEARCH CENTRE (NWRC)

It's difficult to see how the wildlife of Saudi Arabia has any hope of survival until you visit the NWRC. Inaugurated in 1986, it began as a small-scale breeding programme for the highly endangered Houbara bustard (p42), a favourite prey for Bedouin falconers. Under the auspices of Prince Saud al-Faisal, himself a former hunter, the NWRC (which covers 10 sq km plus an extra 70 sq km where grazing is excluded) has expanded to form part of the highly significant breeding programme of the Arabian oryx (p41). It is from here that almost 150 oryx have been reintroduced into the wild since 1995. Also present are small numbers of Nubian ibex, onagers and gazelle.

The **NWRC** (☎ 745 5188; fax 745 5176; ☾ daylight Sat-Wed, 8am-1pm Thu) is not a tourist attraction as such, but visitors are usually welcome if you make arrangements at least 10 days in advance. To get there, take the road from Taif towards Abha and then the northeast turn-off to Sudayrah after about 20km. The NWRC is on your right after about 10km.

BUS

The **Saptco bus station** (☎ 736 3195; Airport Rd) is 2.5km north of the centre. Daily departures include Riyadh (SR120, 10 hours, 10 daily), Jeddah (SR30, three hours, 12 daily), Dammam (SR185, 13 hours, one daily) and Abha (SR100, nine hours, three daily) via Al-Baha (SR37, four hours). For Muslims only there are five daily buses to Mecca (SR20, two hours).

Getting Around

Getting around the centre is easy enough on foot. Taxis and small utilities (they'll find you if you stand on the pavement looking vaguely interested) charge SR5 to SR10 to the bus station from the centre or SR50 to the airport.

AROUND TAIF

While not quite as dramatic as the scenery around Abha further to the south, the landscapes around Taif are nonetheless worth a few days' exploring.

Al-Hada   الهدا

This small village, around 20km northwest of Taif, offers outstanding views down over the edge of the escarpment. The sense of being in a traditional Hejazi village comes from the stone houses and watchtowers, less so from the Sheraton Hotel which rises out of the centre.

A **cable car** (one way SR20; ⏲ 10am-6pm Thu-Sat Oct-Mar, daily Apr-Sep) runs down off the cliffs (25 minutes one-way).

Share taxis to Al-Hada (SR8) leave intermittently (more often on weekends) from the large car park on the corner of King Faisal and Shubra Sts in Taif.

Al-Shafa   الشفا

Al-Shafa is one of the Hejaz's hidden gems. At almost 3000m above sea level and 24km southwest of Taif, Al-Shafa doesn't get the crowds or passing traffic that can afflict Al-Hada, but it does have breathtaking views down Wadi Niyat and north–south along the escarpment. Here too, you'll find stone houses and watchtowers. You'll need your own transport to get here.

BIRKAT AL-KHURABAH
بركات الخورابة

The stone cisterns of Birkat al-Khurabah, 130km northeast of Taif, date back 1000 years

---

THE ZUBAYDAH ROAD

Around AD 800 Zubaydah, the favourite wife of Caliph Haroun Al-Rashid (of *Arabian Nights* fame), set out from Baghdad to perform the pilgrimage to Mecca. Along the way she nearly died of thirst, a not uncommon occurrence at the time, even for those who were part of a well-resourced royal entourage.

Spurred into action by the memory of her ordeal and determined that no other pilgrims should suffer as she did, Zubaydah funded a massive network of cisterns which began at Kufa (near the modern city of Najaf in southern Iraq), passed through Rafah and then Kufa, near Buraydah. From there it turned southwest, continuing across the desert to Mecca, some 1500km from the road's starting point. Though some of the facilities along what came to be known as the Darb Zubaydah, or the Zubaydah Road, eventually fell into disuse, many others were carefully maintained for centuries and a few are still in use today (largely by Bedouins to water their animals – few, if any, pilgrims travel the Zubaydah Road any more).

---

and were adapted to provide water to pilgrims crossing Arabia (above). Take a moment to stand on this desert plain and imagine the 10,000-strong haj caravan emerging from the north in a cloud of dust and descending year after year, century after century, on these great stone pools amid the seemingly trackless wastes of western Arabia.

Getting There & Away

From Taif take the Riyadh expressway. At Exit 54, turn north and follow the road 71km through Ashayrah and Faisaliah to the small settlement of Birkah. The track to Birkat al-Khurabah (a further 11km) turns right on the south side of town.

YANBU   ينبع

☎ 04 / pop 165,000

TE Lawrence used Yanbu, which he famously described as 'half a city of the dead', as a launching pad for raids on the Hejaz Railway. With a booming port, refineries and petrochemical plants, Lawrence's description of Yanbu hardly holds, but this is still far from the Kingdom's most attractive corner. The only reason to come here is that the Red Sea's waters off Yanbu offer improbably excellent diving opportunities.

Orientation & Information

King Abdul Aziz St is the main thoroughfare and runs perpendicular to the north–south road from Jeddah. The 25km-long industrial zone stretches south of the town.

Diving

For information on diving in the area, see p107. There are three dive centres with offices in Yanbu:

Durrah Dive Center (☎ 396 8174)
Red Sea Divers (☎ 392 7396; redseadivers@arab.net.sa)
Yanbu Divers (☎ 322 4246; hashim@yanbudivers.com)

Sleeping & Eating

Middle East Hotel (☎ 322 1281; fax 322 4770; King Abdul Aziz St; s/d SR70/110) The simple rooms here are fine, but can it be a bit of a depressing place to retreat to, surrounded as it is with heavy industry.

Al-Hayat Hotel Yanbu (☎ 322 3888; fax 322 7021; s/d SR300/350) Located 5km south of the centre on the road to the industrial complex, this place is overpriced which is perhaps why it routinely offers discounts of up to 40%, at which point it becomes good value.

Radhwa Holiday Inn (☎ 322 3767; fax 322 7281; s/d SR295/375) The Holiday Inn is 7km south of the centre and is suitably well appointed if not luxurious. It has a small dive shop.

There are cheap eateries along King Abdul Aziz St.

Getting There & Away

The airport is 10km northeast of the centre. **Saudia** (☎ 322 6666; King Abdul Aziz St), a few doors east of the Al-Higgi Hotel, flies to Jeddah (SR110, twice daily).

Madain Saleh
& the North

مدائن صالح و الشمال

CONTENTS

MADAIN SALEH
& THE NORTH

Northern Saudi Arabia is home to the Kingdom's richest source of pre-Islamic sites, including Saudi Arabia's most visited site and some of its least known treasures. The astonishing Madain Saleh is the most impressive site in Saudi Arabia and should be on every visitor's itinerary. With Petra-like, rock-carved tombs in an extraordinary desert setting, Madain Saleh is one of the most rewarding ancient sites anywhere in the world. The nearby town of Al-Ula is less recognised, but is also an impressive open-air gallery to ancient civilisations and is surrounded by stunning red cliffs and abundant palm trees. This is Saudi Arabia at its best.

Cutting through the heart of the same territory, the Hejaz Railway also tells important historical stories. This is where the legend of Lawrence of Arabia was born – the ruined tracks and substations stand as lonely sentinels to the days of trade and pilgrim caravans as well as charting the fortunes of the battles between TE Lawrence and the Arab Revolt against the once-mighty Ottoman Empire. Along the length of the tracks is some of Saudi Arabia's most beautiful and accessible desert scenery, culminating in the stunning monoliths of Wadi Hisma in the north.

Further to the west, the Jouf region is remote, evocative of a once-impenetrable Arabia and home to the unusual and unexplained Standing Stones of Rajajil. Not far away, Doma al-Jandal is as surprising as it is historically significant.

With their proximity to some of the Middle East's most important ancient Empires – the Babylonians, Ottomans and Nabataeans among them – this region is worth the effort to get here. The distances between some of the sites are considerable, but every one of them is worth the time spent travelling.

HIGHLIGHTS

- Finding yourself spellbound by the Nabataean rock-hewn tombs of **Madain Saleh** (p117)
- Picking your way through **Old Al-Ula** (p116) with its building blocks of ancient civilisations
- Following the **Hejaz Railway** (p122) with its abandoned air and echoes of TE Lawrence
- Enjoying the mystery of the remote **Standing Stones of Rajajil** (p124)
- Crossing the breathtaking red and yellow landscapes of **Wadi Hisma** (p122)

★ Standing Stones of Rajajil

★ Wadi Hisma

★ Madain Saleh
★ Al-Ula

★ Hejaz Railway

| ▪ TELEPHONE CODE: 04 | ▪ POPULATION: 675,000 | ▪ AREA: 212,000 SQ KM |

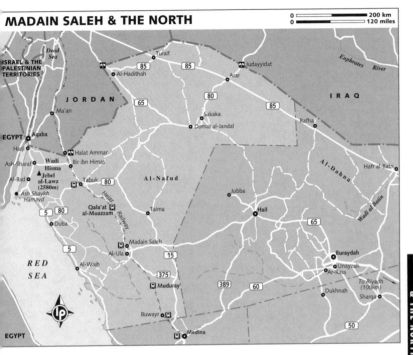

MADAIN SALEH & THE NORTH

0 ———— 200 km
0 ———— 120 miles

AL-ULA

العلا

☎ 04

Al-Ula, the gateway to Madain Saleh, is a small town in the heart of some exceptionally beautiful country. Palm groves run down the centre of the wadi (river bed, dry except in the rainy season) and forbidding red sandstone cliffs line two sides. Apart from the nearby tombs of the Nabataeans, the delightful mud-brick Old Al-Ula is one of the best preserved old towns in Saudi Arabia and the surrounding area has ample evidence (tombs, rock inscriptions) of habitation dating back more than two millennia.

History

Al-Ula's history of settlement predates that of Madain Saleh. Inhabited as early as 500 BC as a staging post on the frankincense trade route from Yemen to Egypt, came under the sway of the Lihyan dynasty from around 400 BC. The Lihyanites left behind many reminders of their past, several of which are still evident throughout the wadi. With the ascendancy of the Nabataeans (see

Who Were The Nabataeans? p123), much of what is now Al-Ula was deserted in favour of Madain Saleh.

Orientation & Information

Al-Ula lies along the western side of the narrow wadi. The southern section of town is home to the museum, a small Internet café (behind the museum) and an ATM for the Arab National Bank (opposite the museum). The old town sits between the two sections of the new town. Both hotels are signposted throughout town.

Sights & Activities

AL-ULA MUSEUM OF ARCHAEOLOGY AND ETHNOGRAPHY

The **museum** (☎ 884 1536; admission free; ☼ 8.30am-2pm Sat-Wed) has the usual informative displays about Saudi Arabia's geology and the legacy of the Al-Sauds, but the displays of pilgrimage routes have a special resonance here because of the critical role which trade played in Madain Saleh's evolution. There are also some good displays on the Nabataeans.

The guides who organise tours (p117) are usually able to arrange for the museum to be opened outside normal opening hours.

AL-KHURAIBBA TOMBS

These tombs date to the Lihyanite era (and hence predate the Nabataeans). They're cut into the cliff-face along the eastern wall of the wadi around 2km north of the Madain Saleh Hotel. 'Al-Khuraibba' literally means 'the abandoned place'. The tombs (small horizontal windows cut into the cliff face) are not open to the public and can only be viewed from a distance. Above the fifth tomb from the left are two carved lions, which is a highly unusual motif in Saudi Arabia.

OLD AL-ULA

Although rapidly crumbling, **Old Al-Ula** is one of the most fascinating old towns in Arabia. The mud town stands on the site of the biblical city of Dedan which is mentioned in Isaiah (21:13) as the home base of Arab caravans and in Ezekiel (27:20–21) as a trading partner of the Phoenician city of Tyre. The buildings that you'll see mostly date back a few hundred years, although some of the bricks from much earlier Lihyanite settlements have been reused. The town is unusual in Arabia for having predominantly two-storey houses; pilgrims from the north settled in the area, bringing with them external influences in architecture.

Originally, the old quarter was enclosed by walls with just two gates and consisted of around 500 houses. It was occupied until the late 1970s. Throughout the town, there are some superb doors made from palm trunks. Rising up from the centre of the old town are the remnants of **Qala'at Musa Abdul Nasser**, the remaining stones of which seem to merge with the natural outcrop of rock. From the rise below the Qala'at, some **carved human figures** are visible high on the cliff face to the northwest. At the southern end of the old town, is a crude but effective **sundial** above a roof. It was from here that the start of Ramadan was once announced.

The palm trees and maze of low mud-brick walls directly across the road from here were once farms whose owners lived in the old town.

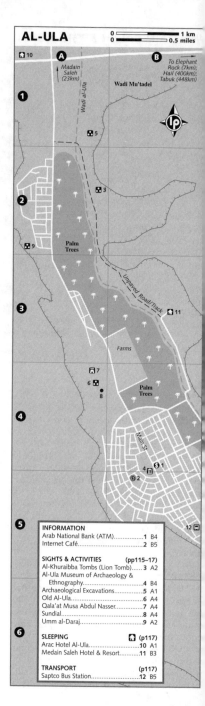

AL-ULA

0 — 1 km
0 — 0.5 miles

INFORMATION	
Arab National Bank (ATM)	1 B4
Internet Café	2 B5

SIGHTS & ACTIVITIES	(pp115–17)
Al-Khuraibba Tombs (Lion Tomb)	3 A2
Al-Ula Museum of Archaeology & Ethnography	4 B4
Archaeological Excavations	5 A1
Old Al-Ula	6 A4
Qala'at Musa Abdul Nasser	7 A4
Sundial	8 A4
Umm al-Daraj	9 A2

SLEEPING	(p117)
Arac Hotel Al-Ula	10 A1
Medain Saleh Hotel & Resort	11 B3

TRANSPORT	(p117)
Saptco Bus Station	12 B5

UMM AL-DARAJ

At the northwestern end of town, Umm al-Daraj (Mother of Steps) is worth a brief detour. It contains a former Lihyanite sacrificial altar, weathered steps climbing up the hill and a few rudimentary Lihyanite inscriptions. From the top of the steps there are fine views out over the wadi. You'll need a guide to find Umm al-Daraj, but it's included on most tour itineraries. There's an exceptional **Lihyanite temple** atop the rock for those with considerable rock-climbing experience.

Tours

Al-Ula's two hotels arrange packages which include accommodation, all your meals, site permits, a tour around Madain Saleh and Al-Ula and transfers to/from the airports at Hail or Medina. Costs escalate if you are on your own.

Medain Saleh Hotel and Resort (☎ 884 2888; info@mshotel.com.sa; 3 days & 2 nights from SR950pp) This operates a professional outfit and has the two best guides for Madain Saleh – Hamid Ben Bouazza and Patrick Pierard – both of whom speak French and English.

Arac Hotel Al-Ula (☎ 884 4444; hotelalula@arac.sa) This charges SR1600 per vehicle for a return transfer from Medina airport (minimum of five people), SR450 for a five-seater full-day tour of Madain Saleh, plus SR220/245 for a single/double. Its guides tend to be drivers with limited knowledge of the sites.

There are also a number of tour agencies who specialise in tours to Madain Saleh. They include:

Bin Zaid Travel (☎ 419 4688; www.binzaidtravel.com.sa; Riyadh)

Xplorer Tours (☎ 02-667 5669; Jeddah)

Golden Eagle Services (☎ 492 2550; goldeneagletours@ hotmail.com; Riyadh)

Reeman Travel Agency (☎ 02-651 3905; fax 653 4649; Jeddah)

Rehlat Travel (☎ 466 0726; www.rehlat.com; Riyadh)

Samal Lagi (☎ 02-664 0638; ops@samallaghi.com; Jeddah)

Sleeping & Eating

Medain Saleh Hotel & Resort (☎ 884 2888; info@ms hotel.com.sa; s/d SR180/220) This place has the best location, overlooking the wadi from underneath the eastern cliff face and with distant views of Old Al-Ula. The rooms (with satellite TV) are very comfortable, the restaurant is excellent and the staff friendly.

Arac Hotel Al-Ula (☎ 884 4444; hotelalula@arac.com .sa; s/d Dec-May SR220/245, Jun-Nov SR190/220) The rooms here are equally good, but the roadside location is less appealing. It is, however, closer to Madain Saleh and the management are friendly. The restaurant is decent; if you're staying here you won't have much choice.

Getting There & Away

Unless you're coming with your own car, most people fly from Riyadh to Hail or from Jeddah to Medina; see opposite for details of packages that include airport pick-ups.

There are daily Saptco buses to Al-Ula from Jeddah (SR110, eight hours), Riyadh (SR170, 3½ hours) and Tabuk (SR70, five hours).

AROUND AL-ULA

There are numerous natural and archaeological sites in the area – ask the authoritative Patrick Pierard at the Madain Saleh Hotel (see opposite) for advice.

Elephant Rock (Saharat al-Fil) is a wonderful natural rock formation which towers above the sands in a landscape of red rocky monoliths; it's a superb spot that some operators choose for an overnight camping stop. Also known as Mammoth Rock, it's 11km northwest of Al-Ula; take the road to Madain Saleh from Al-Ula town centre for 4km, then turn right at the corner on which Arac Hotel Al-Ula is located. The rock is 7km further on, over the sand to the left along well-worn tracks.

MADAIN SALEH   مدائن صالح

If you can only visit one place in Saudi Arabia, make it Madain Saleh which rises up from the sands in a landscape of rare beauty. This crossroads of ancient civilisations, pilgrims, explorers, trade caravans and armies finds its most remarkable expression in the elaborate stone carved temples of the Nabataeans. The Nabataeans, who carved the astonishing city of Petra (in Jordan) chose Madain Saleh as their second city. Although the tombs are less spectacular here than those in Petra, the landscape of sweeping sand and wonderful rock formations is stunningly beautiful. The tombs are also in an excellent state of preservation, due largely to the fact that the local stone is much harder than that found at Petra.

History

The name Madain Saleh (Mada'in Salih) may have been associated with the Midianites of the Old Testament whose empire included parts of northwestern Arabia, or it may be from the Quranic story of Salih (opposite).

Madain Saleh was the Nabataeans' second city and stood at the midpoint of the caravan route between Mecca and Petra in Jordan. Its history rose and fell with the fortunes of the Nabataean capital at Petra. When Petra was, after a period of Nabataean autonomy, finally taken by the Romans in AD 106, Madain Saleh fell into a decline from which it never recovered. The Romans reoriented trade away from the Arabian interior, instead preferring the ports of the Red Sea. In later centuries the pilgrim road from Damascus to Mecca passed through Madain Saleh.

Charles Doughty, in the 1880s, was the first European to see the tombs, having heard in Petra that there was another similar city to the south. He described it as 'that fabulous Medáin Salih, which I was come from far countries to seek in Arabia'. Chapter IV, Volume I of *Travels in Arabia Deserta* contains more extensive descriptions.

Information

You need a permit (p173) to visit Madain Saleh (admission free; ☉ 8am-sunset); most hotels and tour operators arrange permits on your behalf if you fax them your details a week in advance. Video cameras are not allowed inside the site.

The most detailed guide to Madain Saleh is the pocket-sized *Al-Ula & Mada'in Salih* (SR65), available in the gift shop of the Madain Saleh Hotel & Resort (p117) and some branches of the Jarir Bookstore.

The Site

Madain Saleh is home to 131 tombs, 45 of which carry inscriptions in late Aramaic script above the doors. These inscriptions detail the period of the tomb's construction and for whom it was built; these inscriptions are translated on signs in front of the tombs. The only permanent structures built by the Nabataeans were tombs or religious sites; originally nomadic, the Nabataeans later settled in relatively flimsy adobe houses, the meagre remains of which are yet to be excavated and lie inside the fenced-off area in the centre of the site.

Throughout the site there are directional signs to the main tombs. The names given to the tombs or the areas were not the names used by the Nabataeans, but are instead used by local Bedouin and now adopted by archaeologists. Most tours take you around the site in a clockwise direction.

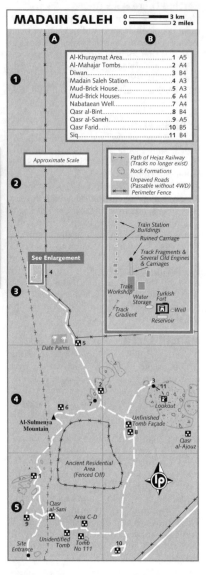

MADAIN SALEH

0 ——— 3 km
0 ——— 2 miles

Al-Khuraymat Area............................1	A5
Al-Mahajar Tombs..........................2	A4
Diwan..3	B4
Madain Saleh Station......................4	A3
Mud-Brick House............................5	A3
Mud-Brick Houses..........................6	A4
Nabataean Well..............................7	A4
Qasr al-Bint...................................8	B4
Qasr al-Saneh...............................9	A5
Qasr Farid....................................10	B5
Siq...11	B4

Approximate Scale

├─ ┼─ ┤ Path of Hejaz Railway (Tracks no longer exist)
Rock Formations
— Unpaved Roads (Passable without 4WD)
✕─✕─✕ Perimeter Fence

Train Station Buildings
Ruined Carriage
Track Fragments & Several Old Engines & Carriages

See Enlargement

Train Workshop
Water Storage
Turkish Fort
Well
Track Gradient
Reservoir

Date Palms

Lookout

Al-Sulmenya Mountain

Unfinished Tomb Façade

Qasr al-Ajouz

Ancient Residential Area (Fenced Off)

Qasr al-Sani

Area C-D

Site Entrance
Unidentified Tomb
Tomb No 111

THE MUSLIM HISTORY OF MADAIN SALEH

Sometime around the year 2000 BC, Salih appeared as a Prophet in northwestern Arabia, preaching monotheism in a city where 47 gods were worshipped. The people demanded a sign of Salih's lone God as proof of His existence: a red-coloured, pregnant camel was to emerge from a rock outside the town at a specified time. When a red, pregnant camel did indeed emerge as promised, local pagan priests were enraged. They declared that anyone believing in the sign would be punished, and one of the town's richer citizens hired several men to kill the miraculous camel. The camel's unborn calf, however, survived the attack and returned to the cleft in the rock from which the mother had emerged. Salih then announced that the killers of the camel and other unbelievers had three days to live. On the third day God caused an earthquake to destroy the town and all but a few believers were killed as punishment for their having doubted Him and His prophet.

The city punished by God was almost certainly Al-Ula (called Al-Hijr in the Quran). To this day many Saudis refuse to visit Madain Saleh because they believe the area to be cursed by God. According to other Muslim scholars, the believers who escaped the earthquake fled to Jerusalem and became the forerunners of the Nabataeans, who founded Petra and, later, Madain Saleh.

QASR AL-SANEH

Not the most spectacular of tombs, **Qasr al-Saneh** is nonetheless a good place to start, as it reveals many of the essential elements of Nabataean funerary architecture – the relatively unadorned façade, the two five-step motifs at the top, a simple interior burial chamber with shelves for corpses and low ceilings, and inscriptions above the doorway. Built around AD 50, Qasr al-Saneh was in use for just 50 years before the Nabataean kings were overwhelmed by Rome.

AL-KHURAYMAT

This area, about 750m north of Qasr al-Saneh, has some of the best preserved **tombs** in Madain Saleh. With around 20 tombs carved into the rockface, you'll see some impressive griffin-like figures with human heads, lions' bodies and wings, that adorn the corners of the pediment. Look also for step-pyramid reliefs atop some tombs, and rose-like designs above some doors; these symbolise plates on which blood fell during animal sacrifice. You'll also see some external burial shelves carved into the rock just outside the entrance; these were for people who died before the tombs could be completed.

NABATAEAN WELL & AL-MAHAJAR

The fence designed to keep you from falling into the **Nabataean Well** effectively blocks the best views. One of around 60 wells in the area, this well has wall supports built from railway sleepers pilfered from the Hejaz Railway.

Across the track from the entrance to the well, the **Al-Mahajar tombs** are unremarkable, but nonetheless photogenic because they're all lined up in a row.

MADAIN SALEH STATION

At the northern edge of the site, is the **Madain Saleh Station** of the Hejaz Railway (p122). The site has been restored to within an inch of its life and therefore lacks the lonely and decrepit charm of the substations elsewhere. The complex, built in 1907, consists of 16 buildings which include a large workshop (with a restored WWI-era engine), shells of other railway carriages and a rebuilt Turkish fort where Doughty stayed for several weeks and which served as a resting place for pilgrims travelling to Mecca.

DIWAN

The *diwan* (meeting room), carved into a hillside to shield it from the wind, is one of the few examples of nonfunerary architecture in Madain Saleh. The name owes more to modern Arab culture than to the Nabataeans, who probably used the area as a cult site. Opposite the hollowed-out room are niches cut into the rock where Nabataean deities could be carved (some deeply weathered examples remain) or statues placed by pilgrims.

Running south from the Diwan is a narrow passageway between two rock faces. Known as the **Siq**, it is lined with more small altars. At the far end, you enter a striking natural amphitheatre with weird and wonderful rock formations. Carved into the eastern wall you can see *qanats* (water channels), while at the southern end there are some well preserved

NABATAEAN ARCHITECTURE

The tombs at Madain Saleh were constructed largely between 100 BC and AD 76. The step designs atop the tombs' façades carry traces of Assyrian design, although the more Nabataean motif of two sets of steps descending inwards towards each other largely prevails. All such designs in Madain Saleh (although not in Petra) consist of five steps, which may represent the five deities of the Nabataeans. Also evident are the multiple step pyramids which drew heavily on Egyptian influence.

The tombs at Madain Saleh also display clear Greek and Roman influences in their decoration, particularly in the styling of the pediments and in the use of columns and pilasters around the tomb doorways. The use of griffins and animal figures with human heads (above the doors on some tombs) also speak strongly of Hellenistic ideas, although the use of falcons and urns are more specifically Nabataean in origin.

As you'll see from some of the unfinished tombs around Madain Saleh, the tombs were carved from the top down. Carvers generally dug out grooves from the rock before using iron chains to dislodge cubic slabs of stone, after which time the exposed façade was smoothed. It was difficult, painstaking work that could take four carvers up to 2½ years to complete. If they discovered a layer of soft or oxidised sandstone, the work had to be abandoned.

It is notable that Madain Saleh contains no royal tombs. All the kings and Nabataean notables were buried in the capital, Petra, so the tombs belong to local families. The degrees of ornamentation that you'll see in Madain Saleh are largely dependent upon the wealth of the owners.

sacrificial altars. As you pass through the cleft in the rock turn around and look up; you should see several ancient carvings of human figures, camels and writing in an early form of Arabic.

After passing through the mini-Siq go straight for 50m and then climb up and to the right to a **lookout** with a breathtaking view over the site.

QASR AL-BINT

Qasr Al-Bint (Girl's Palace) comprises, when taken as a whole, a wonderful row of façades which make for dramatic viewing from across the site, particularly as you pass between Al-Khoraymat and the Nabataean Well. The east face has two particularly well preserved tombs. If you step back and look up near the northern end of the west face you'll distinguish a tomb that was abandoned in the early stages of construction and would, if completed, have been the largest in Madain Saleh; only the step façade was cut.

QASR FARID

Qasr Farid is the largest tomb of Madain Saleh and certainly the most stunning. The tomb is no more or less adorned than many of the others, but its stand-alone location makes it an exceptionally beautiful spot just before sunset. Carved from a single, free-standing monolith of rock, it's visible from

miles away, and the craggy mountains away to the east are spectacular.

Getting There & Away

The road from Al-Ula (23km) is easy to find. The site entrance is marked off the road with a blue 'Antiquities' sign.

TABUK   تبوك
☎ 04 / pop 403,000

Tabuk, in the far northwest of Saudi Arabia is a military town with a reputation for conservatism. That may be why few travellers come here, but it does have an old fort and a station of the Hejaz Railway. There are also some worthwhile sights within striking distance of the town (p122).

Orientation & Information

Most of Tabuk's essential services are on or near Prince Fahd bin Sultan St (largely a pedestrian zone) which cuts east–west through the centre of town. Here you'll find banks and the post office; the hotels are all close by.

Sights
TABUK FORT

Built in 1655 by the Ottomans as a staging post along the pilgrimage route from Damascus to Mecca, **Tabuk Fort** (Prince Fahd bin Sultan St; admission free; ☼ dusk-dawn) is not the most impressive fort in Saudi Arabia, but it is one of the oldest. Restored in the 1990s, its highlights include the carved Quranic verses above the doorway, the blue-and-white Turkish tilework and the small interior courtyard. A permit is required to enter the fort; see p173.

HEJAZ RAILWAY STATION
Tabuk was one of the major stations of the Hejaz Railway (p122). The buildings, which stretch nearly 500m along the street, were first built in 1906 and rebuilt again in the 1990s. The three identical two-storey houses served as barracks for Turkish soldiers, while the main station office was in the larger, one-storey building near the water tower.

Sleeping
Youth Hostel (☎ 422 6308; Sporting City; dm SR10) The youth hostel is 14km north of the centre; ask for the *bayt ash-shabab* (youth hostel).

Al-Tweijri Hotel (☎ 424 0028; s/d with bathroom SR60/90) Tabuk's cheapest hotel, off Prince Fahd Bin Sultan St, is basic but as clean as you can expect for the price. It doesn't get many tourists so expect wary staff.

Al-Adel Hotel (☎ 422 1749; fax 423 8237; s/d SR75/110) The Al-Adel, located east of the Hejaz Railway, is comfortable and quite good value although some rooms are on the small side.

Moroj Hotel (☎ 423 3490; fax 422 6039; s/d SR75/110) Located east of the Hejaz Railway, on the big street parallel to, and one traffic light east of, the street with the railway station, this place

is comfortable, spacious and good value. Staff are friendly once they warm up.

Al-Hamdan Hotel (☎ 422 4790; fax 422 3735; s/d SR130/180) Located on the same street, east of Hejaz Railway, this is a small step up in price and quality, and you may even get CNN on the satellite dish. Bathrooms are well-maintained.

Tabuk Sahara Hotel (☎ /fax 422 1212; Medina Rd; s/d SR325/380) Undoubtedly the best place to stay in Tabuk. It's out in the suburbs and is very comfortable if ageing a little.

Eating
Expect loads of cheap Turkish restaurants; don't expect fine dining.

Mone Restaurant (☎ 423 7645; Prince Fahd Bin Sultan St; meals from SR10) Mone is the best of the Turkish places with a menu that is unusually extensive. The food is cheap and the ambience bright and breezy. The white beans with meat served over rice (SR10) make a great change from grilled chicken.

Caravan Restaurant (☎ 422 9630; meals from SR15) For variety, it's hard to beat Caravan, one short block south of Prince Fahd Bin Sultan St, where the Filipino noodle dishes are great and it also serves Chinese and Pakistani dishes.

Getting There & Away
Saudia (☎ 422 1434, ☎ 802 22222), on the same street as the Al-Adel and Moroj Hotels, has daily flights to Jeddah (SR280), Riyadh (SR390) and Medina (SR190), as well as less

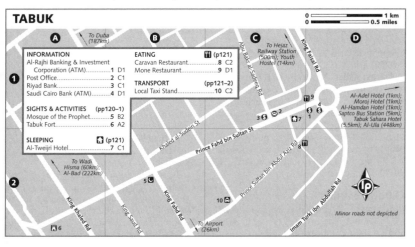

TABUK

| | | | 0 ▬▬▬▬▬ 1 km |
| | | | 0 ▬▬▬▬▬ 0.5 miles |

INFORMATION
Al-Rajhi Banking & Investment
  Corporation (ATM)..............1 D1
Post Office.............................2 C1
Riyad Bank............................3 C1
Saudi Cairo Bank (ATM)........4 D1

SIGHTS & ACTIVITIES   (pp120–1)
Mosque of the Prophet..........5 B2
Tabuk Fort............................6 A2

SLEEPING   🏠 (p121)
Al-Tweijri Hotel.....................7 C1

EATING   🍴 (p121)
Caravan Restaurant................8 C2
Mone Restaurant...................9 D1

TRANSPORT   (pp121–2)
Local Taxi Stand...................10 C2

To Duba (187km)
To Hejaz Railway Station (500m); Youth Hostel (14km)
Al-Adel Hotel (1km); Moroj Hotel (1km); Al-Hamdan Hotel (1km); Saptco Bus Station (5km); Tabuk Sahara Hotel (5.5km); Al-Ula (448km)
To Wadi Hisma (60km), Al-Bad (222km)
To Airport (26km)
Minor roads not depicted

THE HEJAZ RAILWAY

The Hejaz Railway, with its echoes of TE Lawrence and the Arab Revolt, cuts across northwestern Arabia with abandoned and evocative stations, substations and garrison forts.

The official idea of the railway was to make it easier for pilgrims to reach Medina and Mecca, cutting the journey time from Damascus from six weeks to just four days. Construction began in 1900. In addition to the tracks and station buildings, forts were also built every 25km for garrisons of Turkish soldiers whose role was to protect the railway from bandits. The line opened in 1908, stretching over 1600km through largely desert terrain; the planned extension to Mecca was never built.

The Hejaz Railway was unpopular from the outset, despite making the lives of pilgrims infinitely easier. Many Arabs saw the project as a means of reinforcing Turkish military and political aims in the region and supplying the occupation troops. The fact that the Turkish military used money earmarked for religious purposes further angered the Hejazis. Bedouin operators of the pilgrim caravans and those who benefited from the passing pilgrim traffic were suddenly stripped of their livelihoods. In response, the trains were frequently stopped and raided.

During WWI, the Ottomans sided with Germany (who had helped build the railway). Sherif Hussein, the Hashemite ruler of the Hejaz, made an alliance with the British to drive out the Turks. Harnessing the hostility of the local Bedouin, TE Lawrence helped to orchestrate the Arab Revolt, attacking trains and sabotaging the tracks. The Turkish garrison in Medina was soon cut off from the remainder of the Ottoman forces whose empire was crumbling. The railway became unviable and ceased to run after 1918.

The railway was quickly dismantled, with many sleepers and other building materials appropriated by locals for use elsewhere. Many of the stations and substations remain, however, and they're well worth visiting. The **stations** which have been almost completely rebuilt are at **Tabuk** (p121), **Madain Saleh** (p119) and **Medina**.

There are at least 19 substations between Medina and Madain Saleh. They sit alongside the Medina–Al-Ula road for part of the way, but to see all of them, you'll need to take the slower alternative route which continues northwest around 40km north of Medina. Our favourites in this section include **Buwayr** (95km north of Medina) where you'll find an almost-complete train (an engine and 10 cars in various states of decomposition, along with three buildings) and **Muduraj**, a further 100km north, where there are locomotives and carriages damaged by the bombardments of the Arab Revolt as well as some of the best scenery along the line. The road is accessible in a 2WD vehicle, although you'll feel more comfortable in a 4WD.

North of Madain Saleh, there are a further 13 substations. Probably the best is **Qala'at al-Muazzam**, 148km north of Al-Ula, with its caravanserai, fort, decrepit carriages and some pieces of track.

---

frequent departures to Abha (SR480), Hail (SR230) and Taif (SR390).

The **bus station** (☎ 423 7139; Medina Rd) is 5km from the town centre, just west of the Tabuk Sahara Hotel. Daily departures include Riyadh (SR210, 17 hours, two daily) via Hail (SR110, 10 hours) and Buraydah (SR150, 14 hours); Jeddah (SR140, 13 hours, three daily) via Yanbu (SR95, nine hours); Sakaka (SR90, six hours, two daily); and Al-Ula (SR70, five hours, one daily).

AROUND TABUK

Wadi Hisma is as beautiful as any place you'll see in Arabia. The turn-off (west) is 60km north of Tabuk at the town of Bir ibn Himas.

Comparable to Wadi Rum, just across the Jordanian border, the red-stone mountains rise up individually from the sands in stunning formations.

Continue west until Ash-Sharaf (112km), then turn south to **Al-Bad** (50km), which has half a dozen reasonably well-preserved and unadorned **Nabataean tombs** cut into the hillside. They're only visible from the road, but their setting is quite picturesque.

The road continues south to **Duba** (168km), a former staging post on the frankincense road and now home to an attractive **fishing harbour**. From here the road leads back over the mountains to Tabuk (187km) with some lovely scenery along the way.

If you don't have your own car, the Tabuk Sahara Hotel in Tabuk (p121) may be able to arrange transport, as can the Madain Saleh Hotel in Al-Ula (p117).

SAKAKA ساكاكا
☎ 04 / pop 55,000

Remote and rural Sakaka has a host of little-visited archaeological sights, particularly the **standing stones of Rajajil** (p124) 25km from town. Lady Anne Blunt and her husband Wilfred visited Sakaka (which they called Meskakeh) in 1879; Lady Blunt's book, *A Pilgrimage to Najd*, provides a rare portrait of Arabian society in that era.

Orientation & Information

Sakaka's main street runs north from a single large intersection for approximately 4.5km. The intersection is dominated by Sakaka's main mosque and its biggest hotel, the Al-Nusl. Along or near this street you will find most of Sakaka's restaurants and services. The post office, banks and bus station are all nearby.

Sights

According to Lady Blunt in *A Pilgrimage to Najd*, 'Meskakeh [Sakaka], like Jof [Al-Jandal], has an ancient citadel perched on a cliff about a hundred feet high, and dominating the town'. **Qasr Za'abel** (admission free; ☒ 8am-1.30pm Sat-Wed), at the northern end of town, actually dates only from the early 19th century. Restored in 1994, the fort has lost something of its antique charm, although the hilltop perch, irregular shape and four towers make it worth a look. Inside, you'll find the usual *diwan* and the commander's house. A permit (p173) is required to enter, but the exterior is more interesting.

Jabal Burnus, the rocky outcrop just east of Qasr Za'abel, has rock carvings of dancing figures with their arms raised in the air across the upper face. The carvings date from the 6th century BC.

The fort-like **Beit Ibrahim Al-'Aishan** overlooks Sakaka's main intersection. Believed to be more than 50 years old, it's remarkably well preserved and gives some insight into the style of houses Wilfred and Anne Blunt would have seen when they visited.

Sleeping & Eating

Al-Nusl Hotel (☎ 625 0353; fax 625 0408; s/d SR350/450) This place wins our vote for the most tastefully designed hotel in Saudi Arabia. The rooms surround glass-domed courtyards cooled by traditional wind towers. Throughout the public areas there are displays of antiquities and artefacts. The hotel is an ideal base to explore the area and offers packages that include tour guides and transportation.

WHO WERE THE NABATAEANS?

There are many theories about where the Nabataeans came from, although all agree that they were Arabian in origin; possible homelands include the central Najd plateau, the northern shores of the Arabian Gulf or the Hejaz. Most scholars do agree that the Nabataeans were early Bedouins who lived a nomadic life before settling as farmers in the area in the 6th century BC. They developed a specialised knowledge of desert water resources (using water channels known as *qanats*) as well as the intricacies of the lucrative trade caravan routes. These two skills would form the foundations of the Nabataean empire.

Nabataean wealth, which was derived initially by plundering trade caravans, shifted to exacting tolls (up to 25% of the commodities' value) upon these same caravans as a means of securing Nabataean protection and guiding the caravans to water. Through a mixture of shrewd diplomacy and military force, the Nabataeans kept at bay the Seleucids, Egyptians, Persians and later, for a time, the Romans.

The Nabataeans never really possessed an 'empire' in the common military and administrative sense of the word, but rather, from about 200 BC, they had established a 'zone of influence' that stretched to Syria and Rome and south into the Hadramaut.

Apart from tomb inscriptions in Aramaic, the Nabataeans left no written history and their story is largely told through archaeological excavations and non-Nabataean sources. Little is also known of what happened to the Nabataeans after the fall of Petra and Madain Saleh. Thereafter they disappeared from history to an unknown fate.

THE OTHER MT SINAI?

One of the most persistent controversies in Biblical archaeology is the real location of Mount Sinai. Always assumed to have been on the Sinai Peninsula in Egypt, some now claim that Jebel al-Lawz in northwestern Saudi Arabia, northeast of Al-Bad, is the true location. Biblical references place Mt Sinai in the land of ancient Midian (within modern Saudi borders). Further, Paul wrote of 'Mount Sinai in Arabia' (Galatians 4:25) while the 'Arabia' of the Old Testament would have encompassed the Land of the Dedanites (near Al-Ula). Jebel al-Lawz has a strange blackened peak, something which supporters of the Sinai-in-Arabia theory claim is consistent with the story of a mountain scorched from above (Exodus 19:18). For more alleged evidence for this theory, see www.baseinstitute.org/Sinai_1.html.

As you'd expect, this theory is one which has stirred considerable debate and even anger among mainstream archaeologists and the Saudi authorities aren't exactly rushing to verify the story. They have, however, closed off the site to visitors.

Al-Andalus Hotel (☎ 633 1100; fax 633 1331; s/d SR90/130) This place, 9km from the main intersection on the road to Tabuk, is terrific value and has spacious, comfortable rooms with satellite TV.

Al-Buraq Restaurant-3 (meals SR9-20) Located about 1.5km west of the main intersection, this is an excellent cheap place to eat with seasoned kebabs that are slightly better quality than the usual.

Of the others, **Al-Deera Restaurant** (meals SR10) and **Sunset Restaurant** (meals SR10), both 600m north of the main intersection, serve a decent roasted chicken, rice and salad.

Getting There & Away

The airport (which appears in Saudia timetables as Jouf) is 28km southwest of town on the road to Domat Al-Jandal. There are two daily **Saudia** (☎ 624 4444; King Abdul Aziz St) flights to Riyadh (SR290), and less frequent services to Jeddah (SR300) and Hail (SR120).

Buses go from the **Saptco bus station** to Tabuk (SR90, six hours, two daily), Riyadh (SR200, 14 hours, two daily) and Dammam (SR190, 14 hours, one daily).

Getting Around

Sakaka has very few taxis and the only car-hire agencies are at the airport and Al-Nusl Hotel.

AROUND SAKAKA

Surrounded by some of the loneliest country in Arabia, approximately 25km west of Sakaka, stand the mysterious clusters of 3m-high stone pillars of **Rajajil** (Standing Stones; admission free; ☉ 8am-1pm Sat-Wed). Little is known

of their history, but they're thought to date from around 2000 BC and are covered in ancient Thamudic graffiti. Archaeologists guess that the stones belonged to a Bronze Age cult centre and once served an astrological purpose. According to a local legend, the stones are *rijal al-hajar* (men of stone) who were punished by God for their unfaithfulness.

The main set of four pillars is left of the gate, while several smaller (but more vertical) clusters of pillars are scattered around the enclosure.

To visit the site, you'll need a permit (p173) and a guide (ask at your hotel).

DOMAT AL-JANDAL   دومت الجندل

Domat al-Jandal is one of Saudi Arabia's little-known gems. This modest town boasts a ruined fortress, a historically significant fort and a good museum.

History

In 688 BC, Domat al-Jandal (then known as Adummatu) was mentioned in an Assyrian text as the seat of the King of the Arabs. This part of Arabia is identified with the Biblical Midian, a region known to the ancient Egyptians as Kashu. Domat al-Jandal itself appears in many Bible atlases as 'Dhuma'.

Domat al-Jandal was besieged three times by Muslim armies, including by the Prophet Mohammed himself in AD 624, before falling in 630. Two years after Mohammed's death, Domat al-Jandal tried to renounce Islam during the period known as the Rida (apostasy wars). A Muslim force under Khalid Bin al-Waled retook Domat al-Jandal in the period from 633 to 634.

Orientation & Information

The museum and Qasr Marid are 1.2km east of town, south off the main Tabuk–Sakaka road. Domat al-Jandal has few services and the only hotels are at Sakaka, 50km away.

Sights

JOUF REGIONAL MUSEUM

Informative sections on the antiquities of the Jouf region can be viewed at the **Jouf Regional Museum** (☎ 622 2151; admission free; ☺ 8am-2pm Sat-Wed). Reproductions of Lady Blunt's sketches of Sakaka and Domat al-Jandal (which she referred to as 'Jof') are also on display.

QASR MARID

There are foundations dating to Nabataean times at **Qasr Marid** (☺ sunrise-sunset), and Roman-era records of Queen Zenobia's expedition to the area in the 3rd century AD mention Marid by name. The fortress was repaired in the 19th century and became the local seat of government until the new fort built by the Al-Rashids supplanted it.

The main mud structure has towers at the four corners and some pre-Islamic brickwork is visible around the building's lower levels. The ramparts provide great views over the town and oasis.

Permits are not needed but photos are forbidden.

MOSQUE OF OMAR

This mosque is one of the oldest in Saudi Arabia and is believed to have been founded by the second caliph (successor of the Prophet Mohammed), Omar bin al-Khattab

(who ruled until AD 644) when he stopped here en route to Jerusalem.

Still in use, the mosque's lone minaret is one of the few surviving sections of the original mosque. Though not particularly tall, its carved door with red geometric patterns, windows and passageway through the bottom are wholly unlike other mosques you'll see. The mosque is off-limits to non-Muslims.

OLD DOMAT AL-JANDAL

The old mud quarter adjacent to the Mosque of Omar has been settled for almost 1000 years. Although the buildings standing there today are not that old, earlier building materials have been used (even earlier Nabataean inscriptions are visible on some stones). A clear path runs through the houses and wandering through the ruins is a pleasant way to pass an afternoon.

CITY WALL

A small portion of Domat al-Jandal's once formidable city wall has been restored and can be viewed without a permit in the desert just outside town. From the top of the wall you can easily follow the fortification's line along the low ridge to the east and along the hill to the west where the rest of the wall used to run. The watchtowers along the wall were hollow all the way to ground level.

Getting There & Away

Taxis, if you can find one, charge SR50 for the 50km trip from Sakaka, but you're better off arranging transport through your hotel in Sakaka.

Asir عسير

CONTENTS

Asir is the jewel in Saudi Arabia's crown with stunning natural wonders and distinctive cultural heritage. Here you'll find the sort of scenery that you'd never expect to see in Arabia. Home to enchanting stone, slate and mud-brick architecture nestled among towering mountains of rare beauty; forests barely a hundred kilometres from the Empty Quarter; and valleys which drop steeply down to the Red Sea coastal plain, the Asir deserves as much time as you can give it.

The name Asir means 'Difficult Country', a reference to its historical inaccessibility and hostility to those who tried to rule it from afar. Evidence of that inaccessibility remains, but modern solutions to this have been custom-built for tourists. Spectacular scenery abounds in the Asir National Park, some of it in the shadow of Saudi Arabia's highest mountain, Jebel Soudah, with plunging cliffs and modern cable cars from which to view them. Even better, the village of Habalah, accessible only by cable car, is one of the Kingdom's most breathtaking locations.

Of the towns of the Asir, Abha is pleasant and the perfect base for exploring the more mountainous country which begins on its outskirts. But the most fascinating town is Najran, hard up against the Yemeni border with closer historical ties to Yemen than Saudi Arabia. Indeed, Asir was largely an independent kingdom with links to Yemen until it was conquered by Abdul Aziz in 1922. The cultural influence of Najran's hybrid Yemeni-Saudi heritage lives on, however, and is most evident in its evocative architecture that rises up from amid the palm trees, finding its highpoint in the fort at Najran. You'll also come across lively souqs (markets), sometimes with women traders.

Another major drawcard is the temperate summer climate of the Asir mountains. You'll really appreciate this if you spend any time down on Asir's rarely visited coastline, off which lies the idyllic Farasan Islands. A visit here is a great way to round out your visit to Saudi Arabia's most surprising corner.

ASIR

HIGHLIGHTS

- Imagining yourself in Yemen while among the mud architecture and souqs of **Najran** (p135)
- Riding the cable car down off the precipice at **Jebel Soudah** (p133)
- Marvelling at the fearlessness of the ancients at the 'hanging village' of **Habalah** (p133)
- Disappearing off the beaten track and under the water at the **Farasan Islands** (p140)
- Seeking out Saudi Arabia's rare greenery in the forests around **Al-Baha** (p128)

Al-Baha
Jebel Soudah
Habalah
Najran
Farasan Islands

▪ TELEPHONE CODE: 07　　▪ POPULATION: 3.8 MILLION　　▪ AREA: 248,000 SQ KM

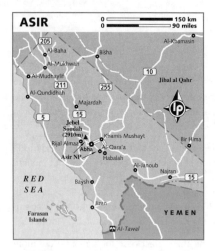

ASIR

AL-BAHA
الباحت
☎ 07

Al-Baha makes a decent stop on the road between Taif and Abha. Spend just enough time here to visit the nearby Shahba and Raghdan forests, two of almost 53 forests in the region. The only other attraction (which can wear off quite quickly) is Al-Baha's air of provinciality.

History
The tribes in the Al-Baha region trace their ancestry to the famous pre-Islamic state of Saba. Some historical accounts claim that they also established the famous state of Aksum in Abyssinia.

Orientation & Information
The Taif–Abha road cuts east–west through the heart of town. What few services there are can be found near the intersection of this road and Al-Aqiq Rd, which runs north–south through the centre. Along Al-Aqiq Rd are the post office, Saudia office and a couple of hotels, while the youth hostel and airport (30km from town) are both north of town. Along the Taif–Abha Rd near the intersection with Al-Aqiq Rd are the bus station and most of the restaurants.

Sights
There are two national forests in Al-Baha. If you've been in Saudi Arabia for a while, the chance to surround yourself with greenery is something of a novelty.

The entrance to **Shahba Forest** is just over 3km (uphill) north of the centre (take the Al-Aqiq Rd north for 1km, turn left then follow the signs), but it's a further 2km before you'll believe that the forest exists. A narrow paved road runs through the forest with tracks running off either side to small white-roofed pavilions, each with a barbecue.

The other stand of trees within striking distance of the town centre is **Raghdan Forest** (signposted off the Taif–Abha Rd in the centre), which covers an area of 600 sq km. Raghdan is about 5km north of Al-Baha city centre.

Sleeping & Eating
Summer prices mentioned here are generally from May to September.

Youth Hostel (☎ 725 0368; Sporting City; dm SR10) Just for something different, the youth hostel is so far north of the downtown area (12km) as to almost be in the next town.

Al-Baha Hotel (☎ 725 1007; fax 725 2625; Al-Aqiq Rd; s/d SR50/80, summer SR75/110) Al-Baha's only cheapie is pretty basic; the fact that prices include a service charge is a bit of a mystery. The rooms have ceiling fans but no heating.

Al-Baha Palace (☎ 725 2000; fax 725 4724; s/d SR210/280, summer SR260/335) On a hill southwest of the centre, this is Al-Baha's finest and it wears its four stars well. There's a good restaurant and great views.

Al-Zulfan Hotel (☎ 725 1053; Taif-Abha Rd; s/d SR200/260, summer SR250/350) This place is not quite as good as the Al-Baha Palace and doesn't have a whole lot of charm but it does have a reasonable restaurant.

Cheap food in Al-Baha means Turkish or Egyptian fare, mostly on the Taif–Abha road between the Al-Zulfan Hotel and the bus station.

Istanbul Servet Restaurant (snacks SR2-3, meals SR10) Across the street from the Al-Zulfan Hotel, this place good salads and *kofta* (meat balls).

Al-Bokhara Restaurant (snacks SR2-3, meals SR10) Closer to the bus station Al-Bokhara isn't bad. It's open all day, including for breakfast. A plate of *fool* (fava bean paste) and all the tea you can drink costs SR3.

Getting There & Away
There are daily **Saudia** (☎ 725 4444) flights to Riyadh (SR290) and Jeddah (SR120) from Al-Baha's small airport.

TONY WHEELER

Masmak Fortress (p86), Riyadh

TONY WHEELER

Historic mud architecture,
Dir'aiyah (p91)

Elephant Rock (p117), near Al-Ula

ANTHONY HAM

CHRIS MELLOR

Coral-and-wood houses, Al-Balad (p99), Jeddah

Al-Khuraibba tombs (p116), Al-Ula

Modern sculpture on the corniche (p102), Jeddah

There are buses to Abha (SR70, six hours, three daily), Khamis Mushayt (SR70, 6½ hours, three daily) and Taif (SR40, four hours, six daily), some with onward service to Jeddah (SR70, seven hours).

ABHA أبها

☎ 07 / pop 155,000

Abha (2200m above sea level) and its mountainous hinterland run contrary to everything people imagine about Saudi Arabia. With its mild climate and its position spread across a number of hills which are alternately bathed in sunshine and shrouded in mist, Abha is a compact and pleasant town and a good base for exploring the nearby Asir National Park. There you'll find exceptional mountain vistas (including Saudi Arabia's highest peak); well-preserved houses of stone and mud, with distinctive façades ridged with horizontal slate protrusions for deflecting rain and providing shade; and an infrastructure as close to a tourist industry you'll find in the Kingdom.

Kids will also enjoy the **funpark** located on the shores of Lake Saad, next to the Abha Palace Hotel (see p131). It often doesn't open during weekdays in the quieter winter months, but is almost always open on weekends (from Thursday night to Saturday). Entry costs SR5/2 for adults/children.

Orientation

The town centre is roughly demarcated by King Saud, King Faisal, King Khaled and Prince Abdullah Sts. Just about everything you'll need in the town itself is found within, or just outside these boundaries.

Information

Tourist information remains largely the preserve of the upmarket hotels; see p130 for details. The Asir National Park Visitors Centre (p130) has some information about the park but little about how to explore it.

There are banks all along the four main streets and most have ATMs which accept international cards. The post office and government telephone office are side by side on King Saud St. Private call cabins abound.

There are two **Internet cafés** (✆ 9am-10pm Sat-Thu, 4-10pm Fri) on the extension of King Faisal St. The one closest to the centre has 'ADSL' in English on its sign, while the other is next to a Saptco booking office.

Sights & Activities

SHADA PALACE

Built in 1927 as an office/residence for a local Saudi governor, **Shada Palace** (Admission free; ✆ 9am-1pm & 4.30-7.30pm Sat-Thu), off King Khaled St, is one of the few traditional buildings left in Abha. Its squat, mud-walled tower provides an interesting counterpoint to the modern buildings which surround it.

The building itself is arguably more interesting than the exhibits (local handicrafts and household items). The whitewashed walls are adorned with brightly painted geometric patterns, particularly the staircase which leads to the sitting rooms and the palace's former residential quarters on the upper two floors. The absence of windows gives the whole place a feel that is at once strictly private and claustrophobic. Don't forget to climb up onto the roof, although you'll find the high walls conceal any views. In ancient times, these high walls enabled the women of the royal household to sit in privacy and enjoy the cooling summer breeze.

TRADITIONAL HOUSES

There's not much of Old Abha left in the town, but there are a few examples of **traditional architecture** which can be viewed from the outside. The most well-preserved house is on King Khaled Street, next to the Great Mosque; pointing a camera anywhere around here would be tempting fate. There's another well-preserved façade just north of the intersection between King Faisal and King Fahd Sts.

JEBEL AL-AKHDAR CABLE CAR

The local predilection for cable cars is not restricted to the mountains outside Abha. From the amusement park complex alongside the Abha Palace Hotel (see Sleeping p131), a 7km **cable car** (SR30 return; ✆ 10am-6pm Wed-Fri Oct-Mar, 9am-9pm daily Apr-Sep) runs up to the southeast then turns northwest across the escarpment for stunning views on the way to the Asir National Park Visitors Centre. It then continues to the somewhat ambitiously named Jebel al-Akhdar (Green Mountain), affording great views across Abha along the way. The opening hours are not necessarily accurate and you'd be lucky to find it operating outside the high season.

ASIR

ABHA

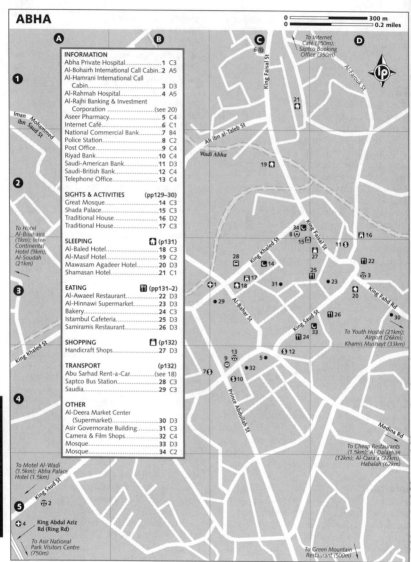

0 _____ 300 m
0 _____ 0.2 miles

To Internet
Café (350m);
Saptco Booking
Office (350m)

INFORMATION
Abha Private Hospital...................1 C3
Al-Bohairh International Call Cabin..2 A5
Al-Hamrani International Call
   Cabin.................................3 D3
Al-Rahmah Hospital....................4 A5
Al-Rajhi Banking & Investment
   Corporation ....(see 20)
Aseer Pharmacy........................5 C4
Internet Café..........................6 C1
National Commercial Bank............7 B4
Police Station..........................8 C2
Post Office.............................9 C4
Riyad Bank............................10 C4
Saudi-American Bank.................11 D3
Saudi-British Bank...................12 C4
Telephone Office....................13 C4

SIGHTS & ACTIVITIES   (pp129–30)
Great Mosque........................14 C3
Shada Palace.........................15 C3
Traditional House....................16 D2
Traditional House....................17 C3

SLEEPING   (p131)
Al-Baled Hotel.......................18 C3
Al-Masif Hotel.......................19 C2
Mawasam Agadeer Hotel............20 D3
Shamasan Hotel......................21 C1

EATING   (pp131–2)
Al-Awaeel Restaurant................22 D3
Al-Hinnawi Supermarket.............23 D3
Bakery.................................24 C3
Istambul Cafeteria...................25 D3
Samiramis Restaurant................26 D3

SHOPPING   (p132)
Handicraft Shops.....................27 D3

TRANSPORT   (p132)
Abu Sarhad Rent-a-Car...........(see 18)
Saptco Bus Station...................28 C3
Saudia................................29 C3

OTHER
Al-Deera Market Center
   (Supermarket).....................30 D3
Asir Governorate Building...........31 C3
Camera & Film Shops................32 C4
Mosque...............................33 D3
Mosque...............................34 C2

ASIR NATIONAL PARK VISITORS CENTRE
High above the southern edge of the Ring Rd sits the **Asir National Park Visitors Centre** (☎ 224 2567; admission free; ☼ 4-8pm summer). The information they have is somewhat sparse, but it's worth stopping by to see the scale model of the park and the breathtaking views from the upper floor observation deck. Inside the centre there are displays on the park's flora and fauna. If you come when it's busy, only families may be allowed in. If you come when it's quiet, it may not be open.

Tours
The three upmarket hotels in the region arrange weekend packages (from Wednesday

night to Friday lunch) which include two nights full-board accommodation, airport transfers and all sightseeing around Abha. Rates vary depending on demand and some require a minimum number of participants; prices are usually per double room. Each also requires that you are staying in their hotel:

Abha Palace Hotel (☎ 229 4444; fax 229 5555; abha palace@hotmail.com; packages from SR490) Abha.

Inter-Continental Hotel (☎ 224 7777; fax 224 4113; abha@interconti.com; packages from SR 550; Jun-Sep only) Al-Soudah.

Trident Hotel (☎ 223 3466; fax 222 0828; per person SR595) Khamis Mushayt.

Sleeping

In summer (from May to September), don't even think of arriving without a reservation, especially on weekends (Wednesday and Thursday) when prices rise by more than 50%.

BUDGET

Youth Hostel (☎ 227 0503; Sporting City; dm SR10) You'd have to be pretty desperate to stay here. It's not that the place itself is bad – it's the usual tidy youth hostel standard – but at 20km west of Abha, it's a long way from anywhere and there's no public transport.

MID-RANGE

The following six places all have satellite TV but only Arabic-language channels.

Shamasan Hotel (☎ 225 1808; s/d SR80/120, summer SR110/165) This hotel, off King Faisal St, is probably the best mid-range choice in Abha. The rooms are nothing special but are clean, and within walking distance of the centre.

Mawasam Agadeer Hotel (☎ 229 9733; King Saud St; s/d SR70/110, summer SR120/160) Another good choice, although not as accustomed to receiving tourists. This place is friendly and the rooms are decent value. The tiled floors don't exactly keep you warm in winter, but they're well-kept.

Al-Baled Hotel (☎ 226 1451; fax 224 7433; King Khaled St; s/d SR80/120, summer SR130/180) Not quite as well-maintained, the rooms here are big and bare but comfortable enough.

Al-Masif Hotel (☎ 224 2651; fax 224 2162; King Faisal St; s/d SR120/150, summer SR160/250) Also close to the centre and friendly, Al-Masif is probably not worth the extra compared to the Shamasan, but is good if you can negotiate a reduction.

Hotel Al-Bouhaira (☎ 224 6458; fax 224 7515; As-Soudah Rd; s/d SR150/250, summer SR250/350) You pay extra here for the view over Abha and Al-Saad Lake, which, given the setting, may just be worth it. It's a pleasant place and the rooms are good and spacious.

Motel Al-Wadi (☎ 229 1470; Nahran Rd; s/d/apt SR90/150/250, summer SR150/260/450) This place doesn't have the views but it does have quiet Lake Saad frontage and good (if a touch soulless) rooms with large balconies.

TOP END

Abha Palace Hotel (☎ 229 4444; fax 229 5555; abha palace@hotmail.com; Nahran Rd; s/d SR295/450, summer SR495/650; ▢ ▣ ▨ P) The Abha Palace has everything you could want from a five-star hotel – luxurious, spacious and tastefully furnished rooms; excellent service; and a good location overlooking Lake Saad about 1.5km south of the city centre. The hotel also arranges excellent guided tours of the region.

Inter-Continental Hotel (☎ 224 7777; fax 224 4113; abha@interconti.com; s/d summer SR495/675; ▢ ▣ ▨ P) Perched atop the escarpment in Al-Soudah (see p133) and originally designed as a palace for a Saudi prince, the Inter-Continental is extravagant and lavish in all the right places, not to mention huge and scenically located. Be warned, however, that to get a view of the mountains you must opt for one of the villas (from SR1500) on the hotel grounds. The hotel is only open from June to September.

Eating

Green Mountain Restaurant (☎ 229 7867; ◷ lunch & dinner; starters from SR10, mains from SR30) As the name suggests, this place sits atop the Green Mountain which overlooks Abha. The food is patchy and a touch overpriced, but the views over Abha more than make up for it. You can also smoke *sheesha* (water pipe) or just enjoy a drink on the outside terrace. Highly recommended.

There's not much fine dining to be found in Abha, but cheap and cheerful kebab and grilled chicken places abound. Some of the better ones are **Samiramis Restaurant** (King Saud St) and **Al-Awaeel Restaurant** (cnr King Saud & King Fahd Sts). The **Istambul Cafeteria** (sandwiches SR3) is located near the Al-Hinnawi supermarket and has grilled chicken, egg, beef or liver sandwiches.

ASIR

If you're planning a picnic in the national park, the Al-Hinnawi supermarket isn't bad, while there's a bakery along King Saud St.

Shopping

The only things in Abha which you won't find elsewhere are women's caftans embroidered with traditional Asiri patterns. There are several small **handicraft shops** near the Shada Palace that are worth seeking out; prices start at SR150.

Getting There & Away

AIR

Saudia (☎ 223 7777; King Khaled St; ☺ 9am-6pm Sat-Thu) has an office in the centre. There are several daily departures to Jeddah (SR190) and Riyadh (SR280), and one to Dammam (SR390). There are less frequent departures for Medina (SR310), Taif (SR140), Tabuk (SR460) and Sharurah (SR190).

BUS

The main **Saptco station** (☎ 224 3174; King Khaled St) is opposite the Great Mosque; the ticket office is in the small trailer near the southern end of the parking lot.

There are departures to Jeddah (SR120, 12 hours, 11 daily), Taif (SR100, 10 hours, three daily) and Jizan (SR45, five hours, two daily). For Riyadh, you must go to Khamis Mushayt.

Local buses run between the Abha and Khamis Mushayt bus stations every half-hour from 6.30am to 10.30pm (SR3, 35 minutes).

Getting Around

The airport is 26km from town, signposted from the Abha–Khamis Mushayt road.

You won't find many taxis in Abha; most hotels will pick you up from the bus station or airport. For exploring Asir National Park you'll need to either take a tour (see p130) or hire a car; there are car-hire agencies at the airport. In the centre, try **Abu Sarhad Rent-a-Car** (☎ 229 8335; King Khaled St).

AROUND ABHA
Asir National Park

Saudi Arabia's first national park contains some of the Kingdom's most spectacular scenery, with mountains reaching nearly 3000m before plunging down onto the coastal plain. The park encompasses some 450,000 hectares stretching from the Red Sea coast, across the mountains and east into the desert. Although you're unlikely to see any, the park, particularly the inaccessible mountain ridges above 1500m, is one of the last refuges of the Arabian leopard (see p41). More likely, you'll come across Hamadryas baboons and an array of birdlife (see p41).

The park's territory is not contiguous with a number of pockets of land – separated by towns, villages and farmlands – fenced off for protection. The park is divided into two main sections: the mountains northwest of Abha and the plains to the southeast. In each section which is open to the public, you'll find a camp site/picnic area (no charge).

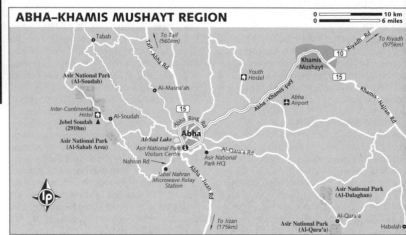

ABHA–KHAMIS MUSHAYT REGION

0 — 10 km
0 — 6 miles

Tabab
To Taif (560km)
To Riyadh (975km)
Khamis Mushayt
10
Youth Hostel
Asir National Park (Al-Soudah)
Al-Masna'ah
15
Abha Airport
Inter-Continental Hotel
Al-Soudah
Jebel Soudah (2910m)
Abha Ring Rd
15
Asir National Park (Al-Sahab Area)
Al-Sad Lake
Abha
Asir National Park Visitors Centre
Al-Qara'a Rd
Asir National Park HQ
Nahran Rd
Jabal Nahran Microwave Relay Station
Asir National Park (Al-Dalaghan)
To Jizan (175km)
Asir National Park (Al-Qara'a)
Al-Qara'a
Al-Qara'a
Habalah

AL-SOUDAH

Al-Soudah is jaw-droppingly beautiful. Located close to the summit of the Kingdom's highest peak, Jebel Soudah (2910m), this is the place to come for precipitous cliffs, deep valleys and mountain tops disappearing into the clouds. There is a camp site a few kilometres beyond the Inter-Continental Hotel (for details on the hotel, see p131).

There's no better way to enjoy the views than taking the **As-Sawdah Cable Car** (☎ 229 1111; SR50 return; 2-5pm Thu-Fri Oct-Mar, 9am-9pm daily Apr-Sep); it's well signposted on the approaches from Abha. Disappearing over the edge of the escarpment, it drops down into the valley with wonderful views all the way, including stone villages, terraced fields, juniper forests off in the distance and even the occasional defensive watchtower.

At the foot of the cable car, take a bus or taxi ride (15 minutes) to **Rijal Almaa**, a traditional, centuries-old village of multistorey, stone fortress houses. One of the houses has been beautifully restored and converted into the **Alma Museum** (☎ Abha 229 1111; admission SR20; 9am-8pm Sat-Thu, 2-8pm Fri). The five-storey façade spread across five conjoined buildings is extraordinary with its austere stone and clay offset by white-washed window frames. The interior's 19 rooms are crowded with almost 2000 exhibits, including household items, costumes, weaponry, jewellery and sacred texts, all from the local area. It's a praiseworthy local initiative which is very professionally run and worth supporting.

AL-DALAGHAN & AL-QARA'A

The main park areas southeast of Abha are **Al-Dalaghan** (Dalgan), 26km from Abha, and, further down the same road, **Al-Qara'a** (Qara), after which the road is named. Both areas consist of a large area of rounded boulders and small evergreen trees; Al-Qara'a sits on the edge of the escarpment, which means that the scenery is better. Wild baboons can often be seen in both areas.

HABALAH

Don't miss Habalah, 60km southeast of Abha and like no place on earth. Although a little overwhelmed by the modern paraphernalia which surrounds it, this deserted village is a fascinating remnant of old Arabia.

To reach the ruins of the village, take the **cable car** (☎ 254 1919; adult/child return SR30/15;

THE HANGING VILLAGE OF HABALAH

Habalah is a place apart. The name means 'rope valley' or 'the ropes', a reference to the fact that this village, built of stone hewn from rock at the foot of sheer 300m cliffs, was once accessible only by *habal* (rope ladders). The village was settled about 350 years ago by members of the Khatani tribe who sought the most inaccessible location as a means of protection from the Ottomans. Despite seeming to cling to the precipice, the village was almost self-sufficient, sustained by terraced farms growing coffee, fruit and vegetables as well as being used for raising sheep, chickens and goats. If you look carefully along the rim of the cliff above the village you can still see the iron posts to which ropes were tied to lower people, goods and frightened livestock to the village. Remarkably, it was inhabited until about 1980.

10am-6pm Wed-Fri Oct-Mar, 9am-9pm daily Apr-Sep). It's a short ride and not for the faint-hearted, but the views en route are breathtaking and among the best you'll see in the Kingdom.

Once down in the village, leave behind the modern terracing and drinks stalls and scramble across the farming terraces and between the decrepit houses. It takes a considerable feat of imagination to picture living here – a simple look up the cliffs or down the valley can conjure up something akin to claustrophobia. The best preserved houses are 100m north and south of the cable car station; look for the carved interior doors.

If you can't face the descent (or if the cable car is not running), it's still well worth the 60km drive out from Abha. The visitors centre next to the upper cable car station has restaurants, a quite extensive children's playground and an open terrace from where the views to the village, valley and distant mountains are wonderful. It costs SR6/3 for adults/children to enter the complex, a fee that's waived if you take the cable car or if the gatekeeper feels like it.

Most people choose to visit from Abha, but if you can't tear yourself away you can stay at one of the **villas** (☎ 226 0336; fax 226 2503; 2-bedroom villas incl breakfast from SR500).

KHAMIS MUSHAYT   خميس مشيط
☎ 07 / pop 300,000

Surrounded by farms in one of the King-dom's most fertile corners, the sprawling city of Khamis Mushayt (Khamis) has an air of prosperity, which only partly com-pensates for the fact that the town, although pleasant enough, has little to see. The main reason to come here is for the weekly souq, which is held on Thursday (*yowm al-khamis* means Thursday in Arabic).

Khamis Mushayt also occupies a some-what ambivalent place in modern Saudi Arabia – it was from the giant King Khaled Air Base that US 'Stealth' bombers attacked Baghdad during the 1991 Gulf War.

See p130 for details of tours to explore the region.

Orientation & Information
Apart from the bus station which is northeast of the city centre, the central souq area is the only place you're likely to need. Surrounding the markets are two of the hotels, cheap res-taurants and banks; the Arab National Bank (with ATM) is opposite the square.

Khamis Souq
Like all the souqs across the southwest of the Kingdom, **Khamis souq** (🕙 9am-1pm & 5-11pm Sat-Thu, 5-11pm Fri) has a decent selection of silver jewellery; there's more here than further south in Najran, although the quality is not as consistent. The **silver souq** (🕙 9am-1pm & 5-11pm Sat-Thu, 5-11pm Fri) can be difficult to find; start in the main square with your back to the Mushayt Palace Hotel, turn left, then left again around the side of the building. From there, turn right across a small intersection and continue straight for about 100m. On your left you should see an alley with a col-lection of about a dozen silver shops.

Amidst the clamour of household goods, fruit and vegetables and silver jewellery, you'll also be able to follow your nose to the **spice souq** where cloves, henna and car-damom are abundant, though these days frankincense is extremely rare. Other local products to watch out for are woven mats and baskets with pyramidal lids which are typical of this part of the Asir.

Sleeping & Eating
Al-Azizia Hotel (☎ 222 0900; fax 222 1128; Main Square; s/d std SR80/100, deluxe SR130/160; summer s/d std SR120/150, deluxe SR195/240) This place is central, friendly and pretty good value. The stand-ard rooms are simple if uninspiring and come with a small TV; the deluxe rooms are more tastefully decorated and have a large TV (Arabic channels only).

Mushayt Palace Hotel (☎ 223 6220; fax 223 5272; s/d SR160/180, summer SR270/312) Central and just across the square from Al-Azizia Hotel, the Mushayt Palace has simple rooms and foreign-language satellite channels.

Al-Fersan Hotel (☎ 222 1453; fax 222 0683; Abha Khamis Mushayt Rd; s/d SR70/90, summer SR110/140) Al-Fersan, 4km west of the city centre on the south side of the road, has not aged par-ticularly gracefully. It does have the cheap-est habitable rooms in Khamis Mushayt, although you'll need to factor in taxi fares to get to the market.

Trident Hotel (☎ 223 3466; fax 222 0828; cnr Abha Khamis Mushayt Rd & King Faisal Rd; s/d SR269/391, sum-mer SR345/460) Undoubtedly the best hotel in Khamis Mushayt, the Trident has attractive rooms and good service. It also organises weekend sightseeing and accommodation packages to help you make the most of your time in Asir.

Chinese Palace Restaurant (King Faisal Rd; starters from SR8; mains from SR30) For a reasonably up-market meal, try this restaurant about 100m down the street from the Trident Hotel. The food is not exactly spectacular, but it can be a welcome change after days of grilled chicken and rice.

Plenty of small Indian, Turkish and Fili-pino restaurants surround the main square particularly in the small streets behind the Mushayt Palace Hotel. At all of them, expect to eat well in basic dining areas for around SR10. The friendly Turkey Restaurant, im-mediately behind the Mushayt Palace Hotel, is probably the pick of the bunch.

Getting There & Away
Khamis Mushayt's Saudia office is on the Abha–Khamis Mushayt road one block northwest of the Trident Hotel. See the p132 for air services from the Abha airport.

The **bus station** (☎ 221 8040) is around 3km northwest of the main square and is Saptco's hub for all of Asir. Departures include Jeddah (SR100, 12 hours, 12 daily), Riyadh (SR135, 14 hours, 10 daily), Bisha (SR42, four hours, two daily), Taif (SR105, 10 hours, three daily), Jizan (SR43, five hours, four daily),

ASIR

Najran (SR45, five hours, three daily) and Dammam (SR210, 18 hours, two daily).

Local buses to Abha (SR3, 35 minutes) leave every half-hour from 6.30am to 10.30pm, either from the main square or from the bus station.

NAJRAN   نجران
☎ 07 / pop 117,000

The oasis at Najran, surrounded by mountains and close to the Yemeni border, is one of Saudi Arabia's hidden gems. With towering mud-brick, fortress-like homes strung out along the wadi (riverbed, dry except during the rainy season) and an exceptional mud-brick fort, Najran is like nowhere else in the Kingdom. Najran is also home to a fascinating cultural mix that owes as much to the northern Yemeni highlands as it does to the rest of Saudi Arabia. Najranis are both garrulous and deeply conservative and here you'll see local Bedouin women with henna tattoo marks and men wearing the *jambiyya* (silver dagger) in their belts.

History

Wadi Najran's fertile soil, plentiful water supply and strategic location have ensured it a colourful past. The small farming settlements here prospered in ancient times from passing frankincense trade caravans (see The Frankincense Trade below) which came over the mountains of Yemen and then branched off to the Hejaz or Riyadh.

Najran's forerunner, Al-Ukhdood, was already an important city during the 6th century BC when the Sabaeans swept over much of this corner of Arabia. By the 1st century BC, the wadi was known as far away as Greece; Greek geographer Strabo described Al-Ukhdood as a town with seven wells.

The Himyarites arrived around AD 250 and the town became a Christian settlement (see the Trench p139). Christianity gave way to Islam in 630–31 (10 AH) and, within a generation, the town's Christians were expelled from the country in line with a saying of the Prophet that 'there shall not remain two religions in the land of Arabia'.

Najran was part of the First Saudi Empire in the late 18th and early 19th centuries, whereafter the town was fought over by the independent kingdoms of Asir and Yemen. Saudi troops finally took control of the city in 1934, one of the last places in the Kingdom to come under Saudi rule. Shortly thereafter the Imam (religious leader) of Yemen ceded Najran to King Abdul Aziz.

Orientation & Information

Najran is strung out over nearly 30km. It's an easy place to find your way around, but it's not possible to do so without a car because of the large distances involved, and the dangers to pedestrians around the busy streets.

The roads to Najran from Riyadh and Abha intersect at what could loosely be called the centre of the modern town. The east–west continuation of the road to/from Riyadh is King Abdul Aziz Rd. Just about everything you'll need (hotels, restaurants, transportation, and banks) are located on or just off this main road, particularly west of the intersection in Faisaliyeh.

THE FRANKINCENSE TRADE

The far south of the Arabian Peninsula (modern Yemen and neighbouring Oman) is one of the few places in the world where frankincense is grown. The fact of its scarceness alone was sufficient to make this strange, aromatic plant from the deserts of the south one of the most lucrative products in the ancient world, exporting to, among other places, Rome, where southern Arabia was known as 'Arabia Felix'. In 25 BC, the Roman general Aelius Gallus marched on southern Arabia to establish Roman control over the trade. En route, his army passed through the Asir highlands and conquered Najran, but he was forced to return empty-handed due a lack of water. Arabia kept its secrets.

The trade in frankincense reached its peak in the 2nd century AD when 3000 tonnes of frankincense – by then a staple in rituals of the world's major religions – were exported from southern Arabia to Greece, Rome and the wider Mediterranean. Theirs was a luxury trade. Apart from frankincense, the caravans carried spices, ebony, silk and fine textiles from India, as well as rare woods, feathers, animal skins, and gold from East Africa.

The trade declined in the 3rd century, but there remained sufficient wealth and markets for Arabia to survive on frankincense proceeds and in relative comfort for a further three centuries.

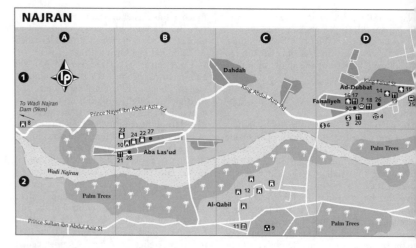

Sights & Activities

NAJRAN FORT (QASR AL-IMARA)

Najran's most outstanding monument, **Najran Fort** (Admission free; ☾ 8am-sunset), has all the signature characteristics of the Asir region: mud-brick fortifications, fairy-tale turrets, crenellations with whitewash flourishes and small windows suggesting more than they reveal. Throughout the fort (which was also a palace), superbly carved doors and window shutters open onto whitewashed rooms with ceilings supported by palm-trunk beams.

Construction began in 1942 and the fort's 60 rooms were designed to form a self-sustaining complex – perhaps a reflection of the fact that Najran's new Saudi rulers had less than complete faith in the Imam of Yemen's renunciation of his claim to Najran. The fort fell out of everyday use in 1967, when Saudi–Yemeni relations stabilised.

The main entrance of the fort is through a beautifully carved **door**. At the end of the entrance passageway on the right, a small **courtroom** faces onto the decidedly claustrophobic **prison cell**. Further around to the right are the **dining room**, **kitchen** and **slaughter room**, as well as the fort's **mosque**; note the tiny, almost perfunctory, 'flight' of three steps next to the mihrab (vaulted niche, which indicates the direction of Mecca). Next to the mosque, in the centre of the southern courtyard, stands a restored **well** which dates to pre-Islamic times.

The large building in the centre of the complex was the **prince's palace** – downstairs was the preserve of animals, while the upper floor included the residence of the royal entourage. From there a bridge leads to the rooms above the fort's entrance. Straight ahead is the **prince's office**. On the north side is the room of the prince's secretaries, while south is the long **majlis** (reception room), where the king held audiences. Up on the roof of the main gate is what local guides call the **secret room** – it was here that sensitive matters of state were discussed away from prying ears.

At ground level, the northern courtyard contains (from east to west) the **servants' quarters**, **communications room** and **garrison barracks**.

The fort is around 14km west of the intersection of the Abha–Riyadh road.

NAJRAN MUSEUM

This **museum** (☎ 542 5292; fax 542 5120; Prince Sultan ibn Abdul Aziz St; admission free; ☾ 8am-2pm Sat-Wed) is compact but excellent. Alongside the usual generic Saudi displays are informative sections on the frankincense trade, Arabia's southern kingdoms and the history of Wadi Najran and Al-Ukhdood. Of particular interest are the photographs taken by the author/diplomat/explorer/spy Harry St John Philby in 1936.

AL-UKHDOOD

Immediately behind the museum are the scattered remnants of **Al-Ukhdood** (Admission free; ☾ sunrise-sunset). Founded as early as the 7th century BC, this former farming community

Scale: 0 — 2 km / 0 — 1 mile

EATING (p138)
Al-Ramal Ash-Shaabi.................17 D1
Cafeteria Al-Beek........................18 D1
Horizon...19 D1
Restaurant Al-Khifr....................20 D1
Samerames Restaurant...............21 B2

SHOPPING (p138)
Basket Souq..................................22 B2
Dagger Souq.................................23 B2
Souq al-Harim.............................24 B2

TRANSPORT (p138)
Saptco Bus Station......................25 D1
Saudia...26 D1

OTHER
Date Souq.....................................27 B2
Fruit & Vegetable Souq...............28 B2
Mosque...29 E1
Municipality Building.................30 D1
Prince's Palace.............................31 E1

INFORMATION
Al-Rajhi Banking & Investment
    Corporation (Ladies' Branch).......1 E1
Al-Rawdah Pharmacy.......................2 E1
Arab National Bank (ATM)..............3 D1
International Call Cabin....................4 D1
King Khaled Hospital........................5 E1
National Commercial Bank (ATM)...6 D1
Petrol Station...........................(see 6)
Post Office..7 D1
Saudi-American Bank.............(see 20)

SIGHTS & ACTIVITIES (pp136–7)
Al-Aan Palace.................................8 A1
Al-Ukhdood....................................9 C2
Najran Fort (Qasr Al-Imara).........10 B2
Najran Museum............................11 C2
Traditional Houses.......................12 C2

SLEEPING (p137)
Najran Holiday Inn.......................13 F1
Najran Hotel.................................14 D1
Okhdood Hotel.............................15 D1
Youth Hostel................................16 D1

urvived possibly until the 10th century AD. Such was its significance that it was mentioned in the Quran (see the Trench p139).

Most of the extensive site is probably only of interest to those with a specialist archaeological interest, although picking your way through the crumbling stone walls and searching for Thaumudic inscriptions can be a pleasant way to pass an afternoon.

A permit is required to visit the site (p173).

AL-AAN PALACE
One of the best preserved pieces of Asiri architecture remaining in Najran is the **Al-Aan Palace** (Saadan Palace; Prince Nayef ibn Abdul Aziz Rd). From its vantage point overlooking the wadi, the mud palace rises five-storeys high. Local guides claim it dates back 300 years, but it was probably the home of a wealthy sheikh in the early 20th century.

The palace is closed to visitors, but the views over the wadi from the parking lot adjacent to the main gate are superb.

WADI NAJRAN DAM
Najranis are very proud of their dam; it's the largest dam in the Kingdom and allows the control of water flowing from the Yemeni highlands without fears of flash flooding. Frankly, there's not a lot to see at the dam itself, so unless dams are your thing, you could probably give it a miss. Around 6km before the dam, there is a checkpoint; without a local guide, you may not be allowed to pass.

Tours
The Najran Holiday Inn (below) has excellent tours of Najran and the surrounds. Half-day tours (SR150) take in all the major sites, while full-day tours (SR250) allow you more time at each and also take in the souqs and a drive past some of the older houses in the wadi. They can also arrange overnight camping expeditions in the Empty Quarter or excursions to Bir Hima (p146).

Sleeping
Youth Hostel (☎ 522 5019; dm SR10) Najran's youth hostel, off King Faisal St, is small, but clean and friendly and is in the Faisaliyeh district about 5km west of the intersection of the Abha–Riyadh roads; ask for the *bayt ash-shabab* (youth hostel).

Okhdood Hotel (☎ 522 2614; fax 522 2434; King Faisal St; s/d SR100/150) Not a bad choice, the Okhdood has aged considerably, but the rooms are simple and generally tidy and come with satellite TV.

Najran Hotel (☎ 522 1750; fax 522 2993; s/d 90/130) Near the Okhdood, and clearly visible from King Abdul Aziz Rd, the Najran Hotel is similar if slightly better value.

Najran Holiday Inn (☎ 522 5222; fax 522 1148; www.holiday-inn.com; King Abdul Aziz Rd; s/d SR400/550) In need of renovation, the Holiday Inn, 4.5km east of the Abha–Riyadh roads intersection, is nonetheless the best hotel in Najran and a good base from which to explore the city. The rooms are comfortable though they lack the attention to detail you'd expect for the price.

ASIR

THE TRADITIONAL HOUSES OF NAJRAN

The old houses which are so distinctive of the region are dotted throughout the wadi, although sadly most are decaying and uninhabitable. Those who have been to northern Yemen will recognise the design with smaller windows at ground level to keep out intruders, and widening windows the higher you go (up to 11 storeys, although few such houses remain). The ground level was generally for animals, while human inhabitants lived upstairs. Often these houses are clustered together around a central courtyard, so that members of the same family or tribe could live together in the same *howi* (compound). Also worth watching out for are the mud watchtowers and turrets around the perimeter. The designs date back 4000 years although most of what you'll see was built no more than 50 years ago.

The greatest concentration of these houses is to be found along the dirt tracks and amid the palm trees of the Al-Qabil district, across the road to the north of the museum. While you could try to find these on your own, you're likely to have better luck if you go with a guide (see p137).

Eating

Al-Ramal Ash-Shaabi (Main Rd; mains from SR5) This is one of Najran's best bets, near the youth hostel (turn right out of the hostel and right again). The kebabs and grilled chicken dishes are excellent. At breakfast they do great *hadas* (a spicy bean dish eaten with pita bread) for SR5. Look for the models of two Yemeni-style houses framing the entrance.

Samerames Restaurant (Grilled chicken/mutton & rice SR10) Out near the fort, this restaurant is so-so, but one of the few options for lunch if you're at this end of town.

There are very few restaurants east of the intersection of the Abha–Riyadh roads, while there are plenty to the west of it, particularly along King Abdul Aziz Rd in the Faisaliyeh area. Among these, Restaurant Al-Khifr is fast and cheerful, as are Horizon and Cafeteria Al-Beek; the sign for the latter is only in Arabic. As with all Najran's cheapies, *shwarmas* (grilled meat in pita bread) or grilled chicken with aromatic rice are the order of the day and you'll eat well for SR10.

Shopping

Najran has some small but worthwhile souqs and the region is particularly noted for its silver jewellery which mostly comes from Yemen. Immediately south of Najran Fort is the **Souq al-Harim** (Ladies' Souq) where, unusually for Saudi Arabia, women run shops and serve male customers. They sell Bedouin jewellery, including *qiladah* (triangular pendants with a single stone), *hazm* (belts) and *iqd* (necklaces). You may even come across the odd pendants made from Maria Theresa dollars. Remember that these women are some of the toughest bargainers you'll encounter.

Najran is also famous for its basket weaving; some of the stuff in the markets come from Yemen. The **basket souq** is across the road from the Souq al-Harim.

The **dagger souq**, around 400m west of the fort, is worth visiting just for the atmosphere. It's very small but lined with old men selling (mostly to locals) a range of daggers which some of them still wear. It can be difficult to find without a local guide who, in any event, will be more likely able to get you a realistic price (from SR100 up to SR25,000) if you intend to buy.

Getting There & Away

AIR

The **Saudia** (☎ 522 3333; King Abdul Aziz Rd) office is located about 3km west of the Abha–Riyadh roads intersection. There are daily flights to Riyadh (SR280) and Jeddah (SR250), and less frequent flights to Dammam (SR390), Jizan (SR150) and Sharurah (SR120).

BUS & SERVICE TAXIS

The **Saptco bus station** (☎ 522 1781; King Abdul Aziz Rd) is 1.7km west of the Abha–Riyadh roads intersection. There are daily departures for Riyadh (SR135, 12 hours, three daily), Jeddah (SR130, 14 hours, two daily) via Abha (SR40, 3½ hours) and Khamis Mushayt (SR40, three hours), and Sharurah (SR50, 3½ hours, one daily).

Getting Around

The airport is around 20km northwest of Najran; a taxi should cost around SR30 depending on your negotiating skills.

None of Najran's taxis have meters and most operate as shared shuttles between

Faisaliyeh and Najran Fort at SR3 per person. If you want the taxi to yourself expect to pay at least SR10.

JIZAN   جزان
☎ 07 / pop 71,000
This grubby, southern Red Sea port is a jumping-off point for Farasan Island. The town does have an Ottoman-era fort and a lively old souq, but most people only stay long enough to catch a boat to the island, especially outside the winter months when the heat and humidity can be unbearable.

Orientation & Information
The heart of the town is between Al-Tawhid Square (the huge roundabout where the road from Abha and the airport road converge) and the corniche (coastal road). The bus station is just off the corniche. The post office and telephone office are two doors apart in a side street that branches off the corniche opposite the main entrance to the port. The airport is about 5km northeast of the centre.

Sights
All the sights in this somewhat grubby port can be seen in an hour. The **Ottoman Fort** overlooking the town is quite evocative, but, as it sits in a police compound, enjoy it from a distance and don't even think of pointing a camera in its direction.

By contrast, the **old souq** is one of the last traditional souqs left in the Kingdom.

There's not really much for the traveller to buy (pottery is the main attraction in these parts and you may find the odd stall), but the atmosphere and smells are what you come here for.

Sleeping & Eating
Youth Hostel (☎ 322 1875, ext 242; Sports City; dm SR10) If you've stayed in Saudi youth hostels before, you'll know what to expect – simple, men-only accommodation that is kept pretty clean.

Al-Hayat Gizan Hotel (☎ 322 1055; fax 317 1774; Corniche; s/d SR230/300; 🛋) This four-star place south of the centre (next to the sea port) is very comfortable and the best place to stay in town.

Atheel Hotel (☎ 317 1101; fax 317 1094; Main Roundabout; s/d incl breakfast SR150/250; 🛋 🛋) This is the next best choice and the swimming pool is a plus.

Gizan Sahari Hotel (☎ 322 0440; fax 317 1386; s/d SR120/160, without bathroom SR75/120) In town, just north of the Main Rd between the roundabout and the corniche, this place is fine for a night but nothing more. The hotel has no sign in English.

Lulua Al-Sahel Broast & Restaurant (mains SR10) The pick of the cheap restaurants around Jizan. On the main road near the junction with the corniche, you'll feast on large servings of rice with chicken, meat or vegetables (SR10).

Turkey Restaurant (mains SR10) Back by the big roundabout, this is another good place to get a quick meal.

Getting There & Away
There are several daily **Saudia** (☎ 323 3333) flights to Jeddah (SR200) and to Riyadh (SR320), with less frequent departures for Najran (SR150) and for Sharurah (SR190). Note that Jizan is spelled 'Gizan' in Saudia's timetables.

The **Saptco bus station** (☎ 317 1265) is just off the corniche between the junction with the Main Rd and the entrance to the port. There are buses to Jeddah (SR105, 10 hours, five daily) and Abha (SR32, five hours, four daily).

To get to Farasan Island, covered launches (SR350 divided by number of passengers, 55 minutes) cross from the fishing port in Jizan to the island around the clock. A car ferry also sails from the main harbour to Farasan

THE COASTAL PLAIN OF TIHAMAH

Western Saudi Arabia is dominated by mountains which run from the Gulf of Aqaba to the Bab el-Mandab straits which separate Yemen from Africa. In the shadow of these mountains stretches the Tihamah plain, 2100km in length but rarely wider than 40km.

While Mecca and Medina are the spiritual homes of Islam, the people of the Tihamah played an extraordinary role in taking Islam to the world. In the 11th century, with Islamic communities across North Africa splitting into schismatic sects and vulnerable to attacks by local Berber tribes, the Bani Hilal, a tribe from the Tihamah, were enlisted by the Fatimid rulers in Cairo to migrate en masse. The result was devastating: 200,000 Bani Hilal families swept across North Africa displacing the Berber tribes. In an unprecedented demographic shift, the Bani Hilal laid the foundations for Arab and Orthodox Islam's dominance across the Maghreb. Members of the Bani Hilal remain in the Tihamah, but their connections to the outside world are utterly unlike the more insular traditions of the tribes of the Arabian interior.

The journey has also been made in reverse. Over the centuries, many of the pilgrims who passed through on their way to Mecca decided to stay. As a result, the plain south of Jeddah and all the way to Jizan, is one of the most culturally diverse regions in this kingdom of arms-length multiculturalism. The largest communities are descendants of East African pilgrims who never went home. Their influence is evident in the clothing (bright colours are the norm), the architecture (thatched roofs are common) and the spiritual landscape (this is one of the most liberal places in the Kingdom). When the traveller Wilfred Thesiger passed through here in the 1940s, he painted a picture of a world wholly different from the rest of Arabia: '...we wandered through the Tihama, the hot coastal plain that lies between the Red Sea and the mountains, passing through villages of daub and wattle huts reminiscent of Africa. The people here were of uncommon beauty, and pleasantly easy and informal in their manners. We watched them, dressed in loin-cloths and with circlets of scented herbs upon their flowing hair, dancing in the moonlight to the quickening rhythm of the drums at the annual festivals...'

Island (free of charge, four hours, from 7am Saturday to Wednesday).

FARASAN ISLANDS جزر فرسان
☎ 07

This little bit of unspoiled paradise would be the site of a booming resort if it were anywhere but Saudi Arabia. As it is, it's quiet and a wonderful escape from the mainland.

Farasan, the main island, is part of an archipelago which lies about 40km off the coast of Jizan. It's the only island with any significant number of inhabitants (most of the other islands are little more than tiny outcrops of rock). The area is rich in marine life and diving is a possibility here; the shallow, plankton-rich waters are home to rays, dolphins, the giant whale shark and a huge variety of fish. The islands also have some of the few remaining stretches of coastal mangrove – the habitat of the endangered dugon – on the Red Sea.

On land, the Farasan and several of the larger islands are home to a distinct island species of small striped gazelle. Birds are another drawcard for getaway nature-lovers; the islands lie on major migratory routes.

The small town of Farasan has several surviving traditional houses built from coral with intricately decorated and carved façades. These were the homes of former merchants and pearl dealers, and one the **House of Rifai**, is now a small museum. There's also a small **Turkish Fort** on the edge of the main town. Both of these attractions are accessible only if you arrange a visit with the Farasan Hotel.

Farasan Hotel (☎ 316 0876; farasanhotel@yahoo .com; r SR250), next to the hospital in the town centre, is the impressive hub and sole operator of the island's fledgling tourism industry. It organises land tours, beach picnics, sea excursions and full-day and overnight guided sea trips for fishing, snorkelling and reef diving off the 70 islands (from SR250 per person inclusive; minimum six passengers). Apart from that, the rooms are comfortable, there's a restaurant and the staff are very helpful.

The Empty Quarter

الربع الخالي

CONTENTS

There is something about deserts which has a peculiar hold over the Western imagination and they don't come any more evocative than the Rub al-Khali, the Empty Quarter. Having drawn such eminent explorers as Wilfred Thesiger, Bertram Thomas and Harry St John Philby, and fed some of the finest pieces of travel literature, the Empty Quarter is home everything that is so curiously inspiring to those who don't have to live there – sand dunes as if sculpted by an artist, an abundance of solitude and the fleeting footprints of nomads and their camels. This is a desert like no other, and includes the largest continuous body of sand on the planet. It remains one of the last great empty spaces on the world map and, in its heart, there are still places where few human beings have ever passed.

The history of the Empty Quarter is written not in books but in the oral history of story-telling as recounted around the Bedouin campfire. For the Bedouins, the history of the Sands is a story of daring raids, tribal wars and alliances and the endless search for water.

Shadowed on its western extremity by a modern road, the Empty Quarter is easy to enter, but as it is even easier to get lost, it should only be done after careful planning. Along its fringe stand ancient cities (Al-Faw) and evidence of ancient civilisations (Bir Hima) who enjoyed a much more bountiful land than exists here today and left behind rock art telling their story. And not far into the desert, a few hardy animals remain, most notably in the 'Uruq Bani Ma'arid Protected Area, south of Sulayyil, which is one of the last refuges for the Arabian oryx.

If you can't understand all the fuss about deserts, then save yourself the considerable trouble of visiting. But if you love deserts, don't miss the Empty Quarter.

HIGHLIGHTS

- Sleeping under the stars, surrounded by sand dunes and soaking up the silence on a **tour** (p145) in the heart of Arabia near Sharurah

- Marvelling at the achievements of Harry St John Philby and Wilfred Thesiger in **Sulayyil** (p144)

- The dramatic scenery on the road between **Najran** and **Sharurah** (p146)

- Imagining the great trading caravans crossing the sands to the ancient city of **Al-Faw** (p146)

- Enjoying the pre-Islamic rock carvings of **Bir Hima** (p146)

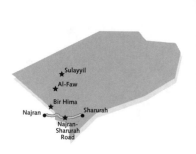

- AREA: 655,000 SQ KM

EMPTY QUARTER

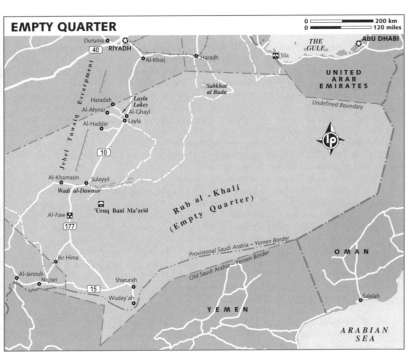

LAYLA   ليلى

Although officially part of Riyadh Province, the agricultural town of Layla (which, according to local legend, was named after the heroine in a Bedouin love story) stands on the northwestern fringe of the Empty Quarter. These days, it's little more than a waystation along the road from Riyadh to Najran or Abha; a place to eat and fill your petrol tank.

Never one to be impressed by towns, Wilfred Thesiger described Layla, then with a population of 4000, as being dun-coloured and full of flat-roofed mud buildings. Although the population has grown and modern buildings have replaced the old, you're unlikely to be more impressed than Thesiger upon arrival. Incidentally, it was here that Thesiger met Harry St John Philby who had earlier secured Thesiger's release from captivity at Sulayyil.

Layla is also a conservative town, a former stronghold of the *ikhwan*, the Wahhabi brotherhoods who helped Ibn Saud come to power but who later turned against him (p24).

If you find yourself stuck here for the night (try very hard not to), there are a few very basic **rest houses** (per person SR50) along the main road at both the northern and southern ends of town. They're often attached to petrol station and restaurant complexes, signed only in Arabic and not places where women will be welcome. Prices are negotiable as truck drivers pay by the hour.

Around Layla

West of Layla runs the **Jebel Tuwaiq Escarpment** which offers some superb scenery and picturesque villages which are worth visiting if you have the time. From Layla, a small road runs west-northwest up onto the escarpment and the villages of **Wasit** then **Al-Ahmar** (70km). From 14km north of Layla, a similar road runs northwest off the highway up to **Haradah** (74km) via **Al-Ghayl**, while 37km southwest of Layla another road leads west up to **Al-Haddar** (60km). For all of these roads, a 4WD vehicle is recommended.

Northwest of Layla are the so-called **Layla Lakes**, Saudi Arabia's only two natural lakes,

THE SANDS

The Empty Quarter (Rub al-Khali), the 'Abode of Silence', conjures up all that was romantic and forbidden about Arabia. European adventurers all dreamt of conquering it, while the Bedouin, who called it simply 'the Sands', looked upon it as a formidable world of necessity, less enamoured with the beauty of a sand dune than concerned about the number of days' travel to the next well.

The Rub al-Khali covers 655,000 sq km, an area larger than France. The Rub al-Khali is connected to the northern Al-Nafud desert (65,000 sq km) by a sand corridor known Al-Dahna which crosses the Riyadh Dammam Highway northeast of the capital. In the southwest, the desert is 800m above sea level and descends gradually to sea level in the northeast. Beneath the sands are gypsum and gravel plains, while east and northeast are *sabkhas* (salt flats). In the far east are the quicksands of Umm al-Samim (mostly in Oman), visited by explorer and writer Wilfred Thesiger and reputed by Bedouins to have swallowed up entire raiding parties.

The breathtakingly sculpted sand dunes for which the Empty Quarter is famous can rise over 300m and form vast chains of longitudinal dune ridges stretching over hundreds of kilometres, while you'll also encounter lone barchan (crescent-shaped) dunes of rare beauty. Pushed by the wind, sand dunes can move at a rate of up to 30m per year, something which villages on the desert fringe can only partially counteract through the planting of wind-breaks such as tamarisk trees.

The desert is also home to a surprising diversity of wildlife, including the Arabian wolf, Cape hare, sand cat, red fox, caracal (desert lynx) and spiny tailed lizard, although your chances of seeing any of these are extremely small. Sadly, numerous species have been driven to the edge of extinction by hunting, overgrazing and damage to vegetation by 4WD vehicles. Those which are no longer seen in the Sands include the striped hyena, jackal and honey badger, while several species have been reintroduced: the Arabian oryx (see The Return of the Arabian Oryx p40), the ostrich, houbara bustard (p41) and sand gazelle are among them.

In all this space, there are just 37 known species of plants, only 20 of which are found in the desert proper. However, on the rare occasions that it does rain (less than 35mm a year), plants which can survive for years beneath the surface come to life and carpet the sands lightly with green.

which were once rich in birdlife and a popular spot for water-skiing for Riyadh expats. However, the water has been receding for years and the only people to visit are locals on weekend picnics. You'll need a 4WD and directions from a local to reach the lakes.

SULAYYIL السليل

☎ 01

The main reasons to come to Sulayyil, 552km southwest of Riyadh, are to launch an expedition into the Empty Quarter (see Visiting the Empty Quarter opposite) or as a stopping-off point for your visit to Al-Faw (p146). Otherwise, it's a singularly unattractive town.

Wilfred Thesiger was imprisoned here in the late 1940s on the orders of Ibn Saud and he was greeted by spitting elders, taunting children and generally 'fanatical and unpleasant' people who freely expressed their hope that the infidel would soon be put to death. As a Muslim under the protection of Ibn Saud, Harry St John Philby was received much more graciously a decade earlier.

Sleeping & Eating

Muslim or not, the days of hostile receptions from the inhabitants of Sulayyil are long past, but the quality of accommodation is anything but welcoming; there are very basic rest houses (with cheap restaurants attached) like those in Layla all along the main road (most petrol stations have one). About 30km south of Sulayyil there's a **Sasco Rest House** (Saudi Automotive Services Company; tw SR150, mini-apartments SR250) which is infinitely preferable. Room are less for Sasco members; see p181. There's also a restaurant, supermarket and mechanic's shop on the premises.

Getting There & Away

There are **Saudia** (☎ 784 0185) flights between Riyadh (SR210, four weekly) or Jeddah (SR220, two weekly) and Sulayyil (listed as Wadi al-Dawasir in Saudia timetables).

Three **Saptco** (☎ 782 1367) buses a day travel between Riyadh (SR70, seven hours) and Najran (SR70, five hours), or between Riyadh and Khamis Mushayt (SR80, seven hours), and stop at Sulayyil.

VISITING THE EMPTY QUARTER

Exploring the Empty Quarter requires more preparation than any other destination in Saudi Arabia.

The first thing you need to decide is whether you wish to travel by 4WD vehicle or by camel. The latter is something of a rarity these days. While more faithful to the journeys undertaken by desert explorers and the Bedouin, and certainly a more leisurely way to enjoy the beauty of the natural surrounds, travelling by camel does limit the distance you'll be able to cover. The second decision you'll have to make is whether to travel independently or as part of an organised group. Travelling independently is cheaper (provided your travelling party owns two 4WD vehicles) but easier and highly recommended are the tour companies who can provide vehicles (if you need them) or camels, and arrange all permits, provisions and guides. Costs vary widely, depending on the length of your trip (from day-trips and overnight stays through to a week-long trip), the number of vehicles (or camels) required (two is a minimum) and the degree of comfort in which you wish to travel (from sleeping under the stars to tents, tables and cloth napkins). Unless you're joining a pre-arranged group (which is rare), you have considerable choice in the itinerary you wish to follow.

Recommended tour companies who can make the arrangements are:

Bin Zaid Travel (☎ 01-419 4688; www.binzaidtravel.com.sa) Riyadh.

Najran Holiday Inn (☎ 07-522 5222; fax 522 1148) Najran.

Rehlat Travel (☎ 01-466 0726; www.rehlat.com) Riyadh.

Samal Lagi (☎ 02-664 0638; mostafaaa@zajil.net) Jeddah.

To travel in the Empty Quarter, it's necessary to first obtain permission from the **NCWCD** (National Commission for Wildlife Conservation and Development; ☎ 01-441 8700; fax 01-441 0797; ncwcd@zajil.net) in Riyadh; much of the Empty Quarter is a protected area and you may encounter rangers on your travels. To get permission, send a fax addressed to 'Professor Abuzinada, Director' outlining who you are – include a copy of your passport or *iqama* (resident's permit), when and where you want to travel and how many people and vehicles will make up your party. Permission is free and rarely denied.

Most expeditions start and end at either Shararah (p146) or Sulayyil (p144) from where superb desert scenery is easily accessible; you can make your own way there or make arrangements through the tour company. If travelling independently, plan on spending at least a few days in the towns buying provisions and tracking down a reliable local guide (you'll need an Arabic speaker).

The Empty Quarter is not for amateurs and even the most experienced desert drivers can encounter difficulties in unfamiliar terrain, especially here where reliable maps are not available. As a bare minimum, always remember the following (if it sounds like too much hard work, anyone who has ventured into the Sands will tell you that it's worth it):

▧ At least two 4WD vehicles are essential in case of breakdown.

▧ If possible, carry a satellite phone for emergencies.

▧ Always travel with a local guide.

▧ Carry a comprehensive tool and first-aid kit.

▧ Don't travel without sand ladders, tyre inflation devices and shovels.

▧ Always notify the local authorities of your proposed route and duration of your expedition.

▧ Carry your passport/*iqama* at all times.

▧ Carry more petrol and water than you think you'll need (six litres of water a day per person is considered a minimum).

▧ Bring a hat, sunglasses and light clothes, and warm clothes and sleeping bags for cold nights.

▧ Always check clothes and bedding for scorpions.

AROUND SULAYYIL

The 12,000 sq km **'Uruq Bani Ma'arid Protected Area**, southeast of Sulayyil, is where the future of the Arabian oryx will be determined; almost 149 oryx have been released into the area since 1995 as part of an impressive programme of reintroducing this iconic beast back into the wild. The sight of the oryx once again roaming the Sands is heart-warming, but not one that's easy to enjoy. Casual visitors are not welcome in the area, but permission can sometimes be obtained through the **NCWCD** (National Commission for Wildlife Conservation and Development; ☎ 01-441 8700; fax 01-441 0797; ncwcd@zajil.net) in Riyadh.

AL-FAW   القاو

Al-Faw (Qaryat Al-Faw) is one of the most important archaeological sites in Saudi Arabia. Nestled under the limestone cliffs of the Jebel Tuwaiq Escarpment on the western fringe of the Empty Quarter, Al-Faw was once a great trading centre – a staging post for camel caravans crossing the desert between the Gulf and Yemen.

Al-Faw was at the height of its prosperity from the late 2nd century BC until early in the 1st century AD. It was a surprisingly large city (1500m by 1700m) surrounded by 20m-high walls, beyond which lay fields of irrigated wheat. The city had a fortified two-storey souq (market), a palace, temple, houses and a number of tombs. The outlines of many of these are still evident in the low-slung ruins. The inhabitants of Al-Faw used a pre-Arabic script and there are some inscriptions still visible on the walls of the escarpment behind the town.

To get an idea of how Al-Faw must once have appeared, there are excellent audio-visual displays and a reconstructed tomb in Riyadh's National Museum (p85). The ongoing archaeological excavations are being carried out by the Department of Archaeology at **King Saud University** (☎ 01-467 4942, 01-467 8135) in Riyadh and the artefacts recovered are among the most important in the Kingdom. If Al-Faw captures your imagination, call the university and they may let you view the wall paintings and bronze statues which were found here; the miniature dolphin is especially beautiful.

A site permit (p173) is required to visit Al-Faw, so make sure that you arrange this before setting out; it's a long way back to the capital if you don't. There are no official opening hours but the archaeologists live on site during winter and guards are always present. Photography is discouraged.

Getting There & Away

Al-Faw can only be reached by private vehicle. From Sulayyil, take the main highway west for 40km and then the turn-off south to Najran. The turn-off to Al-Faw is 76km south of the Najran turn-off, near a petrol station and a large radio tower. The site is 1km east of the road; a 4WD is necessary.

BIR HIMA   بير حمى

The pre-Islamic rock art (see The Rock Art of Arabia p95) at Bir Hima, carved into the eastern foothills of the Asir Mountains, is one of the most important rock art sites in Saudi Arabia. That said, the engravings found at Jubba (p95) are more impressive and extensive and Bir Hima's remote location, at once a highlight in itself and a handicap to easy access, ensures that very few people visit. Most of what you'll see (human figures, giraffes) dates from around 5500 BC, although there are more recent examples scattered around.

A site permit (p173) is required to visit the site.

Bir Hima is 25km northwest off the Riyadh–Najran road; the turn-off is 89km northwest of Najran (look for the signs to 'Hima'). The easiest way to visit is as part of a tour run by the **Najran Holiday Inn** (see p137; ☎ 07-522 5222; fax 07-522 1148).

SHARURAH   شرورة

☎ 07 / pop 52,000

Sharurah is frontier Saudi Arabia, lying deep in the Empty Quarter, 327km east of Najran. A generation ago Sharurah and other settlements like it were hopelessly remote wells known only to a handful of Bedouins. Wilfred Thesiger passed close to here but makes no mention of the town which, in all likelihood, didn't exist. Even today, it's hard to see why it does. It's a sleepy place and one which has few charms of its own, but getting here is half the fun and what lies beyond the town limits is what you come here for.

The **road to Sharurah** from Najran passes through exceptional scenery, including some 60km through a veritable canyon of towering **sand dunes** rising 100m or more on either side of the road. Even if you're not planning the

WILFRED THESIGER & THE DESERT EXPLORERS

For the explorers of the 19th and early 20th centuries, the uncharted deserts of Arabia presented an open and exotic challenge. To be the first European to cross the Empty Quarter was the ultimate prize and many were haunted less by the empty spaces on maps than by the prospect of another European beating them to it.

Sir Richard Burton, Charles Doughty, TE Lawrence and Lord and Lady Blunt all harboured the dream and undertook desert journeys of great significance but ultimately failed to cross the Empty Quarter. Finally, in 1930, Bertram Thomas, a softly-spoken British civil servant, made the first crossing of the Rub al-Khali, travelling from Salalah in Oman to Doha in Qatar. His book, *Arabia Felix*, is a hard-to-find classic. A few months later, Harry St John Philby travelled from Riyadh to Sulayyil, tortured by the knowledge that he could never be the first.

Wilfred Thesiger, who had spent years travelling in Ethiopia and the Sahara before taking a job researching locusts in Arabia, was different. Where previous explorers had undertaken desert travel in spite of great discomfort, Thesiger once remarked that the most fascinating aspect of his journey was not seeing the landscape, but seeing it in such testing conditions. He set himself the challenge of travelling as the Bedouin did and of rising to and overcoming the everyday difficulties – hunger, thirst and fatigue – that were inherent in their lifestyle.

Although not immune from seeking personal glory, Thesiger added a new dimension to desert travel, earning the respect of the Bedu and developing a profound respect and empathy for his desert comrades. Equally importantly, while Thesiger recognised the Empty Quarter as an opportunity to make a name for himself as a traveller, he also saw the empty expanses of the desert as places where he could find tranquillity and companionship with the Bedouin, his fellow travellers. He wrote that without such consolations his expeditions would have been 'meaningless penance'.

By the time of Thesiger's death, aged 93, in 2003, his journey had already become the stuff of legend and his account of it, *Arabian Sands*, 1959, was acclaimed as a masterpiece. In the decades after leaving Arabia, he railed against the 'advances' of modern technology and their impact upon his Bedu friends. Even into his 80s, Thesiger lived in Kenya in a tin-roofed house with neither electricity nor running water.

expense of an expedition beyond Sharurah, this road is like nowhere else in the world and one of *the* great desert highways.

Sleeping & Eating

Despite its potential for desert tourism, the town has just two hotels; Western visitors prefer to sleep in the Sands. There are a few cheap restaurants dotted around the town centre.

Hotel Al-Mahmal (☎ 532 1137; Main Rd; s/d SR80/120) The most modern hotel, but understand that this is a relative concept. The rooms are comfortable if ageing and the staff are friendly in an understated kind of way.

Al-Hammami Hotel (☎ 532 1578; s/d SR70/110) This place, off Main Rd, also isn't bad and the rooms, while not so well-kept, have kitchenettes. The staff are at once wary and moderately friendly; a tourist is something of a novelty here.

Naseef Al-Qamar (snacks SR2-3, meals SR8) This is an Egyptian-run restaurant on the street

that runs between the two hotels, offering the usual chicken and rice selections as well as Egyptian dishes like *molokiyya* (stew of green, leafy vegetables with chicken or beef). The owner enjoys a conversation (he speaks a little English), not surprisingly given how far he is from home.

Samiramis (meals SR8-10) A cheap option along the main road with typical grilled chicken and rice meals.

Getting There & Away

The only direct and daily **Saudia** (☎ 532 1666; Main Rd) flights to Sharurah are from Riyadh (SR280) and Jeddah (SR320); there are several direct flights a week between Sharurah and Abha (SR190), Najran (SR120), Taif (SR310) and Jizan (SR190).

Saptco (☎ 532 0834) has one bus daily to/from Najran (SR50, 3½ hours).

The Najran–Sharurah road is well-maintained and surprisingly busy. That said, never set out without a full tank of petrol, food, water, a spare tyre, and full confidence

THE BEDU (BEDOUIN)

The Bedu (Bedouin), who represent 15% of the Saudi population, are one of the world's great nomadic people.

The traits historically associated with the Bedu are legendary and include: a refusal to surrender to outside authority; a fierce loyalty to family and tribe; the primacy of courage and honour; the purity of language and dialect as preserved in poetry and desert legends; a belief in the desert codes of hospitality, blood feuds and mutual obligations; the tradition of *razzia* or raiding against travellers or other tribes. Wilfred Thesiger observed that their way of life was extremely hard, yet they at all times expected of each other the qualities of patience, good humour, generosity, loyalty and courage.

Since the early days of Al-Saud rule in Arabia, the Bedu have formed the Al-Sauds' last line of defence against opponents, even though Ibn Saud largely outlawed their raiding, blood feuds and cycles of retribution. Although they're looked down upon by many city-dwelling Saudis, the Bedu remain the bedrock of Saudi society.

Some 1.8 million Bedu still claim to live a nomadic lifestyle in Saudi Arabia. Motorised 4WD vehicles may have largely replaced the camel, water may now be carried in plastic containers instead of goatskins and Bedouin families may take radios with them across the desert, but many of their essential characteristics remain – only the Bedu truly understand the freedoms, hardships and perils of the Sands. Even in Riyadh you may still see a Bedouin man driving a small Japanese-built pick-up truck, from the back of which his camel is serenely observing the world.

Those who are still nomadic live in movable encampments of black goat-hair tents, following grazing fields for their livestock and sources of water. If you do happen upon a Bedouin encampment, you should always approach with tact and discretion. Although most Bedouins are hospitable there are some who want nothing to do with foreigners. If the residents want to invite you in for coffee, it will be obvious, regardless of any language barrier which may exist (see Dos & Don'ts p48).

in the reliability of your car. There are several petrol stations in the middle 100km of the trip. Don't do this trip alone and don't venture off the road. Also, keep your documents (passport/*iqama* and car ownership/rental papers) handy for the rigorous checkpoints along the way (the porous Yemeni border is not far away).

AROUND SHARURAH

For advice on exploring the desert around Sharurah, see Visiting the Empty Quarter p145.

If you thought that Sharurah was remote, **Wuday'ah**, 53km due south of Sharurah, feels like you've dropped off the end of the earth. Home to a military garrison, a Saudi border post and not much else, Wuday'ah is wonderfully removed from civilisation and the road crosses a seemingly endless plain of red sand stretching toward Saudi Arabia's often unmarked border with Yemen. The journey is not as remarkable as from Najran to Sharurah and the scenery is patchy, but you're unlikely ever to find yourself in a more remote spot.

Eastern Province

المنطقة الشرقية

The Eastern Province is the centre of Saudi Arabia's colossal oil industry and, as such, you're more likely to live and work here than want to visit. The province has the longest history of Westerners living and working on Saudi Arabian soil and the sprawling satellite towns of Dammam, Al-Khobar and Dhahran are prosperous and have a relatively liberal atmosphere. The region has possibly Saudi Arabia's richest concentration of high-quality restaurants offering a variety of cuisines.

Although you may not realise it at first glance, the Eastern Province is rich in history. Ports along the Gulf coast, and a few inland oases along the caravan routes, once grew fabulously wealthy connecting Arabia to Europe and the riches of the East. Going back even further, some claim this to be the true homeland of Abraham. By the early 20th century, Eastern Arabia had been swept up into the Al-Saud dominions and oil came to overshadow everything. Even so, the rubble of ancient history is still present at Tarut, Thaj and even Jubail.

The ports of the Eastern Province were also once the endpoint of epic journeys by camel caravans carrying frankincense from across the deserts of Arabia in Yemen. The region's ties to the desert survive, most notably in the Bedouin market of Nairiyah and in the town of Al-Hofuf which stands at the heart of what many claim is the largest oasis in the world.

But everything in this part of the Kingdom comes back to oil and for many visitors the enduring highlight will be the state-of-the-art Aramco museum in Dhahran and the comforts of the infrastructure which have accompanied almost half a century of oil wealth.

HIGHLIGHTS

- Dining in Al-Khobar's excellent **restaurants** (p154)
- Learning everything there is to know about oil at the Saudi **Aramco Exhibit** (p156) in Dhahran
- Imagining the world of traders and pirates from the fort on **Tarut Island** (p157)
- Haggling in the traditional Bedouin market at **Nairiyah** (p158)
- Exploring **Al-Hofuf** (p159), the largest oasis in the world

- TELEPHONE CODE: 03
- POPULATION: 3.5 MILLION
- AREA: 672,000 SQ KM

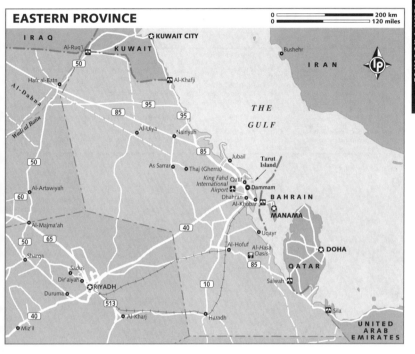

EASTERN PROVINCE

DAMMAM الدمام

☎ 03 / pop 725,000

The provincial capital, Dammam, is the longest settled and largest town of the Dhahran-Dammam-Al-Khobar group, but nonetheless has the feeling of a town whose time has passed. It's pretty run-down compared with Al-Khobar, and Westerners are something of a rarity on the streets here. Even its markets, once lively with the wiles and wares of haj pilgrims from across the Gulf, have largely fallen silent.

Orientation & Information

Central Dammam spreads south of the intersection between King Abdul Aziz St and 11th St.

There are banks and international call cabins all over the town centre and the **main post office** (9th St) is also quite central. Dammam has the cheapest Internet cafés in the Kingdom: SR3 or SR4 per hour is the norm. **Sharkiya Internet Cafe** (per hour SR3; ☺ 24hr), located off King Saud St and **Internet Wave** (Prince Mansour St; per hour SR4; ☺ 24hr) are among those worth trying.

There's a branch of the **Jarir Bookstore** (☎ 809 0441; Corniche) opposite the Sheraton.

Dammam Museum of Archaeology & Ethnography

The **museum** (☎ 826 6056; 4th fl, 1st St; admission free; ☺ 7.30am-2.30pm Sat-Wed), at the railroad crossing and opposite the Al-Waha Mall, contains Stone Age tools, Hellenistic pottery, Bedouin crafts, silver jewellery and information on the archaeological sites (eg Thaj, Tarut Island) of Eastern Province; frustratingly, not everything's labelled in English.

Sleeping

Gulf Flower Hotel (☎ 826 3691; fax 827 0709; 9th St; s/d SR99/110) This is the best mid-range place in Dammam, with rooms that have aged but not as dramatically as the others in this price range. Some rooms are bigger than others, but all come with balcony and BBC on the satellite dish.

Safari Al-Danah Hotel (☎ 832 0063; s/d SR80/120) The rooms at this place, off King Saud St, are clean and comfortable, if a little uninspiring and run-down. The TV picks up CNN.

GREATER DAMMAM

0 |====| 4 km
0 |====| 2 miles

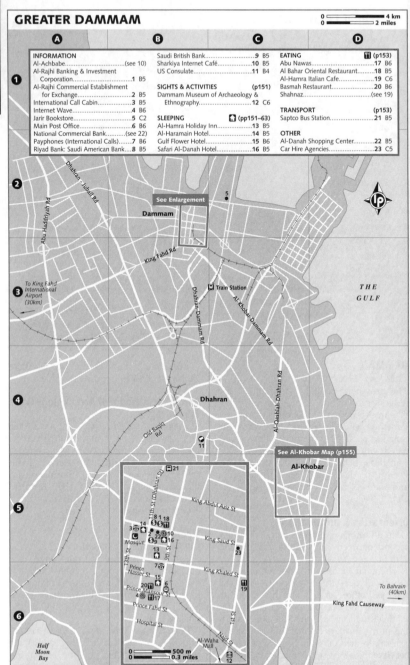

A

INFORMATION
Al-Achbabe.....................................(see 10)
Al-Rajhi Banking & Investment
  Corporation...1 B5
Al-Rajhi Commercial Establishment
  for Exchange.......................................2 B5
International Call Cabin............................3 B5
Internet Wave..4 B6
Jarir Bookstore...5 C2
Main Post Office......................................6 B6
National Commercial Bank.............(see 22)
Payphones (International Calls).............7 B6
Riyad Bank: Saudi American Bank....8 B5

B

Saudi British Bank.....................................9 B5
Sharkiya Internet Café...........................10 B5
US Consulate..11 B4

SIGHTS & ACTIVITIES   (p151)
Dammam Museum of Archaeology &
  Ethnography.......................................12 C6

SLEEPING   🏠 (pp151–63)
Al-Hamra Holiday Inn...............................13 B5
Al-Haramain Hotel..................................14 B5
Gulf Flower Hotel....................................15 B6
Safari Al-Danah Hotel............................16 B5

C

EATING   🍴 (p153)
Abu Nawas...17 B6
Al Bahar Oriental Restaurant...............18 B5
Al-Hamra Italian Cafe............................19 C6
Basmah Restaurant................................20 B6
Shahnaz...(see 19)

TRANSPORT   (p153)
Saptco Bus Station.................................21 B5

OTHER
Al-Danah Shopping Center...........22 B5
Car Hire Agencies..................................23 C5

D

See Enlargement
Dammam

To King Fahd
International
Airport
(30km)

Train Station

THE
GULF

Dhahran

See Al-Khobar Map (p155)
Al-Khobar

To Bahrain
(40km)
King Fahd Causeway

Half
Moon
Bay

0 |====| 500 m
0 |====| 0.3 miles

SITE PERMITS FOR EASTERN PROVINCE

The Dammam Museum is the place to obtain permits for visiting the Eastern Province's main archaeological sites of Qatif, Tarut Island and Thaj. The only exceptions are sites in the Al-Hofuf area, for which permits must be obtained in Riyadh (see Site Permits p173).

Al-Haramain Hotel (☎ 832 3838; fax 832 5785; s/d SR90/120) Located off King Saud St, this hotel has adequate rooms, though they're not as gleaming as the corridors might suggest. Neither is the place run as efficiently as it could be.

Al-Hamra Holiday Inn (☎ 833 3444; fax 833 0944; King Khaled St; s/d SR402/485) This is the best hotel in the town centre. It's semiluxurious and they may give you a discount if you ask nicely. There's a gym, business centre and good restaurant.

Eating

Al-Bahar Oriental Restaurant (King Saud St; meals around SR10) For cheap meals, it's hard to go past this restaurant, located opposite the entrance to the Al-Danah Shopping centre. For SR10, you get two main Chinese/Filipino dishes, rice, soft drink and a small dessert. They're a friendly lot and it's outstanding value.

Shahnaz (☎ 833 2243; King Khaled St; starters/mains from SR10/30, set meals from SR60; ⊙ lunch & dinner) This Iranian restaurant, 50m east of the corner with 1st St, is superb top-end value with char-grilled dishes the specialty; the char-grilled lobster (SR78) is a sensation. Highly recommended.

Al-Hamra Italian Cafe (☎ 833 2243; King Khaled St; starters/mains from SR10/18; ⊙ lunch & dinner) In the same building as Shahnaz and run by the same people, this is a good place if you're craving a tomato and mozzarella salad (SR12).

Other good choices include:

Basmah Restaurant (Prince Mansour St; mains SR10-15) Good Iranian dishes including *fatar* (seasoned bread).

Abu Nawas (Prince Mansour St; mains SR10-15) Lebanese food.

Getting There & Away

AIR

King Fahd International Airport (p176) is a busy international and domestic regional hub, although this huge, new complex still manages to feel under-utilised. Most airlines are based in Al-Khobar; see p156. **Saudia** (☎ 894 3333; Gulf Centre, Prince Turki St, Al-Khobar) has flights to:

Destination	Cost (SR)	No of daily departures
Abha	390	1
Buraydah (Gassim)	290	2
Hail	320	1
Jeddah	390	3
Najran	390	1
Riyadh	150	8
Taif	360	1

BUS

The **Saptco bus station** (☎ 832 0202; 11th St) is around 700m north of the city centre. Intercity services include Al-Hofuf (two hours, SR30, eight daily), Riyadh (4½ hours, SR60, ten daily), and Jeddah (19 hours, SR210, two daily) via Taif (16 hours, SR180).

Local bus No 9 goes to Qatif (30 minutes, SR3) and some bus Nos 11 continues on to Darin on Tarut Island (45 minutes, SR3).

TRAIN

The train station is southeast of the city centre, off the Dammam–Al-Khobar expressway. There are three trains daily to/from Riyadh (four hours, 2nd/1st class SR50/70) via Al-Hofuf (1½ hours, SR20/30), except for Thursday when there is only one.

Getting Around

Buses (SR15) run from the bus station to the airport approximately every 45 minutes. A taxi between the airport and Dammam costs about SR50.

AL-KHOBAR الخبر
☎ 03 / pop 196,000

Al-Khobar (Khobar) is the newest of the three cities that make up Greater Dammam. In many ways it is also the most attractive with its long corniche along the Gulf waterfront. It has also taken on the air of an expatriate village and is the most liberal (and pedestrian-friendly) city in the Eastern Province with some of the finest restaurants in Saudi Arabia.

Orientation

Al-Khobar follows a compact grid design. The central business area is bounded by

28th St (Pepsi Cola St) to the north, Dhahran St to the south, the Gulf to the east and King Abdul Aziz St to the west. Everyone refers to Prince Turki St as the corniche.

Information

BOOKSHOPS

Jarir Bookstore Al-Rasheed Mall (☎ 889 0019; 1st fl; 9am-noon & 4-10.30pm Sat-Thu; 4-10.30pm Fri); Corniche (☎ 894 3311; btwn 11th & 12th Sts; 9am-2pm & 4-11pm Sat-Thu; 4-11pm Fri) Excellent selection.

INTERNET

Al-Khobar has numerous Internet cafés, including:

Café Sahara (2nd fl, Al-Rasheed Mall; per hr SR10; 9.30am-11.30pm Sat-Thu, 4-11.30pm Fri)

Email Cafe (Corniche; per hr SR10; 9am-4am Sat-Thu, 2pm-4am Fri)

Golden Cafe (King Abdul Aziz St; per hr SR5; 24hr) Near 4th St.

MEDICAL SERVICES

King Fahd University Hospital (☎ 887 3333; 30th St) Has a good accident-emergency department.

MONEY

There are numerous banks around town, especially along King Khaled St and on the side streets just off it, between 1st and 3rd Sts.

POST

The **main post office** (Corniche) is located near the Gulf.

Sights

There's a pleasantly landscaped stretch of greenery with good walkways along the **waterfront**. There are plans for marina complexes along here.

The **King Fahd Causeway**, a 25km-long engineering marvel, links Saudi Arabia with Bahrain. There are spectacular views from the twin towers on the artificial island halfway along. Although it wasn't running when we were there, a **steam boat** periodically takes tourists on a scenic, 40-minute ride to King Fahd Causeway.

Sleeping

There's not much in the way of cheap accommodation in Al-Khobar.

Bustan Hotel (☎ 894 6550; fax 895 4405; Prince Hamoud St; s/d SR80/150) This is the best choice for those who are counting their riyals. The staff

are friendly, and the rooms are tidy and come with satellite TV and minibar.

Park Hotel (☎ 895 0005; info@parkhotel.com.sa; Corniche) This long-standing local institution, an expat-favourite, was due to close for renovation just after our visit.

Al-Nimran Hotel (☎ 867 5618; mail@alnimran.com; 28th St; s/d SR250/280) A business-oriented hotel, Al-Nimran is not the most personal place but it's good value. The rooms are very comfortable and there's a good coffee shop.

Gulf Meridien (☎ 864 6000; www.lemeridien-alkhobar .com; Corniche; s/d SR500/585) Al-Khobar's finest has all the luxury that you would expect for the price. It also has the added advantage of being close to the water amid more greenery than exists elsewhere in town.

Algosaibi Hotel (☎ 882 2882; www.algosaibi-hotel .com; Prince Abdullah Ben Jalawi St; s/d SR400/520) This isn't a bad option, especially for its Olympic-sized swimming pool and its bowling alley.

Eating

Eating out well is one of the joys of Al-Khobar and you'll find a greater variety of multinational cuisines here than anywhere else in the Kingdom. The area bounded by Dhahran St, 4th St, the Gulf and Prince Bandar St is filled with good, cheap restaurants, with a preponderance of Indian/ Pakistani and Southeast Asian food.

Turkey Cock (28th St; kebabs SR12, set meals SR15) A good choice for cheap, filling meals, across from the Pepsi Cola bottling plant. Excellent set meals include a main dish, salad, rice and a drink. The kebabs are also good.

New Chiangmai Seafood Restaurant (☎ 894 5197; Prince Mossaed St; starters SR10, mains SR15; lunch & dinner) This place is outstanding, provided you don't get a headache from the lurid décor. There are over 100 menu items to choose from – the Thai dishes are the best (they also serve Chinese and Filipino), and the servings enormous.

Chinese & Grill Restaurant (☎ 898 7336; 28th St; starters SR8-12, mains SR14-25; lunch & dinner) There are hundreds of choices here. It's not the most stylish place, but the food is good and the servings large. Check out the chef's specials which generally focus on seafood; they're expensive (lobster with garlic sauce costs SR60) but worth it.

Copper Chandni (☎ 887 7868; 28th St; starters SR10-22, mains SR20-45; lunch & dinner) This affordable Indian restaurant has an understated but

AL-KHOBAR

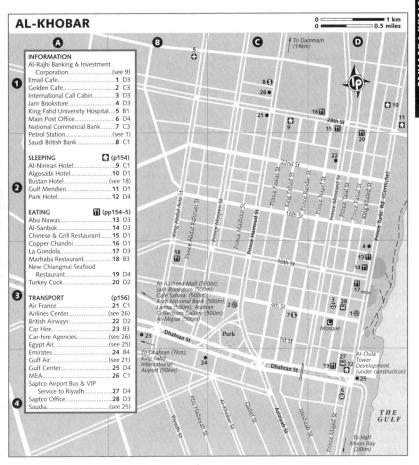

0	1 km
0	0.5 miles

INFORMATION
Al-Rajhi Banking & Investment
  Corporation.........................(see 9)
Email Cafe.....................................**1** D3
Golden Cafe.................................**2** C3
International Call Cabin............**3** D3
Jarir Bookstore............................**4** D3
King Fahd University Hospital...**5** B1
Main Post Office.........................**6** D4
National Commercial Bank.......**7** C3
Petrol Station.............................(see 1)
Saudi British Bank.....................**8** C1

SLEEPING 🏠 (p154)
Al-Nimran Hotel..........................**9** C1
Algosaibi Hotel..........................**10** D1
Bustan Hotel.............................(see 18)
Gulf Meridien.............................**11** D1
Park Hotel...................................**12** D4

EATING 🍴 (pp154–5)
Abu Nawas.................................**13** D3
Al-Sanbok...................................**14** D3
Chinese & Grill Restaurant.......**15** D1
Copper Chandni.........................**16** D1
La Gondola.................................**17** D3
Marhaba Restaurant..................**18** B3
New Chiangmai Seafood
  Restaurant.................................**19** D4
Turkey Cock...............................**20** D2

TRANSPORT (p156)
Air France...................................**21** C1
Airlines Center.........................(see 26)
British Airways...........................**22** D2
Car Hire.....................................**23** B3
Car-hire Agencies...................(see 26)
Egypt Air..................................(see 25)
Emirates.....................................**24** B4
Gulf Air....................................(see 21)
Gulf Center.................................**25** D4
MEA...**26** C1
Saptco Airport Bus & VIP
  Service to Riyadh...................**27** D4
Saptco Office.............................**28** D3
Saudia.......................................(see 25)

unmistakeable sense of style. The food and service are excellent.

Marhaba (☎ 898 6484; Prince Hamoud St; starters SR10, mains from SR18; ☾ lunch & dinner) Good Indian food, especially the sesame seed fish (SR30) is served here. You can also eat outside by the pool of the neighbouring Al-Bustan Hotel.

Abu Nawas (☎ 889 1378; 12th St; starters from SR8, mains SR15-30; ☾ lunch & dinner) This Lebanese restaurant is good for take-away, but the upstairs dining area is also pleasant; the mezzes are particularly good.

La Gondola (☎ 889 1002; 10th St; starters from SR15, mains SR30-75; ☾ lunch & dinner) A great place for a splurge, La Gondola has an Italian chef, a creative and varied menu and friendly waiters. This place has class, and you won't find

better Italian food in Saudi Arabia (nor in many other places). Highly recommended.

Al-Sanbok (☎ 865 3867; Corniche; starters from SR20, mains from SR35; ☾ lunch & dinner) This wins the prize from many expats for the best seafood in Al-Khobar. The lavish setting is perfectly complemented by the beautiful cooking and artistic presentation. You choose the fish yourself and prices depend on weight – you could easily spend SR150 for two but it's well worth it. Its Ramadan buffets are also something of a local institution.

Shopping

Saudi Arabia's mall culture has come to Al-Khobar in a big way, which doesn't really compensate for the complete absence of atmospheric and traditional souqs (markets). Those in search of local handicrafts should expect to pay a steep price.

Al-Rasheed Mall (off Dhahran Rd) This is the largest mall, and was for a time the largest in the Middle East. Just about every brand name has an outlet here.

Lamsa (☎ 899 6683; www.lamsa-arabia.com; ground fl, Al-Rasheed Mall; 9am-noon & 4-11pm Sat-Thu, 4-11pm Fri) Probably the best (and most expensive) handicraft shop, specialising in traditional clothing and an array of silver items.

Other handicraft shops include:
Arabian Collections Gallery (☎ 864 2959; sales@arabian collections.com; ground fl, Al-Rasheed Mall; 9am-noon & 4-11pm Sat-Thu, 4-11pm Fri) Paintings and lithographs on Arabian themes.
Al-Migsar (☎ 865 0155; 1st fl, Al-Rasheed Mall) Slightly cheaper general handicrafts.

Getting There & Away
AIR
For details of flights from King Fahd International Airport, see p153.

Airline Offices
Most airlines have offices at the **Airlines Center** (King Abdul Aziz St). Airlines with offices in Al-Khobar:
Air France (☎ 864 0411; cnr of King Abdul Aziz & 28th Sts)
British Airways (☎ 882 3006; King Khaled St btwn 21st & 22nd Sts)
Egypt Air (☎ 899 9519; cnr Dhahran St & Corniche)
Emirates (☎ 897 9797; Dhahran St)
Gulf Air (☎ 898 0804; cnr King Abdul Aziz & 28th Sts)
Middle East Airlines (MEA; ☎ 864 6118; Airline Centre, King Abdul Aziz St)
Saudia (☎ 894 3333; cnr Dhahran St & Corniche)

BUS
Inter-city buses leave from Dammam (p153). The only exception is a Saptco **VIP Express service** (☎ 895 0005, toll free ☎ 800 124 9999; Prince Mossaed St) between Al-Khobar and Riyadh (four hours, SR90), which leaves from behind the Park Hotel building. There are loads of advantages to this service – it's nonstop, there's a touch more comfort, you arrive in Olaya St in Riyadh and you don't need to get to the bus station in Dammam.

The **Saptco office** (☎ 894 6724; Prince Talal St) mainly connects Al-Khobar with Qatif (45 minutes, SR4) and Tarut Island (1¼ hours, SR5).

CAR
There are loads of local and international car-hire agencies on King Abdul Aziz near the corner of 28th St, close to the Airlines Center.

Getting Around
The easiest way to get to/from the airport is a Saptco bus (SR15) which travels between the airport arrivals hall and Prince Mossaed St, behind the Park Hotel building in Al-Khobar, 19 times a day from 6am until 11.30pm.

Taxis are everywhere and you shouldn't pay more than SR15 for the longest journey within Al-Khobar or SR25 to Dammam (this is one situation where it's better not to use the meter).

AROUND AL-KHOBAR
Half Moon Bay, 28km from downtown Al-Khobar, is a very popular retreat for expats living in the Eastern Province. With its clean beaches, diving facilities (probably the best in the Eastern Provinces) and liberal atmosphere, it's not hard to see why. The best place to stay is the **Holiday Inn** (☎ 03-896 3333; www.holiday-inn.com; d from SR475); prices skyrocket in August.

DHAHRAN الظهران
☎ 03 / pop 102,000
Dhahran is the home of Saudi Arabia's oil industry and is the base of Aramco, the grandaddy of Saudi oil companies. The wells surround the region evidenced by vast swathes of pipes and pumping stations. Much of Dhahran is like an exclusive club, a small and self-contained American city which consists of an Aramco compound, shops, residential areas and the University of Petroleum & Minerals. It even has its own US Consulate. There is not much here for the casual visitor apart from the Aramco Exhibit, although the existence of this strange island in the middle of conservative Saudi Arabia is interesting in itself.

Aramco Exhibit
A welcome change from the usual displays on domesticating camels and Arabia's geological evolution, the **Aramco Exhibit** (☎ 876 2421; admission free; 8am-6.30pm Sat-Wed, 9am-noon & 3pm-6.30pm Thu, 3pm-6.30pm Fri, families only Thu & Fri) is one of the best museums in the country. Designed as a comprehensive layperson's

THE WORLD'S LARGEST OIL PRODUCER

Under the terms of Saudi Arabia's first oil agreement in the 1930s, the government of the fledgling Kingdom of Saudi Arabia received an annual rental fee of just UK£5000 in gold along with a loan of UK£50,000 in gold and a royalty payment of four shillings gold per net ton of crude production. In return, Socal (Standard Oil Company of California) and its partners were gifted exclusive rights for exploration, production and export without having to pay a cent in Saudi taxes.

By 2003 Saudi Arabia had proven oil reserves of 261.8 billion barrels, the Saudi government had complete ownership over oil production, and annual net export oil revenues were expected to reach US$70 billion. Ghawar is the largest oil field in the world and the refinery and tanker stations at Ras Tanura are similarly large-scale. Every day, more than 8.5 million barrels of oil are pumped from more than 800 oil wells across Saudi Arabia and projections based on known reserves alone suggest that oil will continue to flow for at least the next 70 years. Hardly surprising, therefore, that industry analysts have dubbed Saudi Arabia the world 'mother lode' of oil reserves.

And yet, all is not rosy for the world's largest oil producer. With 75% of budget revenues and 90% of export earnings dependent upon oil, the Kingdom remains extremely vulnerable to regional instability and internal pressures. In 1991 production was shut down after Iraqi missile attacks on Saudi oil storage facilities. It took more than a year for production to return to prewar levels. With memories of the 1973 Arab oil embargo and allegations of a lukewarm Saudi response to the September 11 terrorist attacks, Western governments have begun looking for alternative, less vulnerable sources of oil. With unemployment pushing close to 20%, one of the world's fastest rates of population growth and a concomitant fall in per capita oil export revenues (US$2296 per person in 2002 as opposed to US$23,820 in 1980), there is also concern that a young, restive and disaffected population could pose a threat to the stability of the Kingdom. Add to this the fact that there have been no significant finds of oil since the mid 1990s and there is considerable concern among long-term planners about what life will be like after oil.

guide to the oil industry (detailing how oil is formed, found, extracted and refined and a short history of Aramco), there's an emphasis on explaining the technical side of the industry. There are also fascinating displays on Arab science and technology (timekeeping, astronomy and alchemy). Apart from anything else, it's fun, especially for kids, with lots of buttons to push, user-participation displays and quizzes.

Getting There & Away

A taxi to Dhahran from Dammam or Al-Khobar shouldn't cost more than SR25. Expect to pay SR50 from the airport.

QATIF
القطيف

pop 140,000

This oasis town 13km north of Dammam is one of the centres of Saudi Arabia's Shiite community, and, as such, is a politically sensitive place. Riots here at the height of Iran's Islamic Revolution (p25) in 1980 have ensured that the Saudi authorities keep a close eye on Qatif; expect a larger than usual police presence.

Qatif is only of passing interest to the visitor. **Al-Qalah**, the town's fortified old quarter which was once home to 30,000 people, was torn down by the government in the early 1990s. The only remnants are near the taxi stand on King Abdul Aziz St, close to the intersection dominated by the Saudi Hollandi Bank.

Qatif can be reached from the Dammam (20 minutes, SR3) and Al-Khobar (45 minutes, SR4) bus stations.

TARUT ISLAND
جزيرة تاروت

pop 53,000

Tarut Island is one of the most romantic destinations in the Eastern Province. This strategically significant island and erstwhile port and military stronghold has drawn armies (most notably the Portuguese) and traders since ancient times. Evidence has also been unearthed to suggest that this was an important centre of the Sumerian civilisation of southern Mesopotamia some 5000 years ago, making it one of the oldest inhabited sites in Arabia. It again became significant during the 3rd millennium BC when it was part of the Bahrain-based Dilmun Empire. It became a well-known entrepôt for pearls, lapis lazuli and other precious stones, connecting Arabia to Egypt and Persia, a role it served until well into the 20th century.

Apart from the fort, the island is worth exploring for the **old houses** made of palm fronds, the **decorative doors** in Tarut village (1km from the fort) and the **fishing harbour** at Darin on the south side of the island where traditional **dhows** are still built.

Tarut Fort

This large, austere and well-restored bastion of mud and stone stands amid palm trees and looks out over the distant waters of the Gulf – waters which have been fought over throughout human history. The original structure was built by the Portuguese in the late 16th century. The fact that it also lies on top of layers of earlier civilisations only adds to its allure.

Apart from its sentinel-like location, the overwhelming impression is one of solidity, in stark contrast to the other ruins around the Eastern Province. Inside the fort, the **staircase** is particularly interesting – the lighter coloured portions are thought to be about 5000 years old. If the **ramparts** are open, the views are great and you can see old mud houses in the vicinity. There are also the remains of a **well** in the centre of the fort.

You need a permit from Dammam Museum to enter; see p151 for details.

Qasr al-Darin

Qasr al-Darin, the other fort on Tarut Island, is poorly preserved but still worth a visit and it's a pleasant spot for a picnic. Built in 1875 to guard the main seaborne approaches to the island at the height of the pearl trade, the fort once covered over 8.3 sq km. You may also see the remains of the last of the cannons although they're slowly disappearing under the sand.

Getting There & Away

Tarut Island is connected to the mainland town of Qatif by a causeway and is around 50km north of Dammam. You can reach the island by bus from the Dammam (45 minutes, SR3) and Al-Khobar bus stations (1¼ hours, SR3), but you're better off with your own car which will enable you to explore the island.

JUBAIL الجبيل

☎ 03 / pop 195,000

Jubail, around 90km north of Dammam, encapsulates the history of the Eastern Province. Once a small fishing village, Jubail was the first base for Saudi Arabia's oil industry and is now an industrial super-city with sprawling petrochemical plants, refineries and export paraphernalia. Although you may still see the occasional wooden dhows in the water off the coast, Jubail is overwhelmingly a monument to industrial development.

North of Jubail are the modest ruins of a 4th-century **Nestorian church**, which is a rare sight in Saudi Arabia although the site is closed and can only be viewed from a distance.

Of the places to stay, the **Jubail Intercontinental Hotel** (☎ 341 7000; fax 341 2212; s/d SR450/550), on the waterfront around 1km south of the centre, is semiluxurious and geared towards the business traveller, while the **Ash-Sharq Hotel** (☎ 362 1155; fax 362 4161; Jeddah St; s/d SR180/250), in the heart of Jubail City, is a local expat hang-out and a great place to have lunch or a (nonalcoholic) beer.

The only way to get to and from Jubail is by taxi, the rate depends on your negotiating skills.

NAIRIYAH النعيرية

The wonderful **Bedouin market** in Nairiyah solves the problem of what to do with your Friday morning. Located about 250km north of Dammam, this market is something of a local legend and draws Bedouins from as far away as Qatar and Abu Dhabi. For the Bedouins themselves the market is a major spot for buying and selling sheep, goats, house wares and the occasional camel. For foreigners the attraction has long been the Bedouin weavings (mostly rugs) sold by women tending stalls off to one side of the main market; be wary of hard-nosed negotiating techniques and don't even think of getting a good price if you point your camera at any of them; women should wear *abayas* (black robe that covers the clothes) and some form of head covering.

Few people stay the night in Nairiyah, but those that do stay at the **Al-Sharafi Hotel** (☎ 373 0772; fax 373 1688; s/d SR100/140), a surprisingly comfortable and well-run choice with pleasant and friendly staff. The hotel is signposted throughout town.

From Dammam, take the Jubail express-way to the Abu Hadriyah turn-off and then follow the signs to Nairiyah. Once in town head for the large mosque with a low green dome and follow the crowd.

Get an early start as the market usually disappears by 10am.

THAJ ثاج

The ruined **Thaj Fortress** is 94km south of the Nairiyah market and the two can easily be combined in a visit; a permit (see Site Permits p173) is needed to enter. Today Thaj is a desert village little different from others in the region, but 2000 years ago it was a thriving city set beside a substantial lake.

Much of Thaj's history is the stuff of uncertain legend (see The Lost City of Gherra), but the site was definitely occupied from at least 400 BC, reached its height in the 1st century AD and was in ruins by the 6th century AD. Although it was a large city (its still-traceable walls ran 600m along each side and were 4m thick), little remains above ground. Its lonely location, however, is a big attraction.

The site is open more or less whenever you can get the guard to unlock the gate. Your best chance of finding the guard in the vicinity are mornings (from 9am to noon) or late afternoon (from 4pm to 7pm), except during prayer times.

AL-HOFUF (AL-HASA) الهفوف
☎ 03 / pop 300,000

Al-Hofuf (which means 'the whistling of the wind') is arguably the highlight of any visit to the Eastern Province. The Al-Hasa (The Wells) Oasis, of which Al-Hofuf is a part, is claimed by some to still be the largest oasis in the world with over 1.5 million palm trees. The palm groves seem to stretch forever and, although the rapidly growing town is slowly overtaking the sea of green, it's still possible to imagine the excitement felt by travellers who had reached the safety of the oasis after days of desert travel. Hofuf has a good souq, an interesting fort and a feeling unlike anywhere else in the Kingdom.

History
In ancient times, the area that Al-Hofuf occupies lay under the ocean. Later, in the early days of Islam, Al-Hofuf was something of a refuge for persecuted religious minorities, particularly the troublesome and heretical Qamartians in the 10th century who had stolen the black stone from the Kaaba. The Ottomans, who called the area Lahsa,

---

THE LOST CITY OF GHERRA

Gherra is one of the elusive prizes of Arabian archaeology. The 1st century AD Roman scholar, Pliny the Elder, and the Greek geographer Strabo (who lived in the late 1st century BC and early 1st century AD) both identify Gherra as a great city in Arabia. Gherra traded with Babylon by sea and with the frankincense-growing regions of South Arabia by land.

Strabo wrote that the incense trade had made the city's population some of the wealthiest people on earth and that they possessed 'a great quantity of wrought articles in gold and silver'. It was a city whose people, he wrote, lived in 'very costly houses; its doors and walls and ceilings are variegated with ivory, gold and silver set with precious stones'.

Both authors agree that it had a wall, but they give differing accounts of its location. Strabo placed Gherra on a 'deep gulf 200 stadia from the sea' while Pliny states that the city was located on a bay opposite Tylos (Bahrain) and that it had a wall some 8km in circumference.

A number of locations around Eastern Arabia have been suggested as the site of Gherra. These include the Al-Hasa Oasis, one part of which is called Qara, a name that may be derived from Gherra. Thaj is another leading contender as is Uqayr, on the coast near Qatif. The confusion stems, in part, from uncertainty over whether Gherra was a coastal city or an inland city that controlled a port on the coast.

None of these places exactly fit either description. Thaj is large enough to be Pliny's Gherra and coins found here support the theory, but it's much too far inland, even accounting for the somewhat wider Gulf of ancient times. It's also too far north to be 'opposite' Bahrain. Uqayr has a port and is opposite Bahrain but does not appear to have ever been large or rich enough to fit the description.

Like all great mysteries, the true location of the lost city of Gherra remains unknown and open to speculation to this day.

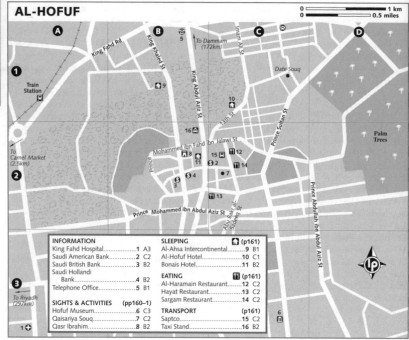

AL-HOFUF

INFORMATION			SLEEPING	⬛ (p161)
King Fahd Hospital	1	A3	Al-Ahsa Intercontinental	9 B1
Saudi American Bank	2	C2	Al-Hofuf Hotel	10 C1
Saudi British Bank	3	B2	Bonais Hotel	11 B2
Saudi Hollandi				
Bank	4	B2	EATING	🍴 (p161)
Telephone Office	5	B1	Al-Haramain Restaurant	12 C2
			Hayat Restaurant	13 C2
SIGHTS & ACTIVITIES	(pp160–1)		Sargam Restaurant	14 C2
Hofuf Museum	6	C3		
Qaisariya Souq	7	C2	TRANSPORT	(p161)
Qasr Ibrahim	8	B2	Saptco	15 C2
			Taxi Stand	16 B2

ruled it twice, from 1549 to 1680 and again from 1871 until Abdul Aziz conquered the area in 1913. In between, the Al-Sauds took the oasis in the 1790s and Al-Hasa was one of the last Wahhabi strongholds in the 18th century. A hundred years ago a substantial portion of Europe's dates came from here and it is still one of the world's leading areas for high quality date production.

Orientation & Information

The centre of Al-Hofuf is compact; King Abdul Aziz St is the main commercial street and intersects with Prince Mohammed ibn Fahd ibn Jalawi St to form a central square where the bus station is located. There are several banks and international call cabins around the main intersection.

Sights & Activities

HOFUF MUSEUM

There's a big map of the oasis at the entrance to the exhibit hall of the **Hofuf Museum** (☎ 580 3942; Prince Sultan St; admission free; ⊗ 8am-2pm Sat-Wed). It also has good sections on Eastern Province archaeology and displays showing

the Arabian peninsula disappearing and re-appearing from under the oceans up until well after the Ice Age. The museum is about 5km southeast of the main intersection.

QASR IBRAHIM

Dominating the centre of town is the heavily restored **Qasr Ibrahim** (Prince Mohammed ibn Fahd ibn Jalawi St; admission free; ⊗ dawn-dusk), with its austere solidity offset against the almost childlike crenellations atop the walls. The fort's earliest structure is the restored, white **Quba Mosque** (1571), around which the remainder of the fort grew from the 17th century. Next to the mosque is the **jail**, complete with **underground cells**. Abdul Aziz was not one to enjoy the pleasures of the **hammam** (Turkish bath) and so he used the one near the northwest corner of the compound – to store dates. Near the *hammam* is a small excavated area showing the underground system which was used for heating water. The views from the **ramparts** are also good.

The present fort dates from the beginning of the 19th century. The Turkish garrison once sheltered here, surrounded by hostile

Najran fort (p136), Najran

Stall holder, basket souq
(p138), Najran

Locally made baskets and ceramic bowls, basket
souq (p138), Najran

Lionfish on red coral, Red Sea (p107)

Anathais on a coral reef, Red
Sea (p107)

Yellow coral, Red Sea (p107)

Cuttlefish on a coral reef, Red Sea (p107)

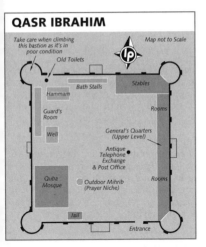

QASR IBRAHIM

Take care when climbing this bastion as it's in poor condition

Map not to Scale

Old Toilets

Bath Stalls

Stables

Hammam

Guard's Room

Rooms

Well

General's Quarters (Upper Level)

Antique Telephone Exchange & Post Office

Quba Mosque

Outdoor Mihrib (Prayer Niche)

Rooms

Jail

Entrance

local tribes, until Abdul Aziz conquered Al-Hofuf with a debilitating siege in 1913.

You'll need a permit to visit the interior; see Site Permits p173 for details.

QAISARIYA SOUQ

Until a tragic fire in 2001, this was one of the last and certainly the most extensive covered souqs in Saudi Arabia. The authorities have largely rebuilt the souq and it has inevitably lost much of its old-world charm. That said, it's still one of the few places in the country where hand-made Arabian coffee pots, as opposed to mass-produced ones imported from Pakistan, can still be found. Several shops also have good collections of Bedouin weavings and a few have old silver jewellery.

HOFUF CAMEL MARKET

A wonderful opportunity to experience a tradition extending back centuries is available at the **Hofuf Camel Market**, off King Fahd Rd southwest of the centre. It's a working market and not a tourist attraction, trading in camels, sheep and goats. Colourful stalls laden with the halters, bridles, blankets and other paraphernalia of camel saddlery and breeding dot the walkways and are usually run by Bedouin women. Sightseers are rare and women may feel uncomfortable here. The action starts around 6am.

Organised Tours

The Al-Hofuf and the Al-Ahsa Intercontinental hotels offer a number of sightseeing tours, including throughout the oasis, to the souq and to nearby Kailabiyah (17km northeast of Hofuf and the holy site of the Juwatha Mosque, now just a whitewashed prayer enclosure). Some of these can be combined with accommodation and meals packages.

Sleeping

Bonais Hotel (☎ 582 7700; fax 582 1168; King Abdul Aziz St; s/d SR100/150) The cheapest hotel in town is simple, central and reasonable value.

Al-Hofuf Hotel (☎ 587 7082; hofhtl@nesma.net.sa; 13th St; s/d SR400/485) This four-star hotel is very well-run with good rooms and friendly staff who offer discounts if things are quiet.

Al-Ahsa Intercontinental (☎ 584 0000; www.inter continental.com/alahsa; s/d from SR250/325) Opulence is the byword in this newly constructed hotel off King Khaled St. It's built in the style of a fort, the luxury rooms and villas overlook the palm trees, and the restaurants and the service are excellent. It offers a range of rates and weekend packages, some of which include meals and tours. This is one place where paying extra is worth every riyal.

Eating

Apart from those located in the hotels, Al-Hofuf lacks good restaurants. A local specialty is whole-wheat bread; follow your nose to the nearest bakery.

Al-Haramain Restaurant (mains SR15) For cheap meals of chicken, rice and salad try this place opposite the bus station.

Sargam Restaurant (mains under SR10) Also near the bus station, Sargam has good, cheap Indian food.

Hayat Restaurant (Off King Abdul Aziz St) A good place to look for fresh juice and Arabian sweets.

Getting There & Around

Saptco (☎ 587 3688; cnr King Abdul Aziz St & Prince Mohammed ibn Fahd ibn Jalawi St) operates services to Dammam (two hours, SR30, eight daily), Riyadh (four hours, SR55, five daily) and Jeddah (16 hours, SR190, one daily).

The **train station** (☎ 582 0571; King Fahd Rd) is about 2km northwest of the centre. Three trains a day (except Thursday when there is only one) pass through en route to Dammam (1½ hours, 2nd/1st class SR20/30) or Riyadh (2½ hours, SR30/40).

Metered taxis congregate around the main intersection.

Directory

CONTENTS

ACCOMMODATION

For a country not renowned for its tourism industry, Saudi Arabia has a surprisingly good network of hotels aimed largely at local and international businesspeople, pilgrims and tourists from within the country.

Throughout this book, quoted prices are for a room with private bathroom unless stated otherwise and do not include the 15% service charge which is added to your bill by all top-end hotels. In Abha, Taif and other mountain regions, expect prices to increase by almost 50% in summer, when demand is high. Where 'summer' is used in the Sleeping sections of this book, it refers to the months from May to September.

Saudi law requires the presentation of a passport (those on visitors' visas) or an *iqama* (residence permit for expats) to check in at any hotel or hostel. Women travelling alone need a letter from their sponsor to check into any hotel, and the sponsor should contact the hotel in advance.

Camping

The only camping grounds are in the Asir National Park (p132). There are no facilities such as water or electricity provided, but camping is free; sites are allocated on a first-come, first-served basis. In the Empty Quarter, camping in the desert is popular.

PRACTICALITIES

- *Arab News* and the *Saudi Gazette* (SR2 each) are English-language daily newspapers of a reasonably high standard. International newspapers are readily available from Jarir Bookstores in Riyadh, Jeddah, Buraydah, Al-Khobar, Al-Hofuf and Dammam, but are usually two or three days old.

- Jeddah Radio (96.2 FM) broadcasts in English and French, and the BBC World Service (www.bbc.co.uk/worldservice /programmes/index.shtml) is available on short-wave (11.760kHz, 15.310kHz or 15.575kHz), check the website for frequencies for different programmes.

- Satellite TV (CNN, BBC, RFI) is widely available; Saudi Arabia TV Channel 2 also broadcasts programmes in English (everything from *Blue Heelers* to *Islam Q&A*) and news in French (8pm).

- Like France and Greece, Saudi Arabia uses the SECAM video system, which is incompatible with many European and North American systems.

- Electrical current is 110VAC and 220VAC. European two-pin plugs are the norm, although three-pronged British plugs are also used.

- Saudi Arabia uses the metric system (weights in grams, distances in metres); for conversion charts see the inside back cover.

Hostels
These days very few Westerners stay at Saudi Arabia's *buyut ash-shebab* (youth hostels). Most would be excellent value if they weren't (with few exceptions) located miles from anywhere and accessible only by private transport. There's one in most medium-sized towns, they're almost always clean, rarely crowded and very well maintained. Most offer single or double rooms with a private bathrooms and cost SR10 per person. Stays are usually limited to three nights. Saudi hostels are open only to men.

Saudi Arabia is an IYHF member and hostel cards are always required. Foreigners can purchase cards for SR35 per year from any hostel. The *Saudi Arabian Youth Hostels Federation Handbook* (available for free at all of the bigger hostels) contains complete listings of the Kingdom's 19 hostels and their facilities.

Hotels
Cheap hotels range from basic and bleak to simple and tidy. Most (but not all) have shared bathrooms kept in varying stages of decay and you should also get an Arabic-language TV. Expect to pay from SR40 for a single and up to SR80 for a double.

Mid-range hotels are generally excellent value for money. For a few more riyals (from SR80 to SR200 for singles, and from SR100 to SR250 for doubles), you'll be staying in comfortable and often spacious rooms with satellite TV (usually with English-language channels) and private bathrooms. These days, such hotels rarely get foreign visitors, so staff will often go out of their way to be helpful. Most medium-sized towns have at least one hotel in this price range.

Saudi Arabia also has an excellent selection of five-star hotels, ranging from international chains to local, privately owned hotels, and even many smaller towns have one. Quoted rates start at SR400/550 for singles/doubles, but these can usually be negotiated down to around SR300/375. Asking for 'the corporate rate' or booking in advance over the Internet also helps. Hotels in this price range offer supremely comfortable rooms, as well as swimming pools, business centres, fitness centres and all the other luxury bells and whistles. Top-end hotels, particularly those in Asir and Jeddah, also offer cheaper weekend package deals; always book ahead, as they're excellent value.

At all but the cheapest hotels in the mountains (which have ceiling fans) count on your hotel room having air-conditioning.

ACTIVITIES
For a country with sprawling cities, booming population growth and a massive oil infrastructure, it's surprisingly easy to get away from it all and enjoy the natural wonders of the Arabian Peninsula.

Beaches
Saudi Arabia has some good beaches along the Red Sea Coast, but none that you would describe as idyllic. Women are made to feel uncomfortable swimming or sunbathing in anything vaguely resembling a swimsuit at a public beach. All of the top-end hotels in Jeddah (p104) have private beaches where you can wear what you like (although going topless would be inadvisable). Entry generally costs SR50 per person (more on weekends; guests enter free of charge). Other good private beaches include Al-Nakheel Beach (p106) north of Jeddah and Half Moon Bay (p156) southwest of Al-Khobar.

Camel Trekking
If you have visions of following in the footsteps of legendary British explorer Wilfred Thesiger (see Wilfred Thesiger & the Desert Explorers p147), remember that part of his later disillusionment with Arabia stemmed from the fact that 4WD vehicles had largely replaced the camel. You may find something on offer in Sharurah (p145), but it takes at least a week to get far enough into the desert to make it worthwhile travelling this way. If you don't have time for this, you could always take a token camel ride at the camel markets on the outskirts of Riyadh (p91) and Al-Hofuf (p161). At these markets, owners will sometimes let you ride their camel for around SR15.

Diving & Water Sports
The Red Sea coast off Jeddah offers superb diving and would surely be a magnet for the divers of the world were Saudi Arabia less difficult to enter. All year, reef fish (triggerfish, wrasse grouper and surgeonfish) abound. Pelagic fish (jacks, tuna, Spanish mackerel and barracuda) have extensive breeding grounds,

---

DODGING PRAYER TIMES

In Saudi Arabia, *everything* closes during *salat* (prayer time). This is strictly enforced and can last for up to 30 minutes. If you are already inside a restaurant and eating, the staff may let you hang around and finish your meal (with the curtains drawn and they may not let you out until prayers are finished), but most won't serve you unless they're convinced that you can finish in time. The food courts of big shopping centres (particularly in Riyadh) are perhaps the most lenient in this respect. If you're inside an Internet café when prayers start, you'll probably be allowed to stay. Shop owners, however, will invariably show you the door, politely but firmly, to avoid problems with the mutawwa (religious police). Offices (including that of the airline Saudia) will also stop answering phones.

Prayer times vary throughout the Kingdom and from day-to-day, and there are at least four during business hours that you need to watch out for. A list of prayer times appears daily on pages two or three of *Arab News*.

---

unspoiled by over-fishing and virtually un-dived. Whale-shark season runs from April to June. There are also numerous wrecks in the area, many of which offer adventurous diving.

The best dive sites are all along the Red Sea Coast from the Farasan Islands (p140) near the Yemeni border, Shwayba (south of Jeddah), and from Jeddah north to Rabigh and Yanbu. For details on diving opportunities, see Red Sea Diving p107, and visit the comprehensive www.saudidiving.com, which has a full list of dive centres.

The best shore diving and facilities can be found at Al-Nakheel Beach (p106) near Jeddah, a seaside compound with superb reef-wall dives. Soft corals, clownfish, yellow monos and Spanish dancers all occupy the reef within 100m north of the entry point.

4WD

There are ample opportunities to leave behind the tarmac roads and explore Arabia's superb desert interior. The most rewarding desert journeys are undoubtedly among the sand seas of the Empty Quarter around Sharurah (p146) and following the route of the old Hejaz Railway (see the Hejaz Railway p122). Although the latter is relatively straightforward, there are some essential rules to travelling in the Empty Quarter; see p141.

If you're going to be in the Kingdom for any length of time and have access to a 4WD vehicle, the three guides *Desert Treks from Riyadh* by Ionis Thompson, *Off-Road in the Hejaz* by Patrick Pierard and Patrick Legros, and *Desert Treks from Al Khobar* by Jon Carter, offer an excellent range of off-road expeditions; each costs SR20 from any Jarir Bookstore.

BUSINESS HOURS

See the inside cover for a summary of country-wide opening hours for shops, post offices, banks, offices and restaurants. In addition to the official hours, you'll find souqs (markets) and many other shops open on Friday evenings from 4pm or 5pm to 8pm, especially in larger towns.

CHILDREN

Families form the centre of Saudi life and children are an integral part of social and public life. As such, visiting children will often find the experience of Saudi Arabia to be much easier than their parents do, as children have more opportunities for interaction than most adults and can also get away with more. Saudi Arabia has a surprising number of amusement parks designed for children, but enjoyed by small and big kids alike. They're usually family-only affairs (ie men are not allowed to enter unless accompanied by children or family), cost SR5/2 per adult/child and just about any medium-sized town has one. Some examples are along the North Corniche in Jeddah (Map p100) and next to the Abha Palace Hotel in Abha (p131). For a small listing of some amusement parks in the Kingdom, visit www.funguide.com /parks/park.pl?saudiara.

There are other sites and activities that kids will love, including the National Museum in Riyadh with its interactive displays, and cable-car rides in Abha. The Hejaz Railway is best explored after watching *Lawrence of Arabia*, and reaching Habalah makes a great trip, with baboons along the roadside en route, a cliff-top Ferris wheel, and a cable car to a village once reached only by ropes. See Top Tens p11.

It's also the case that children often find the life of the expat to be far easier than their parents do (see p51).

For more comprehensive advice on traveling with children, pick up a copy of Lonely Planet's *Travel with Children*, written by Cathy Lanigan.

Practicalities

Baby food and disposable nappies (including many Western brands) are widely available in supermarkets and pharmacies. Most mid-range and top-end hotels are happy to accommodate kids (usually in the form of an extra bed) but only the international chains can provide cots. If you're living in a compound, there's often some form of childcare available and there are international schools in most major cities (see p61).

Most reputable international airlines allow babies (up to two years of age) to fly for 10% of the adult fare, and usually provide nappies (diapers), tissues, talcum powder and all the other paraphernalia needed to keep babies clean, dry and half-happy. For children between the ages of two and 12, the fare on international flights is usually 50% of the regular fare or 67% of a discounted fare.

CLIMATE CHARTS

Central Saudi Arabia is renowned for its fierce, dry summers with cool evenings, while the Red Sea and Gulf coasts are usually warm and humid. The Asir mountains of the southwest are noticeably cooler. See p9 for an overview of Saudi Arabia's climate.

CUSTOMS

When you go through customs on arrival, forbidden items such as alcohol, drugs, pork products and anything deemed pornographic or politically sensitive (broadly defined) will be confiscated and harsh punishments imposed for carrying these. Laptop computers are generally fine, as are still and video cameras, but always be prepared for questions. Smokers will enjoy the 600 cigarette customs allowance, and 'a reasonable quantity' of perfume is permitted.

DANGERS & ANNOYANCES

Although muggings and other violent street crime are virtually nonexistent, Saudi Arabia presents its own unique challenges to visitors. For information to help you avoid

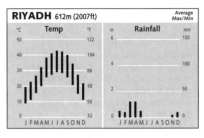

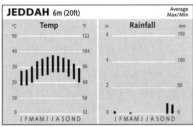

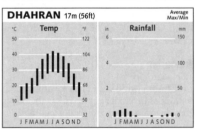

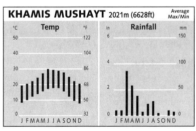

social faux pas, see Dos & Don'ts p30; for more on Saudi Arabia's laws, see p168; and for dangers pertaining to women, see p174.

Mutawwa

Formally known as the Committee for the Propagation of Virtue and the Prevention of Vice, the mutawwa, or religious police, have a fearsome reputation as a squad of moral vigilantes out to enforce their own special brand of Islamic orthodoxy. Made up of pious religious youths and some disillusioned foreign-educated men, the mutawwa are largely untouchable by other branches of the security services, unless their actions cause great embarrassment to the government (who finance them).

They've become less visible in Jeddah and Al-Khobar in recent years, but remain active elsewhere, especially in Riyadh.

Women are most likely to be confronted by the mutawwa, usually for not covering their heads in public. Using a public phone during prayer times also attracts attention. Mutawwa at their most authoritative (hence not to be argued with) when accompanied by uniformed police.

The best way to deal with the mutawwa is to avoid them. However, if you do find yourself facing an angry-looking religious policeman, keep calm and be polite but firm. Above all, don't turn the situation into a confrontation. If they're asking something reasonable of you, at least by local standards, do it. Afterwards, always report the incident to your embassy.

Ramadan

Ramadan (see p47) is observed throughout the Muslim world but nowhere with as much fervour as in Saudi Arabia. To say that life in the Kingdom moves slowly during Ramadan is an understatement. Even worse, hungry and nicotine-starved officials abound, especially during the day. Public observance of the fast is mandatory here; smoking or eating in public could result in arrest.

Road Safety

If you've spent any time in the Kingdom, you won't be surprised that Saudi Arabia has the highest road-death rate in the world. Rules, such as they are (see p183), are not often respected. Although you need to be careful everywhere, the general rule is that the driving gets worse the further west you go; Jeddah can be a nightmare.

Terrorism

In May 2004, 22 civilians were killed during an attack on the Petroleum Centre building and subsequent siege on an expatriate housing compound in Al-Khobar.

Before then, the most devastating attacks carried out in the Kingdom against Western targets were in Riyadh (November 1995, May

---

GOVERNMENT TRAVEL WARNINGS

Most governments have travel advisory services detailing potential pitfalls and areas to avoid. Some of these services:

Australian Department of Foreign Affairs & Trade (☎ 02-6261 1111; www.dfat.gov.au/consular /advice/)

Canadian Department of Foreign Affairs & International Trade (☎ 1-800-267-6788; www .voyage.gc.ca/dest/index.asp)

New Zealand Ministry of Foreign Affairs & Trade (☎ 04-439 8000; www.mft.govt.nz/travel/)

UK Foreign and Commonwealth Office (☎ 0870-6060290; www.fco.gov.uk/travel/)

US Department of State (☎ 202-647-4000; www.travel.state.gov/travel_warnings.html)

2003, November 2003) and Al-Khobar (Jun 1996). Saudi authorities initially blamed riva Western gangs fighting for control of th trade in illegal alcohol, but, prior to the 200 attack, had belatedly (but forcefully) begun t crack down on terrorist activity and allege Al-Qaeda cells.

The 2004 attack occured despite dramati cally tightened security around residentia compounds and embassies. Always remai vigilant, especially around compounds an other places frequented primarily by Wes erners. You should also register your pres ence with your embassy upon arrival in th Kingdom and keep a close eye on recer warnings issued by Western governments.

DISABLED TRAVELLERS

If mobility is a problem, most top-end hote and official sites have some form of whee chair access. Where they don't (Madai Saleh is an obvious case in point), local o ficials, guides and hotel staff are willing t help in any way that they can. Nonethele the trip will require careful planning, so g as much information as you can before yo go. The British-based Royal Associatio for Disability and Rehabilitation (RADAR publishes a useful guide called *Holidays & Travel Abroad: A Guide for Disabled Peopl* It's available from **RADAR** (☎ 020-7637 5400; 2 Mortimer St, London W1N 8AB).

DISCOUNT CARDS

Saudi Arabia's youth hostels are mem bers of Hostelling International (HI) and membership card is generally required in order to stay. Prices listed throughout this book are the rates for HI cardholders.

There is no official discounting policy for holders of student cards, but some official sites will offer discounts if you ask for them and upon presentation of official student accreditation (international or local).

EMBASSIES & CONSULATES

Generally speaking, your embassy won't help much in emergencies if the trouble you're in is remotely your own fault. Embassies will not be sympathetic if you end up in jail after committing a crime locally, even if such actions are legal in your own country. In genuine emergencies you might get some assistance (such as a new passport), but the embassy would expect you to have insurance. On the more positive side, some embassies post useful warning notices about local dangers or potential problems.

Saudi Embassies & Consulates

Following are the Saudi embassies and consulates in major cities around the world:

Australia (☎ 02-6282 6999 38; Guilfoyle St, Yarralumla, 2600 ACT)

Canada (☎ 613-237 4100; 99 Bank St, Suite 901, Ottawa, Ontario, K1P 6B9)

France (☎ 01-4766 0206; 5 Ave Hoche, 75008, Paris)

Germany (☎ 030-889 250; Kurfürstendamm 63, 10707, Berlin)

Ireland Apply through the Saudi embassy in the UK.

The Netherlands (☎ 361 4391; Alexanderstraat 19, 2514 JM, The Hague)

New Zealand Apply through the Saudi embassy in Australia.

UK (☎ 020-7917 3000; 30 Charles St, London W1X 7PM)

USA (☎ 202-342 3800; 601 New Hampshire Ave NW, Washington, DC, 20037)

Embassies & Consulates in Saudi Arabia

Embassies and consulates generally open from 9am to 4pm, Saturday to Wednesday. The British also handle diplomatic matters for citizens of Canada, Australia and New Zealand. The diplomatic quarter in Riyadh, where most embassies and consulates are located, is 10km northwest of central Riyadh.

Australia Riyadh (☎ 488 7788, after hours 488 7812; Diplomatic Quarter)

Bahrain Riyadh (☎ 488 0044; Diplomatic Quarter)

Canada Riyadh (☎ 488 2288; Diplomatic Quarter)

France Riyadh (☎ 488 1255; Diplomatic Quarter)

Germany Riyadh (☎ 488 0700; Diplomatic Quarter)

Iran Riyadh (☎ 488 1916; Diplomatic Quarter)

Ireland Riyadh (☎ 488 2300; Diplomatic Quarter)

Jordan Riyadh (☎ 488 0039; Diplomatic Quarter)

Kuwait Riyadh (☎ 488 3500; Diplomatic Quarter)

New Zealand Riyadh (☎ 488 7988; Diplomatic Quarter)

Oman Riyadh (☎ 482 3120; Diplomatic Quarter)

Qatar Riyadh (☎ 482 5685; Diplomatic Quarter)

UAE Riyadh (☎ 482 6803; Diplomatic Quarter)

UK Jeddah (☎ 654 1811) One block east of the Sheraton Hotel; Riyadh (☎ 488 0077; Diplomatic Quarter)

USA Dhahran (☎ 330 3200; Aramco Compound); Jeddah (☎ 667 0080; Falasteen St); Riyadh (☎ 488 3800; Diplomatic Quarter)

FESTIVALS & EVENTS

Saudi Arabia's only, big, institutionalised cultural occasion is the **Jenadriyah National Festival**, see p87 for details. For information about Islamic holidays see p168.

FOOD

Throughout this book, restaurant information includes whether the restaurant is open for breakfast, lunch and/or dinner. For more information about the times of these meals in Saudi Arabia, see inside front cover.

Most restaurants in Saudi Arabia have 'family' and 'male-only' sections; families sometimes have to sit inside what feels like a train compartment so that they're unable to see, or be seen by, the other families. Even the waiter may back into the 'compartment', offering a menu in an outstretched hand!

For a comprehensive insight into Saudi Arabian food, see p44.

GAY & LESBIAN TRAVELLERS

Homosexuality is regarded as a heinous crime by many Saudi Arabians (at least publicly) – this is not a good place to come out. The benefit of compound living is that expats are largely left to themselves within the walls of the compound, allowing a little more freedom. Two men sharing a hotel room is not uncommon, although single beds are always the only option. Although you may see Saudi men walking along the street hand-in-hand, this implies no sexual dimension and the sight of two Westerners doing the same would attract unwanted attention. Saudi law imposes harsh penalties for homosexual acts (imprisonment, public flogging and even death).

ISLAMIC HOLIDAYS

Hejira Year	New Year	Prophet's Birthday	Ramadan Begins	Eid al-Fitr	Eid al-Adha
1425	22.02.04	01.05.04	14.10.04	13.11.04	21.01.05
1426	11.02.05	20.04.05	03.10.05	02.11.05	10.01.06
1427	31.01.06	09.04.06	22.09.06	22.10.06	30.12.06
1428	20.01.07	29.03.07	11.09.07	11.10.07	19.12.07

HOLIDAYS

No holidays other than Eid al-Fitr (Festival of Breaking the Fast, celebrated at the end of Ramadan) and Eid al-Adha (Feast of Sacrifice, marking the pilgrimage to Mecca) are observed in the Kingdom. Saudi National Day is celebrated on the 23 September. The above table lists the approximate dates for the major Islamic holidays until the end of 2007.

INSURANCE

A travel insurance policy to cover theft, loss and medical problems is a good idea, particularly as Saudi Arabian medical treatment can be expensive (see p186 for more on health insurance). Some insurance policies specifically exclude dangerous activities, which can include scuba diving, motorcycling, even trekking, so always check your policy if you intend to do any of these activities.

INTERNET ACCESS

Internet cafés are present in many Saudi Arabian towns. Connections aren't as fast as you're used to at home, but they're still generally quite good. Internet cafés can also be a good place to pass prayer time as some (but not all) don't kick you out; they just draw the curtains and don't let anyone enter (or leave). One hour's surfing usually costs between SR3 and SR10.

If you need to access a specific account of your own, you'll need to carry three pieces of information with you: your incoming (POP or IMAP) mail server name, your account name and your password. Your ISP or network supervisor will be able to give you these. With this information, you should be able to access your Internet mail account from any Net-connected machine, provided it runs some kind of email software (Netscape and Internet Explorer both have mail modules).

For more information on travelling with a portable computer, see www.teleadapt.com or www.warrior.com.

In Saudi Arabia, connecting your computer to a local Internet server is relatively easy. Prices for Internet cards from Saudi Internet companies start at SR10 for ten hours (per hour costs reduce the more hours you buy); the best companies are Awal Net, Nesma and Saudi Net. Cards are available from computer shops, from the Jarir Bookstore (Riyadh, Jeddah, Buraydah Dammam, Al-Khobar and Al-Hofuf) and some stationery stores. A good place to ask advice is **Arab Stationery** (☎ 736 0400; King Faisal St) in Taif where the staff upstairs have their finger on the pulse. You'll also need a telephone cable (access points are available in most top-end hotel rooms) and you'll need to change your proxy settings (instructions are on the cards).

LEGAL MATTERS

Saudi Arabia is one of the most insular societies on earth, and its strict brand of Islam takes some getting used to. Things which are illegal include:

- alcohol (see below)
- pork products
- theatres and cinemas
- shops, businesses or restaurants remaining open at prayer time
- women driving
- women travelling without a male relative; domestic flights on Saudia are exempt from this rule.

Alcohol

Alcohol is strictly illegal in Saudi Arabia, although it does exist. Embassy diplomatic bags are exempt from customs searches, while home-made alcohol is often available within the confines of expatriate compounds.

Only a fool would try to bring alcohol into the country or to move the stuff around. If you get caught, plan on spending a minimum of three months in prison, possibly a lot longer. Flogging is also part of the

SHARIA'A LAW

One of the main criticisms (and macabre fascinations) directed at Saudi Arabia by the international media is its strict imposition of Sharia'a law, which prescribes amputation of a hand for theft, and execution (usually public beheadings) for murder, rape, drug trafficking, adultery, renouncing Islam and homosexual acts. In the case of murder, the family of the victim has the power to grant clemency, seek blood money (around SR120,000 for the life of a Muslim) or demand the death penalty. The consumption of alcohol is strictly prohibited, and if you are caught in public with a drink (or with evidence on your breath), expect to be jailed and then deported. There are no exceptions to this rule, and the Saudi authorities will not listen to excuses. Public floggings also occur but are rare in cases of Westerners.

Sharia'a law remains largely unchanged since the time of the Prophet Mohammed. Although mixed with elements of tribal justice, the main sources of Sharia'a law are the Quran, Sunnah (the sayings of Mohammed), *ijma* (the consensus of Islamic scholars on areas not covered by Quran) and *qiyas* (legal norms based on Islamic analogies). Sharia'a law is administered by courts of first instance (presided over by between one and three *qadis* (religious judges) depending on the seriousness of the offence), then a court of appeal, while the king retains the ultimate power to pardon.

Although it seems barbaric to many Westerners, many Muslims view Sharia'a law as an essential pillar in maintaining public order, guaranteeing the rights of individuals to be safe from acts of disorder and safeguarding business interests (non-payment of debt can be punished by imprisonment), with an emphasis on defending Islamic values.

Should you find yourself in breach of Sharia'a law, there's very little your embassy will be able (or willing) to do, and conditions inside Saudi prisons are notoriously harsh.

standard punishment, though this is rarely applied to Westerners. When released from prison you will be deported and blacklisted.

Car Accidents

If you're involved in a traffic accident you must get a police report, before you leave the scene. Outside the cities (where traffic police are everywhere), call the police or wait for a police car to drive past; in remote areas take down the number plate of the other person's vehicle and photograph the scene (if you have a camera). When you go to the police station for the inevitable paperwork, try to get an Arabic-speaking friend to accompany you.

Note that you won't be able to get your car repaired locally without this documentation (by law you must provide a police report), and may even be prevented from leaving the Kingdom, if you cannot explain serious damage to your car's body work. If you should find yourself in this situation, contact your embassy for advice or your sponsor's legal advisors.

MAPS

The best maps of Saudi Arabia are the Farsi Maps. They are available at branches of the Jarir Bookstore throughout the Kingdom (SR20 each). The series includes many gen-

eral maps for most regions and excellent city maps for, among other places, Riyadh, Jeddah, Al-Ahsa (Al-Hofuf), Hail, Abha, Taif, Mecca and Medina. Most comprehensive of all is their *Atlas of Saudi Cities & Regions* (SR75), which contains detailed maps of all regions and medium-sized towns.

Probably the best country map available is the *Africa North East & Arabia*, published by Michelin.

MONEY

The unit of currency is the Saudi riyal (SR) and one riyal (SR1) equals 100 halalas. It's a hard currency and there are no restrictions on its import or export. Notes come in SR1, SR5, SR10, SR20, SR50, SR100, SR200 and SR500 denominations. Coins come in 25 halalas and 50 halalas denominations.

The riyal is pegged to the US dollar (SR3.75), but the rates against other Western currencies change constantly. See the inside front cover for a list of exchange rates current at the time of publication.

For details about the cost of travelling in Saudi Arabia, see p9.

ATMs

As you'd expect in this oil-rich country, banks (with ATMs) are almost as common as petrol stations. The banks which we found to be the most reliable include the National Commercial Bank, Saudi British Bank, Arab National Bank, Saudi Hollandi Bank and Saudi American Bank. In this car-loving society, you'll also find hundreds of drive-thru ATMs.

Always keep your receipts from ATMs; we've received reports from travellers who have withdrawn money from their savings account, only to find that their credit card has also been debited. If this happens, contact your bank in your home country.

Cash

Cash is readily exchangeable in most banks and by moneychangers, which can be found in the souqs of the major cities. Most hard currencies are accepted; US dollars, UK pounds, euros and the currencies of other Gulf countries are the most common. You may encounter difficulties changing marked or damaged notes. The exchange desks at top-end hotels offer poor rates.

One bank that has been recommended for changing cash is Al-Rajhi Banking & Investment Corporation. Be aware that queues in banks can be tediously long, especially on Thursday and Saturday.

Credit Cards

Major international credit cards are widely accepted throughout the Kingdom in top-end hotels, upmarket restaurants, airline offices and many shops.

Tipping

Tipping of around 10% is generally expected in mid-range and top-end restaurants and by service staff at top-end hotels. Rounding up for taxi drivers and waiters in other restaurants is not expected, but is always appreciated, as many such people are quite poorly paid.

Travellers Cheques

With the availability of ATMs (and the replacement policies of international card companies), few people now use travellers cheques. Most banks will exchange them, as will some moneychangers, and most charge a standard SR10 commission. The Saudi-British Bank doesn't usually request proof of purchase before cashing travellers cheques.

PHOTOGRAPHY & VIDEO

Although photography in public places and tourist sites is generally fine, three basic rules apply: never photograph government buildings, airports, police stations, mosques or anything vaguely connected with the security services. Never photograph people without their permission and never photograph women (even in a general street scene); even asking permission to do can be considered a grievous insult.

Bear in mind that Saudis are even more sensitive about videos than they are about still cameras. Videos are prohibited at some archaeological sites (eg Madain Saleh), and using a video camera pretty much anywhere is an excellent way to attract the attention of the police.

Film is easy to find in the Kingdom's main cities, but check that it hasn't passed its expiry date. There are numerous shops specialising in one-hour photo processing but most of these places only handle colour prints. Slides or B&W film tend to take a lot longer, sometimes a week or more, and the results are often less than satisfactory.

For detailed technical advice, get a copy of Lonely Planet's *Travel Photography: A Guide to Taking Better Pictures,* written by internationally renowned travel photographer, Richard I'Anson. It's full colour throughout and designed to take on the road.

POST

Just about every town in the Kingdom has a post office, although the queues can be long, especially at the end of the month when many foreign workers are sending their salaries home to their families. For details of opening hours for Saudi post offices, see the inside front cover.

Airmail postage for letters/postcards sent to addresses outside the Arab world is SR2/1.5. Within Saudi Arabia and to other Arab countries, postage is SR1/0.75. Small packets (up to 1kg) sent by air to destinations outside the Arab world cost SR7.5 for the first 100g and SR4 for each additional 100g. Registering a package or letter costs SR4 internationally and SR3 inside the Arab world.

Any parcel you want to post to an address outside the Kingdom must first be taken to the post office open so that Saudi customs can inspect it. If the parcel includes video tapes these may be viewed by customs before you can mail them out. Outside the main cities that could take a while.

If you're living in Saudi, you'll need to get a post box at the local post office (there are no door-to-door deliveries in the Kingdom) or make arrangements through the company you work for. If you're visiting, you'll need to find a friend who'll let you get mail through his or her company, or talk to your sponsor about using his company address. Note that there are no poste restante facilities and American Express does not hold mail.

SHOPPING

Saudi Arabia is not the treasure trove of exotic Arabian bazaars that you might expect; there simply isn't the market for it. That said, there are some handicrafts worth seeking out.

Among the best buys in the Kingdom is 'silver' Bedouin jewellery; the silver is often mixed with nickel to keep pieces affordable and to strengthen them. Look for quality and consistency in the crafting, particularly in the detailed work around the edges of individual pieces. Ultimately, Bedouin silver is something you purchase for aesthetic reasons, not as an investment.

Much of what you see in Saudi Arabia is of Yemeni origin. The best places to track down silver pieces are the Souq al-Harim in Najran (p138), Khamis Souq in Khamis Mushayt (p134) and handicraft shops in Riyadh (p89), Jeddah (p105) and Al-Khobar (p156).

Another excellent buy are curved *khanjar* or *jambiyya* (silver daggers) many of which are still worn on men's belts in the south. The best place to shop for them is the small Dagger Souq (p138) in Najran or the handicrafts stores in bigger cities.

Woven Bedouin bags and rugs make great souvenirs. The best place to look is the Qaisariya Souq in Al-Hofuf (p161) or the Friday Bedouin market in Nairiyah (p158), although not all pieces these days come from Saudi Arabia. For a wide selection of carpets from across the Middle East, head to Jeddah's Afghan Souq (p105).

Other popular buys include small pottery incense burners (found in Jizan), traditional coffee pots (found in Al-Hofuf or the handicraft stores in large cities; check underneath to ensure they're not made in Pakistan) or gold jewellery (the gold souqs in Riyadh, Taif and Jeddah are especially large).

See p11 for a list of the most traditional souqs. For more Western items, one expat ventured the following:

> There is hardly anything that you don't get here…[you can get] 'millions' of kinds of canned food…exotic foods as well as spices…There are all brands of cosmetics, shoes, clothes. All fashion designers have shops in Saudi Arabia, and the sale prices are great, you may find 70-90% deals. Gold and silver is cheaper than in most places.
>
> *Anonymous, Jeddah*

Bargaining

The simple rule is that almost any price for handicrafts is negotiable. In shops, prices are officially fixed but a 'special discount' is invariably possible. Only at souq stalls will you find the tradition of full-scale haggling very much alive.

TELEPHONE

Saudi Arabia has an excellent telecommunications system. Almost every town has a telephone office through which international calls can be made, and some offer fax, telex and/or telegraph service. Long-distance calls can also be made from payphones; cards from private carriers (Salwa is the most popular) can be bought at most bookshops and groceries. There are also international call cabins on just about every street corner.

Local calls within a Saudi Arabian city cost SR1 per minute (more from hotels), while long-distance calls within the country start at SR2 per minute.

For a list of useful phone numbers in Saudi Arabia, see the inside front cover.

International Calls

See the inside front cover for international codes for dialling to and from Saudi Arabia. The following table shows international dialling codes and charges from Saudi Arabia.

	country code ☎	cost per minute (SR)
Australia	61	5.8
France	33	3.5
Germany	49	3.5
Ireland	35	3.5
New Zealand	64	5.8
UK	44	3.5
USA/Canada	011	3.2

Mobile Phones

The mobile phone network run by STC operates on the GSM system. Rechargeable, prepaid chips are available locally in SR100 and SR200 denominations. However, you need to be a resident to apply for one of these. There is presently no way to rent a mobile phone in the Kingdom short-term.

TIME

The time in Saudi Arabia is GMT plus three hours. Clocks aren't changed for summer time so the time difference vis-a-vis many other countries changes a couple of times a year. See the World Time Zones Map p192.

TOILETS

There are very few public toilets on the streets, but all the major shopping centres have them and most hotels and restaurants seem quite willing for you to use their toilets, although in the case of restaurants, it helps if you're eating there. If travelling by road, roadside restaurants have public toilets, although they're usually poorly maintained and rarely clean. Most toilets in the Kingdom are Western-style, although in some cheaper hotels and restaurants, particularly older ones, you still find squat toilets (a hole in the ground).

TOURIST INFORMATION

Although there's a tourism ministry in Saudi Arabia, tourist information is not really within their brief and there are no tourist offices. That said, there are numerous top-end hotels that run tours and can offer a wealth of information about local sites. Among the better ones of these are in Al-Ula (p117), Najran (p137), Abha (p130), Farasan Islands (p140), Jeddah (p99). Diving operators (p107) are also useful sources of tourist information, as are the companies who arrange visas (p172). The obvious drawback is that you may have to use their services.

VISAS

In the early days of the oil boom, Ibn Saud, the founder of Saudi Arabia, stated that 'My kingdom will survive only insofar as it remains a country difficult of access, where the foreigner will have no other aim, with his task fulfilled, but to get out.' Little has changed and Saudi Arabia remains one of the most difficult places in the world to visit. There are, however, exceptions: tour-

ists travelling on expensive package tours, people travelling with visitor (business) visas and those with transit visas.

Residence (work) visas for living and working in the Kingdom are organised by your employer; see p56 for details. Visa extensions must be obtained by your sponsor.

Remember that all business in Saudi Arabia is conducted according to the Muslim calendar. When you collect your visa, ask someone at the embassy to write down the Western date on which it will expire.

Haj & Umrah

For haj (pilgrimage to Mecca) visas there's a quota system of one visa for every 1000 Muslims in a country's population. Exactly how this system is administered varies from country to country.

Umrah (pilgrimage outside the haj season) visas are issued to any Muslim requesting one, although applications must be made in your country of nationality or legal residence. All you need is to show a round-trip plane ticket to Jeddah. If you're not from a Muslim country or don't have an obviously Muslim name, you'll be asked to provide any official document that lists Islam as your religion. Converts to Islam must provide a certificate from the mosque where they went through their conversion ceremony.

Umrah visas are valid for one week and only for travel to Jeddah, Mecca and Medina and on the roads connecting them to one another. They also allow travel on the road between the holy cities and the border. Haj visas are similarly limited to the holy sites and don't allow travel around the country before or after your pilgrimage.

Tourist Visas

In recent years, the Saudi authorities have begun issuing tourist visas, although ever-so-tentatively and only for those willing to travel as part of a group organised by a recognised tour company. The visas themselves are issued under the sponsorship of Saudi Arabian Airlines under their 'Discover Saudi Arabia' programme.

For a list of approved international and Saudi Arabian tour companies, visit www.saudiairlines.com/tours/discoversaudi arabia.jsp. At the time of writing, the only international companies offering tours to Saudi Arabia were:

SITE PERMITS

To visit virtually any fort, ruin or archaeological site you must first obtain a permit from the Director General of the Department of Antiquities at the **National Museum in Riyadh** (fax 01-411 2054; PO Box 3734, Riyadh 11418).

File the permit application in the morning and return a day later to collect it. If you're not in Riyadh, fax your details, and include a fax number to which the permit can be faxed back. Resident foreigners must present their *iqama* (residence permit), but those in the country on a visitor visa need only present the visa in their passport. The hotels in Madain Saleh and other tour operators can usually arrange the permits if you give them enough notice.

The only exceptions are Tarut Island and Thaj in Eastern Province, for which permits must be obtained at the Dammam Museum (p151). Note that permits for sites around Al-Hofuf are obtained in Riyadh.

Sites which require permits include:

- Murabba Palace, Riyadh (p85)
- Al-Qashalah Fortress, Hail (p94)
- Rock carvings, Jubba (p95)
- Madain Saleh (p117)
- Tabuk Fort (p120)
- Standing Stones of Rajajil (p124)
- Al-Ukhdood, Najran (p136)
- Rock art, Bir Hima (p146)
- Al-Faw (p146)
- Tarut Fort, Tarut Island (p157)
- Thaj (p159)
- Qasr Ibrahim, Al-Hofuf (p160)

Apart from museums (for which permits are not required), significant sites which do not require permits include:

- Masmak Fortress, Riyadh (p86)
- Old City of Dir'aiyah (p91)
- Naseef House, Jeddah (p101)
- Old Al-Ula (p116)
- Hejaz Railway substations (p122)
- Qasr Marid, Domat al-Jandal (p125)
- Shada Palace, Abha (p129)
- Najran Fort, Najran (p136)

Explorator (☎ 01-42 60 80 00; www.explo.com) Operating from France; French-language website.
Intermédes Art & Voyages (☎ 01-45 61 90 90; 60 rue La Boëtie 75008 Paris; www.intermedes.com) Operating from France; French-language website.
Worlds Apart (☎ /fax 510-836 2952; 730 29th Street C-12, Oakland, CA 94609, USA; www.worldsapart.org)

Transit Visas

Three-day transit visas are issued to people driving between Jordan and either Kuwait or Yemen. Those driving between Jordan and Bahrain or the United Arab Emirates (UAE) are usually granted seven-day visas. They're occasionally issued for transit by plane or bus, but to get one you must prove that there was no other way to get to your destination.

To obtain a transit visa you must visit the embassy with your vehicle's *carnet de passage* and proof that you already have a visa for the country at the other end of the road. Always check with the Saudi embassy for the prevailing regulations well in advance of travelling.

Visitor (Business) Visas

To get the ball rolling you must have a Saudi sponsor (a company or an individual). The sponsor applies to the Saudi Chamber of Commerce and Industry for approval and, if approval is granted, an invitation letter will then be sent to you (or direct to the embassy).

Once you have received this letter, you will need to make an application in your country of nationality or permanent residence.

It depends on the Saudi embassy to whom you are making your application (always phone the embassy to check), but most commonly you will require a letter from your company outlining the nature of your business in Saudi Arabia, and a letter of support from your local chamber of commerce.

Armed with this paperwork, you should receive a visa from the embassy, sometimes even on the same day (if you visit in person) but more often within ten days if applying by post.

WOMEN TRAVELLERS

Let's be honest about it: Saudi Arabia is the most difficult country in the world for Western women to travel in. The strict segregation of the sexes and the prohibition on female drivers ensures that you'll invariably need to be in the company of a male relative when in public. Bizarrely, even lingerie shops are staffed by men.

Restrictions

Restaurants usually have a family section where women, whether accompanied or not, must sit; those that don't have a family section won't serve women. To prevent chance encounters, some places (like one floor of the Al-Mamlaka Mall in Riyadh's Kingdom Tower) are open only to women (small compensation for those places where women are prohibited). Museums and some sights have special women-only hours and banks catering only to female customers are common.

Unaccompanied women cannot travel by inter-city bus or train, although the rules have relaxed in recent years and many expat women now do so without problems. A woman leaving the country usually has to be accompanied to the airport by her husband, even if he is not travelling, or, in the case of unmarried women, by a company representative carrying a letter authorising her departure. On arrival in the Kingdom they must be met at the airport by the sponsor or his representative.

An unaccompanied woman cannot check into a hotel without a letter from her sponsor and women must *never* be in the company of a single male, unless chaperoned by a married couple. Again, things are changing but talk to long-term expats for advice before venturing beyond these rules.

Sexual Harassment

Sexual harassment against women is quite widespread, although it rarely extends beyond the ubiquitous leers and obscene comments, usually in Arabic. Although men will stare they are far less likely to touch; if they

do, the social opprobrium that comes from having touched a woman in public is one of your most effective weapons in these situations. Making a fuss and asking '*inta Muslim?*' (are you a Muslim?) sufficiently loudly for others to hear is a good way to send them on their way.

Remember that for every Saudi man who looks on a foreign woman as a sex object there's another who's genuinely alarmed at the thought of even being in the same room as her.

What to Wear

You're required by law to wear the *abaya* (a black robe that covers the body) in public and this is enforced in all but a few circumstances; it's not usually necessary for non-Muslim women to cover their head. The *abaya* can become the bane of your life, but some expat women have found some positives:

> Sometimes I really don't like it because it's black and not very appealing. But there were times when I loved to have my *abaya*, and I guess a couple of moms agree. When you have little kids you often look very messy, having food, spit or whatever all over your clothes and this a couple of times a day. An *abaya* covers everything up. And you can go into the finest shops without any problems.
>
> *Anonymous, Jeddah*

In the rare times that you're not concealed in an *abaya*, you should always cover your shoulders and not wear clothing that is even vaguely tight or revealing. The mutawwa are particularly active in Riyadh, Buraydah and Tabuk; you should always carry a head covering in case you come across a particularly persistent mutawwa.

Long-term expats always have a host of mutawwa stories, some amusing, some sobering:

> A friend and her husband were stopped by a mutawwa because she didn't cover her hair. So, as mutawwas are not allowed to talk to women when the husbands are around, he said to the husband to tell his wife to cover her hair. The husband was very quick and

answered, 'She never does what I want so what can I do, you talk to her'. So the mutawwa left...helpless, probably thinking 'poor man'.

Another guy, who was in a car with a female colleague, made a mistake when the mutawwa asked him the same. The guy said, 'But she is not my wife.' Both went to prison for a day until released through their employers.

One day I went to the antique souq and of course was stopped by a big GMC with a mutawwa inside...the usual: 'Woman, woman, cover, cover'. I turned around, went to the car and said, 'Good evening, couldn't you wish me a nice evening before you yell at me,' and something like, 'I don't mind covering my hair, but please try to be more friendly'. That guy had a certain sense of humour, smiled and left. A couple of days later, same place same car, same yell: 'Woman, woman, cover, cover' I turned around and the guy recognised me. He smiled and said, 'Thank you, ma'm, thank you!' ...and left.

Anonymous, Riyadh

Transport

CONTENTS

GETTING THERE & AWAY

ENTERING THE COUNTRY

Those who get impatient waiting in queues should be prepared for the fact that immigration procedures at Saudi airports can take an age. Provided your visa is valid, you're unlikely to encounter any difficulties. Queues are lengthy and slow-moving, however, as officials assiduously check that the documents of all foreign workers are in order, and passport and visa details are entered into the computer by one-finger typists. One trick is to join the queue immediately adjacent to the 'Diplomatic Passports' queue as this clears quickly and is then often opened up for lesser mortals.

THINGS CHANGE...

The information in this chapter is particularly vulnerable to change. Check directly with the airline or a travel agent to make sure you understand how a fare (and ticket you may buy) works and be aware of the security requirements for international travel. Shop carefully. The details given in this chapter should be regarded as pointers and are not a substitute for your own careful, up-to-date research.

Once through immigration, the days of rigorous bag searches at Saudi Arabia's airports are largely a thing of the past, at least for Western travellers, although they still occur occasionally and your bags will be put through an X-ray (for more on what to expect at customs, see p165).

If you're arriving by land, procedures are similar, although expect long delays if you're bringing your own car into the Kingdom as your *carnet de passage en douane* (effectively a passport for the vehicle that acts as a temporary waiver of import duty) and other documents are checked and your car searched.

For details on tour companies who organise tours (and visas) to Saudi Arabia, see p172.

Passport

Gulf Cooperation Council (GCC) nationals (but not GCC residents) don't need a visa in their passport – everyone else does.

Those with even the vaguest evidence in their passport of having been to Israel will be denied entry, even if the Saudi embassy that granted your visa somehow missed it. Jews are not permitted to enter the Kingdom, so those with Jewish-sounding names are also unlikely to be allowed to enter, although you won't have been granted a visa in the first place if put your religion as Jewish on your visa application form (or entry card upon arrival).

AIR
Airports & Airlines

There are three airports handling international traffic in Saudi Arabia:

King Abdul Aziz International Airport (JED; ☎ 02-684 2227) In Jeddah.

King Fahd International Airport (DMM; ☎ 03-883 5151) In Dammam.

King Khaled International Airport (RUH; ☎ 01-221 1000) In Riyadh.

AIRLINES FLYING TO & FROM SAUDI ARABIA

The national carrier is **Saudia** (Saudi Arabian Airlines; ☎ 01-488 4444; www.saudiairlines.com; cnr Prince Turki ibn Abdul Aziz & Olaya Sts, Riyadh) which flies to dozens of destinations across the Middle

East, Europe, Asia and the USA and Asia. It has a reasonable safety record, although it has had three fatal incidents since 1970 (see www.airsafe.com for details).

Other airlines servicing the country:

Air France (☎ 01-476 9666; www.airfrance.com) Hub: Paris.

Air India (☎ 02-661 4928; www.airindia.com) Hub: Delhi.

Biman Bangladeshi Airlines (☎ 02-665 3023; www .bimanair.com) Hub: Dhaka.

British Airways (☎ 01-465 0216; www.british-airways .com) Hub: London.

Egyptair (☎ 02-644 1515; www.egyptair.com.eg) Hub: Cairo.

Emirates (☎ 01-465 5485; www.emirates.com) Hub: Dubai.

Gulf Air (☎ 01-462 6666; www.gulfairco.com) Hub: Bahrain.

Iran Air (☎ 02 -665 4619; www.iranair.org) Hub: Tehran.

Kuwait Airways (☎ 01-463 1218; www.kuwait -airways.com) Hub: Kuwait.

Lufthansa (☎ 01-463 2004; www.lufthansa.com) Hub: Frankfurt.

MEA (Middle East Airlines; ☎ 01-465 6600; www.mea.com .lb) Hub: Beirut.

Oman Air (☎ 02-664 8666; www.oman-air.com) Hub: Muscat.

Pakistan International Airlines (☎ 01-464 2123; www .piac.com.pk) Hub: Lahore.

Philippine Airlines (☎ 01-477 2228, ext 237; www.philip pineair.com) Hub: Manila.

Qatar Airways (☎ 02-667 5182; www.qatarairways.com) Hub: Doha.

Royal Jordanian Airlines (☎ 01-218 0850; www.rja.com .jo) Hub: Amman.

Turkish Airlines (☎ 01-463 1600, ext 5; www.turkishair lines.com) Hub: Istanbul.

Syrian Arab Airlines (☎ 01-461 4678; www.syrian-air lines.com) Hub: Damascus.

Tickets

When you're looking for the cheapest air fares, go to a travel agent rather than directly to the airline, who generally sell fares at the official listed price. The Internet is a great place to start comparing prices, but online super-fast fare generators are no substitute for a travel agent who knows all about special deals and can offer advice on everything from which airline has the best vegetarian food to the best travel insurance to bundle with your ticket.

Jeddah tends to be cheapest place to buy tickets for African destinations, while

Riyadh is good for most destinations in the Middle East.

For Saudi Arabia, high season, when fares are most expensive, is roughly from mid-December to early January and from June to August.

For buying international air tickets in Saudi Arabia, there a multitude of travel agencies, but it's hard to go past **Ace Travel** (Map 100; ☎ 02-660 5120; abe@goacetravel.com; Falasteen St, Jeddah).

Africa

Rennies Travel (www.renniestravel.com) and **STA Travel** (www.statravel.co.za) have offices throughout Southern Africa. Check their websites for branch locations.

Saudia and Egypt Air fly daily to Cairo (one-way/return around SR1200/1500) from Jeddah (prices are more expensive from Riyadh and Dammam), and Saudia flies weekly to Nairobi (SR1500/2000). For other destinations in Africa, you'll either need to go via these hubs or fly to Europe or Dubai for connections.

Asia

STA Travel proliferates in Asia, with branches in **Bangkok** (☎ 02-236 0262; www.statravel.co.th), **Singapore** (☎ 6737 7188; www.statravel.com.sg), **Hong Kong** (☎ 2736 1618; www.statravel.com.hk) and **Japan** (☎ 03 5391 2922; www.statravel.co.jp). Another resource in Japan is **No 1 Travel** (☎ 03 3205 6073; www.no1-travel.com); in Hong Kong try **Four Seas Tours** (☎ 2200 7760; www.fourseastravel.com/English).

In India, **STIC Travels** (www.stictravel.com) has offices in dozens of cities, including **Delhi** (☎ 11-233 57 468) and **Mumbai** (☎ 22-221 81 431). Another agency is **Transway International** (www .transwayinternational.com).

The large number of foreign workers entering Saudi Arabia from Asian countries means that there are sometimes good deals are available. Sample one-way/return fares are: Bangkok (SR1600/3000) and New Delhi (SR1500/2500).

Australia & New Zealand

STA Travel (☎ 1300 733 035; www.statravel.com.au) and **Flight Centre** (☎ 133 133; www.flightcentre.com.au) have offices throughout Australia. For online bookings, try www.travel.com.au.

In New Zealand, both the **Flight Centre** (☎ 0800 243 544; www.flightcentre.co.nz) and **STA Travel** (☎ 0508 782 872; www.statravel.co.nz) have branches throughout the country. For online bookings try www.travel.co.nz .

There are no direct flights between Australasia and Saudi Arabia; you'll need to go via Bangkok, Singapore or Dubai.

Continental Europe

Return fares to Saudi Arabia from Europe generally cost from €600 to €800. One recommended agent in Italy is **CTS Viaggi** (☎ 06 462 0431; www.cts.it). In the Netherlands, try **Airfair** (☎ 020 620 5121; www.airfair.nl).

Recommended agencies in France:
Anyway (☎ 0892 893 892; www.anyway.fr)
Nouvelles Frontières (☎ 0825 000 747; www.nouvelles -frontieres.fr)
Voyageurs du Monde (☎ 01 40 15 11 15; www.vdm.com)

Recommened agencies in Germany:
Expedia (www.expedia.de)
Just Travel (☎ 089 747 3330; www.justtravel.de)
STA Travel (☎ 01805 456 422; www.statravel.de)

Middle East

For flying to or from Riyadh, sample one-way/ return fares include: Bahrain (SR300/400), Damascus (SR1200/1500), Doha (SR400/ 550), Dubai (SR650/900), Kuwait (SR600/ 800) and Muscat (SR1000/1400).

Recommended agencies:
Al-Rais Travels (www.alrais.com; Dubai)
Egypt Panorama Tours (☎ 2-359 0200; www.eptours .com; Cairo)
Orion-Tour (www.oriontour.com; Istanbul)

UK

Return flights to Saudi Arabia shouldn't cost more than £500, although prices rise around Christmas as expats head home.

Recommended travel agencies in London:
Flightbookers (☎ 0870 010 7000; www.ebookers.com)
Flight Centre (☎ 0870 890 8099; www.flightcentre .co.uk)
North-South Travel (☎ 01245 608 291; www.northsouth travel.co.uk) North-South Travel donate part of their profit to projects in the developing world.
STA Travel (☎ 0870 160 0599; www.statravel.co.uk)

USA & Canada

Discount travel agents in the USA are known as consolidators and San Francisco is the ticket consolidator capital of America, although some good deals can be found in Los Angeles, New York and other big cities.

The following agencies are recommended for online bookings:
American Express (www.itn.net)
Cheap Tickets (www.cheaptickets.com)
Expedia (www.expedia.com)
Lowestfare (www.lowestfare.com)
Orbitz (www.orbitz.com)
STA travel (www.sta.com)
Travelocity (www.travelocity.com)

Travel Cuts (☎ 800-667-2887; www.travelcuts.com) is Canada's national student travel agency. For online bookings try www.expedia.ca and www.travelocity.ca.

Expect to pay at least US$1400 for a return ticket to Saudi Arabia from North America; it's often cheaper to go via Europe.

LAND
Border Crossings

Saudi Arabia has land border crossings with Bahrain (King Fahd Causeway), Jordan (Halat Ammar and Al-Hadithah, although the former is much more efficient and used to Western travellers), Kuwait (Al-Khafji and Al-Ruq'i), Qatar (Salwah), the United Arab Emirates (Sila) and Yemen (Al-Tawal) .

At the time of research, all of these were trouble-free and relatively efficient (see p176), apart from the Yemeni border which closes occasionally during diplomatic disputes (the official border recently changed) and at other times is notoriously slow and rigorous, due to the prevalence of smugglers in the region.

For Oman, you'd need to be Wilfred Thesiger to contemplate crossing by land, while the Iraq–Saudi Arabia border was closed at the time of research.

For details of cross-border bus services from Riyadh, Jeddah and Dammam, see below.

Bus

Such are the distances involved, very few Westerners travel to surrounding countries by bus, with the exception of the Dammam– Bahrain and Dammam–Qatar routes.

Saptco (Saudi Arabian Public Transport Company; ☎ 800 124 9999; www.saptco.com.sa) has the best international bus services, although companies from surrounding countries also cover the same routes for the same price. Departures are primarily from Riyadh, Jeddah and Dammam; you can board these buses at other points along the routes, but they originate in these three cities, making departure times (and seat availability) anything but precise.

The following times are estimates; if taking these routes, allow for variations. From Riyadh's Al-Aziziyah Bus Station (p90), weekly departures include: Amman (SR240, 20 hours), Cairo (SR410, 36 to 40 hours), Damascus (SR240, 30 hours), Istanbul (SR350, 48 to 70 hours), Kuwait (SR185) and Sana'a (SR330, 20 hours). For Bahrain (SR130, six hours), Qatar (SR160, 7½ hours) and the UAE (SR230, 10 hours), you'll change buses at Dammam.

From Jeddah's bus station (p106), buses depart at least once a week for: Amman (SR230, 20 hours), Cairo (SR350, 36 hours), Damascus (SR230, 30 hours) and Istanbul (SR300, 48 to 72 hours).

From the Dammam bus station (p153), there are regular daily departures for Bahrain (SR100, one hour) and buses once a day to Doha (SR130, five hours), Kuwait (SR110, five hours), Abu Dhabi (SR210, 10 hours) and Dubai (SR210, 13 hours).

Car & Motorcycle

If driving, or riding a motorcycle, you'll need the vehicle's registration papers, liability insurance, a driving licence (preferably an international driving licence in addition to their domestic licence) and a *carnet de passage en douane*. Contact your local automobile association for up-to-date details on the documentation required.

If all of your documents are in order, don't expect problems, but do expect long delays entering the country. The procedures are quicker on the most popular crossing points (eg the borders with Bahrain, Jordan, Qatar and the UAE), unless you get a customs official who's a car lover and will find all sorts of spurious reasons to inspect more closely. Elsewhere (especially the Saudi–Yemeni border), entering with your own vehicle is more trouble than it's worth.

SEA

Car (and passenger) ferries operate between Jeddah and Suez or Port Safaga (both in Egypt), Port Sudan (Sudan) and Musawwa (Eritrea).

As a general rule, the food on these boats is dreadful, the trip interminable, Red Sea–humidity fierce and schedules erratic; you'd be better off flying. Westerners are almost unheard-of on any of these routes. For current schedules and prices contact **Ace Travel** (Map p100 ; ☎ 660 5120; abe@goacetravel.com; Falasteen St; ☒ 9am-1.30pm & 4.30-8pm Sat-Wed, 9am-1.30pm Thu) in Jeddah. You may find other ticket offices between Al-Mina'a and Al-Dahab Sts, south of Ba'najah St, also in Jeddah.

Egypt

The crossing to Egypt takes anywhere between 36 hours and three days and costs SR250/550 in deck/1st class. Fares for small cars start at SR600. The crossing to Port Safaga is shorter but leaves you in the middle of nowhere (although close to Hurghada) in Middle Egypt with little public transport on offer.

Boats to either port usually leave once every seven to 10 days. Sailings increase around the Saudi school holidays (the beginning and end of summer and in January), and during Ramadan and the haj.

Eritrea

Ferries sail irregularly (around twice a month) between Musawwa and Jeddah (deck/2nd/1st class SR320/370/420, 20 hours).

Sudan

Sailings for Port Sudan also take place a couple of times a month (deck/2nd/1st class SR320/370/420, 12 hours). Make sure that your Sudanese visa is valid for sea-borne entry.

GETTING AROUND

Saudi Arabia has an extensive and well-developed transport infrastructure with air and road options to most destinations in the Kingdom, as well as a train service in the east.

The days when expats required a travel letter from their sponsor before leaving their city of residence have, thankfully, passed. In order to travel legally, you'll just need your *iqama* (residence permit) and passport if an expat, and just your passport if you're here on a visitor visa.

AIR

All domestic air services in the Kingdom are operated by **Saudia** (Saudi Arabian Airlines; ☎ 01-488 4444; www.saudiairlines.com), which covers the whole country. Services between major

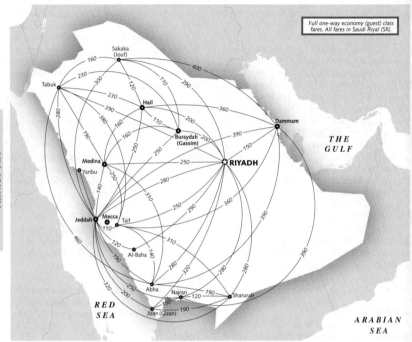

Full one-way economy (guest) class fares. All fares in Saudi Riyal (SR).

centres are frequent, generally run on time and are very reasonably priced. Unlike international tickets, domestic Saudia tickets are the same price whether bought from an agency or direct from Saudia. The Air Fares Chart shows inter-city Saudia fares current at the time of research. See also Getting There & Away in the regional chapters.

BUS

All domestic bus services are operated by **Saptco** (www.saptco.com.sa). Although Saudi Arabia has one of the highest rates of road fatalities in the world, Saptco buses have a reputation for safety and relatively careful driving, making this probably the safest way to travel by road. Most Western expats travel by air or by private vehicle, but Saptco remains worth considering as they have comfortable, air-con buses that run on time. On longer routes the buses have an on-board toilet and in all cases the buses make rest stops every few hours.

Women are not allowed to ride inter-city buses unless accompanied by their husband or a male relative. There are no obviously segregated areas on the buses, but the front

seats are for women and families and the back half for men; if a woman boards a half-full bus, expect the men to move en masse to the back.

Given the long distances in Saudi Arabia, some journeys are best made by air (eg Riyadh–Jeddah, Riyadh–Najran and Jeddah–Dammam), but for some regions (eg getting around the Asir in the southwest or getting to/from Al-Ula near Madain Saleh) buses will be your only option if you don't have your own wheels or join a tour.

The other obvious advantage of taking the bus is that you get to see more of the countryside along the way than you do from a plane.

For contact details of Saptco offices around the country (they're usually located in the bus stations), see the individual city entries.

Classes

One class fits all when it comes to Saptco buses, which range from the ageing-rapidly to the brand-new; regardless of which you get (it's a question of luck), you'll pay the same.

TIPS FOR GETTING AROUND SAUDI ARABIA

■ Fly wherever possible – it's cheap, efficient and saves loads of time (p179).

■ Book Saudia flights over the Internet (www.saudiairlines.com).

■ Between Riyadh and Al-Khobar, take the VIP bus service (p180).

■ For bus travel, return tickets are 25% cheaper (p181).

■ Don't hesitate to take the bus, even if no other expats do (p180).

■ For the novelty value, it's hard to be beat the train from Riyadh to Al-Hofuf (p185).

■ Medina bus station is off-limits to non-Muslims, but the airport is outside the prohibited zone.

■ If driving and involved in an accident, don't leave the scene until the police arrive (p168).

■ When hiring a car, make sure the insurance covers 'blood money' (p183).

The only exception is the **Saptco** (☎ 800 124 9999) VIP Express Service (SR90, four hours) which runs between the Howard Johnson Olaya Palace Hotel (p88) in Riyadh and the Park Hotel (p154) in Al-Khobar. Although considerably more expensive than the standard Riyadh–Dammam fare (SR60), you won't have to take a taxi to/from Dammam (if you're staying in Al-Khobar). It's also quicker as it doesn't stop along the way and a light meal is served. For details see p156 or contact Saptco.

Costs
Bus fares are approximately one-half of the equivalent air fare. If you're planning a return trip, purchasing a return ticket works out 25% cheaper (eg the one-way Najran–Jeddah fare is SR130, but a return ticket costs just SR190). If you don't know your exact return date, this can be changed later.

For prices of inter-city bus tickets, see Getting There & Away under the individual city entries.

Reservations
Bus tickets can be bought a day in advance. It is wise to do so for longer journeys (especially where there are few daily services) during the haj season if you're going anywhere near the Hejaz, or in summer when demand can be high. When purchasing your ticket, you'll need to show your passport (for visitors) or *iqama* (for expats). There are no seat reservations but when you purchase a ticket your name will be added to a passenger list for the specific bus you request; if you

want a window seat, get on board quickly to 'reserve' the seat of your choice.

For shorter journeys with more regular departures (such as Jeddah–Taif or Riyadh–Dammam), you shouldn't have to wait too long for a bus to depart and advance reservations are not usually necessary, as long as you turn up an hour or so before you want to travel.

CAR & MOTORCYCLE
Despite its impressive public transport system, Saudi Arabia remains a country which glorifies the private car (and the large private car above all others) to an extent rivalled only by the USA. Which is why most of the cars you'll see in Saudi Arabia are American models.

Motorcycles are an extremely rare sight on Saudi roads.

Automobile Associations
The **SATA** (Saudi Automobile & Touring Association; www .sata-sa.com) has offices in Riyadh (☎ 01-456 7693 or toll free ☎ 800 124 1002), Jeddah (☎ 02-693 9494) and Dammam (☎ 03-837 2579) and is affiliated with international automobile associations. If you're a member of such an organisation in your home country, you're entitled while in Saudi Arabia to breakdown and towing services (for a fee if outside the three main cities), advice and mechanical assessments on car purchases, customs information and legal advice in the event of traffic accidents. If you live in the Kingdom, you can join SATA for a range of additional benefits.

For a full listing of SATA-approved mechanics, contact **Sasco** (Saudi Automotive Services Company; ☎ 01-419 1951; www.sasco-sa.com).

TRANSPORT

ROAD DISTANCES (KM)

	Abha	Al-Hofuf	Dammam	Hail	Jeddah	Jizan	Mecca	Medina	Najran	Riyadh	Sakaka	Tabuk
Al-Hofuf	1300											
Dammam	1450	170										
Hail	1530	950	1050									
Jeddah	650	1280	1370	870								
Jizan	190	1500	1640	1595	725							
Mecca	660	1180	1290	885	80	670						
Medina	1070	1190	1290	465	410	1135	425					
Najran	280	1240	1370	1635	1025	470	940	1335				
Riyadh	1015	290	385	704	960	1245	870	870	980			
Sakaka	1970	1290	1205	900	1340	2065	1350	930	2200	1205		
Tabuk	275	1605	1680	670	1105	1850	1110	695	2080	1310	475	
Taif	580	1090	1204	990	170	775	90	530	860	790	1450	1220

Bringing Your Vehicle

Few people bring their own vehicle to Saudi Arabia, if only because they'd need to transport it all the way there.

For an explanation of the documents required if you're bringing your car into Saudi Arabia, see p181; always check with your local automobile association about the period of validity for your *carnet de passage* if you're planning to remain in the Kingdom for an extended period as, Saudi import duties can be high.

Driving Licence

There's no official list showing which countries' national licences are accepted and which are not, but if you're on a visitor's visa and want to hire a car, you should always have your International Driving Licence handy. This is obtainable from the automobile association in the country where your national licence was issued or through **Ace Travel** (Map p100; ☎ 02-660 5120; abe@goacetravel.com; Falasteen St, Jeddah). Licences from other Gulf Cooperation Council (GCC) countries are only accepted from GCC nationals and residents.

If you're going to be in the Kingdom for more than three months, you'll need to get a local driving licence which will usually be arranged by your employer.

Fuel & Spare Parts

Saudi Arabia is a famously cheap place to fill up your petrol tank, but not, as some would have you believe, virtually free. Prices have (unpopularly) risen in recent years as a result of budgetary squeezes. In all but the most remote petrol stations (where you'll pay a few halalas more), you'll pay 91 halalas per litre. Petrol stations abound (even the smallest towns seem to have one) and the general rule is that if the road is sealed, a place to fill up will appear sooner rather than later. The exception is along the quieter roads of the north (particularly the Jouf region around Sakaka, and near the Iraqi border) where you could conceivably run out of petrol within sight of an oil pipeline.

Hire

You'll find international and local car-hire agencies in most medium-sized towns in the Kingdom. Hire rates are fixed by the government and the extent of available discounts is agreed in advance by the companies; shopping around will only save you a few riyals. Insurance and the collision-damage waiver are mandatory and usually included in the quoted price, but always ask before signing on the dotted line. A credit card imprint or cash deposit is usually required as a guarantee.

If you're going to be taking the car to different parts of the country it's a good idea to stick to the larger agencies. If you get into trouble or decide to drop the car off early, a company with offices around the Kingdom is likely to have a much better support network or convenient drop-off points than a small, local agency.

Rates generally start at SR90/600 per day/ week, including full insurance, for the smallest cars and can rise to over SR200/1200 for 4WDs. There is usually an additional charge of between 75 halalas and SR1.5 per km, although most agencies offer the first 100km free.

Motorcycles are difficult, if not impossible, to hire.

Insurance

Comprehensive insurance is included in the rates charged by car-hire agencies. If you are buying a car, one former resident recommends that your insurance covers 'blood money'. This insurance will pay the compensation that relatives have the right to under Sharia'a (Quranic law), keeping you out of jail if you kill or injure someone accidently.

The paperwork involved in purchasing a car in Saudi Arabia is enough to drive even a saint to distraction. The few expats who do buy cars usually do so from other expats, simply because it saves considerable time in bureaucratic wrangling. Company cars are still a fairly standard part of an expat's employment contract (there are exceptions, such as language teachers).

One final thing to remember if you do decide to buy a car here is that the Saudi authorities normally won't allow you to borrow money from a Saudi bank during your first two years' residence.

Road Conditions

Although you'll undoubtedly come across exceptions, all but the smallest of Saudi Arabia's roads are tarmac and generally in good condition.

Road Hazards

The way other people drive in Saudi Arabia is a serious danger to life and limb, a risk which is greater the further west you go (especially in Jeddah), although driving in Riyadh isn't exactly good for your nerves. As one expat family in Jeddah told us, the worst thing for women is that they can't drive, while the worst thing for men (because of the dangerous driving) is that they can! To get an idea of who are the worst drivers, spend a day with a Pakistani, Indian or Bangladeshi taxi driver in a big city and you'll soon learn they're angels compared to young Saudi men in fast, expensive cars.

Take particular care driving after heavy rain. It rains infrequently, but when it does the roads become very slippery. One resident advised us that most Saudi roads don't have drains, and the covers of manholes are sometimes removed to compensate for this.

As one expat observed, the situation for pedestrians is even worse:

It is too fast, drivers are unpredictable and often don't know how to drive at all. Pedestrians have no rights at all. Crossing the street is always a major experience and dangerous whether you do it on zebra stripes or anywhere else. Sometimes you just give up and don't cross the street at all, even if you intended to do something on the other side.

Alanna Lee, Jeddah

Road Rules

Yes, there are some and they do extend beyond women not being allowed to drive. The most obvious rules include:

- Driving in Saudi Arabia is on the right side of the road.
- Right turns are allowed at red lights unless specifically forbidden (if you don't plan to turn right, get over into one of the left lanes or someone is likely to come up behind you and lean on their horn until you move).
- The speed limit in towns is usually 50km/h or 60km/h.
- The speed limit on open highways is 120km/h (but can drop to 90km/h or 100km/h), so watch for signs.
- Speeding fines average around SR100 (paying fines at the police station time-consuming, but preferable to spending a night in jail or not being allowed to leave the country because of an unpaid fine).
- Not carrying a valid driving licence can result in a night in jail and a hefty fine.
- Leaving the scene of an accident is a serious offence and can result in fines of over SR1000, imprisonment and (at best) deportation.

HITCHING

Hitching is common in the Kingdom among the less well-off, particularly in rural areas with little public transport, but is unwise for Westerners in the current climate. Apart from anything else, anyone

TRANSPORT

TRANSPORT

DON'T BE SURPRISED IF YOU FIND...

Driving in Saudi Arabia can be an unpredictable experience, so it's entirely possible that you'll encounter any or all of the following events while driving in the Kingdom:

- people overtaking you at 160km/h
- local farmers driving at less than 40km/h on the open road (and just around the next bend)
- people overtaking you on all sides, including via the emergency stopping lane
- children as young as ten driving in rural areas
- cars ignoring traffic lights until at least five seconds after they've turned red
- overtaking despite oncoming traffic
- overtaking on mountain curves
- high speed in the fog of the Asir Mountains
- traffic police looking on with a look of studied concern as the cars speed past
- traffic police with radar guns on major highways (especially around Riyadh).

---

trying it would attract the unwelcome attention of the first policeman who happened by.

LOCAL TRANSPORT
Bus
Municipal bus systems operate in Riyadh, Jeddah and the Dammam–Al-Khobar area of the Eastern Province. Few Westerners take them and routes can be confusing, but they're cheap (SR3). Riyadh and Jeddah also have private minibus systems (also SR3) which operate more or less along the municipal routes.

Taxi
Taxis in the Kingdom's main cities have meters, but whether or not they use them varies from region to region. They're turned on as a matter of course in Riyadh, but some of the capital's drivers like to take unsuspecting Westerners by the most roundabout route possible. In Jeddah, the drivers use their meters but only if asked. Taking a taxi between the three cities of Dammam, Al-Khobar and Dhahran, is actually best done without a meter (agree on a price before setting out). In Abha, you'll do well to find a taxi at all.

Metered rates are standardised throughout the Kingdom: flagfall is SR5, plus SR1.6 per kilometre and 70 halalas per minute waiting time. On the whole, Saudi Arabia is a pretty cheap place to take a taxi, although distances in the larger cities can be huge.

Service-Taxis
Service-taxis (shared taxis) operate throughout the Kingdom, but there's little reason to use them. Seats (between five and 11 per car) are sold individually (rather than hiring the whole car) and they leave when full which can take a while; arrive early if you plan to go anywhere. Fares are generally the same as or slightly higher than the equivalent bus fare. Service-taxis usually cluster around the bus station in each city and touts sometimes circulate nearby calling out their destinations.

TOURS
There's a professionally run tourism industry, targeted at expats and Saudis living within the Kingdom, which visitors can take advantage of. The tentative opening up to tour groups from abroad (see p172 for details on agencies organising such tours) has led some operators to expand their operations and it can be a convenient, hassle-free way to visit the Kingdom's most impressive sites.

Apart from the haj, the major destinations where tours are possible include Madain Saleh (p117), the Asir region around Abha (p130) and Najran (p137).

Riyadh (p84) and Jeddah (p99) have the largest selection of companies offering tours around the Kingdom.

The Red Sea has some wonderful diving opportunities and many professional dive centres able to organise dive packages (see Red Sea Diving p107), while many top-end hotels in western Saudi Arabia offer accommodation-and-diving packages.

TRAIN

Saudi Arabia has the only stretch of train track in the entire Arabian Peninsula. Trains travel between Riyadh and Dammam via Al-Hofuf and leave three times daily in each direction, except Thursday, when there's only one departure in each direction.

With prices around the same as the equivalent bus journey, the levels of comfort (and novelty value) make the train an excellent way to travel.

Classes

Saudi trains have both 1st- and 2nd-class carriages; there's not a lot of difference between the two but you'll have more space to yourself in 1st class. Women have their own compartments. The service includes a restaurant car, and sandwiches, coffee, tea and soft drinks can be purchased from vendors in the passenger section.

Costs

The journey from Riyadh to Dammam (2nd/1st class SR50/70, four hours) goes via Al-Hofuf (SR30/40, 2½ hours). From Al-Hofuf you'll continue to Dammam (SR20/30, 1½ hours).

Reservations

The trains are rarely crowded but it's nonetheless worth buying your ticket a day or so in advance, or in the morning for the evening train. The process of scrutinising people's IDs both when tickets are purchased and when going through security before boarding can be a bit slow. Also note that the ticket windows in the stations close at prayer time, meaning you'll have to get there early if departure and prayer times coincide (see Dodging Prayer Times p164).

TRANSPORT

Health Dr Caroline Evans

Prevention is the key to staying healthy while travelling in Saudi Arabia. Infectious diseases can and do occur here, but they're quite rare. The most common reason for needing medical help in Saudi Arabia is as a result of accidents – some of the driving has to be seen to be believed. Fortunately, Saudi Arabia has possibly the best medical facilities in the Middle East.

BEFORE YOU GO

A little planning before departure, particularly for pre-existing illnesses, will save you a lot of trouble later. See your dentist before a long trip; carry a spare pair of contact lenses and glasses (and take your optical prescription with you); and carry a first-aid kit with you.

It's tempting to leave it all to the last minute – don't! Many vaccines don't ensure immunity for two weeks, so visit a doctor from four to eight weeks before departure. Ask your doctor for an International Certificate of Vaccination (otherwise known as the yellow booklet), which will list all the vaccinations you've received. This is mandatory for countries that require proof of yellow-fever vaccination upon entry, but it's good to carry it wherever you travel.

Travellers can register with the **International Association for Medical Advice to Travellers** (IMAT; www.iamat.org). Its website can help travellers find a doctor with recognised training. Those heading off to very remote areas may like to do a first-aid course, (Red Cross and St John Ambulance can help) or attend a remote medicine first-aid course such as offered by the **Royal Geographical Society** (www.rgs.org).

Bring medications in their original, clearly labelled, containers. A signed and dated letter from your physician describing your medical conditions and medications, including generic names, is also a good idea. If carrying syringes or needles, be sure to have a physician's letter documenting their medical necessity.

INSURANCE

Find out in advance if your insurance plan will make payments directly to providers or reimburse you later for overseas health expenditures (in many countries doctors expect payment in cash). If you have to claim later, ensure you keep all documentation. It's also worth ensuring your travel insurance will cover repatriation home or to better medical facilities elsewhere, including aeromedical evacuation. For dental treatment, your travel insurance will not usually cover you for anything other than emergency procedures.

RECOMMENDED VACCINATIONS

The World Health Organization (WHO) recommends that all travellers, regardless of the region they are travelling in, should be covered for diphtheria, tetanus, measles, mumps, rubella and polio, as well as hepatitis B. While making preparations to travel, take the opportunity to ensure that all of your routine vaccination cover is complete. The consequences of these diseases can be severe and outbreaks do occur in the Middle East.

MEDICAL CHECKLIST

Following is a list of other items you should consider packing in your medical kit.

▪ antibiotics (if travelling off the beaten track)
▪ antidiarrheal drugs (eg loperamide)
▪ acetaminophen/paracetamol (Tylenol) or aspirin
▪ anti-inflammatory drugs (eg ibuprofen)
▪ antihistamines (for hay fever and allergic reactions)
▪ antibacterial ointment (eg Bactroban) for cuts and abrasions
▪ steroid cream or cortisone (for allergic rashes)
▪ bandages, gauze, gauze rolls
▪ adhesive or paper tape
▪ scissors, safety pins, tweezers
▪ thermometer
▪ pocket knife
▪ DEET – containing insect repellent for the skin
▪ pyrethrin – containing insect spray for clothing, tents, and bed nets
▪ sun block
▪ oral-rehydration salts
▪ iodine tablets (for water purification)
▪ syringes and sterile needles (if travelling to remote areas).

ONLINE RESOURCES

There is a wealth of travel health advice available on the Internet. **Lonely Planet.com** (www.lonelyplanet.com) is a good place to start. The **World Health Organization** (www.who.int/ith/) publishes a superb book called *International Travel and Health*, which is revised annually and is available online at no cost. Another website of general interest is **MD Travel Health** (www.mdtravelhealth.com); this provides complete travel health recommendations for every country and is updated daily, also at no cost. **The Centers for Disease Control and Prevention** (www.cdc.gov) website is a very useful source of traveller's health information.

TRAVEL HEALTH WEBSITES

It's usually a good idea to consult your government's travel health website before departure, if one is available.
Australia (www.dfat.gov.au/travel/)
Canada (www.travelhealth.gc.ca)
United Kingdom (www.doh.gov.uk/traveladvice/)
United States (www.cdc.gov/travel/)

FURTHER READING

Lonely Planet's *Travel With Children* is packed with useful information including pretrip planning, emergency first aid, immunisation and disease information and what to do if you get sick on the road. Other recommended references include *Traveller's Health* by Dr Richard Dawood (Oxford University Press) and *International Travel Health Guide* by Stuart R Rose, MD (Travel Medicine Inc). *The Travellers' Good Health Guide* by Ted Lankester (Sheldon Press) is especially useful for volunteers and long-term expatriates working in the Middle East.

IN TRANSIT

DEEP VEIN THROMBOSIS (DVT)

Deep vein thrombosis occurs when blood clots form in the legs during plane flights, chiefly because of prolonged immobility. The longer the flight, the greater the risk. Though most blood clots are reabsorbed uneventfully, some may break off and travel through the blood vessels to the lungs, where they may cause life-threatening complications.

The chief symptom of deep vein thrombosis is swelling or pain of the foot, ankle, or calf, usually on just one side. When a blood clot travels to the lungs, it may cause chest pain and difficulty breathing. Travellers with any of these symptoms should immediately seek medical attention.

To prevent the development of deep vein thrombosis on long flights you should walk about the cabin, perform isometric compressions of the leg muscles (ie contract the leg muscles while sitting), drink plenty of fluids, and avoid alcohol and tobacco.

JET LAG & MOTION SICKNESS

Jet lag is common when crossing more than five time zones; it can result in insomnia, fatigue, malaise or nausea. To avoid jet lag try drinking plenty of fluids (nonalcoholic) and eating light meals. Upon arrival, seek exposure to natural sunlight and readjust your schedule (for daily activities such as meals and sleep) as soon as possible.

Antihistamines such as dimenhydrinate (Dramamine) and meclizine (Antivert, Bonine) are usually the first choice for treating motion sickness. Their main side-effect is drowsiness. A herbal alternative is ginger, which works like a charm for some people.

IN SAUDI ARABIA

AVAILABILITY & COST OF HEALTHCARE

Saudi Arabia has some of the best medical facilities in the Middle East, with well-trained doctors and nurses who are often expats. It's highly unlikely that Saudi Arabia will have reciprocal arrangements with your own country and you should be prepared to pay for all medical and dental treatment.

Medical care is not always readily available outside major cities. Medicine, and even sterile dressings or intravenous fluids, may need to be bought from a local pharmacy. The travel assistance provided by your insurance may be able to locate the nearest source of medical help, otherwise ask at your hotel. In an emergency contact your embassy or consulate.

Standards of dental care are variable and there is an increased risk of hepatitis B and HIV transmission via poorly sterilised equipment.

For minor illnesses such as diarrhoea, pharmacists can often provide valuable advice and sell over the counter medication. They can also advise when more specialised help is needed.

INFECTIOUS DISEASES
Dengue Fever

Otherwise known as break-bone fever, dengue is spread through the bite of the mosquito. It causes a feverish illness with headache and muscle pains like a bad, prolonged, attack of influenza. There may also be a rash. Mosquito bites should be avoided whenever possible.

Diphtheria

Diphtheria is spread through close respiratory contact. It causes a high temperature and severe sore throat. Sometimes a membrane forms across the throat requiring a tracheostomy to prevent suffocation. Vaccination is recommended for those likely to be in close contact with the local population in infected areas. The vaccine is given as an injection alone, or with tetanus, and lasts 10 years.

Hepatitis A

Hepatitis A is spread through contaminated food (particularly shellfish) and water. It causes jaundice, and although it is rarely fatal, can cause prolonged lethargy and delayed recovery. Symptoms include dark urine, a yellow colour to the whites of the eyes, fever and abdominal pain. Hepatitis A vaccine (Avaxim, VAQTA, Havrix) is given as an injection: a single dose will give protection for up to a year while a booster 12 months later will provide a subsequent ten years of protection. Hepatitis A and typhoid vaccines can also be given as a single dose vaccine, hepatyrix or viatim.

Hepatitis B

Infected blood, contaminated needles and sexual intercourse can all transmit hepatitis B. The disease can cause jaundice, and affects the liver, occasionally causing liver failure. All travellers should make this a routine vaccination. (Many countries now give hepatitis B vaccination as part of routine childhood vaccination.) The vaccine is given singly, or at the same time as the hepatitis A vaccine (hepatyrix). A course will give protection for at least five years. It can be given over four weeks, or six months.

HIV

HIV is spread via infected blood and blood products, sexual intercourse with an infected partner and from an infected mother to her new-born child. It can be spread through 'blood to blood' contacts such as contaminated instruments during medical, dental, acupuncture and other body piercing procedures and sharing used intravenous needles.

Saudi Arabia requires a negative HIV test as a requirement for Residence visas (ie work visas) – not for Haj, Visitor (Business) or Transit visas.

Leishmaniasis

Spread through the bite of an infected sand fly, leishmaniasis can cause a slowly growing skin lump or ulcer. It may develop into a serious life-threatening fever usually accompanied with anaemia and weight loss. Infected dogs are also carriers of the infection. Sand-fly bites should be avoided whenever possible.

Leptospirosis

Leptospirosis is spread through the excreta of infected rodents, especially rats. It can cause hepatitis and renal failure that may be fatal. It is unusual for travellers to be affected unless living in poor sanitary conditions. It causes fever and jaundice.

Malaria

The prevalence of malaria varies throughout Saudi Arabia. There is a risk of infection throughout the year in the south, (apart from in the high altitudes of the Asir region) and also in some western regions. The risk of malaria is minimal in most cities, however, check with your doctor if you are considering travelling to any rural areas. It is important to take antimalarial tablets if the risk is significant. For up-to-date information about the risk of contracting malaria in Saudi Arabia, contact your local travel health clinic.

It is possible to contract malaria from a single bite from an infected mosquito. Malaria almost always starts with marked shivering, fever and sweating. Muscle pains, headache and vomiting are common. Symptoms may occur anywhere from few days to three weeks after the infected mosquito bite. The illness can start while you are taking preventative tablets if they are not fully effective, and may also occur after you have finished taking your tablets.

Meningitis

Meningococcal infection is spread through close respiratory contact. A Quadrivalent vaccine is advised for those attending haj pilgrimages (in Mecca and Medina along the west coast) but not for those travelling to other parts of the country. A meningococcal vaccination certificate covering the A and W135 strains is required as a condition of entry if attending a haj pilgrimage, and from all travellers arriving from the meningitis belt of sub-Saharan Africa. Visas for pilgrimages are not issued unless proof of vaccination is submitted with the visa application.

Poliomyelitis

Polio is generally spread through contaminated food and water. It is one of the vaccines given in childhood and should be boosted every 10 years, either orally (a drop on the tongue), or as an injection. Polio may be carried asymptomatically, although it can cause a transient fever and, in rare cases, potentially permanent muscle weakness or paralysis.

Rabies

Spread through bites or licks on broken skin from an infected animal, rabies is fatal. Animal handlers should be vaccinated, as should those travelling to remote areas where a reliable source of post-bite vaccine is not available within 24 hours. Three injections are needed over a month. If not vaccinated, you will need a course of five injections starting within 24 hours or as soon as possible after the injury. Vaccination does not provide you with immunity, it merely buys you more time to seek appropriate medical help.

Rift Valley Fever

This haemorrhagic fever is spread through blood or blood products, including those from infected animals. It causes a 'flu-like' illness with fever, joint pains and occasionally more serious complications. Complete recovery is possible. An outbreak of Rift Valley fever occurred in the Hejaz in the late 1990s, so check the prevailing situation before travelling.

Schistosome

Otherwise known as bilharzia, this is spread through the fresh-water snail. It causes infection of the bowel and bladder, often with bleeding. It is caused by a fluke (parasitic flatworm) and is contracted through the skin from water contaminated with human urine or faeces. Paddling or swimming in suspect freshwater lakes or slow-running rivers should be avoided. There may be no symptoms. Possible symptoms include a transient fever and rash, and advanced cases of schistosome may cause blood in the stool or in the urine. A blood test can detect antibodies if you have been exposed and treatment is then possible in specialist travel or infectious disease clinics.

Tuberculosis

Tuberculosis (TB) is spread through close respiratory contact and occasionally through infected milk or milk products. BCG vaccine is recommended for those likely to be mixing closely with the local

HEALTH

population. It is more important for those visiting family or planning on a long stay, and those employed as teachers and health-care workers. TB can be asymptomatic, although symptoms can include a cough, weight loss or fever which can appear months or even years after exposure. An X-ray is the best way to confirm if you have TB. BCG gives a moderate degree of protection against TB. It causes a small permanent scar at the site of injection, and is usually only given in specialised chest clinics. As it's a live vaccine, BCG should not be given to pregnant women or immunocompromised individuals. The BCG vaccine is not available in all countries.

Typhoid

This is spread through food or water that has been contaminated by infected human faeces. The first symptom is usually fever or a pink rash on the abdomen. Septicaemia (blood poisoning) may also occur. Typhoid vaccine (typhim Vi, typherix) will give protection for three years. In some countries, the oral vaccine Vivotif is also available.

Yellow Fever

Yellow-fever vaccination is only required for visitors who have been to a yellow-fever infected country (and is not necessary otherwise). This normally means if arriving directly from an infected country or if the traveller has been in an infected country during the last 10 days. We would recommend, however, that travellers carry a vaccination certificate if they have been in an infected country during the previous month, to avoid any possible difficulties with immigration. There is always the possibility that a traveller without an up-to-date certificate will be vaccinated and detained in isolation at the port of arrival for up to 10 days, or even repatriated. The vaccination must be given at a designated clinic, and is valid for 10 years. It is a live vaccine and must not be given to immunocompromised or pregnant travellers.

TRAVELLER'S DIARRHOEA

To prevent diarrhoea, avoid tap water unless it has been boiled, filtered or chemically disinfected (iodine tablets). Eat only fresh fruits or vegetables if cooked or if you have peeled them yourself and avoid dairy products that might contain unpasteurised milk.

Buffet meals are risky, food should be piping hot; meals freshly cooked in front of you in a busy restaurant are more likely to be safe.

If you develop diarrhoea, be sure to drink plenty of fluids, preferably an oral rehydration solution containing lots of salt and sugar. A few loose stools don't require treatment but, if you start having more than four or five stools a day, you should start taking an antibiotic (usually a quinolone drug) and an antidiarrheal agent (such as loperamide). If diarrhoea is bloody, persists for more than 72 hours, or is accompanied by fever, shaking chills or severe abdominal pain you should seek medical attention.

ENVIRONMENTAL HAZARDS
Heatstroke

Heat exhaustion occurs following heavy sweating and excessive fluid loss with inadequate replacement of fluids and salt. This is particularly common in hot climates when taking unaccustomed exercise before full acclimatisation. Symptoms include headache, dizziness and tiredness. Dehydration is already happening by the time you feel thirsty – aim to drink sufficient water to produce pale, diluted urine. The treatment of heat exhaustion consists of fluid replacement with water or fruit juice or both, and cooling by cold water and fans. The treatment of the salt loss component consists of consuming salty fluids (as in soup or broth) and adding a little more table salt to foods than usual.

Heatstroke is much more serious. This occurs when the body's heat-regulating mechanism breaks down. Excessive rise in body temperature leads to the cessation of sweating, irrational and hyperactive behaviour, and eventually loss of consciousness and death. Rapid cooling by spraying the body with water and fanning is an ideal treatment. Emergency fluid and electrolyte replacement by intravenous drip is usually also required.

Insect Bites & Stings

Mosquitoes may not carry malaria but can cause irritation and infected bites. Using DEET-based insect repellents will prevent bites. Mosquitoes also spread dengue fever.

Bees and wasps only cause real problems to those with a severe allergy (anaphylaxis), who should carry an adrenaline injection or similar.

Scorpions are frequently found in arid or dry climates. They can inflict a painful bite which is rarely life threatening.

Bed bugs are often found in hostels and cheap hotels. They lead to very itchy lumpy bites. Spraying the mattress with an appropriate insect killer will do a good job of getting rid of them.

Scabies are also frequently found in cheap accommodation. These tiny mites live in the skin, particularly between the fingers. They cause an intensely itchy rash. Scabies is easily treated with lotion available from pharmacies; people who you come into contact with also need treating to avoid spreading scabies between asymptomatic carriers.

Snake Bites

Do not walk barefoot or stick your hand into holes or cracks. Half of those bitten by venomous snakes are not actually injected with poison (envenomed). If bitten by a snake, do not panic. Immobilise the bitten limb with a splint (eg a stick) and apply a bandage over the site, firm pressure, similar to a bandage over a sprain. Do not apply a tourniquet, or cut or suck the bite. Get the victim to medical help as soon as possible so that antivenin can be given if necessary.

Water

Tap water is not safe to drink throughout the Middle East, although some expats in Saudi Arabia do so with no problems. Stick to bottled water or boil water for ten minutes, use water purification tablets or a filter. Do not drink water from rivers or lakes, this may contain bacteria or viruses that can cause diarrhoea or vomiting.

TRAVELLING WITH CHILDREN

All travellers with children should know how to treat minor ailments and when to seek medical treatment. Make sure the children are up to date with routine vaccinations, and discuss possible travel vaccines well before departure. as some vaccines are not suitable for children aged under one year old.

In hot, moist climates any wound or break in the skin may lead to infection. The area should be cleaned and then kept dry and clean. Remember to avoid contaminated food and water. If your child is vomiting or experiencing diarrhoea, lost fluid and salts must be replaced. It may be helpful to take rehydration powders for reconstituting with boiled water. Ask your doctor about this.

Children should be encouraged to avoid dogs or other mammals because of the risk of rabies and other diseases. Any bite, scratch or lick from a warm-blooded, furry animal should immediately be thoroughly cleaned. If there is any possibility that the animal is infected with rabies, immediate medical assistance should be sought.

WOMEN'S HEALTH

Emotional stress, exhaustion and travelling through different time zones can all contribute to an upset in the menstrual pattern. If using oral contraceptives, remember some antibiotics, diarrhoea and vomiting can stop the pill from working and lead to the risk of pregnancy – remember to take condoms with you just in case. Condoms should be kept in a cool dry place or they may crack and perish.

Emergency contraception is most effective if taken within 24 hours after unprotected sex. The **International Planned Parent Federation** (www.ippf.org) can advise about the availability of contraception in different countries. Tampons and sanitary towels are not always available outside of major cities in the Middle East.

Travelling during pregnancy is usually possible but there are important things to consider. Have a medical check-up before embarking on your trip. The most risky times for travel are during the first 12 weeks of pregnancy, when miscarriage is most likely, and after 30 weeks, when complications such as high blood pressure and premature delivery can occur. Most airlines will not accept a traveller after 28 to 32 weeks of pregnancy, and long-haul flights in the later stages can be very uncomfortable. Antenatal facilities, like the rest of the Saudi medical service, is generally excellent, particularly in medium-sized towns and cities. Taking written records of the pregnancy, including details of your blood group, are likely to be helpful if you need medical attention while away. Ensure your insurance policy covers pregnancy, delivery and postnatal care.

HEALTH

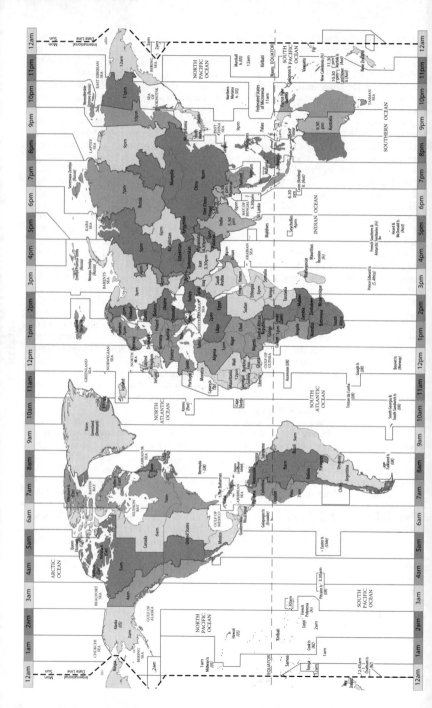

Language

CONTENTS

English is widely spoken throughout the Saudi Arabia, but a few words of Arabic can do a lot to ease your passage through the region.

Learning a few basics for day-to-day travelling doesn't take long at all, but to master the complexities of Arabic would take years of consistent study. The whole issue is complicated by the differences between Classical Arabic (*fus-ha*), its modern descendant MSA (Modern Standard Arabic) and regional dialects. The classical tongue is the language of the Quran and Arabic poetry of centuries past. For long it remained static, but in order to survive it had to adapt to change, and the result is more or less MSA, the common language of the press, radio and educated discourse. It is as close to a *lingua franca* (common language) as the Arab world comes, and is generally understood – if not always well spoken – across the Arab world.

For most outsiders trying to learn Arabic, the most frustrating element remains understanding the spoken language (wherever you are), as there is virtually no written material to refer to for back up. Acquisition of MSA is a long-term investment, and an esoteric argument flows back and forward about the relative merits of learning MSA first (and so perhaps having to wait some time before being able to communicate adequately with people in the street) or a dialect. All this will give you an inkling of why so few non-Arabs, or non-Muslims, embark on a study of the language.

Mercifully, the words and phrases a traveller is most likely to use are fairly standard throughout Saudi Arabia. The words and phrases that follow should be understood anywhere in the region.

SAUDI ARABIC

The Arabic spoken in Saudi Arabia is known as Gulf Arabic (GA) which tends to be more more formal than, say, Egyptian or Moroccan Arabic. This is due in large part to the fact that orthodox Wahhabi Islam is the ruling orthodoxy in Saudi Arabia, where religion plays a much more prominent role in public life than in other Arab countries. As a result, Classical Arabic (the language of the Quran) makes more forays into daily conversation than possibly anywhere else in the world. More specialised or educated language tends to be pretty much the same across the Arab world, although pronunciation may vary considerably – Gulf Arabic tends to stem from the Bedouin Arabic of the desert and, as such, can sound quite harsh to the Western ear. An Arab from, say, Jordan or Iraq will have no problem.

PRONUNCIATION

Pronunciation of Arabic can be tongue-tying for someone unfamiliar with the intonation and combination of sounds. This language guide should help, but bear in mind that the myriad rules governing pronunciation and vowel use are too extensive to be covered here.

Vowels

Technically, there are three long and three short vowels in Arabic. The reality is a little different, with local dialect and varying consonant combinations affecting the pronunciation of vowels. This is the case throughout the Arabic-speaking world. More like five short and five long vowels can be identified; in this guide we use all of these except the long **o**.

THE STANDARD ARABIC ALPHABET

Final	Medial	Initial	Alone	Transliteration	Pronunciation
ـا			ا	aa	as in 'father'
ـب	ـبـ	بـ	ب	b	as in 'bet'
ـت	ـتـ	تـ	ت	t	as in 'ten'
ـث	ـثـ	ثـ	ث	th	as in 'thin'
ـج	ـجـ	جـ	ج	j/g	as in 'jet'; sometimes as the 'g' in 'go'
ـح	ـحـ	حـ	ح	H	a strongly whispered 'h', like a sigh of relief
ـخ	ـخـ	خـ	خ	kh	as the 'ch' in Scottish *loch*
ـد			د	d	as in 'dim'
ـذ			ذ	dh	as the 'th' in 'this'; also as **d** or **z**
ـر			ر	r	a rolled 'r', as in the Spanish word *caro*
ـز			ز	z	as in 'zip'
ـس	ـسـ	سـ	س	s	as in 'so', never as in 'wisdom'
ـش	ـشـ	شـ	ش	sh	as in 'ship'
ـص	ـصـ	صـ	ص	ṣ	emphatic 's'
ـض	ـضـ	ضـ	ض	ḍ	emphatic 'd'
ـط	ـطـ	طـ	ط	ṭ	emphatic 't'
ـظ	ـظـ	ظـ	ظ	ẓ	emphatic 'z'
ـع	ـعـ	عـ	ع	'	the Arabic letter *'ayn*; pronounce as a glottal stop – like the closing of the throat before saying 'Oh-oh!' (see Other Sounds on p195)
ـغ	ـغـ	غـ	غ	gh	a guttural sound like Parisian 'r'
ـف	ـفـ	فـ	ف	f	as in 'far'
ـق	ـقـ	قـ	ق	q	a strongly guttural 'k' sound; also often pronounced as a glottal stop
ـك	ـكـ	كـ	ك	k	as in 'king'
ـل	ـلـ	لـ	ل	l	as in 'lamb'
ـم	ـمـ	مـ	م	m	as in 'me'
ـن	ـنـ	نـ	ن	n	as in 'name'
ـه	ـهـ	هـ	ه	h	as in 'ham'
ـو			و	w	as in 'wet'; or
				oo	long, as in 'food'; or
				ow	as in 'how'
ـي	ـيـ	يـ	ي	y	as in 'yes'; or
				ee	as in 'beer', only softer; or
				ai/ay	as in 'aisle'/as the 'ay' in 'day'

Vowels Not all Arabic vowel sounds are represented in the alphabet. For more information on the vowel sounds used in this language guide, see Pronunciation on p193.

Emphatic Consonants To simplify the transliteration system used in this book, the emphatic consonants have not been included.

a	as in 'had'
aa	as the 'a' in 'father'
e	short, as in 'bet'; long, as in 'there'
i	as in 'hit'
ee	as in 'beer', only softer
o	as in 'hot'
u	as in 'put'
oo	as in 'food'

Consonants

Pronunciation for all Arabic consonants is covered in the alphabet table on p194. It's important to note that when double consonants occur in transliterations, both are pronounced. For example, *al-Hammam* (toilet), is pronounced 'al-ham-mam'.

OTHER SOUNDS

Arabic has two sounds that are very tricky for non-Arabs to produce, the 'ayn and the glottal stop. The letter 'ayn represents a sound with no English equivalent that comes even close. It is similar to the glottal stop (which is not actually represented in the alphabet) but the muscles at the back of the throat are gagged more forcefully – it has been described as the sound of someone being strangled. In many transliteration systems 'ayn is represented by an opening quotation mark, and the glottal stop by a closing quotation mark. To make the transliterations in this language guide (and throughout the rest of the book) easier to use, we haven't distinguished between the glottal stop and the 'ayn, using the closing quotation mark to represent both sounds. You should find that Arabic speakers will still understand you.

TRANSLITERATION

It's worth noting here that transliteration from the Arabic script into English – or any other language for that matter – is at best an approximate science.

The presence of sounds unknown in European languages and the fact that the script is 'defective' (most vowels are not written) combine to make it nearly impossible to settle on one universally accepted method of transliteration. A wide variety of spellings is therefore possible for words when they appear in Latin script – and that goes for places and people's names as well.

While striving to reflect the language as closely as possible and aiming at consistency, this book generally spells place, street

and hotel names and the like as the locals have done. Don't be surprised if you come across several versions of the same thing.

ACCOMMODATION

I'm looking for ...	*ana badawar ala ...?*
a youth hostel	*bayt al-shabaab*
hotel	*funduq*

I'd like to book a ...	*ana aloga eHjaz ...*
Do you have a ...?	*fee aindakoum ...?*
(cheap) room	*ghurfa (rakheesa)*
single room	*ghurfa muferda*
double room	*ghurfa muzdawaja*

May I see the room?	*mumkin ashuf al-ghurfa*
May I see other rooms?	*mumkin ashuf ghuraf thaania*
How much is this room per night?	*cham ujrat haathil ghurfa fil-leila*
This is very expensive.	*hatha ghali jeddan*
Do you have any cheaper rooms?	*fi ghuraf arkhas*
This is fine.	*hatha zein*

for one night	*lee layla wahda*
for two nights	*lee layla ten*
It's very noisy.	*hathee feeha dajeh kaseer*
It's very dirty.	*hathee waskha kaseer*
Where is the bathroom?	*wayn el-Hammam*
I'm leaving today.	*ana musafer al-youm*
We're leaving today.	*neHna musafereen al-yom*

address	*al-anwaar*
air-conditioning	*mookayif/kondishen*
blanket	*al-bataaniyya*
camp site	*al-mukhayam*
hot water	*al-mayya saakhma*
key	*al-miftaH*
manager	*al-mudeer*
shower	*al-doosh*
soap	*al-saboon*
toilet	*al-Hammam*

CONVERSATION & GREETINGS

Arabs place great importance on civility and it's rare to see any interaction between people that doesn't begin with profuse greetings, enquiries into the other's health and other niceties.

Arabic greetings are more formal than in English and there is a reciprocal response to each. These sometimes vary slightly, depending on whether you're addressing a man or a woman. A simple encounter can become a drawn-out affair, with neither side wanting to be the one to put a halt to the stream of greetings and well-wishing. As an *ajnabi* (foreigner), you're not expected to know all the ins and outs, but if you come up with the right expression at the appropriate moment they'll love it.

The most common greeting is *al-salaam alaykum* (peace be upon you), to which the correct reply is *wa alaykum al-salaam* (and upon you be peace). If you get invited to a birthday celebration or are around for any of the big holidays, the common greeting is *kul sana wa intum bikher* (I wish you well for the coming year).

Arrival in one piece is always something to be grateful for. Passengers will often be greeted with *al-Hamdu lillah al al-salaama* – 'thank God for your safe arrival'.

Hello.	*al-salaam alaykum*
Hello. (response)	*wa alaykum al-salaam*
Hello. (informal)	*marHaba/ya marHaba*

It's an important custom in Saudi Arabia to ask after a person's or their family's health when greeting, eg *chayf es-saHa?* (How is your health?), *chayf al-ahal?* (How is the family?). The response is *bikher il-Hamdu lillah* (Fine, thank you).

Goodbye.	*ma'al salaama*
Goodbye. (response)	
(to a man)	*alla ysalmak*
(to a woman)	*alla ysalmich*
(to a group)	*alla ysallimkum*
Goodbye.	
(to a man)	*Hayyaakallah*
(to a woman)	*Hayyachallah*
(to a group)	*Hayyakumallah*
Goodbye. (response)	
(to a man)	*alla yHai'eek*
(to a woman)	*alla yHai'eech*
(to a group)	*alla yHai'eekum*
Good night.	
(to a man)	*tisbaH ala-kher*
(to a woman)	*tisbiHin ala-kher*
(to a group)	*tisbuHun ala-kher*
Good night. (response)	
(to a man)	*wa inta min ahlil-kher*
(to a woman)	*wa inti min ahlil-kher*
(to a group)	*wa intu min ahlil-kher*
Welcome.	*ahlan wa sahlan/marHaba*
Welcome to you.	
(to a man)	*ahlan beek*

(to a woman)	*ahlan beechi*
(to a group)	*ahlan beekum*
Pleased to meet you.	*fursa sa'ida* (also said to people as they are leaving)
Pleased to meet you. (response)	
(by an individual)	*wa ana as'ad*
(by a group)	*wa iHna as'ad*
How are you?	*kief ul-hal*
(to a man)	*shlonik/kef Halak*
(to a woman)	*shlonich/kef Halik*
(to a group)	*shlonkum/kef Halkum*
Fine, thanks.	*bkher al-Hamdu lillah* or *tammam*
(by a man)	*zein al-Hamdu lillah*
(by a woman)	*zeina al-Hamdu lillah*
(by a group)	*zeinin al-Hamdu lillah*
What's your name?	
(to a man)	*shismak*
(to a woman)	*shismich*
(to a group)	*shisimkum*
My name is ...	*ismi ...*
I'm ...	*ana ...*
Where are you from?	*min wayn inta?*
I'm from ...	*ana min ...*
Do you like ...?	*inta/inti bitHib ...?* (m/f)
I like ...	*ana bHib ...*
I don't like ...	*ana ma bHib ...*
Yes.	*aiwa/na'am*
No.	*la'*
Maybe.	*mumkin*
Please.	
(to a man)	*min fadhlak*
(to a woman)	*min fadhlich*
(to a group)	*min fadhlekum*
Thank you.	*baraka Allah beek* (God bless you) or *shukran*
You're welcome.	*afwan/al-afu*
Excuse me.	
(to a man)	*lau samaHt*
(to a woman)	*lau samaHti*
(to a group)	*lau samaHtu*
After you.	*atfaddal*
OK.	*zein/kwayyis/tayib*
No problem.	*mafee mushkala*
Impossible.	*mish mumkin*
It doesn't matter/ I don't care.	*ma'alish*

DIRECTIONS

How do I get to ...?	*keef boosal lil ...?*
Can you show me the way to ...?	*mumkin tdallini ala tareeq lil ...?*
How many kilometres?	*cham kilometa?*
What street is this?	*shoo-hatha sharai?*

to/for	lil
left	shimaal/yasaar
right	yimeen
straight	ala tool
street	shaari'
number	raqam
city	madina
village	qaria
at the next corner	thani mafraq
this way	matn hina
here/there	hina/hinak
in front of	chiddaam
near	gareeb
far	ba'eed
north	shimaal
south	janub
east	sharg
west	gharb

SIGNS

Entrance	مدخل
Exit	خروج
Information	معلومات
Open	مفتوح
Closed	مغلق
Prohibited	ممنوع
Police	شرطة
Men's Toilet	حمام للرجال
Women's Toilet	حمام للنساء
Hospital	مستشفي

HEALTH

I'm ill.	ana maareed
My friend is ill.	sadeeyee maareed
It hurts here.	bee yu ja nee hina

I'm ...	andee ...
asthmatic	azmit raboo
diabetic	al-sukkar
epileptic	al-saraa

I'm allergic ...	andee Hasasiyya ...
to antibiotics	min al-mudad alhayawee
to aspirin	min al-asbireen
to bees	min al-naHl
to nuts	min al-mukassarat
to penicillin	min al-binisileen

antiseptic	mutahhir
aspirin	asbireen
Band-Aids	dammad lazeg

EMERGENCIES

Help me!	saa' idoonee!
I'm sick.	ana maareed/mareeda (m/f)
Call the police!	itasell bil shurta!
doctor	al-tabeeb
hospital	al-mustashfa
police	al-shurta
Go away/Get lost!	imshee!
Shame on you!	istiHi a'la Haalak!
(said by woman)	

chemist/pharmacy	al-sayidaliyya
condoms	kaboot
contraceptive	waseela lee man'al-Haml
diarrhoea	is-haal
fever	sukhooma
headache	suda' ras/waja' ras
hospital	mustashfa
medicine	dawa
pregnant	Haamel
prescription	wasfa/rashetta
sanitary napkins	fuwat saHiyya
stomachache	waja' feel bat-n
sunblock cream	marham wagee min ashat alshams
tampons	tambaks (as in 'Tampax')/ fuwat saHiyya leel Hareem

LANGUAGE DIFFICULTIES

I understand.	
(by a man)	ana fahim
(by a woman)	ana fahma
I don't understand.	
(by a man)	ana mu fahim
(by a woman)	ana mu fahma
Do you speak English/ French/German?	titkallam ingleezi/fransawi/ almaani
I don't speak Arabic.	ma-atkallam arabi
I want an interpreter.	ana abga mutarjem
Could you write it down, please?	mumkin tiktbha lee, min fadlach
How do you say ... in Arabic?	chayf tegool ... bil'arabi?

NUMBERS

0	sifr	٠
1	waHid	١
2	ithneen	٢
3	thalatha	٣
4	arba'a	٤
5	khamsa	٥
6	sitta	٦

LANGUAGE

7	saba'a	٧
8	tamaniya	٨
9	tis'a	٩
10	ashra	١٠
11	Hda'ash	١١
12	thna'ash	١٢
13	thalathta'ash	١٣
14	arbatash	١٤
15	khamistash	١٥
16	sittash	١٦
17	sabi'tash	١٧
18	thimanta'ash	١٨
19	tisita'ash	١٩
20	'ishreen	٢٠
21	waHid wa 'ishreen	٢١
22	itnayn wa 'ishreen	٢٢
30	thalatheen	٣٠
40	arbi'een	٤٠
50	khamseen	٥٠
60	sitteen	٦٠
70	saba'een	٧٠
80	thimaneen	٨٠
90	tis'een	٩٠
100	imia	١٠٠
200	imiatayn	٢٠٠
1000	'alf	١٠٠٠
2000	'alfayn	٢٠٠٠
3000	thalath-alaf	٣٠٠٠

PAPERWORK

date of birth	tareekh al-welada/al-meelad
name	al-ism
nationality	al-jenseeya
passport	jawaz al-safar/al-bassbor
permit	tasreeh
place of birth	makka al-welada/meelad
visa	ta'sheera/feeza

SHOPPING & SERVICES

I'm looking for ...	ana adawar ala ...
	ana abHath aa'n ...
Where is the ...?	wein al ...?
bank	el-bank
beach	il-shatt/il-shaat'i
embassy	el-safara
exchange office	maktab el-sirafa
laundry	el-ghaseel
market	el-souq
mosque	el-masjid
museum	el-matHaf
newsagents	el-maktaba
old city	el-madina il-qadima
palace	el-qasr
police station	el-makhfar
post office	maktab al-bareed

restaurant	el-mataam
telephone	el-telefon/el-hataf
telephone office	maktab el-Hatef
toilet	el-Hammam
tourist office	maktab el-seeyaHa

nappies (diapers)	Hafadat leel atfal
disposable nappies	bamberz (brand name)
formula (baby's milk)	Haleeb mujafaf leel atfal

I want to change ...	ana abga asrif ...
money	floos
travellers cheques	sheikat siyaHeeya

I want...	ana abga ...
Where can I buy ...?	wein agdar ashtiri
Do you have ...?	indik (to a man)/
	indich (to a woman)
Is there ...?	fee andakum ...?
What is this?	shoo Hadha?
How much?	gedash?
How many?	cham?
It's too expensive.	ghalee/ghalia wa'id (m/f)
There isn't (any).	mafee (walashai)
May I look at it?	mumkin ashoof il?

What time does it open?
   sa'acham yeftaH?
What time does it close?
   sa'a cham yegfell?
I'd like to make a telephone call.
   ana abga sawee mookalama

TIME & DATES

What time is it?	as-sa'a kam
It's ...	as-sa'a ...
one o'clock	waHda
1.15	waHda wa rob'
1.20	waHda wa tilt
1.30	waHda wa nus
1.45	ithneen illa rob' (literally 'quarter to two')

daily	kil yom
today	al-yom
yesterday	ams
tomorrow	bukra/bacher
early	mbach'ir/badri
late	mit'akhir

Monday	yom al-ithneen
Tuesday	yom al-thalath
Wednesday	yom al-arbaa'
Thursday	yom al-khamis
Friday	yom al-jama'a

LANGUAGE

| Saturday | yom as-sabt |
| Sunday | yom al-Had |

The Western Calendar Months

The Islamic year has 12 lunar months and is 11 days shorter than the Western (Gregorian) calendar, so important Muslim dates will occur 11 days earlier each (Western) year.

There are two Gregorian calendars in use in the Arab world. In Egypt and westwards, the months have virtually the same names as in English (January is *yanaayir*, October is *octobir* and so on), but in Lebanon and eastwards, the names are quite different. Talking about, say, June as 'month six' is the easiest solution, but for the sake of completeness, the months from January are:

January	kanoon ath-thani
February	shubaat
March	azaar
April	nisaan
May	ayyaar
June	Huzayraan
July	tammooz
August	'aab
September	aylool
October	tishreen al-awal
November	tishreen ath-thani
December	kaanoon al-awal

TRANSPORT
Public Transport

Where is the ...?	wein al ...
How far is ...?	cham yibe'id ...
the bus stop	mogaf al-bas
the bus station	maHattat al-bas
the train station	maHattat al-qatar
a taxi stand	mogaf el-taks
the airport	al-mataar

boat	markab
bus	al-bas
taxi	el-taks
ticket office	maktab al-tathaaker

I want to go to ...	abga arouH li ...
When does the ... leave?	mata yamshi il ...
When does the ... arrive?	mata tusal il ...
What is the fare to ...?	cham il tathkara li ...
Which bus/taxi goes to ...?	ai bas/tax yrouH il ...

Does this bus/taxi go to ...?	Hathal bas yrouH il ...
How many buses go to ...?	cham bas yrouH li ...
How long does the trip take?	cham sa'aa al-riHla?
Please tell me when we get to ...	lau samaHtit goul li mata nosal li ...
Stop here, please.	'ogaf hina, lau samaHt
Please wait for me.	lau samaHt, intethernee
May I sit here?	mumkin ag'id hina
May we sit here?	mumkin nag'id hina

1st class	daraja oola
2nd class	daraja thaniya
ticket	al-tathkara
to ...	ee/a ...
from ...	min ...

Private Transport

I'd like to hire a ...	ana abga ajar ...
Where can I hire a ...?	wayn mumkin ajar ...?
bicycle	bisklet/dakaja
camel	jamal
car	sayyara
car baby seat	kursi sayyara leel tefl
donkey	Hmaar
4WD	'four wheel'
horse	Hsaan
motorcycle	motosikl
tour guide	daleel seeyaHe/ murshid seeyaHe

Is this the road to ...?	Hal Hatha al-tarig eela ...?
Where's a service station?	wayn maHattet el-betrol/al-benzeen?
Please fill it up.	min fadhlak fawell Ha
I'd like (30) litres.	abga (thalatheen) leeter

diesel	deezel
leaded petrol	betrol bil rasas
unleaded petrol	betrol khali mina rasas

I need a mechanic.	ana abga mekaneeki
The car won't start.	el-sayyara ma bet door
I have a flat tyre.	nzel el-doolab
I've run out of petrol.	khalas el-betrol/al-benzeen
I've had an accident.	ana a'malt Hads

Glossary

You may come across the following terms and abbreviations during your travels in Saudi Arabia. For terms relating to food and drink, see the Food & Drink chapter. More terms relating to the haj are covered in that chapter.

Abbasids – Baghdad-based ruling dynasty (AD 749–1258) of the Arab/Islamic Empire
abaya – long, black robe worn by women in public
abu – father of; occurs commonly in Arabic names
agal – double, black wooden braid worn by Saudi men to keep their *gutras* in place; sometimes spelled *igal*
ahl al-kitab – People of the Book (Jews and Christians)
ain – water source or spring
Al-Balad – centre of town
Al-Hasa – Eastern Province oasis; sometimes used interchangeably with Al-Hofuf
Allah – God
Al-Rashid – tribal group centred on Hail and historical rivals to Al-Sauds
Al-Saud – ruling tribal group in Saudi Arabia whose homeland is around Riyadh
Aramco – Arabian American Oil Company, now nationalised
ardha – traditional Bedouin dance

banager – Bedouin silver bracelet
Bedu (Bedouin) – indigenous, nomadic people of Arabia
buyut ash-shebab – youth hostel affiliated to Hostelling International

caliph – Islamic ruler; originally referred to the successors of the Prophet Mohammed
Committee for the Prevention of Vice and the Propagation of Virtue – government department administering the mutawwas; see mutawwa
compound – residential area for expats, usually with high security
corniche – coastal road

dillah – coffee-pot
diwan – assembly (in the Ottoman Empire)

eid – feast
Eid al-Adha – feast of Sacrifice marking the pilgrimage to Mecca; sometimes called Eid al-Kebir
Eid al-Fitr – feast of the Breaking of the Fast, celebrated at the end of Ramadan
emir – prince or local sheikh (sometimes spelled Amir)

Fatimids – Muslim dynasty (AD 909–1171) with their capital in Cairo

GCC – Gulf Cooperation Council consisting of Saudi Arabia, UAE, Bahrain, Kuwait, Qatar and Oman
gutra – long, cotton cloth worn by Saudi men to cover the head

haj – the pilgrimage to the holy sites in and around Mecca, the pinnacle of a devout Muslim's life
hajji – one who has made the haj to Mecca
halal – lawful or permitted in Islam
haram – prayer hall; also used to refer to areas forbidden to non-Muslims; something which is unlawful or prohibited in Islam
harissa – spicy chilli paste
hazm – Bedouin silver belts
Hejaz – western region of Saudi Arabia centred on Mecca and Medina
hijab – woman's veil or headscarf
Hejira – Mohammed's flight from Mecca in AD 622; also the name of the Muslim calendar

ibn – son of; occurs commonly in Arabic names
iftar – the breaking of the day's fast during Ramadan; also spelled 'ftur'
ijma – consensus of Islamic scholars on matters not covered by Quran
ilaga – silver feminine version of an *agal*; see *agal*
imam – Islamic equivalent of a priest
iqama – residence permit and identity document for those living in Kingdom
iqd – Bedouin silver necklaces, consisting of up to five panels

jambiyya – silver dagger, often with a leather handle and sheath, worn by Bedouins in the south, *see also khanjar*
jebel – hill or mountain
jihad – holy war

Kaaba – holy stone in the Great Mosque of Mecca and which all Muslims face when praying
khanjar – silver dagger, often with a leather handle and sheath, worn by Bedouins in the south see also *jambiyya*
khutba – sermon in a mosque
kirdan – Bedouin silver collars or chest pieces made of silver mesh

Mahdi – messiah
mahram – male guardian who should accompany women when in public

majlis – traditional meeting where emirs and tribal sheikhs held public audiences; sometimes refers to place of meeting
malek – king
masjid – mosque
madrassa – Quranic school
maydan – town or city square
medina – city; usually refers to the old quarter of a town
mihrab – vaulted niche in a mosque, which indicates the direction of Mecca
minaret – tower of a mosque from which the muezzin calls the faithful to prayer
minbar – the pulpit in a mosque
al-mizmar – traditional dance and musical instrument
muezzin – mosque official who calls the faithful to prayer
mullah – Muslim scholar, teacher or religious leader
mutawwa – religious police charged with upholding Islamic orthodoxy

Nabataean – northern Arabian empire (1st century BC to AD 106), creators of Petra (in Jordon) and Madain Saleh
NCWCD – National Commission for Wildlife Conservation and Development

Ottoman Empire – former Turkish Empire, of which Saudi Arabia was part until the end of WWI

qadi – Islamic judge under Sharia'a (Quranic) law
qala'at – castle or fort
qasr – castle or fort
qibla – the direction of Mecca in a mosque, indicated by the mihrab
qiladah – Bedouin silver, triangular pendants with a single stone set into the centre
qiya – legal norm based on Islamic analogies
Quran – the holy book of Islam

Ramadan – ninth month of the Muslim year, a time of fasting
Ras as-Sana – New Year
ras – cape, point or headland
rawashan – wooden, latticework balconies which are used throughout the old quarter of Jeddah
Rub al-Khali – The Empty Quarter

Saba – southern Arabian kingdom which controlled frankincense routes

Sasco – Saudi Automotive Services Company
SATA – Saudi Automobile & Touring Association
salat – obligation of prayer for Muslims; sometimes refers to prayer times
Sands, The – Bedouin name for the Empty Quarter (Rub al-Khali)
Saptco – Saudi Arabian Public Transport Company
Saudia – national airline of Saudi Arabia
Sawm – Ramadan
Shahada – basic profession of faith for a Muslim
Sharia'a – Quranic law
shebab – male youth
sheesha – water pipe used to smoke tobacco
sheikh – officer of the mosque or venerated religious scholar
sherif – descendent of the Prophet Mohammed and used by Islamic ruler (including the Ottomans)
Shiites – one of two main Islamic sects (see also Sunnis); followers believe that the true imams are descended from Ali
siq – narrow gorge or canyon which often forms a passageway through the rock
souq – market
Sunnah – sayings of Mohammed
Sunnis – the main Islamic sect (see also Shiites) derived from followers of the Umayyad caliphate
sura – chapter of Quran

TCN – Third Country National; often used for non-Western expats
thobe – loose-fitting, ankle length robe made of cotton and worn by Saudi men

umm – mother of; occurs commonly in Arabic names
Umayyads – first great dynasty of Arab Muslim rulers (AD 661–750), based in Damascus
umrah – Muslim pilgrimage to Mecca outside haj season

wasta – slang term for connections used to circumvent Saudi bureaucracy
wadi – valley or river bed formed by watercourse, dry except after heavy rainfall
Wahhabi – conservative and literalist 18th century Sunni orthodoxy prevailing throughout Saudi Arabia

zakat – alms to the poor, sometimes in the form of a tax

Behind the Scenes

THIS BOOK

This 1st edition of *Saudi Arabia* was prepared in Lonely Planet's Melbourne office. It was researched by Anthony Ham. Martha Shams wrote the Haj chapter, Andrew Madden contributed to the Expats chapter and Dr Caroline Evans wrote the Health chapter.

THANKS from the author

Anthony Ham I'm very grateful to the many people who shared their experiences of living and travelling in Saudi Arabia, many of whom didn't know the real purpose of my visit. As many of them still live and work in the Kingdom, some have asked to remain anonymous. Particular thanks go to Bobby Cortez, Ingrid Galal and Alanna Lee. I'm also indebted to Roderick Neilsen, Brendan Hopley and the Moreau family whose descriptions of expat living were invaluable. I couldn't have written the Expats chapter without the insights of my co-author Andrew Madden. I also benefited greatly from my time with Azeem Taj and the boys from Lahore on the road

THE LONELY PLANET STORY

The story begins with a classic travel adventure: Tony and Maureen Wheeler's 1972 journey across Europe and Asia to Australia. There was no useful information about the overland trail then, so Tony and Maureen published the first Lonely Planet guidebook to meet a growing need.

From a kitchen table, Lonely Planet has grown to become the largest independent travel pub-lisher in the world, with offices in Melbourne (Australia), Oakland (USA), London (UK) and Paris (France).

Today Lonely Planet guidebooks cover the globe. There is an ever-growing list of books and information in a variety of media. Some things haven't changed. The main aim is still to make it possible for adventurous travellers to get out there – to explore and better understand the world.

At Lonely Planet we believe travellers can make a positive contribution to the countries they visit – if they respect their host communities and spend their money wisely.

SEND US YOUR FEEDBACK

We love to hear from travellers – your comments keep us on our toes and help make our books better. Our well-travelled team reads every word on what you loved or loathed about this book. Although we cannot reply individually to postal submissions, we always guarantee that your feedback goes straight to the appropriate authors, in time for the next edition. Each person who sends us information is thanked in the next edition – and the most useful submissions are rewarded with a free book.

To send us your updates – and find out about LP events, newsletters and travel news – visit our award-winning website: **www.lonelyplanet.com**.

Note: We may edit, reproduce and incorporate your comments in Lonely Planet products such as guidebooks, websites and digital products, so let us know if you don't want your comments reproduced or your name acknowledged. For a copy of our privacy policy visit www.lonelyplanet.com/privacy.

to Abha, Riyadh's best taxi driver, Zamirul, and the countless others who taught me the other side of the expat experience. Extra special thanks to Hamid Ben Bouazza, Saaed Jumaan Saeed and Humberto da Silveira who opened so many doors. At Lonely Planet, Tony Wheeler forged the path, while the vision of Virginia Maxwell and Lynne Preston kept this project from foundering over the years. Will Gourlay was a pleasure to work with and made this book happen, first by reinventing the wheel and then by somehow keeping me sane throughout. And to my family and friends in Australia and Spain who kept the home fires burning and swallowed their fears for my safety, I can't thank you enough. Above everyone else, to my wife and best friend Marina: *eres un encanto*.

CREDITS

This is the first edition of Saudi Arabia. The title was developed in Lonely Planet's Melbourne office by Virginia Maxwell and Lynne Preston. Lynne commissioned the title. Will Gourlay wrote the brief and Cathy Lanigan assessed the manuscript. Cartography for this guide was developed by Shahara Ahmed. Editing was coordinated by Suzannah Shwer with assistance from Lara Morcombe, Sally Steward, Susannah Farfor and Sally O'Brien. Cartography was coordinated by Marion Byass, with assistance from Chris Thomas, Daniel Fennessy and Sarah Sloane. Kieran Grogan managed the project. The cover was designed by Pepi Bluck and cover artwork was by Wendy Wright. Jacqui Saunders chose the colour images and laid-out the book. Quentin Frayne compiled the Language chapter.

ACKNOWLEDGMENTS

Many thanks to the following for the use of their content:

Globe on back cover © Mountain High Maps 1993 Digital Wisdom, Inc.

204

Index

INDEX

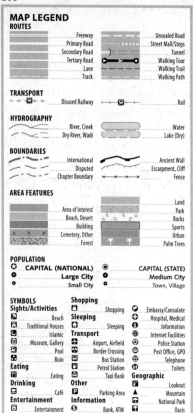

MAP LEGEND

ROUTES

Freeway	Unsealed Road
Primary Road	Street Mall/Steps
Secondary Road	Tunnel
Tertiary Road	Walking Tour
Lane	Walking Trail
Track	Walking Path

TRANSPORT

Disused Railway	Rail

HYDROGRAPHY

River, Creek	Water
Dry River, Wadi	Lake (Dry)

BOUNDARIES

International	Ancient Wall
Disputed	Escarpment, Cliff
Chapter Boundary	Fence

AREA FEATURES

Area of Interest	Land
Beach, Desert	Park
Building	Rocks
Cemetery, Other	Sports
Forest	Urban
	Palm Trees

POPULATION

◎ **CAPITAL (NATIONAL)**	◉ CAPITAL (STATE)
● **Large City**	● Medium City
● Small City	○ Town, Village

SYMBOLS

Sights/Activities
- Beach
- Traditional Houses
- Islamic
- Museum, Gallery
- Pool
- Ruin

Eating
- Eating

Drinking
- Café

Entertainment
- Entertainment

Shopping
- Shopping

Sleeping
- Sleeping

Transport
- Airport, Airfield
- Border Crossing
- Bus Station
- Petrol Station
- Taxi Rank

Other
- Parking Area

Information
- Bank, ATM
- Embassy/Consulate
- Hospital, Medical
- Information
- Internet Facilities
- Police Station
- Post Office, GPO
- Telephone
- Toilets

Geographic
- Lookout
- Mountain
- National Park
- Oasis

LONELY PLANET OFFICES

Australia
Head Office
Locked Bag 1, Footscray, Victoria 3011
☎ 03 8379 8000, fax 03 8379 8111
talk2us@lonelyplanet.com.au

USA
150 Linden St, Oakland, CA 94607
☎ 510 893 8555, toll free 800 275 8555
fax 510 893 8572, info@lonelyplanet.com

UK
72–82 Rosebery Ave,
Clerkenwell, London EC1R 4RW
☎ 020 7841 9000, fax 020 7841 9001
go@lonelyplanet.co.uk

France
1 rue du Dahomey, 75011 Paris
☎ 01 55 25 33 00, fax 01 55 25 33 01
bip@lonelyplanet.fr, www.lonelyplanet.fr

Published by Lonely Planet Publications Pty Ltd
ABN 36 005 607 983

© Lonely Planet 2004

© photographers as indicated 2004

Cover photographs: Domes of the Qoba Mosque, Madinah, Saudi Arabia Nabeel Turner/Tony Stone (front); Spice stall vendor at the Jeddah Souq al-Alawi, Tony Wheeler/Lonely Planet Images (back). Many of the images in this guide are available for licensing from Lonely Planet Images: www.lonelyplanetimages.com.

Printed through Colorcraft Ltd, Hong Kong.
Printed in China